The Complete Book of
PORTABLE
POWER TOOL
TECHNIQUES

Popular Science Books, New York

Distributed to the trade by
Rodale Press, Emmaus, Pennsylvania

The Complete Book of
PORTABLE
POWER TOOL
TECHNIQUES

by R.J. De Cristoforo

Copyright © 1986 by R.J. De Cristoforo

Published by
    Popular Science Books
    Times Mirror Magazines, Inc.
    380 Madison Avenue
    New York, NY 10017

Distributed to the trade by
    Rodale Press
    33 East Minor Street
    Emmaus, PA 18049

Designed by Linda Watts
Produced by Bookworks, Inc.

ISBN 0-943822-69-6

Manufactured in the United States of America

to Mary

Introduction

I grew up with R.J. De Cristoforo. No, I didn't go to school with him; we weren't kids together in the same neighborhood. Nonetheless, I feel like I grew up with him. Like so many of today's craftsmen and craftswomen—both professional and amateur—I've worked with his books and articles for much of my life.

When I first began to take a real interest in working with tools in the early 1960's, 'Cris' had already established himself as a workshop expert. Whenever I'd pick up a magazine such as *Popular Science* or other publications with articles aimed at the do-it-yourself crowd, like as not I'd find some advice from R.J. De Cristoforo. If I went to the library to look up a shop technique or method, I'd usually find Cris' name in the card catalogue. It was no wonder. The last time anyone counted, Cris had over thirty books and a thousand magazine articles to his credit.

But quantity doesn't tell the whole story. Cris' innovations with tools are legendary. In his writings, he has expanded the uses and capabilities of common workshop tools far beyond what even the manufacturers have envisioned. The jigs and shop-built accessories that he has invented have enabled many tool owners (such as myself) to do more and better work than we would have otherwise thought possible. Robert Stevenson, the former Home and Shop Editor of *Popular Science*, put it this way: "For me the arrival of a new article from Cris was always a welcome event, and I shoved other work aside to see what new and surprising ideas his manuscript contained. I was rarely disappointed…it was in these articles that his imagination and ingenuity in the use of power tools came into fullest flower. In the *use* of tools, R.J. De Cristoforo has been a true pioneer."

When I became a workshop editor in the early 1980's, our publishing staff decided to try to put together a complete woodworking encyclopedia from existing books. We scoured the publishers' lists for the best and the most complete books on cabinetry, carpentry, finishing, and so on. Eventually, we chose seven books that we felt were a must for any serious do-it-yourselfer. One of those books was *De Cristoforo's Complete Book of Power Tools, Both Portable and Stationary*, first published by Popular Science Books in 1972. After reviewing all the other books on the market, we felt this was *the* classic text of power tool techniques and methods.

As fate would have it, just a few years later I found myself in the midst of a publishing project to outclass the classic. In the dozen years since Cris had written his first 'definitive' book on power tools, he had amassed dozens of new ideas, jigs, and techniques. He had collected so much new information, in fact, that it was decided that there was enough material for *two* new books—one on stationary tools, and the other on portable tools. The first, *The Complete Book of Stationary Power Tool Techniques*, was published in 1985 by Popular Science Books. As for the second—well, here it is.

Though *The Complete Book of Portable Power Tool Techniques* is intended as a companion volume to De Cristoforo's book on stationary power tools, you'll quickly find that it's a wonderfully useful text all by itself. There are few books on the market that provide such complete information on portable power tools, and none that make such ingenious use of them. It has all the makings of another workshop classic: Not only will the present generation of do-it-yourselfers get a lot of use out of this book; it will be something that our kids will grow up with.

Nick Engler
September, 1986

Contents

1. Using Tools Safely

It's an old truism that a tool is only as good as the worker who uses it. The thought also applies to safety; it's as much in the mind as it is in the hands, or in the tool. Being aware that tools are disinterested helpers, lacking the intelligence that can determine whether their cutting edges are directed toward wood or a finger, must be a constant consideration.

If you use a hand as a backup when drilling a through hole, you ask for trouble. If you are sawing a panel with a circular saw and are thinking about the golf game you're anxious to get to, you're in danger. If you don't position a ladder correctly when, for example, sanding a fascia strip, you might get back to the ground too quickly—with a plop!

It isn't enough to take routine precautions like wearing safety goggles and a dust mask when sanding (Figure 1-1). It's also necessary to preview the operation and to plan it to avoid potential problems.

Getting to know a tool, how it functions, what it can do, how to use it, and its limits are important safety factors. However, be aware that expertise is not a shield that keeps you from harm. In fact, too often expertise breeds overconfidence, a dangerous state of mind. Being a bit afraid of a tool, no matter how well you learn to use it, is as logical as being sure your car's braking system is in dependable condition.

It's significant that a worker's regard for safety can vary from tool to tool. A portable saw might be used with more respect than a portable drill or sander, yet the seemingly less dangerous tools can also do harm. The point is that the degree of damage should not cause the operator to overlook that there should never be damage at all.

Generally, the potential hazards when working with power tools are no different than those of everyday living, but there is an important difference. Your safety in an automobile depends on the care of other drivers as much as on yourself. When you use a tool, you alone control the risk factor. Accept that tools can't think. Don't be complacent because the tool has a guard.

Safety rules provided with a tool, printed in books and magazines, are often ignored. It can't happen to us, but it CAN. And that's the crux of the matter—accepting that you are vulnerable.

Tool Guards

Not many portable tools can be equipped with guards that completely cover what the tool drives. You can't shield the entire length of the blade on a saber saw, so you must always be aware of the exposed cutter under the work and keep hands somewhat in the position shown in Figure 1-2. The

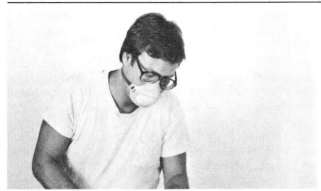

1-1.   Many factors are involved in working safely with power tools—among them protection for eyes (even if you must get special prescription glasses) and lungs. It's also critical to accept that safety is as much in the mind as it is in lists of rules.

1-2.   Blades on some tools, like the saber saw, can't be completely shielded. Always be aware that much of the blade is exposed *under* the workpiece.

same thought applies to other tools like portable routers and sanders. Of course, on these items you'll probably have both hands on the tool. Be careful when you start the operation and when you lift the tool at job's end. Some safety factors have to do with how a particular tool should be used; these will be discussed in other chapters.

The portable circular saw (Figure 1-3) has a swiveling guard that retracts into the fixed upper guard as the cut is made. When the cut is complete, the movable guard automatically returns to cover the bottom area of the blade. This means that during the cut, like the saber saw, part of the blade is exposed *under* the work. While a lot of blade projection may be a more efficient way to saw, it's becoming more common, for safety's sake, to keep the projection to a minimum. Always be aware of that under-the-work danger.

It's amazing how often I've seen the lower guard tied back. It's pointless to go into why this is considered more efficient. Let's just say it's a dumb thing to do.

Some portable tools like grinders, polishers, and disc sanders may have partial guards that are often sold as accessories. Either to save a few dollars or because the operator feels they're in the way, the guards are not always in evidence. If you're going to use a tool it's just common sense to protect yourself as much as possible.

Let's make this point now—if there are demonstration illustrations in this book that don't show a guard when the tool has one, IT'S NOT THAT I'M DISOBEYING MY OWN RULES, BUT ONLY SO THE ACTUAL CUT CAN BE SEEN MORE CLEARLY.

Tool Toting

Portable tools are applied to the work and carried to the site. Too often, a tool is kept running between cuts. It's a much better practice, let alone safer, to allow the tool to stop at the end of a cut and then start it again for the next one. Don't set a tool down until the blade or bit, or whatever, has stopped moving. If you're using an extension cord, plug the tool in at the site. Don't make all electrical connections before walking, or climbing a ladder or scaffold, to where the tool will be used.

Extension Cords

Portable power tools are often used with electrical extension cords for on-site work. The right cord allows the tool to work efficiently. A bad choice can harm the tool and set up some potentially hazardous electrical conditions. The cords needed for tools are a bit different than those used inside for lamps and such, but overall it's just a matter of matching the extension cord to the job.

"Ampacity" is a term that applies to current-carrying capacity in terms of amperes (amps). In this area you can base a judgement by reading the specification plate on the tool which will, or should, state the amperage. If you have several tools and a single extension cord, the cord should be suitable for the tool having the highest amperage rating. The point is, don't use a cord with an amperage rating that is lower than the tool to be powered.

Two factors go together—the tool's amperage and the length of the cord. As one or the other or both of them increase, so must the gauge of the cord's wires. Undersize wires (for the job) cause voltage drop. It's something like feeding a gallon of water at one end of a pipe but getting a pint at the opposite end. Double amperage or double same-size wire length equals double voltage drop. This can result in tool-power loss, excessive heat, and even burnout. "Fatter" wires have less resistance than "thin" ones and help to bring voltage-drop to acceptable levels.

A #12 extension cord, which is usually available only in a heavy-duty grade, is generally acceptable for typical portable power tool use. The chart in Figure 1-4 gives more specific information. Sometimes choices are made on the basis of cost and weight; a #12 is three times a #16 in cost and weight, and even more when compared with #18. A factor though, as we mentioned, is that #12 is usually a heavy-duty grade.

Safety with Cords

The important factor is this—if the tool has a three-prong plug, then the extension must be compatible; three wires, with a three-prong plug at one end and a three-hole receptacle at the other end to receive the tool's plug. Of course, these safety factors are nullified if the starting outlet (where you plug in) isn't correctly grounded or if you don't, when necessary, use a proper grounding-adapter procedure. If in doubt, have the electrical system checked by a qualified electrician so you don't operate with false security.

Tool cords or extensions that can be used on less than 150V will have plugs like the one shown in Figure 1-5A. The grounding pin, WHICH MUST NEVER BE REMOVED, engages with the third, specially shaped hole in the outlet.

1-3.   Portable circular saws have a fixed upper guard and a pivoted lower one that retracts during the cut and then returns to cover the blade when the cut is complete. Tying the lower guard back, as some workers do, is asking for trouble.

An adapter, like the one shown in Figure 1-5B and attached as in Figure 1-5C, can be used to accommodate a conventional two-prong plug. The lug on the adapter must be firmly attached to the outlet box. As we said, for systems like this to work, the box itself must be CORRECTLY GROUNDED. Such adapters should be viewed as temporary measures for use only until a correctly grounded outlet box is installed, preferably by a qualified electrician. These adapters are NOT used in Canada.

Most tools designed for operation on 150-250V will have a plug like the one shown in Figure 1-5D. This must be used with a matching, correctly grounded receptacle that is wired to deliver the correct voltage. DON'T use adapters with this plug design.

The grounding precautions do not apply to modern, double-insulated tools that are equipped with a two-prong plug. These tools have a built-in safety factor that is designed to prevent shorting through parts of the tool you handle so a two-wire extension cord can be used safely. More about this in a bit.

Double Insulation

A double-insulated tool has all the electrical components and the basic insulation required for it to work. But, additionally, its components such as motor, controls, brushes, and so on, are surrounded by what you might call secondary insulation or correctly engineered air space. Should the basic insulation fail, electricity doesn't get to the handle or casing of the tool. You wouldn't be "shocked" even though the failure situation might blow a fuse.

Essentially, this is also true of a three-wire, three-prong setup so long as the system is actually grounded. If, as is often the case, grounding doesn't exist, then the operator becomes the grounding medium and the results, in case of accident or failure, can be unpleasant. But when a three-prong tool is properly installed in a correctly grounded three-hole outlet and correctly used, it's as safe as you can expect any electric tool to be. It's the unknown, or shall we say, "hidden" aspects of the electrical environment that might cause problems. It's also things like removing the grounding prong of a three-prong plug because only a two-hole outlet is available.

The double-insulated tool, among other things, guards against our own mis-deeds. The safety is part of the tool, built into it, and doesn't depend on how the end of the cord is designed.

As good as they are, double-insulated tools are not 100% safe. I don't care to use any electric tool in or around water. Water penetration of uninsulated parts poses a potential hazard. If you touch the metal chuck of a drill while the bit is touching a hidden, hot wire, and if your feet happen to be on a good ground, you might be in for a jolt. A lot of "ifs" but they make a point.

CORD LENGTH	EXTENSION CORDS WIRE SIZE B&S GAUGE					
	AMP RATING OF TOOL (FULL LOAD)					
	0 - 2.0	2.1 - 3.4	3.5 - 5.0	5.1 - 7.0	7.1 - 12.0	12.1 - 16.0
25	18	18	18	18	16	14
50	18	18	18	16	14	12
75	18	18	16	14	12	10
100	18	16	14	12	10	8
150	16	14	12	10	8	8
200	16	14	12	10	8	6
300	14	12	10	8	6	4
400	12	10	8	6	4	4
500	12	10	8	6	4	2
600	10	8	6	4	2	2
800	10	8	6	4	2	1
1000	8	6	4	2	1	0

Note: This table is for 115V tools.

1-4. Choosing the correct extension cord assures sufficient power where it's needed. It's a good idea to have several on hand and to use the shortest one that will do.

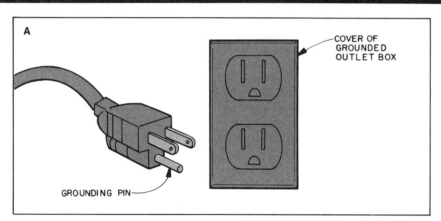

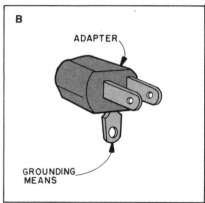

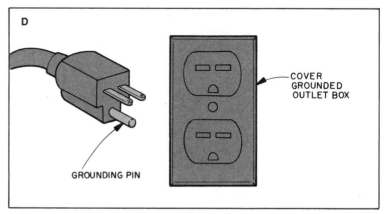

1-5.   Various methods of grounding. You're asking for trouble if you remove the grounding pin from a three-prong grounding plug. These systems work only if the connection is made to a CORRECTLY GROUNDED outlet.

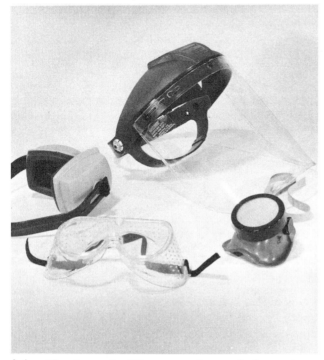

1-6.   All tool users should have a complete set of safety products on hand. These items will protect your eyes, ears, and lungs—BUT ONLY IF YOU USE THEM!

Protecting Eyes, Ears, and Lungs

The safety items displayed in Figure 1-6 should be standard equipment in all shops. The wisdom of using safety goggles and face masks gets a lot of publicity so it isn't difficult to convince most people to use them. However, the harmful effects of dust and noise are often overlooked or ignored.

Headphone-type hearing protectors are as important as any safety device. High frequencies can be generated by high-speed electric motors and even by some woodworking operations. The effects are cumulative; each exposure contributing to possible hearing impairment. Good ear protectors that will screen out high frequencies while still allowing normal conversation, are available and they won't eliminate the woodworking noises you SHOULD hear. They should be used with all powered tools including products like weed cutters, lawn mowers, chain saws, and such.

Don't feel that a dust mask is necessary only when doing sanding chores. Many sawing, routing, and shaping operations can produce particles best kept from your lungs. Be sure to keep the filters in the mask clean and to replace them as often as necessary.

Unauthorized Use

Power tools are intriguing to children. Add to this the desire to imitate dad or mom and you may have a potential disaster.

Unlike many stationary tools, portable tools don't have built-in locks with removable keys so it's best never to leave a tool plugged in when it's not being used. Actually, this is good safety practice anyway. Put tools away when you're through working, preferably in a cabinet with a lock. Put the key in a secret place.

Work Uniform and Shopkeeping

A special uniform to wear when using tools makes sense. Shirt and trousers should fit snugly. Shoes should be heavy, preferably with steel toes and non-slip bottoms. The latter feature is especially important when using a ladder or working on a roof. It's rarely necessary to wear gloves, and a necktie is OUT, period. Avoid any loose clothing that might snag on a tool or shop furniture or on-site objects. Rings, wristwatches, bracelets, and other adornments are hazards. Cover your hair, whether it's long or short, for safety and protection from dust. A hard hat, like those used by construction workers, should also be part of your uniform for use in particular environments.

Treat your shop, or any work area, as if it were a kitchen. Tables, benches, tools, accessories, and so on should be kept in pristine condition. Keep a bench brush and a vacuum cleaner handy, and use them. Don't allow litter, sawdust, and wood scraps to clutter the work area. This creates dangerous hazards that can cause a nasty slip or trip.

Keep tool surfaces like the baseplates on circular saws and saber saws and the surface of a router/shaper table in new-bright condition. Dirty tools aren't nice to work with and rough bearing-surfaces make it more difficult to move the tool and can mar the workpiece. Clean such areas and then apply paste wax rubbed to a polish. Don't use oil; this collects sawdust and dirt, and it doesn't do the workpiece any good.

It's not wise to work in a wet location or to expose tools to rain.

The shop, or any work area, should be well lighted. Extension lights, with the bulb protected in a wire cage, can provide illumination for on-site work.

Good Work Practice

Don't overreach, no matter what the operation or the tool. Don't struggle with workpieces that are too large for you to handle safely. When necessary, ask someone to help but be sure to describe the procedure to the assistant.

Always provide firm support for the workpiece (Figure 1-7). Support stands and small workbenches you can carry about are available commercially. Sawhorses are a great aid, really a must for on-site work. By spacing them correctly you can, for example, support a twenty foot 2x4 or a plywood panel, and when spanned with sturdy lumber they can be used as low scaffolding. Readymade sawhorses like the one shown in Figure 1-8 are available or you can quickly and easily make some with 2x4s and a pair of special brackets (Figure 1-9). Other designs for sawhorses you make from scratch are shown in Figures 1-10 through 1-13.

Don't work with dull tools. You won't get good results. Also, dull tools make it necessary to apply more pressure

1-7.   Good support for the workpiece is essential. You may not have a workbench for on-site work but other means are available. This is the "Versa Ladder" organized to serve as a temporary bench.

1-8.   Readymade sawhorses are available. This one is all metal and can be folded for storage.

1-9.   You can assemble a basic A-frame sawhorse in very little time by using lengths of 2x4 and available sawhorse hardware. Note that no angle-cut is required at the top of the legs. A plywood shelf will increase rigidity.

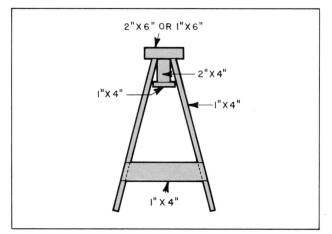

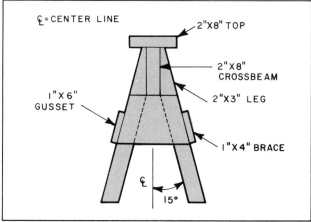

1-10.   This sawhorse design allows assembly without having to cut angles. The width of the 1x4 under the rail and rail support determines the splay of the legs. The 2x6 rail provides more work surface than a 2x4 and allows some room for a screw-on vise.

1-11.   I call this the "toughie" horse. Use lag screws, carriage bolts and nuts, and waterproof glue to assemble all parts. Use straight grain fir and apply several coats of exterior sealer.

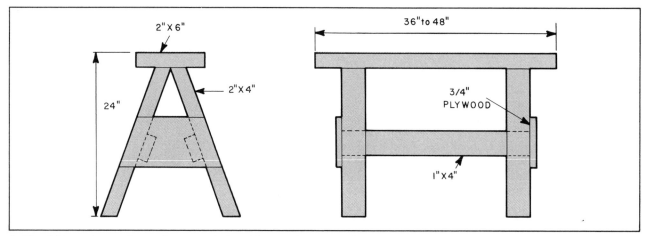

1-12.   This version requires angle-cuts on the legs. The legs should splay from 15 to 20 degrees. It's best to attach the legs to the rail before cutting the gusset.

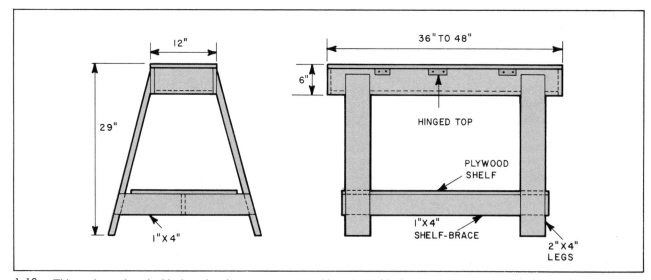

1-13.   This sawhorse does double duty since its top serves as a tool box. Assemble the compartment as a unit before adding other components. You can use a strip of continuous (piano) hinge for the lid instead of conventional ones.

when you move the tool, which establishes a situation where your hands might slip.

Always disconnect the tool when you must change a saw blade or a router bit, or whatever. Don't leave a power tool running when you need to turn to another chore or area of a workpiece regardless of how little time is involved. It's prudent to wait for the cutter to come to a halt before you move away.

Be aware that something is wrong when you must force a cut. Usually, it means that the cutter is dull or that you're trying to cut too deep. Most of the time, extra deep or oversize cuts must be accomplished by making repeat passes.

Don't mix tool-use with socializing. Keeping a conversation going while you're using a tool is not allowed. Politely advise friends and neighbors not to barge into the shop if they hear the noise of a tool. You don't want them to startle you.

Stay alert; keep your mind on the job at hand. Don't use tools when you're tired or upset and, like driving, alcoholic beverages and tool-use don't mix.

Good Tool Practice

It's critical to know the tool, especially if you are using it for the first time. Read and reread the owner's manual that is supplied with the equipment. Learn the tool's applications and, ESPECIALLY, its limitations. Don't use a tool for something it was not designed to do. For example, you don't use

1-14. Ladders are available in wood or metal. Wood is subject to deterioration. A metal ladder is lighter but must never be used near electrical installations. Choose ladders carefully; your safety depends on them.

drill bits in a router or substitute a grinding wheel for the blade on a circular saw. Make it a habit to check all locking devices before turning on the power.

Mount cutters or accessories by carefully following the installation instructions. Don't use saw blades that are larger in diameter than the saw can take. Check the maximum rpm of the blade; it must not be less than the tool's speed.

Don't work with damaged tools or tools with frayed cords. Be sure to mount blades and cutters so they have the correct direction of rotation.

Don't work on pieces too small to be safely held or, at least, grip them firmly in a vise or with clamps. If you need a shaped, narrow piece (router work), form it on a large workpiece and then cut off the part you need.

Be sure you know what you are going to do before you start an operation. If you preview the chore you can judge how best to support the work, how to move the tool, and the best positions for your hands. Often, and especially with new tools and operations you haven't tried before, it's wise to do a dry run. That is, go through the operation with the tool unplugged. Become "tool wise".

There are some operations in woodworking that are done without standard guards. When involved with these, be extra cautious about how you proceed, or choose another method of getting the same result. Never, regardless of what you are doing, use your hands so they are too close to the cutting area. To put it bluntly, a cutting tool can't distinguish between wood and flesh. As we said, they're great helpers but they function with the belief that you know what you're doing.

Ladders

Because portable power tools are often used on-site, and this frequently involves getting to another level, it's important that what you use to get there is strong and used correctly. Since a ladder is the common means, getting a sturdy one is the first step (Figure 1-14). Today, ladders have stickers and labels of various colors so the consumer knows something about the product before he buys it. For example, an industrial grade wooden ladder will have a yellow label. If the same color is on a metal ladder, it's a heavy-duty type. The ladder should also have some information about how it can be used. This also applies to extension ladders—safe overlap lengths, good angle when setting the ladder against a vertical surface, and so on.

Good ladders can be found in wood or metal. Wood ladders are subject to weather-deterioration; metal ones should never be used near electrical lines.

"Versa Ladders" (Figure 1-15) are uniquely designed with pivoting joints so they can be set to different heights, used as scaffolds, or even as work supports.

You can buy accessories for some ladders like the scaffold support shown in Figure 1-16 or the ridge hooks for roof work shown in Figure 1-17.

Basic Ladder Rules

■ Place a solid footing under each foot of the ladder when working on soft ground.

- Tying the bottom rung of the ladder to a fixed object, especially when it's on a slippery surface, is good procedure.
- Don't stand on the top ledge or the paint shelf, or straddle the top of a step ladder.
- Don't overreach in any direction while on a ladder.
- When climbing, keep your weight centered and use your hands on the rungs, not the sides.
- If you're climbing to a roof, have at least three feet of the ladder projecting above the roof line.
- Never try to make a long ladder by splicing together two short ones.

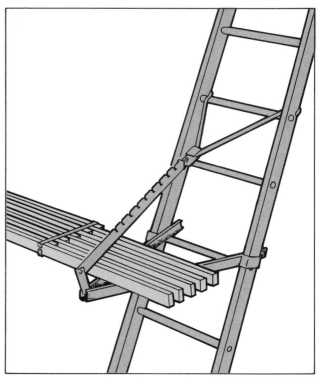

1-16.   Accessories for ladders include special brackets like this one. Consider renting such equipment since you may not need it too often. Knock-down scaffolding is also available at rental places.

1-15.   The unique "Versa Ladder" can be used conventionally or "folded" to serve in other ways, among them, as a scaffold.

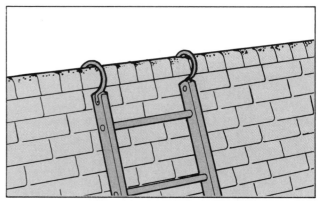

1-17.   Using a ladder on a roof calls for special precautions like these ridge hooks. I would also add a heavy rope tied to an immovable object on the other side of the building. Also, be sure to wear non-slip shoes.

2.

The Portable Circular Saw

Stretch your imagination a bit and you will see that the portable circular saw is something like a table saw or radial arm saw that you hold in your hand. That's one of the virtues of this and other carry-about tools. You bring the tool to the work instead of bringing the work to the tool. For example, you can use the portable saw to trim-cut roof boards or sheathing or deck boards that are already installed, or reduce the length or width of a plywood panel without having to muscle it over the table of a stationary tool.

The usual alternative to the powered saw is a handsaw which requires effort to use and considerably more time to complete a cut (Figure 2-1). The power tool has built-in accuracy features, and when handled correctly cuts straight and square edges with a minimum possibility of human error. Some apprenticeship is necessary but the amateur can quickly get professional results.

The tool was originally developed as an aid for construction people who must size house-framing boards and timbers right on the job. Today there are dozens of models available that look alike and have similar features (Figure 2-2). Different manufacturers offer units that span a broad range of light-duty and heavy-duty tools with differences in size, power, and price.

It's not uncommon to hear the tool referred to as a "Skilsaw"—probably because the Skil people were originators—but other names such as "cutoff saw", "utility saw", and "builder's saw" are also used. The descriptive titles fit but it's an error to limit the saw's use to the area of woodworking implied by the name.

With some know-how, accessories you can buy, and jigs that you make, you can broaden the tool's workscope to include jobs that are routine on stationary equipment. For example, it can be used to form dadoes and rabbets, cut

2-1.   The portable circular saw substitutes electric power for muscle. It took more than 30 seconds to make the handsaw cut, only about 3 or 4 seconds using the power saw. The power tool has built-in accuracy.

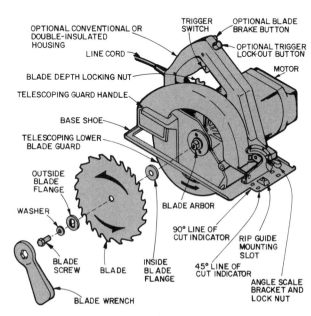

2-2.   Portable saws vary in appearance, size, and weight, but most will have the features shown here.

bevels and miters, do compound cuts, single-cut multiple and similar pieces, and so on.

Types and Sizes

The size of the saw is indicated by the diameter of the blade. The "average" might be around 7¼" or 7½", but the range is from under 5" to better than 10" (Figures 2-3—2-6). Blade diameter is important but should not be the sole factor when making a choice. Also consider its maximum depth of cut—the thickness of material the blade can get through on both straight cuts and 45° bevels. There's no problem if your woodworking will be limited to ¾" lumber or plywood, but it's more realistic to think in terms of 2" lumber. Even here, consider the difference between dressed lumber and rough lumber. Standard 2" dressed lumber is actually 1½" thick, whereas lumber in the rough (not planed) is at least a full 2". So, if lumber in the rough will be part of the work picture, you may need more depth of cut than the person who works on dressed stock only.

Since sharpenings reduce the diameter of a blade, getting one that is just enough for a piece of work when the blade is new may not be wise. Also, a blade that is constantly buried in the cut won't function efficiently and will cause burn marks on itself and the wood. All of which seems to indicate that it's better to overestimate when deciding on capacity. Overall, you should be able to make square and 45° bevel cuts through 2" dressed stock.

Generally, the larger the size the more powerful, heavier, and more expensive the tool will be. Getting the biggest size, regardless of cost, isn't being tool-wise. A smaller saw with

Features to Consider in Circular Saws

2-3.   Skil's 7¼" saw has a burnout protected 2 hp motor and a clutch to help prevent kickback should the blade bind in a cut. A special lock-out switch can be used to prevent accidental starts.

2-5.   Makita's 4⅜" saw weighs only a bit more than six pounds yet it is rated at 7.5 amps so has the power to cut wood, paneling, aluminum, and plastic. It's a high-speed unit; the blade turns at 11,000 rpm.

2-4.   This Porter Cable unit is double insulated and has a heavy-duty wrap-around base with a single sight line that serves as a guide on straight, angle, or bevel cuts. Depth of cut at 90° is almost 2½".

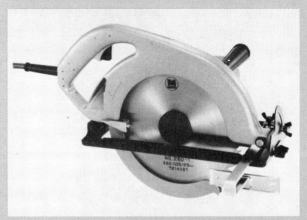

2-6.   Weight, and usually power, goes up with size. This 10¼" saw weighs a bit more than 18 lbs. and is powered with a 12 amp motor for heavy-duty work. Electric brake stops the blade when the trigger is released.

adequate horsepower (say a minimum of 1 hp) may be a better buy, so long as it will perform the tasks with the frequency of use you anticipate, because it may be more comfortable to handle. Looking forward isn't difficult. Are you going to build a house and then add decks and fences, or do major remodeling work? Or do you wish to have the tool on hand for those occasional chores? This can make the difference between choosing a light-duty tool or a heavy-duty version. Here, manufacturers offer help since many catalogs state duty-performance, presenting units as "industrial", "homeowners", and so on. Another aid is the length of the guarantee. A two-year guarantee obviously indicates a tool considered longer-lived than one with a one-year backup.

Blade speed is specified in rpm when the blade is running free. Keeping close to this specification when the blade is working has to do with horsepower and, of course, the material being sawed. Some slow-up will occur under almost all conditions. So consider rpm in this light—a fast turning blade that slows down considerably when cutting isn't really going to be faster than a slower tool that does not bog down. Of course, how the tool is handled—how fast YOU try to cut—affects its cut-consistency, but more about that later.

Because the tool is designed for square cuts and beveled ones, it should have scales that help to preset the tool (Figure 2-7). It's rare that these can be accepted prima facie but they do serve as a beginning. It's always best to make a test cut before going further.

A basic accessory is an edge guide like the one shown in Figure 2-8. It's used when you need to make a straight cut parallel to an outside edge. It may be supplied with the saw or offered as an accessory.

If it can be arranged, it's a good idea to actually test the tool you're interested in, or have the salesperson do it for you with a demonstrator model. Be sure to "heft" it yourself. When all other factors are satisfactory, how the tool feels in your hands can logically determine which saw to choose from a variety of units. Weight and ease of handling can also

be important safety factors. A tool that is too heavy for you, or one that feels awkward when you grip it, can make you uncomfortable and thus be a hazard.

In General

After purchasing the saw, you should spend more than a few minutes practicing to become familiar with the tool and how it handles. Make test cuts on some ¾″ plywood that is clamped securely to a bench, and on a length of 2x4 adequately supported across sawhorses or some similar support. Set the blade projection so it doesn't exceed the thickness of the material by more than ¼″. A greater projection is actually more efficient since the cutting arc is less, but for safety's sake it's best to keep it to a minimum. Place your right hand with a finger on the trigger and your left hand on the secondary grip (Figure 2-9). Position yourself so you are not in line with the path of the saw blade. Place the saw so its weight is supported by the bulk of the stock, not the part that will be cut off.

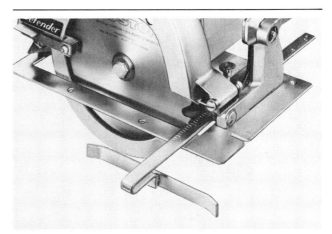

2-8.   An edge guide may be supplied with the tool or offered as an accessory. It's used to guide the saw when making a cut parallel to an edge.

2-7.   Depth of cut and bevel scales don't all look like this. The scales can be used for casual sawing but when accuracy is critical it's best to make a test cut before sawing good stock.

2-9.   It's good practice to grip the saw firmly with both hands. Feed-speed should be just enough to keep the blade cutting. Take a position that keeps your body out of the line of cut.

The upper portion of the saw blade is guarded by a fixed housing. The lower portion is covered by a guard that should automatically telescope into the top housing as you move the tool forward to make the cut. Always be aware that the portion of the saw blade in the cut and the area of the saw blade that extends below the stock are not covered by the guard during the cut. When the cut is complete—the blade has cleared the wood—the lower guard will return and the blade will be completely covered. Move the tool completely off the wood to be sure that this happens. Always let the blade come to a halt before resting the tool.

The teeth on the saw blade will (should) point toward the front of the tool (Figure 2-10). This direction of rotation makes it cut on the "up" stroke and suggests that the good face of the stock should be "down" when you cut since any splintering or feathering will occur where the teeth leave the work. This factor is critical only when the material you are cutting, like a fancy plywood with a single good side, deserves such consideration. Don't let it bother you if, for example, you're cutting wall-framing studs.

Feed Speed

Feed speed (how fast you try to move the tool) should be judged by how the saw is cutting. The thickness and the density of the stock, whether the cut is parallel to or across the grain, the saw blade being used and its condition, are all factors that affect how fast you can go. Actually, you shouldn't be out to set speed records. Usually, the quality of the cut is more important. The rule to obey is to be sure the blade cuts steadily without being forced. Too slow and you won't accomplish much while the blade burnishes and dulls. Too fast and the blade chokes.

Portable circular saws will kick back quickly if you bind the blade by twisting the tool as you make the pass. An answer here, as we'll show, is to use guides that keep the tool moving in a straight line. Binding can also happen on long rip cuts, especially on green wood, because the kerf (the groove formed by the blade) tends to close behind the blade. When your first cut indicates that this is likely to happen on subsequent cuts, it's wise to do something about it. Some operators simply tap a shim into the kerf to keep it open, but a better

idea is to make and use the "kerfer" that is shown in Figures 2-11 and 2-12. An item you can buy, the "KerfKeeper" offered by the Adjustable Clamp Company, is another solution to the problem (Figure 2-13).

Some tools are equipped with a "slip clutch". Its job is to allow the saw blade to slip when the blade is confronted with an adverse situation such as a knot in the wood or mishandling that causes the blade to bind. Even though the motor still turns, the blade does not. The idea works but it's a tricky mechanism simply because its efficiency depends on how the operator adjusts it. Do the job right by carefully following the instructions that come with the tool and by frequently checking the adjustment.

In most cases it's simply a question of tightening the retaining nut on the arbor just so. Tighten the nut too much and the clutch won't work; if it's too loose, slippage can occur to the point where the saw loses efficiency. When the situation is optimum, the slip clutch will protect the motor and help to avoid kickback. The slip clutch can add to safety when operating the saw but remember that the most depend-

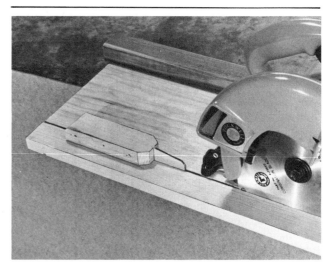

2-11.   The kerf tends to close behind the blade especially on long rip cuts and when cutting green wood. You can make a "kerfer" and use it as shown to prevent the binding hazard.

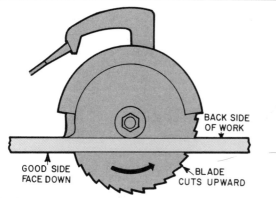

2-10.   Saw blades cut on the upstroke, so the face side of the stock should be down since most splintering and feathering will occur when the teeth leave the cut.

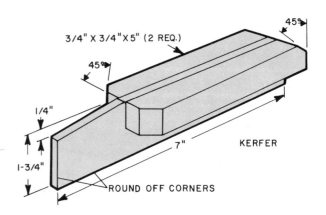

2-12.   One way to make a kerfer.

able safety device should be you. Always work with a sharp blade and move the tool so the blade can do its job without being forced.

Another safety device found on some portable circular saws is an electronic brake. No extra buttons to push or procedures to go through are required for the brake to operate. When you release the tool's trigger, the brake automatically goes into action—the blade says "whoosh" and stops, just like that!

Saw Blades

Most saws will be supplied with a combination blade, a compromise design that can be used for crosscutting, ripping, and even mitering. It's an adequate blade to start with but not the best blade for optimum results on particular cuts and various materials. Use it on plywood and you'll get a good deal of splintering and feathering so the cut edge will require further attention.

Many other blade designs, some of which are shown in Figure 2-14 are available. It's wise to gradually acquire an assortment and to limit each to the chore it does best. There's little point in using a paneling or hollow-ground blade to saw studs and it won't do the blade much good. On the other hand, a hollow-ground blade will produce respectable miters. Smooth plywood cuts result when they are done with a paneling saw or a similar unit simply called a "plywood blade".

If you have a lot of cutting with-the-grain to do, switch to the rip blade. Its fast cutting action puts minimum strain on the motor and its deep gullets quickly throw off rather large waste-chips. The crosscut blade, with its many, small, sharp-pointed teeth severs wood fibers cleanly so you have smoother results when sawing across the grain.

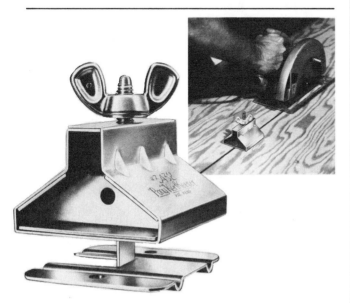

2-13. The "Pony" Kerfkeeper is offered by the Adjustable Clamp Company. It keeps the kerf open, but because it has surfaces that bear against both the bottom and top of the workpiece, it also helps to keep material from sagging during the cut.

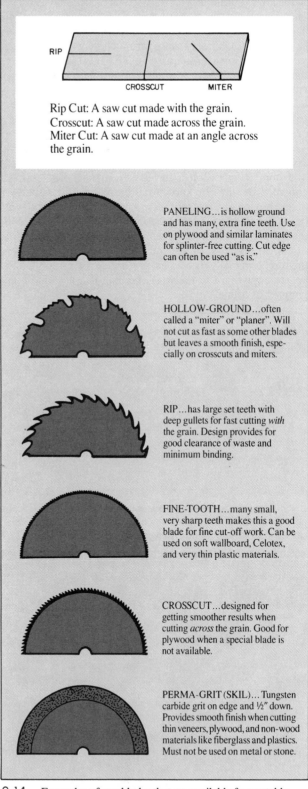

Rip Cut: A saw cut made with the grain.
Crosscut: A saw cut made across the grain.
Miter Cut: A saw cut made at an angle across the grain.

PANELING…is hollow ground and has many, extra fine teeth. Use on plywood and similar laminates for splinter-free cutting. Cut edge can often be used "as is."

HOLLOW-GROUND…often called a "miter" or "planer". Will not cut as fast as some other blades but leaves a smooth finish, especially on crosscuts and miters.

RIP…has large set teeth with deep gullets for fast cutting *with* the grain. Design provides for good clearance of waste and minimum binding.

FINE-TOOTH…many small, very sharp teeth makes this a good blade for fine cut-off work. Can be used on soft wallboard, Celotex, and very thin plastic materials.

CROSSCUT…designed for getting smoother results when cutting *across* the grain. Good for plywood when a special blade is not available.

PERMA-GRIT (SKIL)…Tungsten carbide grit on edge and ½" down. Provides smooth finish when cutting thin veneers, plywood, and non-wood materials like fiberglass and plastics. Must not be used on metal or stone.

2-14. Examples of saw blades that are available for portable power saws. It's wise to start a collection so you can select a blade for optimum results on particular jobs. Always work with sharp blades.

Saw blades that have tungsten carbide teeth (Figure 2-15) are as common today as all-steel blades, and as usable on a portable saw as they are on a stationary machine. They're more costly than other types but they cut easier, smoother, and they stay sharp for much longer periods than steel blades. However, there isn't ONE blade that does everything perfectly. The examples in Figure 2-15 include a rip, crosscut, and combination blade.

Tungsten carbide is tough, but has a degree of brittleness so it can't be abused. Don't place the blades on steel surfaces or store them so their keen edges might be nicked.

Abrasive blades can add to the usefulness of a portable saw. Various types are made for cutting non-wood materials like stone (Figure 2-16), non-ferrous metals, plastics, even concrete. Be sure you know what the disc was designed for before buying and using it. These are special cutters and must be used with respect. Don't use them on wood or even think that you can do grinding on their sides. Carefully follow mounting instructions. A good safety procedure is to allow the disc, especially a new one, to run free for a minute or so before applying it to the work. Forcing is a no-no—safety goggles, of course.

Cutting Techniques

Crosscutting (sawing across the grain of the wood) and ripping (sawing parallel to the grain) are basic functions. Although the tool is often used freehand, you'll get better results and will actually be safer if you establish a guide against which to move the saw. This doesn't have to be more than a strip of wood, clamped or tack-nailed to the workpiece (Figure 2-17). If you keep the tool bearing against the guide, there is little chance that you might inadvertently twist the tool and cause the blade to bind. The distance from the edge of the baseplate to the cutting line is easily established by a one-time test cut. Thus, you will always know where to establish the guide strip for accurate cutting. This dimension can vary depending on the style of saw blade you're using, so you must check it each time you change blades and also after you've had a blade sharpened.

An edge guide, sometimes supplied with the tool and other times offered as an accessory, can also be used on rip cuts (Figure 2-18). While it can be used to establish the width of the piece being cut off, it doesn't have enough bearing surface to relieve you of the responsibility of keeping the saw

2-15.   Blades with teeth of tungsten carbide are also available for portable saws. When properly made they cut better than all-steel saws and stay sharp for much longer periods of time.

2-17.   You'll do a better job of cutting if you use a guide for the saw whenever possible. Keep the edge of the baseplate firmly against the guide throughout the pass.

2-16.   Silicon carbide wheel slices smoothly through 1″ marble slab. It can also cut materials like brick, concrete, and plaster. Be sure to read instructions that come with the wheel. Don't abuse it!

2-18.   The edge guide is used for making cuts parallel to an edge. It doesn't have much bearing surface so keeping the saw moving in a straight line is the operator's responsibility.

moving in a straight line. Both tool-guide examples have been demonstrated on rip cuts, which we'll talk more about later, but the practice also applies to crosscutting.

Crosscuts are often short cuts, across a 2x4, a 1x12, and so on, so it's often more convenient to use a guide that can be held to the work by hand. For example, you can use a common shop square as a guide, or you can make a special guide with more capacity by nailing two pieces of wood together to form an "L". The short leg should bear against the edge of the work while the long leg performs as the guide for the saw. There are quite a few commercial accessories that serve as guides for crosscut work. Two examples are shown in Figures 2-19 and 2-20.

Of course, this and other portable saw cutting can be done freehand by relying on your own expertise to keep the blade on the cutline. In any case, when starting the operation, place the front edge of the base plate firmly on the work with the guide notch in line with the direction of the cut. Start the saw, and after the blade has arrived at full speed, move the tool slowly forward for the actual cutting. Remember that the saw kerf has width so it must occur on the waste side of the stock.

When you approach the end of the cut, the guide-notch area of the base plate will be off the work, so you'll have to watch the blade itself to be sure it stays on the line. This applies more to freehand cutting than when you're moving the saw against a guide. In the latter case you can just concentrate on keeping the edge of the base plate snug against the guide strip throughout the pass.

Keep both hands on the saw (Figure 2-21) if possible. However, there are times when you may need one hand to secure a guide or to keep the work firm. Never work in a situation where you must use a free hand to brace yourself. Always be sure that both you and the tool are firmly planted. If a situation causes doubt, pause, step back and re-evaluate. The importance of being aware of what might occur, and what it demands of you, can't be emphasized too strongly.

Always try to set up so the weight of the saw will be supported by the bulk of the stock. This isn't always possible, especially on on-site work, but many times you can make a choice. For example, let's assume you must trim off the end of a long 2x4. Whether the saw will rest on the waste portion of the wood or on the body of the piece depends on which side of the 2x4 you stand. The same thinking applies if the piece you're cutting off is the one you need. The extra thinking required is in determining which side of the cut mark you want the kerf to be on. Cutting on the wrong side can shorten the piece you need by the width of the kerf.

Sawing Extra-Thick Stock

Sawing through stock that is thicker than the maximum depth of cut of the blade can be accomplished by making matching cuts from opposite surfaces (Figure 2-22). A cut is made on one side, and then the stock is flipped for the second cut. In such cases, layout and correct positioning of the saw for each cut are of primary importance if the two are to mate exactly. When you have many such cuts to make on similar materials, it will pay to make a U-shaped guide that can be clamped to the work so the two cuts will meet exactly. An

2-19.   This commercial jig is adjustable for various stock widths. Squeezing the trigger handle causes the jig to grip the stock between rear and front flanges. Arrow indicates the cutline guide.

2-20.   Protractor type guide can be used for square or angular cuts. It's usually hand-held but there's no reason why you can't clamp it in place if you wish.

2-21.   Keeping both hands on the saw is good practice but not always possible. Place the front of the baseplate firmly on the work—let the blade come to full speed before you make contact.

2-22.   Getting through stock that is thicker than the saw's maximum depth of cut requires half-way cuts from opposite surfaces. Align the blade very carefully after flipping the stock for the second cut.

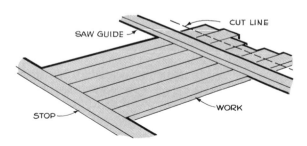

2-23.   One pass trimming of multiple pieces can be done accurately by setting up this way. Clamp or tack-nail the guide strip to the first and last workpieces.

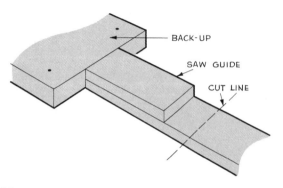

2-24.   A simple setup that lets you cut many pieces of similar length. The saw guide equals the length of the part you want less the distance from the edge of the saw's baseplate to the cutline.

alternative method is to create a setup so the work can be flipped in correct position for the second cut after the first one has been accomplished.

When doing two-pass cutting through thick stock, set the saw-blade projection to the least that will do the job. For example, if you're cutting stock that is 2″ thick, set projection to a bit more than 1″.

Cutting to Length

When it's necessary to cut many pieces to the same length, say studs or deck boards, make a setup like the one shown in Figure 2-23. Many professionals work this way, working freehand and just following a marked line, but accuracy comes easier if you use a stop against which you can butt one end of the pieces and then add a guide for the saw. It isn't necessary to do more than tack-nail or clamp the guide to the first and last piece in the set you are cutting.

Another method you can use to cut pieces of similar length is shown in Figure 2-24. The backup block, or "stop" is secured to a firm surface with nails or clamps. The guide block is the length of the pieces you need less the distance from the baseplate's edge to the saw blade. The guide and the work are butted against the backup and the saw is moved along the guide to make the cut. Some workers hand-hold the guide but it's safer to clamp it in place for each cut you make. The stock from which you're cutting the pieces should be allowed to fall away.

Butt Cuts

The technique that is demonstrated in Figures 2-25 and 2-26 will help when you must trim the ends of boards to make a matching joint. Just overlap the board ends and cut through both of them at the same time. Thus, even a slight error in cutting will not affect how the two ends will join together. The method will work whether the cut is straight, at an angle, long or short, and whether you are ripping or crosscutting. Clamp the pieces together to keep them firm as you saw.

More on Ripping

A good deal of what has been said so far in regard to saw handling applies to rip cuts as well as crosscuts. The primary distinction—whether you are sawing with the grain or across it—often isn't as important as the length of the cut. Choosing the right saw blade is important when you have a lot of ripping to do. If you have one rip cut to make and you already have a combination blade mounted, you won't be faulted for not changing to a rip blade. That's an "out" we all take advantage of. Incidentally, if you are sawing plywood and don't have a special plywood blade, the next best choice is a crosscut blade.

As in crosscutting, and as we have already mentioned, use a clamped or tack-nailed guide strip or an edge guide to help produce straight cuts. A commercial edge guide (Figure 2-27) is okay to use when the width of the cut permits. Remember, however, that it's not as easy to be as accurate with the accessory as you can with a strip of wood. The wood strip will prevent you from being wobbly with the saw.

2-25.   Overlapping pieces this way lets you produce matching edges in a single pass. Be sure pieces are held together and firmly supported.

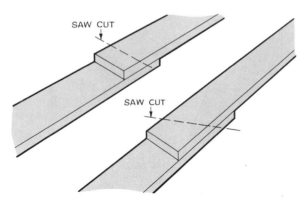

2-26.   The overlap method can be used regardless of whether you are making straight or angular cuts. The idea assures a perfect joint between the cut edges.

2-27.   The position of the edge guide determines the width of the cut. Some edge guides are calibrated but you should check with a rule anyway.

Most saws are designed so the guide can be used on either side of the blade. To choose which side to place the guide, just consider which position involves the least extension of the guide and which provides the most support for the saw. Sometimes a decision has to be based on which end of the work you're going to start from, especially if the board is part of a fixed assembly and you don't have much choice in determining operator position.

With some edge guides you can create a setup by using both a clamped strip and an edge guide. The combination can be useful when it's necessary to cut a number of long pieces of equal width. In this situation the guide rides against the clamped strip and is adjusted after each cut by using calibrations on the guide, if there are any, or by measuring with a rule. Similarity in width of the pieces you saw will depend on how carefully you adjust the guide after each cut.

When material thickness allows it, and you must cut the same amount from a number of pieces, you can do the job by stacking the parts and cutting through them all at the same time. The method is very practical with even the smallest saw when you are working on thin material, say ⅛″ or ¼″ paneling. Of course, the thicker the material, the fewer the number of pieces you can stack. You will work more accurately if you use clamps to hold the parts together.

Angular Sawing

The two basic angular sawing operations are forming bevels or chamfers, which involve working with the blade tilted, and miters, done with the blade in normal position but with the pass made obliquely across the stock. For beveling, the tool is equipped with a tilt scale so the blade can be set to the necessary angle, but when the accuracy of the cut is critical, it's best to use the scale setting only as a guide. Check the test cut with a protractor before you get on with the job. Also, determine if the cutline indicator on the baseplate will work for bevel cuts as well as square ones. Be sure the tilt lock is secure and the leading edge of the baseplate is firmly seated on the wood before the blade makes contact.

The general rules for tool handling and feed-speed apply when making angular cuts. The blade will be working harder simply because it will be going through more wood

2-28.   Guiding a saw through a bevel cut is much easier when you establish a guide strip. You can use the bevel scale to set the blade angle but check the cut with a protractor before cutting good stock.

when at an angle than when it is perpendicular. You'll find it easier to work accurately if you guide the tool against a clamped-on guide strip (Figure 2-28), or work with an edge guide. It's good practice to check the real distance from the cut to the side of the baseplate, especially for angle settings you might use frequently. Do this by actually making a short cut in a board and then measuring from the cut to the edge of the plate that will bear against the guide. Make a note of the dimension and thereafter, whether cutting one piece or many, you'll know exactly where the guide strip should be positioned.

Bevels or chamfers on relatively small pieces can be done efficiently if you take the precautions demonstrated in Figure 2-29. The idea is to supply support for the tool and to keep the workpiece secure.

Miter Cuts

You can accomplish a simple miter cut pretty much as you would a crosscut; either by guiding the saw freehand along a marked line or by using a guide (Figure 2-30). Accuracy will

2-31.   The protractor guide may also be used for angular sawing. It can be hand-held or clamped to the work. Always provide good support for workpieces.

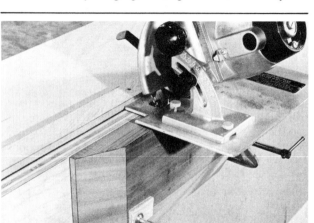

2-29.   You can chamfer or bevel shorter workpieces so long as you clamp them firmly and provide support for the saw. Blades work harder when set at an angle so adjust feed speed to suit.

2-30.   Using a guide strip when sawing miters is as practical as its use on straight cuts. Always support the saw on the bulk of the stock—not the cutoff.

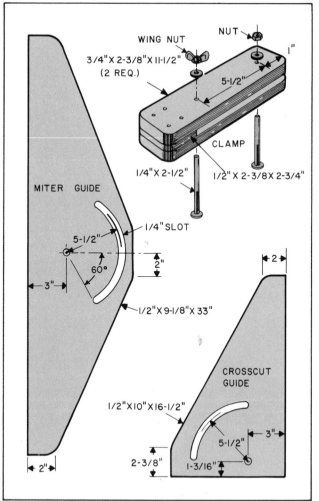

2-32.   Construction details of a guide that can be used for crosscutting and mitering. Jigs like this should be carefully sanded and then protected with applications of sealer.

depend on how carefully you work when marking the cutline and establishing the guide's position. Since miter cuts are made most often across narrow widths, you can use an adjustable protractor as a guide. Protractors, of various designs, are available as accessories (Figure 2-31) and there are others that you can make yourself.

The construction details of a combination unit that has become standard equipment in my shop are shown in Figure 2-32. Half-inch plywood, a piece of ¾″ lumber, and a couple of bolts are all you need to make the guides. For the half-guide (marked "crosscut guide"), establish the length of the arc to provide 45° and 90° settings. Drill end holes first and then cut away the waste with a saber saw. Do the same for the full guide (marked "miter guide").

Actually, both guides can be used for either miters or plain crosscuts (Figures 2-33 and 2-34). The full guide provides a bearing edge for the saw even before the blade makes contact, a feature many commercial guides don't have. If you wish, you can mark settings for particular angles along the clamp edges of the guides.

Another design for a jig that can be used for either crosscutting or mitering is detailed in Figure 2-35. If you're careful about positioning the lock arm and forming the slot that it requires, the extremes of the slot will be auto-stops for 45° and 90° settings.

Making a Miter Box

To cut narrow components, moldings and such, you can make a kind of miter box that is ordinarily used with a backsaw. The basic design, a U-shaped trough with cuts across it, is the same, but for the portable power saw you must add a saw guide and a ledge that provides support for the saw (Figure 2-36). The special box should also be longer than one designed for a handsaw. Provide for left- and right-hand miter cuts by using a saw guide and have a support ledge for each. The depth of the box can't be greater than the maximum depth of cut of the tool. In use, the box should be nailed or clamped to a solid surface. As always, keep hands well away from the cut area.

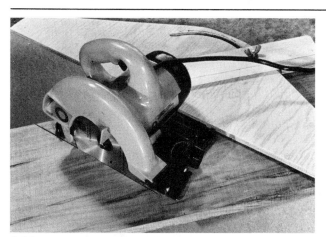

2-33.   The full guide will provide a bearing edge for the saw's baseplate even before the blade makes contact.

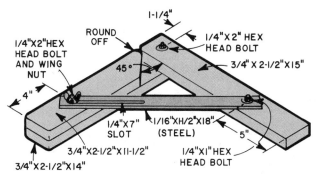

2-35.   Another example of an adjustable guide that you can make. The end points of the slot in the lock bar can be auto-stops for 90° and 45° cuts.

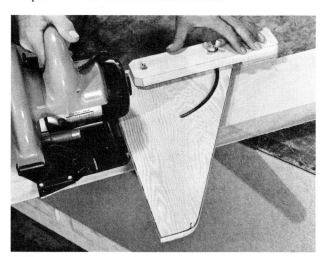

2-34.   You can switch to the second guide if it is more convenient for the job at hand. If you're careful when forming the slotted curve, its extreme points can act as stops for 90° and 45° settings.

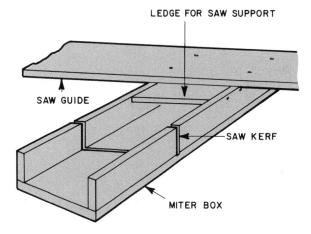

2-36.   You can make a special miter box for use with a portable circular saw. Install guides and saw-support ledges for both left-hand and right-hand miter cuts.

There are many special accessories for doing mitering work with a portable saw that are available commercially. The one shown in Figure 2-37 has a track arrangement to guide the saw. Also, since the track can be tilted, you can do compound angle work. Black & Decker has introduced a "Mitremate" saw guide that can be used with their "Workmate" portable bench and any 7¼″ saw (Figure 2-38). It can be used for angular cuts ranging from 30° to 90° and can also be used as a guide for plain crosscutting on work that is not more than 17″ wide.

The powered miter box (Figure 2-39) is really a stationary tool but it's designed around the type of portable saw we have been discussing. If you wished to imitate its features, and if your unit has a pivoting action to provide for blade projection, you could improvise by following the construction drawings for a "swing saw table" that are shown in Figure 2-40. This must be made very carefully, with ample provision for full use of the saw's guard, and it must be securely attached to a solid bench when it is used.

Notching

You can form notches, say for mid-point lap joints, or form dadoes and grooves, by setting the blade projection to the depth of cut required and then making a series of cuts as

2-39.   A powered miter box is essentially a portable saw mounted on an arm that allows the saw to pivot downward.

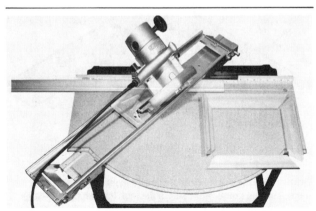

2-37.   Commercial accessory has a track arrangement to guide the saw. Because the track can be tilted and set at an angle, the unit can be set up for compound cuts.

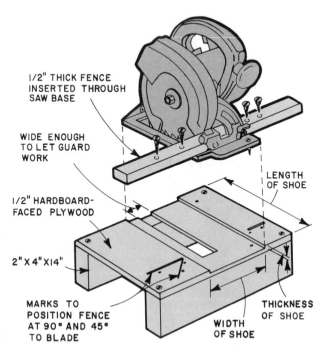

1/2″ THICK FENCE INSERTED THROUGH SAW BASE

WIDE ENOUGH TO LET GUARD WORK

1/2″ HARDBOARD-FACED PLYWOOD

2″ X 4″ X 14″

MARKS TO POSITION FENCE AT 90° AND 45° TO BLADE

LENGTH OF SHOE

THICKNESS OF SHOE

WIDTH OF SHOE

SWING SAW TABLE

2-40.   If you would like to try this idea, you can make a swing saw table that imitates a powered miter box. It will work only if your saw provides a pivot action to achieve depth of cut.

2-38.   The "Mitremate" saw guide is designed for use with Black & Decker's "Workmate" portable bench. Protractor allows settings from 30° to 90° in 5° increments.

shown in Figure 2-41 and 2-42. The cuts can overlap so you completely remove the waste material or they can be spaced so what remains can be removed with a chisel. The only difference between a notch and a groove or a dado is that the latter is likely to be longer. They all are U-shaped.

The best procedure is to make the outline—shoulder—cuts first by guiding the saw with a clamped-on strip of wood. Material between the first cuts can be removed by making repeat passes, either freehand or by relocating the guide strip.

To form the kind of notches that are needed in a stringer for a stairway, you must make two cuts that meet at the base of the angle (Figure 2-43). In order to clean out the waste by using only the saw, each cut must be longer than is needed to form the notch. Extra saw projection minimizes this over-cutting. If this method is not acceptable—for appearance or component strength—then just cut to the line and finish up with a handsaw or saber saw.

Since many similar cuts are required, you can work more accurately by making a template that can be used to guide the saw for each cut. The template (Figure 2-44) situates the saw and also acts as a stop that determines where the cut should end.

The same procedure applies when you must remove a corner from a board or panel (Figure 2-45).

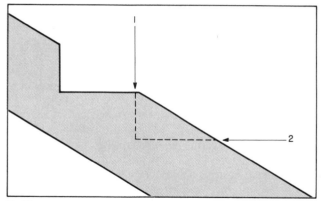

2-43.   This kind of cutout, required, for example, for the treads and risers in stair stringers, needs two cuts that meet at a common point. Overcutting will remove all the waste, or you can saw to the line and finish with a hand saw or saber saw.

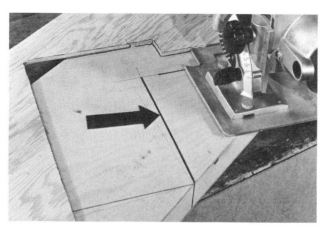

2-44.   When many such cuts are needed, as they are in a stair stringer, making a template to guide the saw for each of the cuts will help you work more accurately.

2-41.   You can cut notches for half-lap joints by making a number of passes and then cleaning away the waste with a chisel, or by making cuts that overlap and removing all the waste.

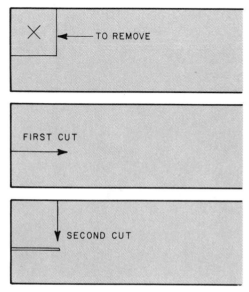

2-45.   The two-pass technique applies when it is necessary to remove a corner from a board or panel.

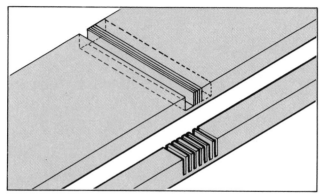

2-42.   You can use the same technique to form dadoes or grooves. Both the notch and the dado are U-shaped; the dado usually being longer.

Making Rabbet Cuts

A rabbet cut is an L-shaped form that is made along the edge of stock or across its end. There are two techniques that you can use with a portable saw. One—set blade projection to the required depth-of-cut and make repeat, overlapping passes to remove the waste. Two—make two cuts that meet at a particular point so the waste is removed as a solid strip.

When you employ the first technique, move the saw along a guide-strip to do the outline—shoulder—cut. Then remove the waste by making repeat passes, either working freehand or by repositioning the guide strip for each of the remaining passes needed to complete the job.

If you use the two-pass technique, which is demonstrated in Figures 2-46 and 2-47, start the job by making the shoulder cut, using a clamped-on strip to guide the saw. The blade projection must be adjusted to conform with the depth of the rabbet. Most times, this is about one half, or maybe a bit more, than the thickness of the stock. The second cut, which must meet the first one, has to be done with the stock placed on edge. This takes a little more organizing since stock-edges are rarely wide enough to supply adequate support for the saw, so a special setup, like the one I use (Figure 2-46), is needed.

The repeat-pass procedure is probably most practical when you need to cut a rabbet on just one piece. If the form is needed on many pieces, then setting up for the two-pass method is better. Actually, when you need many similar pieces, the two-pass idea aids production. For example, assume that you need six or eight components that are an inch or so wide and x-inches long with a rabbet at one or both ends. You can form the rabbet on material—plywood or lumber—that is sufficiently wide and then slice the material into the number of pieces you need.

Making Plunge Cuts

Cuts within a panel, without the need of a lead-in cut from an edge, can be accomplished with a portable circular saw regardless of its design. The basic approach for this operation is to place the saw on the work with the blade situated on the cut-line but with the blade clearing the work surface and with the guard retracted, which it must be in this situation. Then, with blade projection adjusted so it's a bit more than the stock's thickness, pivot the tool downward until it is seated firmly on the base plate (Figure 2-48). This system works if the saw projection on your tool is controlled by a pivoting action. If the tool has an elevator-type depth of cut adjust-

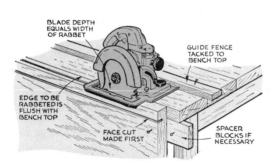

2-46.   This is one way to set up for the second cut when doing a two-pass rabbeting operation. The first cut—the shoulder—was made with the work flat and the saw moved along a guide strip.

2-48.   To start a plunge cut, rest the saw firmly on the front edge of the baseplate and then pivot it slowly downward to penetrate the stock. You can work by lowering the blade with the saw resting on the work. In either case, maintain a firm grip.

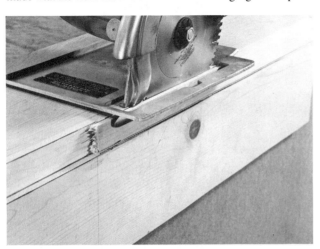

2-47.   The arrangement for the second pass of the rabbet cut can be made on the edge of a workbench. The waste piece has been broken off to reveal what the finished rabbet looks like.

2-49.   As with most other sawing operations, you'll work more accurately when plunge cutting if you set up guide strips for the cuts.

ment, line up the retracted blade with the layout mark and then, with power on, slowly lower the blade until its projection is a bit more than the stock's thickness.

This type of operation can be done freehand but, to assure straight cutting and square edges, use a strip to guide the saw (Figure 2-49). In order to clean out corners by using only the power saw, you must saw beyond the point where corners meet. Maximum blade projection will minimize the over-cutting you must do. If you want to, or must avoid the over cutting, saw only to the line from both directions and then complete the cut with a handsaw or saber saw.

It's advisable, after you have accomplished two or three of the cuts, to nail or clamp a support-piece across the pocket (Figure 2-50). This will prevent the part being cut out from binding the blade as it starts to fall, and maybe twists, as it separates from the body of the panel. The piece that falls away should be tack-nailed to the support piece and the support piece should be clamped to the panel. It's a nuisance to work this way but it contributes to safer operation and cleaner cuts.

The plunge-cutting technique can also be used to form slots (Figure 2-51). Work with a guide strip and cut to lines that determine the terminal points of the slots. You can, of course, add other strips of wood that will act as stops for the beginning and end of the cut. Make overlapping, repeat cuts for wide slots, or do outline cuts and then remove the waste by cutting at each end with a coping saw or saber saw.

Cut a Curve—A Circle?

The portable circular saw really isn't designed for such work but you can cut circles by working very carefully with a pivot-guiding system and being very patient about getting through the stock (Figure 2-52). The radius gauge is a thin strip of wood or metal fastened by the same system used to secure an edge-guide and which uses a nail as a pivot point. Actually, the technique is more feasible on thin material. The kerf that is cut is actually a cove, so feed very slowly and don't attempt very small circles.

Sawing must be done in stages with the first pass just deep enough to break the surface of the wood. Thereafter, increase depth of cut no more than 1/16″ for each pass required. Move the saw slowly and position yourself on the motor side

2-52. We don't recommend using the circular saw as a substitute for a saber saw but it can be used for limited circular sawing if you follow carefully the procedure described in the text.

2-50. Supplying support for the waste piece will keep it from falling away and maybe binding the blade. The support should be attached to both the body of the workpiece and the part being removed.

2-51. Forming slots can be done by using the plunge cutting technique. Use repeat passes or make outline cuts and then remove the waste by making end cuts with a saber saw.

2-53. It's also possible to saw a gentle curve if you first make a number of tangent cuts to remove as much of the waste as possible. What remains must be flexible enough so it can be moved away to keep the blade from binding.

Crosscut and Miter Jig

2-54. A crosscut and miter jig, that you can make, can be used in the shop or for on-site work. Either way, it should rest on a sturdy support.

2-55. Work to be crosscut is placed in the bed of the jig and up against the front fence. The cut is made by moving the saw along the track assembly. Note that you can cut more than one piece at a time.

2-56. For miter cutting, the track assembly is placed at the angle required. The use of lock pins, set in predrilled holes, lets you set the track at frequently-used angles.

2-57. By flipping the stock after making the first cut, the jig can be used for jobs like pointing fence pickets. The arrow points to one of the locking pins. These location holes will stand up better if you use steel bushing.

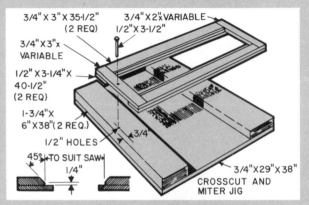

3/4" X 3" X 35-1/2" (2 REQ)
3/4" X 2" X VARIABLE
1/2" X 3-1/2"
3/4" X 3" X VARIABLE
1/2" X 3-1/4" X 40-1/2" (2 REQ)
1-3/4" X 6" X38" (2 REQ.)
3/4
1/2" HOLES
45° TO SUIT SAW
1/4"
3/4" X 29" X 38"
CROSSCUT AND MITER JIG

2-58. Construction details of a crosscut and miter jig that you can make. Cutting accuracy will depend on how carefully you assemble the unit.

of the tool. Be sure to supply good support for any workpiece in which you're making a circular cut.

Cutting a gentle curve is feasible if you first make a series of tangent cuts so that what is left to remove is flexible enough to avoid binding the blade (Figure 2-53). Techniques like this must be used with great care and are not suggested as substitutes for saber-saw work. The chapter on the saber saw and even the router will show other methods of doing circular cutting.

Special Jigs You Can Make

A crosscut and miter jig (Figure 2-54) can set you up for accurate cutting whether you use it in the shop or secure it to sawhorses for on-site work. The jig is used for crosscutting as shown in Figure 2-55. Workpieces are set on the bed of the jig and up against the front fence. The saw makes the cut as it is guided by the tracks.

Angular cutting is possible when the tracking system is placed as it is in Figure 2-56. The setup can be used for mitering or for jobs like the one shown in Figure 2-57. The work is flipped for the second cut; it isn't necessary to change the position of the track.

You can construct a duplicate by following the details in Figure 2-58. The holes for the pivot pin and the position lock-pins should provide a snug fit. Actually, since holes in wood will wear, you can assure continued accuracy by sizing the holes to receive steel bushings.

The distance between the track bars must suit the saw you own; other dimensions should be right for just about any saw. Check the thickness of the front and rear fences against the maximum projection of the saw blade. If necessary, you can pick up more depth-of-cut by using ¼″ instead of ½″ stock for the track base. If your saw does not have a wrap-around base plate, install a solid platform instead of ledges between the track arms. Cut a slot in the platform for the saw blade, positioned so the edge of the base plate will bear against the left track arm.

To crosscut, keep the saw against the rear fence and then feed it forward after the stock is positioned. The kerf in the back fence becomes a guide for lining up the workpiece. The crosscut position is fine for dado work. Adjust the blade projection for the depth of cut you want and then make repeat passes. If you do the outline cuts first, to marks on the work, you won't have to be so careful with the in-between cuts that clean out the waste. Jigs like this should be carefully made, sanded smooth, and then protected with several applications of a sanding sealer.

Jig Setup For Extra-Long Ripping

The setup that is shown in Figure 2-59 can be used when the width of the cut is beyond the capacity of an edge guide or when the waste, or the piece you need, doesn't provide sufficient support for the saw. Using two guide strips makes it possible to work with an edge guide when a cut is required at some midpoint in a panel.

Guide for Extra-Wide Cuts

The jig shown in Figure 2-60 involves a custom-made T-square with a slotted arm and an accessory base for the saw. In use, the saw and the guide move together; something like having an oversize edge guide. The arm of the square that rides against the work must be straight and smooth. Be sure the workpiece's edge is also straight. Irregularities will interfere with moving the saw in a straight line.

Place a strip of self-adhesive measuring tape on the saw side of the square's arm. It will, at least, allow setting the saw at an approximate position. Lock the saw where it should be by actually measuring from the edge of the workpiece.

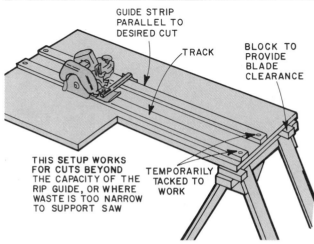

2-59.   Rip cuts that are wider than can be done with an edge guide can be done this way—using guide strips along with the edge guide. An extra strip raises the tool so its motor can clear the guide strip.

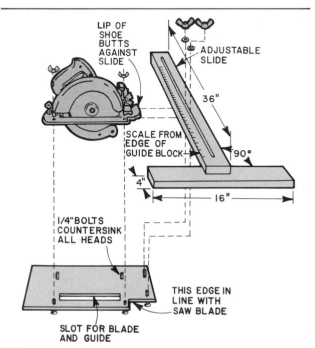

2-60.   This jig is designed so the guide and the saw move together in making extra-wide rip cuts. The saw is locked at a point on the T's arm to establish the width of the cut.

2-61. A very simple project that lets you use a portable saw like a stationary unit. The saw is inverted and supported on blocks so its baseplate becomes part of the unit's table surface.

2-62. An important point to be aware of is that the saw blade will not be completely shielded during the cut—the guard pivots downward so the work moves it beneath the table. We show the blade elevated for photo purposes; actually, it should barely poke through the stock.

Make a Table

You can use a portable saw like a stationary tool for simple crosscutting and ripping if you make a table like the one pictured in Figure 2-61. Cut the opening in the top with a saber saw, suiting its dimensions to match the size of the tool's base plate. Attach the support blocks with glue and screws, and then secure the saw, in inverted position, with flathead screws driven through the base plate into the support blocks.

A VERY CRITICAL point to remember, if you make the table, is that the saw blade will not be guarded when you do ripping or crosscutting (Figures 2-62 and 2-63). Because the tool's guard pivots, it will be moved under the work during the pass. Always be aware of this. Don't try to rip narrow pieces or crosscut short pieces. Always keep hands well away from the cut area. We show a higher-than-necessary blade projection in the photos. For safety sake, set the blade so it barely pokes through the work.

Construction details for a very simple unit are shown in Figure 2-64. The design of the rip fence requires that it be clamped in place when it is used.

How to Make a Panel Saw

You have probably seen an apparatus like the one shown in Figure 2-65 being used in a lumberyard so you know how convenient it can be for initial sizing cuts on large panels. Our project, designed around a portable circular saw, is designed to stand vertically so it can be placed against a wall to take up very little floor space. You can, if you wish, add angled braces at the back so the unit can be freestanding. Another thought is to hinge the braces and add locking arms. Then the project can be used as you choose.

The device is basically a frame with the saw in a carriage that is track-mounted to allow vertical movement. The work is placed in the frame and crosscut by moving the saw downward (Figure 2-65). Cables from sliding-door closers (Figure 2-66) connect to the carriage to counterbalance the weight of the saw and carriage. Spring-type sash balances can be substituted for the door closers but they may not be as

2-63. The exposed-blade precaution also applies to crosscutting. Don't try to cut short pieces or rip narrow ones. Hands must always be well away from the cut area.

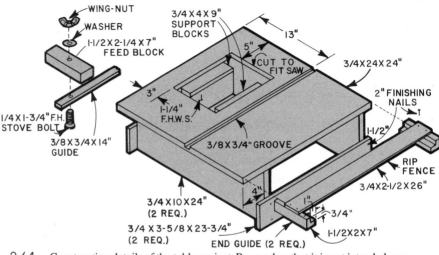

2-64. Construction details of the table project. Remember that it is not intended as a substitute for a stationary tool. The rip fence is secured with clamps at one or both ends.

2-65. A panel saw lets you crosscut standard size panels with minimum fuss. You can make one that allows use of your own portable saw if you follow our instructions.

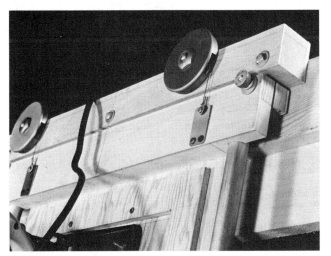

2-66. The weight of the saw and the carriage it rides in is counterbalanced with sliding door closers. Other methods can be used, but remember that counterbalancing is intended only to help the operator move the saw up and down.

2-67. The carriage, with the saw rotated 90°, can be locked in any position along the tracks. Thus the unit can be used for ripping panels as well as crosscutting them.

readily available. Actually you can accomplish the same result by using a steel weight. The steel weight could be attached by cable to the carriage with the cable running over a pulley at the top of the frame.

No matter how you go about counterbalancing the weight of the saw and carriage, don't design things so the saw will be snapped back at the end of a cut. The whole idea is merely to relieve the weight so you can easily move the carriage up or down.

Since the saw can be rotated 90° and the carriage can be locked at any point on the tracks, the project can be used for ripping as well as crosscutting. When ripping, the saw is in a fixed position; the work is moved to make the cut (Figure 2-67).

One inch OD pipe was used for the tracks. Black-iron pipe (¾″) would work okay, or you can use something with a larger diameter if you wish. Just be sure to have the track material on hand before you start constructing the related parts. The reason for the two-piece, bottom track support is to provide a method of adjustment so the tracks can be set parallel (Figure 2-68).

The carriage holds the portable saw securely and permits its vertical action. The saw is bolted to a plywood plate that fits the cutout in the carrier. Both the plate and the cutout are square. This feature permits the saw to be rotated so it can be used for crosscutting or ripping.Construction accuracy is very critical here (See Figures 2-69 and 2-70). The ends of the top and bottom carriage members are drilled for the tube-tracks and slotted so they serve as split clamps. The lock mechanism consists of a bolt and a knurled nut or wing nut (Figure 2-71).

Study the photographs and the construction details that are shown in Figures 2-72 and 2-73 before you start fabrication. There are choices when choosing material. Construction grade fir is okay so long as you're very selective about choosing good, straight stock. It might pay to spend a little more for something like kiln dried straight grain fir. Inferior material can distort enough to destroy the accuracy you build into the tool.

2-68. The bottom support for the tracking tubes is made in two pieces. This allows adjustment so the tubes can be set parallel to each other.

2-69.   The carriage has a cutout that is sized to fit the plates on which the portable saw is mounted.

2-70.   The saw, mounted on plates, fits in the opening in the carriage and is secured with a simple locking mechanism—small pieces of metal bar stock that bear down on the plate on which the saw is mounted.

2-71.   The ends of the top and bottom members of the carriage assembly are drilled to receive the tube-tracks and then slotted so they act as split clamps.

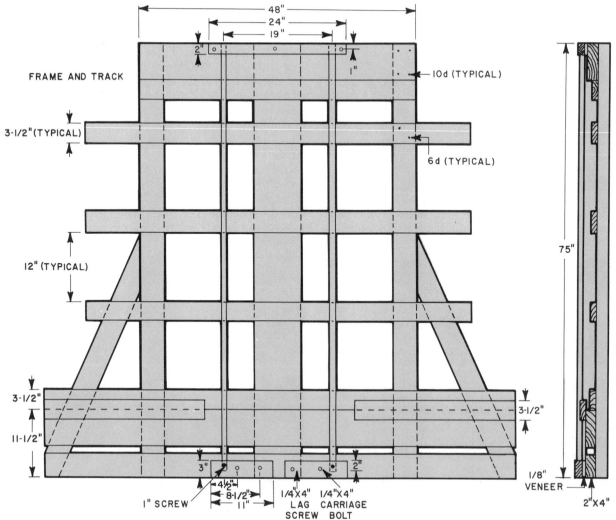

2-72.   Construction details of the frame for the panel saw.

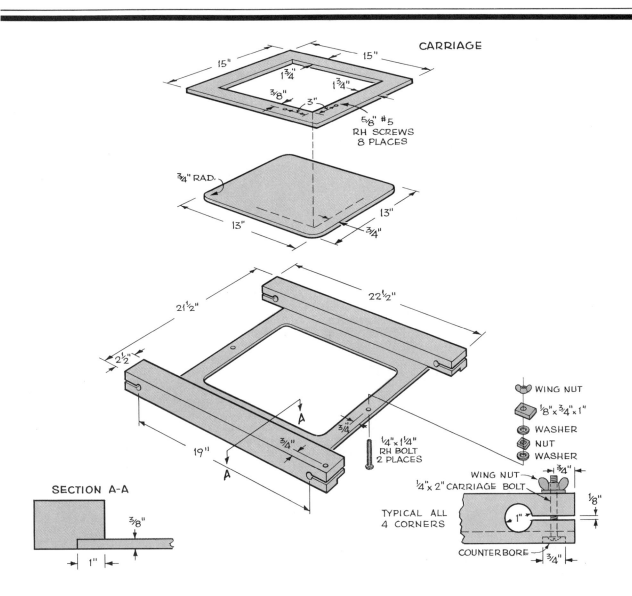

2-73.   This drawing details the construction aspects of the carriage and the saw mounting arrangement.

A Few Practical Commercial Accessories

Portalign's SAW GUIDE is designed for attachment to the base plate of a portable saw (Figure 2-74). When it is used for crosscutting, the saw, in a sense, rides on ball bearings along the arm that serves as a guide (Figure 2-75). Because of the accessory's built-in protractor the saw can be positioned for left or right angle cuts up to 45° (Figure 2-76). The guide capacity of the product is about 15″ on square cuts and across 12″ stock at 45°. The unit can be removed from the saw when it isn't practical for the job on hand.

The SAW MATE is a guide table that uses tracking arms to control the path of the saw (Figure 2-77). It can be used for crosscutting, by keeping the work in place and moving the saw, or for ripping, by securing the saw and moving the work. Miter cuts are possible because the unit's fence can be positioned to hold the workpiece at a particular angle. This type of cut is made as if the saw was being moved for crosscutting. An accessory is shown in Figure 2-78. This can provide a lot of helpful support when working on large panels.

The STRATE-CUT (Figure 2-79) is actually a set of extrusions that can be organized in various ways to provide a guide for a portable saw when crosscutting, ripping, mitering, beveling, and so on. Clamps are provided so the guides can be secured where needed. The guides, because of how they are designed, can extend to more than eight feet, which makes them practical for jobs like ripping a standard panel parallel to its long dimension. Since the STRATE-CUT is basically a guidance system, it can be used with a saber saw or router, or even with a knife for scoring wallboard.

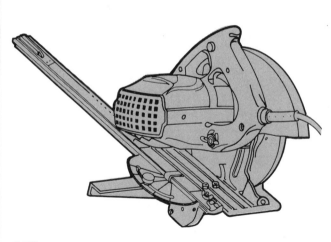

2-74.   This saw guide is attached to the baseplate of the portable tool.

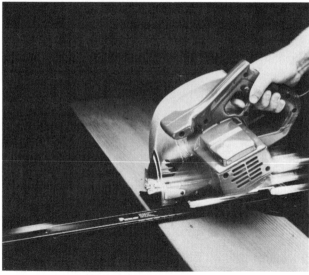

2-75.   The saw, on its "new" mount, rides along the guide arm. Because of a ball bearing slide arrangement, the saw is easy to move.

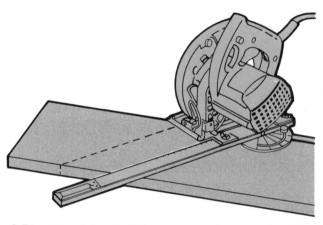

2-76.   The unit has a built-in protractor so the saw can be guided through angular cuts as well as straight ones.

2-77.   A product called "Saw Mate", is a system of tracking arms and a plate on which the portable saw is situated. A pivoting fence lets you position workpieces for angular cuts. The saw still moves in a straight line.

2-78.   An accessory for the "Saw Mate" is another table that provides support for large workpieces, like panels. A router was placed in the photo to show that the accessory can also be used for router operations.

2-79.   The name for this set of parts is "Strate-Cut". The pieces can be assembled in various ways to provide guidance for a portable saw whether it's being used for straight or angular cuts.

3. The Saber Saw

It wasn't too many years ago that the saber saw was introduced and made as big a splash with portable power tool users as the portable circular saw did when it first appeared. The continuing enthusiasm is justified because of the tool's special, practical features. The only tool that might be more popular, at least as a first-choice, is the portable drill.

With a saber saw you can do on-location chores that might be done on a bandsaw or jigsaw in the shop. But even with stationary tools on hand, the size of the workpiece often makes it more convenient to do a sawing job with a tool that can be applied to the work (Figure 3-1).

Of course, the saber saw doesn't make the stationary tools obsolete. In the case of the bandsaw, the hand-held tool can't compete in cutting speed, nor can it rival the big tool on jobs like resawing, pad cutting, or making compound cuts. The concept of the saber saw demands a stiff, relatively wide blade so it's not about to challenge the jigsaw, which can be used with a hair-thin blade, in terms of extremely fine, tight-radius fretwork. Its advantages are in its small, palm-grip size and its portability. However, don't misjudge it because of its size or discount its ability to turn a reasonably tight corner. Scroller designs that allow turning the blade as you move the tool can follow some pretty fancy designs, whereas the tools in general have grown up rough and tough and can easily get through 2″ stock or any plywood. With the correct blade, saber saws can be used on plastics, metals, pipe, and even leather or paper.

One of the tool's exclusive features is its ability to make piercing cuts—internal cuts without a lead-in cut from an edge—without the need of a starting hole. Since the blade is chucked at only one end, it's possible to hold the tool at an angle, resting it firmly on the front edge of the baseplate so the blade's teeth begin to cut as you slowly pivot the tool until the baseplate is solidly on the work (Figure 3-2). Thus, you penetrate the work and arrive at the normal operating position to finish the job. More about this technique later.

What makes the tool more flexible, and even more exciting today, is the great variety of blades that are available and the fact that newer models provide different, specific

3-1. The saber saw makes it easy to work on large panels that might be difficult to muscle over the surface of a stationary tool. Much of the work ordinarily done on a jigsaw or bandsaw can be accomplished with this unique tool.

3-2. One of the features of the saber saw is its ability to do plunge cutting, which simply means making internal cutouts without the need of a lead-in cut from an edge. The technique will be described later in this chapter.

speeds, or allow an infinitely variable choice through the tool's speed range. Thus, you can choose an efficient combination of speed and blade to saw anything from paper to steel. With the right blade you can do heavy-duty work like notching studs or stair stringers and then, merely by changing to another blade design and possibly another speed, go immediately to more delicate work on cabinets and paneling.

Types and Sizes

The type of saw to consider depends, as always, on the kind of cutting you anticipate and the frequency of use. While the tool design, for some reason or other, bears many names—saber or sabre saw, jigsaw, bayonet saw, scroller saw—the basic function of the mechanism is to convert a rotating action into the up-and-down motion required by the saw blade (Figure 3-3). There is a lot of variation in features like horsepower, weight, blade stroke-length, fixed blade or scroller type, and, of course, price (Figures 3-4—3-10).

Generally, you get what you pay for. A manufacturer isn't going to, or can't, put into a light-duty, single speed, $30 tool what goes into a $100 or better, hefty, heavy-duty, variable speed version. This doesn't discount the less costlier models for light, occasional use. However, they may not cut as fast on all materials and they probably won't stand up as well as the "bigger" saws under continuous, hard use conditions. When the tool has a more powerful motor it will cut faster and more smoothly, run cooler, and have a good, solid feel to it. Its longer life will be due, in part, to huskier construction and better bearings. Sometimes, a more expensive tool will have extra refinements like an auxiliary knob that permits a two-hand grip, and removable base-plate inserts that minimize splintering and feathering when sawing materials like plywood.

Cutting capacity isn't much of a question these days. Getting through 1½″ wood is a basic need and it would be difficult to find a unit that won't do it. The capacity factor is often listed as so many inches in softwood and so many inches in hardwood. Many times, the tool's capacity in aluminum or steel is also rated. These areas, though, are affected as much by horsepower as by blade length. Some tools can be used with special, extra-long blades so you can cut through stock as thick as 4″, but they have the horsepower to do it.

Blade speeds—strokes per minute—are variable. A single speed has limited function; a couple of specific speeds is better, whereas a variable speed control allows near-perfect operating conditions for various materials. High cutting speeds used in combination with a tapered or hollow-ground blade generally result in fine, smooth cuts in wood. Slower speeds are better for getting through metals and some plastics.

Blade Action

Some units provide a consistent up-and-down blade motion, whereas others do sawing with a canted blade (the blade slopes away from the vertical), or one that describes a slight orbit while moving up and down, something like a narrow ellipse standing on its long radius. In essence, the last two blade motions cause the blade to move away from the cut

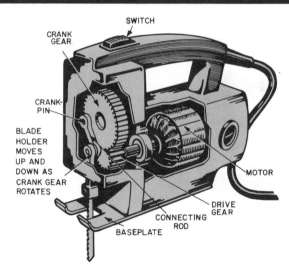

3-3.   Saber saws differ in terms of weight, size, power, and blade strokes per minutes, but all of them convert a rotary motion to the up-and-down action required by the saw blade.

3-4.   This Black & Decker unit is rated "professional." Motor fan is designed to clear dust from the cut area. A 4.5 amp motor, and ball and roller bearing construction make it a tool to last for quite a while. The speeds are variable; the blade has a four-position orbital action.

3-5.   Makita's double insulated, single speed, 3700 spm saw (they call it a jigsaw) is rated at 2.6 amps and can saw up to 2″ in wood and ¼″ in steel. Lever under the housing is actually the on-off switch. Standard equipment includes six blades, a pivot guide, and an edge guide.

3-6.   Skil's scroller model allows the user to select any of three cutting methods. Set the blade to follow tool direction, or lock it at any 90° interval, or rotate it 360° by controlling it with the front knob. Speeds are variable.

3-9.   If you haven't noticed, this tool is working without a trailing electric cord. It's a cordless saber saw that can cut through 2x4s. The battery powered concept is making its mark in all areas of portable tools.

3-7.   Porter Cable calls this double insulated, heavy-duty unit a "bayonet saw." A unique feature is the roller bearing blade support guide which can increase accuracy and add to blade life. A built-in blower keeps the cut area clear.

3-10.   Top handle unit has an auxiliary side knob, a pretty tough worm gear drive, and an oversize baseplate. Blade action is orbital and moves at 4,500 spm. Tool comes with a special insert that can be used to minimize chipping and splintering.

3-8.   Electronics are also becoming part of the power tool scene. New scroller-type saw has electronic analog feedback that maintains the selected speed under load conditions. Speed dial has 20 incremental settings.

area on the downstroke when it isn't working, and move it forward on the upstroke when the teeth are biting into the wood (Figure 3-11).

The idea behind the alternate actions is to reduce power-wasting drag on the blade's downstroke, when it isn't actually working, and to help it keep the kerf—the groove made by the blade—free of waste material. The purpose is to reduce friction so cutting is easier, and to minimize heat build-up that might burn the wood and shorten the blade's use-life.

Basic Accessories

One feature that should be built into the tool is a baseplate that can be tilted from zero to 45°. The adjustable baseplate allows the saw to be used for beveling, cross-bevels (often called "miters"), and even compound cuts—the shapes achieved by moving the tool at an angle across stock but with the blade tilted. You'll probably find this feature useful, so check for it when you judge various models.

Some units are equipped with, or have available as accessories, special inserts that attach to the baseplate in some way to minimize the open area around the blade. Their purpose is to bear down on surface fibers close to the blade and so eliminate or, at least, minimize the degree of chipping that occurs as the blade teeth leave the work on the upstroke. This is especially useful when sawing plywood.

Edge guides are as available for saber saws as they are for circular saws (Figure 3-12). One will probably be included if you buy a saber saw "kit", but any respectable saw should be designed to accept one even if you must buy it as an accessory. Some edge guides do double-duty. The one shown in Figure 3-13 is designed to accept an adjustable point that

can be used as a pivot to guide the saw through circular cuts. Later, we'll show how this is done and how you can make an accessory that serves the same purpose but which has greater capacity.

A saber saw can be used somewhat like a stationary jigsaw by mounting the tool on the underside of an accessory table (Figure 3-14). Since the blade is chucked only at one end, the smallest blade you use must be stiffer than those that are used in a jigsaw. Actually, the setup emulates a stationary jigsaw when it is used with saber saw blades. In either case, work must be fed very carefully to make sure that the blade stays on the cutline. Because the blade is not held taut between upper and lower chucks, feeding too fast, or twisting the work too abruptly when getting around a turn, will result in ruining a workpiece or, at least, in poor quality.

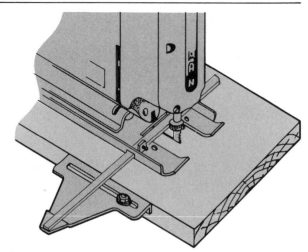

3-12.   Edge guide, often called a rip guide, is used to guide the saw through cuts that are parallel to an edge. The edge against which it bears must be flat and true.

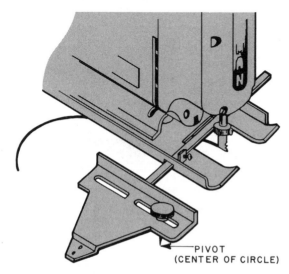

3-13.   Some edge guides are equipped with a trammel point so the accessory can be used to guide the tool through circular sawing. We'll show how you can make pivot guides with greater capacity.

3-11.   Saber saw blades cut on the "up" stroke. All of them move up and down. Some might be canted, others will describe a slight orbit—it depends on how the tool is designed.

The table that is shown in Figure 3-14 is actually a combination unit, one that can be fitted with a saber saw or a portable router. If you are interested in a table, be sure it will accommodate the portable tools you have or plan to add. Usually, it's best to go for tools and accessories that are produced by the same manufacturer.

The Importance of Saw Blades

A close study of saw blades that are available for the saber saw is almost a course in how the tool is used and a view of its many applications. The blades that are profiled in Figure 3-15 are just a sampling of the many varieties that are available. In most cases, a single blade is packaged with the tool. Like the combination blade usually supplied with a table saw, the free blade will be a general-purpose wood cutter,

good for initial sizing cuts but hardly ideal for all applications. To rely on the one blade for all jobs imposes restrictions and limitations that will reduce the quality of your work, and will even increase your shop chores. It's also a fact of saber saw blade-life that they are subject to breakage. Even if you did choose to work with one blade, you should have a reserve package on hand.

A special blade with many teeth and formed with a tapered or hollow-ground cross-section will cut a kerf with minimum feathering and so reduce if not eliminate the follow-through sanding needed to get a perfect edge. It's a good blade to use on plywood—in fact it may be called a "plywood blade"—and it will also do nicely on lumber (Figure 3-16). As a rule of thumb, blades designed for fine cutting, being narrow and having many teeth, produce a

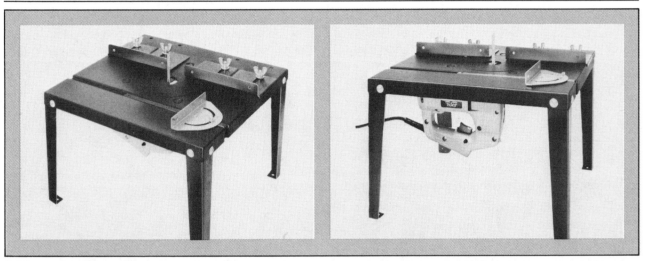

3-14.   Tables are available that allow you to use the saber saw like a stationary tool. Check before buying to be sure saw and table are compatible. Some tables can also be used with a portable router.

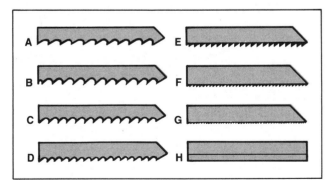

3-15.   This is just a sampling of available saber-saw blades. (A) 7-tooth blade for fast, rough cuts in thick wood and plaster-board. (B) 7-tooth extra long, for sawing logs and timbers up to 4″ thick. Usually 6″ long. (C) 10-tooth, for all-around use on hard-wood, softwood, composition board, plastics. (D) 10-tooth taper-ground, for cuts in plywood, veneer, plastic laminates. (E) 14-tooth, for soft, nonferrous metals (aluminum, copper, brass) up to ¼″ thick. (F) 24-tooth, for fine cuts in thin sheet metal and tubing, either ferrous or nonferrous. (G) 32-tooth, for ferrous metals (iron and steel), pipe, and solid rod and bar stock. (H) Knife blade, for rubber, leather, wallboard, cloth, resilient floor tiles.

3-16.   Taper-ground or hollow-ground blades are best to use when you wish to keep surface chipping and feathering to a minimum. The blades will have many small teeth; are often called plywood blades or scroller blades.

confining kerf and can snap more easily than a wide blade with coarse teeth, so they must be moved carefully and slowly.

Install a blade with wave-set teeth, like those found on common hacksaw blades, and you can use the saber saw almost like a power hacksaw. For jobs on leather, rubber, cardboard, and the like, there is a sharp-edge blade without teeth that installs in the tool like any other blade but cuts like a knife.

If you are involved in remodeling work you can use blades that aren't fazed by an occasional nail, getting through them without damage (Figure 3-17), and others, shaped like the example in Figure 3-18, that allow cutting through moldings and baseboards and other installations that might be flush against a wall (Figure 3-19).

Blades for the saber saw are not expensive enough to prohibit having an all-inclusive assortment that will keep you prepared to cut anything from paper to steel. Actually, being prepared this way can prove to be the most economical arrangement in the long run since you will be less likely to abuse blades by using them on jobs they were never meant to do.

If you plan on using the saw for only occasional wood cutting, then a few dollars will buy the blades you should have. If your work calls for using the tool in depth, then it's wise and economical to purchase assortments. For example, the Sears Craftsman catalog lists an assortment of fifty blades in a storage case for about $26. Buying the blades individually would increase the cost considerably and, as usually happens, you may find yourself without the blade that's best for the job you want to do now.

The blade selection chart in Figure 3-20 doesn't list the blade width or its length or the tooth design, simply because such details would result in repeating blade-use suggestions and would make the chart difficult to use. Actually, the number of teeth per inch is probably the single most important factor except for plywood sawing and similar applications where you want the smoothest cut possible. In such cases, a hollow-ground or taper-back blade design, in addition to many teeth, will produce the best results. The test cuts in Figure 3-21 clearly prove the point.

Normally, you should choose a wide blade (3/8" or 1/2") for straight cutting, especially on heavy stock, and a narrow one (1/4" or less) for forming curves. The thickness of the material should also influence your choice in blade length. Blade lengths can be short (2½" to 3") or long (from 4" to 6"). The lengths can vary according to tool brand, but most manufacturers do supply both long and short blades. The instructions that come with the tool will list available blades that can be used with the tool.

3-17.   Some blades are tough enough to get through an occasional nail without damage or breakage. However, use a blade that's designed for the purpose when you plan on sawing metals.

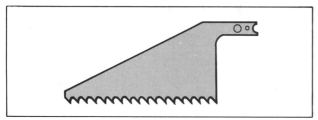

3-18.   All saber saws can be used with blades that are shaped like this. Called offset blades, they're designed so the teeth will be slightly ahead of or in line with the front edge of the tool's baseplate.

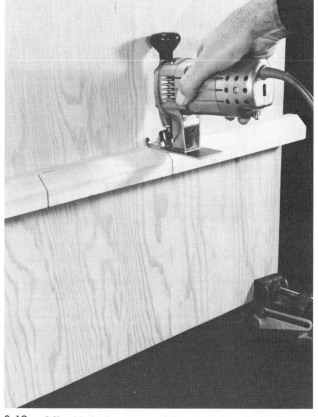

3-19.   Offset blades let you saw right to a surface. A nice feature when, for example, you are removing or repairing sections of molding. Cut just a bit shy to avoid damaging what the material is attached to.

WOOD		
TEETH PER INCH	MATERIAL	RECOMMENDATIONS
3	Lumber, logs	Fast cuts in heavy lumber (up to 6″ thick) of logs to 5″ diameter.
5	Lumber (nail free)	Fast but rough general cutting; good for ripping stock ½″ to 2″ thick.
6	Lumber	As above, but produces cuts a bit smoother.
7 or 8	Lumber, insulation board	Good general-purpose blade, especially for construction work; medium-smooth cuts.
10	Lumber (especially hardwood) under ½″ wallboard	Smoother cuts, but slower on heavy work; for scrollwork; also good for composition board, plastics. (Some saw makers recommend for general-purpose cutting; others offer special taper-back or hollow-ground versions to reduce chipping of plywood, laminates.)
12 or 14	Plywood	Smoothest cuts in plywood and fine scrollwork; also good for materials such as linoleum or rubber tile, hardboards, nylon, Plexiglas, and fiberglass. Also for plastic laminates, though some makers recommend use of 14 (or even 18) t.p.i. metal-cutting blade.
10 (H.S.S.)	Wood with occasional nail	Special steel will stand up under nail-cutting; also good for materials such as asbestos, laminates, etc.
7 (Flush cut or offset)	Lumber	For cutting flush to a wall, as with baseboards and moldings.
Special-purpose knife edge	Leather, cork, cloth, paper, cardboard, rubber, Styrofoam	Material being cut must be firmly held and supported.
METAL		
6 (H.S.S.)	Aluminum, copper, brass, laminates, compositions	Heavy cutting in plate or tubing; sample maximum cut: ½″ in aluminum plate.
10 (H.S.S.)	Same as above	General cutting with smoother finish than above.
14 (H.S.S.)	Aluminum, brass, bronze, copper, laminates, hardboard, mild steel, pipe	General cutting with smooth finish; maximum in steel: ¼″ - ½″ depending on manufacturers' specifications.
18 (H.S.S.)	Same as above	For lighter materials; maximum cuts about ⅛″.
24 (H.S.S.)	Sheet metal, light-gauge steel, thin-wall tubing, Bakelite, tile, etc.	Finest-tooth blade offered by some makers; wave-set.
32 (H.S.S.)	Thin-gauge sheet metals, thin-wall tubing, metal trim	Wave-set blade cuts fine kerf; maximum in steel: ¹⁄₁₆″. For typical hacksaw jobs.
Note: For information on length and width of blades, see text.		

3-20.   Use this chart as a guide when selecting a blade for optimum results on particular materials. Remember that what you can do with a blade is also affected by the power of the saw.

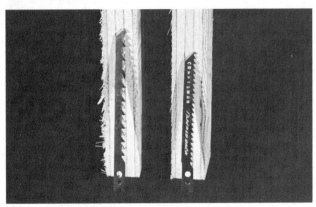

3-21. Wise choice of blades can make a big difference in the quality of the cut. Cut on the left was made with a coarse, few-teeth-per-inch blade. A small-toothed, taper-back blade produced the superior edge.

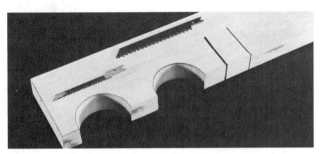

3-22. An interesting factor of blade-use is that a wide, coarse blade can often make as tight a turn as a narrow one. The wider kerf formed by the big blade provides more room for it to turn. The difference will be in the quality of the cut.

3-23. Cutting edges of toothless blades are fused with particles of tungsten carbide. They're indispensable for sawing many non-wood materials. They can also be used on wood but they are not speed demons.

3-24. Ten-inch-long test cuts show the difference in cut-speed of various blades. From the top—seven-teeth-per-inch blade with set teeth, 10-teeth-per-inch taper-back blade, medium grit tooth-less blade. Notice the difference in cut-quality as well as speed.

It's good practice to choose the shortest blade that will do the job and not tax the tool by using it with blades that are longer and bigger than it can handle. For example, the big 6″ blade varieties are not usually recommended for saws that have less than a full 1″ stroke.

Of two similar blades, the one that has set teeth and is "flat ground" will leave rougher edges than one that is taper-ground or hollow-ground. A very important factor to be aware of is that a blade with few, heavy-set teeth per inch will often turn as tight a radius as a narrow blade with many teeth per inch and little or no set (Figure 3-22). It's even possible that the heavy blade might be able to make a tighter turn than the other because the big blade forms a wider kerf which provides more room for the blade to turn.

Bear in mind that when the chart recommends a particular blade for scrollwork, the narrowest, finest-tooth blade you can use in a saber saw can't begin to match the fretwork designs you can cut on a jigsaw when it is fitted with a fine jeweler's blade. The point is made so you won't try to do work that can only result in blade-breakage.

Some manufacturers offer blades that are intended to fit only their saws. If you are ever in doubt about which blade to buy for the tool you own, take an example blade with you and be sure to match the shank end, the end of the blade that is gripped in the chuck. Although the trend has been toward standardization, there are differences in the combinations of teeth per inch, set, lengths, and widths the makers offer. The owner's manual supplied with the tool will state specifics concerning the tool-blade relationships.

All blades, stiff as they might be, can still bend, twist, or arc in the cut. The main cause of such problems is forcing the cut, asking the teeth to chew out more material than they were designed to handle at a particular feed-speed. You can easily tell when you're guilty of poor practice by sound and feel. If the cut isn't progressing steadily without excessive feed pressure, the blade is being overworked, is dull, or isn't the blade design that's best for the job.

Don't use woodworking blades to cut any metal except do-it-yourself materials, such as aluminum, that can be worked with ordinary woodworking tools. In a pinch, however, you can use metal-cutting blades to saw wood, hardboards, and similar materials.

Teflon-coated blades are more expensive. Generally, they reduce friction in any cut, but they are especially practical if you plan to do much work with lumber that is green, damp, or contains much pitch. Whether or not it has a special coating, a blade that has few teeth per inch and lots of set is the best choice for such work. This also applies to any heavy stock. However, in cases when you want a reasonably nice finish, it's not taboo to work with a smoother-cutting blade. Just make the cut more slowly than you would with the recommended blade.

"Toothless" Blades

Relatively new, tungsten carbide blades that came into being for industrial applications, are now available to any power tool user. These blades cut almost anything and have a long-use life. The blades do not have teeth like a regular saw blade; instead, they have countless particles of tungsten carbide granules fused to the blade's cutting edge (Figure 3-23).

Cutting speed is not a strong point of the blades. A group of conventional teeth will chew out more material and do it faster than an edge of grit. Judged under average woodworking conditions, this suggests that the toothless blades do not—and probably aren't meant to—replace regular saw blades. But they do provide a valuable supplement, since no conventional blade can manage to saw through ceramic tile or slate or similar materials—or get through sheet metal that isn't sandwiched between scrap material without excessive burring and edge distortion.

The blades will work on wood, and they leave an impressive, almost sanded edge with minimal feathering, but they don't come close to sawing as speedily as conventional blades. Under test conditions, a medium-grit tungsten carbide saber saw blade took about 50 seconds to make a 10" cut through ¾" douglas fir plywood. A 10-tooth-per-inch, taper-back blade made it in about 19 seconds, while a seven-tooth-per-inch blade with set teeth ran the 10" in about 14 seconds (Figure 3-24).   .

There was, however, quite a difference in the quality of the cuts. Although the taper-back blade (designed for the purpose) left a respectable edge, much more impressive than that left by the coarser blade, the toothless blade was definitely the cut-quality winner.

Tungsten carbide blades are also a good choice when cutting hard metals. Shop tests showed that it took about 92 seconds to get through a 1¼" OD, heavy-walled steel tube with a 32-tooth, wave-set blade, but only about 80 seconds

with a coarse-grit toothless blade. This was not a great difference in time but the other fact that emerged was the difference in the durability of the blades. The conventional blade was obviously tired after the job, whereas the tungsten carbide blade was ready to repeat the chore many times over.

The durability factor applies to the toothless blades generally. There's no question that they will outlast conventional blades by a good margin. But long life and cut-speed are not the prime considerations. The tungsten carbides are the blades to use when you need to use a saber saw to cut ceramic tile, slate, asbestos cement, clay pipe, brick, and other problem materials that you can't touch with a conventional blade.

The chart in Figure 3-25 suggests a practical grit selection for various materials. All of the grit types leave comparatively smooth edges with a minimum of feathering and chipping. The fine grit works best in thin, hard materials when cut quality is important and when chipping and delamination might be a problem. Medium-grit blades can be used if you wish to cut faster or if you find that the waste from the material you're cutting is packing between the tungsten carbide particles. Coarse-grit blades cut the fastest and, since they form a wider kerf, will move around smaller radii than finer-grit blades. This aspect is comparable to being able to make tighter turns with a wide, heavy-set blade than a no-set, narrow blade. There is simply more room in the kerf for the blade to maneuver.

As with any blade, tool speed can be an efficiency factor when working with the toothless blades. Slower speeds are best on materials such as stainless steel and counter top

MATERIAL TO BE CUT	FINE GRIT	MEDIUM GRIT	COARSE GRIT
Fiber Glass (Polyesters, Epoxies, Malamines, Silicones)	X	X	X
Ceramic Tile, Slate, Cast Stone	X	X	
Asbestos Cement, Nail Embedded Wood, Plaster with Nails			X
Chalkboard, Carbon/Graphite, Clay Pipe, Brick	X	X	
Stainless Steel Trim, Sheet Metal to 18 Ga., Ducting, Counter Top Materials, Tempered Hardboard	X		
Plywood, Hardwood Veneer Plywood	X	X	

Note: Use slower speeds with variable speed saws.   Highlighted boxes show most popular grit size.

Select fine grit when a smooth cut is desired in thin, hard materials where precision is important, particularly where splitting, chipping, or delamination is a problem. Use medium-grit blades where faster cutting is needed or when loading of fine-grit blades occurs. The coarse-grit blades cut faster in thick or softer materials where a rougher finish is acceptable. Coarser grit saws will permit up to a 30% smaller radius cut.

Courtesy of Remington Arms Co., Inc.

3-25.   Suggestions for selecting the most efficient grit when using toothless blades to saw various materials.

laminates. Testing has indicated that in all cases it's wise to start at a slow speed and increase spm (strokes per minute) to the point where the blade is cutting most efficiently. It's a procedure to follow, at least for the first time, on each new material you work on.

Always be certain that the blade is locked securely in the chuck. Methods of achieving this can vary depending on the tool. With some, it's a question of tightening a single Allen screw with a small wrench (Figure 3-26). Others may have a screw that bears against the back edge of the blade as well as a lock screw. The owner's manual will tell how to set the blade securely.

It's not a bad idea to check the lock screw occasionally as you work since vibration might cause it to loosen. Always remove the blade when storing the tool.

Operational Speeds

The rule of thumb is, slow speeds with coarse blades, high speeds with finer cutters. This is based on the thought that, generally, you'll be using heavy blades to saw through comparatively tough material like construction grade fir, and smoother cutters when working on something like kiln dried pine or fancy hardwoods and plywood.

An advantage of a tool with a variable speed control is that you can adjust the speed as you work. For example, you can slow down a bit when the blade has to get through a particularly dense grain area or a knot.

Of course, efficient sawing depends on the combination of blade, tool speed, and feed speed—how fast you move the tool. How the job is going tells a lot. The more you use the tool, the more you'll realize that excessive vibration, having to force the tool to keep it cutting, excessive blade slow-down, and a blade that does more rubbing than cutting all indicate that you're not working as efficiently as you should. Tool sense is acquired—it's not a secret skill you must be born with.

Tool Handling

The major cause of substandard work, and even blade break-age, is excessive vibration in the tool or the workpiece. The practice of clamping work to a solid surface, especially pieces that aren't large or heavy enough to sit solidly on their own, makes sense, and helps you work more safely. Much saber saw cutting can be done with just one hand on the tool, but if you're using a heavy-duty tool and the work is secure, there's no reason why you can't hold the tool with both hands to keep it firmly on the work and to move it steadily forward. This has to be done when using the blade turning feature of a scroller saw (Figure 3-27). The hand on the control knob controls the direction of the blade while the other hand keeps the tool moving.

To minimize vibration, apply pressure down on the tool as you move it. This can't be overdone, of course, but the combination action should assure firm contact between the tool's baseplate and the work throughout the pass. Keep the blade running free by avoiding sideways pressure. Remember that the blade is chucked at only one end so its free to twist and bend. Lateral forces can result in blade damage or breakage, burning of the blade and the work, and substandard cut quality in general.

Saber-saw blades cut on the "up" stroke so any splintering or feathering will appear on the surface of the work that is in contact with the baseplate. This makes it necessary to keep the good surface of the stock "down" anytime the finish cut is important (Figure 3-28). This isn't always possible. For example, you may need to saw a hole through some wall paneling that is already installed. In such cases the most you can do to minimize the feathering is saw with a smooth-cutting blade.

A trick that may come in handy is to place a strip of transparent tape over the cutline before you saw. This does the job of keeping surface fibers together as the blade saws through. Another help, if the tool is so equipped, is to use the

3-26.   Be sure the blade is securely locked in the tool's chuck. It's good practice to check occasionally to be sure vibration hasn't caused the blade to loosen. Always remove the blade when storing the tool.

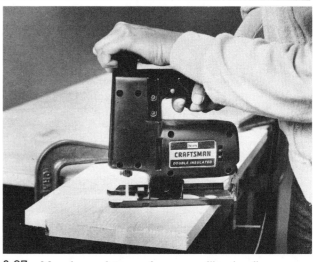

3-27.   Many heavy-duty saws have an auxiliary handle so you can use a two-hand grip. When the scroller feature on a saw like this one is used, one hand controls the blade to keep it on line, the other hand moves the tool.

special insert that minimizes the opening around the saw blade. Like the tape, the insert bears down on surface fibers close to the blade.

Keeping the baseplate in firm contact with the workpiece is the general rule, but the rule can be broken in certain situations. An exception might occur when you encounter a knot in the wood. Here, rocking the tool will help the blade get through the hard area more easily (Figure 3-29). The idea is to pivot the tool up using the toe of the baseplate as a fulcrum and thus decrease the contact area between the blade and the work. Pivoting back down does the same thing. In effect, the method concentrates the cutting power on smaller areas.

The saber saw can be used for pad sawing, which simply means that you stack pieces that must have the same shape and cut through all of them at once (Figure 3-30). The limitation is the length and stroke of the blade. Naturally, you can stack more ¼″ pieces than ¾″ pieces, but in any event, work as if you are sawing solid stock, selecting an efficient combination of blade, stroke speed, and feed speed.

Straight Cutting

While it isn't difficult to make straight cuts by guiding the saw along a marked line, you can do the job more accurately and with less strain if you work with a guide. The most common aid in this area is the "edge guide" which is lighter but otherwise very similar to those available for portable circular saws (Figure 3-31). Sometimes, they are supplied with the saw. If not, they will be available as an extra-cost accessory.

The arm of the guide is inserted through slots (or some similar arrangement) in the baseplate and secured with, usually, small thumb screws. When using one, measure from the inside surface of the guide's fence to a tooth on the blade that points toward the guide. The fence bears against the edge of the stock to maintain a uniform cut-width as you move the

3-29. Rocking the tool a bit when you encounter a knot or a particularly dense grain area, will help sawing go easier. In effect, the method reduces the amount of wood the blade must work on.

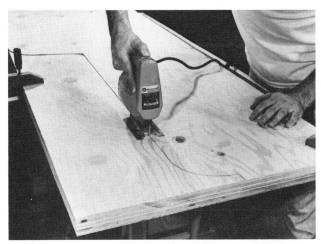

3-30. Pad sawing is simply stacking workpieces so you can produce several similar ones in a single operation. Be sure the pieces are aligned and clamped together.

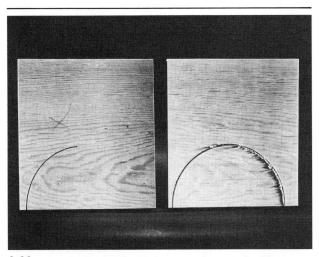

3-28. Remember that the blade cuts on the upstroke. The samples are top and bottom views of a cut made with the same saw blade. The clean cut on the left, which was the bottom of the workpiece during sawing, proves that material should always be sawed with the good surface down.

3-31. Edge guides for the saber saw are similar to those supplied for portable circular saws. Remember that it's just a guide. Keeping the saw moving in a straight line, without twisting, is the operator's responsibility.

saw. Remember that the accessory is a guide. Keeping the saw moving without twisting is your responsibility. Some edge guides are dual purpose. When set up as shown in Figure 3-32, they provide a pivoting action that guides the saw through circular cuts.

When the cut you require is too far from the stock's edge to allow using an edge guide, or when you choose to work without one, you can use a straight piece of wood to guide the saw (Figure 3-33). The guide can be tack-nailed or clamped to the workpiece. Always position the guide so you are allowing for the distance from the edge of the base plate to a tooth that is set in its direction. The guide can be secured either to the piece you need or to the part that's being cut off. Making the cut is just a matter of moving the saw so the baseplate bears constantly against the guide.

The same type of guide can be used for any long cut, like sawing across the small dimension of a plywood panel or for angular cuts. Accessories like the one in Figure 3-34 are available from manufacturers. The advantages are that the guide is a metal extrusion and will have more natural rigidity than a strip of wood, and that it has "built-in" grippers so it's easy to secure without having to resort to tack-nailing or clamps.

Good guides, like the common adjustable square shown in Figure 3-35, for making short, straight cuts can be found right in the shop. For longer cuts, why not use a carpenters square? You can hand-hold the guides as you move the tool along the blade or you can use a clamp.

Any of the guides that were described in the chapter on portable circular saws, including the ones that you can make, can be used with a saber saw for straight or angular sawing.

Extra Thick Cuts

Getting through thick material, say a 4x4 (Figure 3-36), is a matter of working with a longer-than-normal blade. For example, a 6″ blade is long enough to get through 4″ stock. It's assumed, of course, that the tool you have can handle a 6″ blade, but you'll find the answer in the owner's manual.

Most long blades are designed for tough work and so have few, but large teeth with a lot of set—so don't expect perfectly smooth cuts. The general rule is to take it easy. Allow the blade to set its own pace. Forcing the cut won't accomplish anything.

3-32.   Using an edge guide to lead the saw through a circular path. More about this particular technique later on.

3-33.   When the cut is too wide for an edge guide or you choose not to use one, a tack-nailed or clamped strip of wood will assure a clean, straight cut. Just keep the edge of the baseplate against the strip throughout the pass.

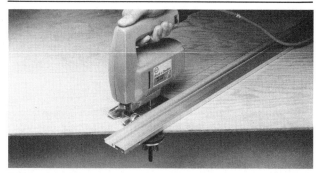

3-34.   Guides should also be used for angular cuts. This commercial unit is a strip of extruded metal with its own clamping arrangement. Working with guides minimizes the possibility of human error.

3-35.   An adjustable square is a fine guide for short cuts. A carpenters square, which has a 24″ blade, can be used on wider workpieces.

Freehand Cutting

Freehand cutting is required on scroll-type cuts (Figure 3-37) where it's not possible to work with a guide, and on jobs like forming scalloped edges where it may be more convenient to work without one (Figure 3-38). This type of sawing demonstrates one of the major features of the saber saw—its ability to do cutting that would ordinarily require a jigsaw or that would have to be done by hand with a coping saw.

3-36.   "Long" saber-saw blades can get through 4″ material but the saw must have sufficient power. The owners manual should tell you the maximum length of blades you can use as well as the tool's capacity in terms of material thickness.

3-37.   Scroll-type cutting calls for narrow blades and very careful tool handling to avoid over-cutting. Scroller-type units are particularly good at this sort of thing since the blade can be controlled independently of the tool's feed direction.

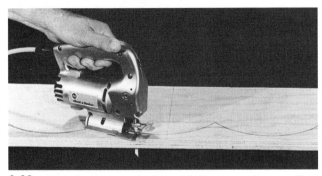

3-38.   Planning the route for the saw helps you work more efficiently. Note that the marked cutline bypasses the point where the arcs meet. This area will be cleaned out after the bulk of the waste has been cut away.

Of course, it's not all roses. The saber saw can't turn on itself or manipulate minute radii. But there are ways to compensate; a common one being to drill holes where lines meet at right angles so all that's left for the saw to do is make straight cuts. Actually, when the design permits, it's a good idea to pre-drill the workpiece wherever an arc fits in. Then you won't have to strain the saw around tight turns.

Note, in the illustration that shows a scalloped edge being formed (Figure 3-38), the marked cutline bypasses the point where the arcs meet. The saw is brought back to clean out the corner after the bulk of the waste has been removed. The technique eliminates the need to make a lot of lead-in cuts.

Making tight turns, doing scroll-type work, calls for careful tool-handling. A slow feed, just barely enough to keep the blade working, produces best results. Always anticipate where a straight line flows into a curve and start the turn a fraction before you get there. A common error is to over-cut at this point so back-tracking is needed to get to the point where the curve begins.

Curves and Circles

The general rule is, don't force blades to follow curves or make turns they are obviously struggling to make. There are techniques you can use that allow a blade to follow a curve it couldn't ordinarily do. In some cases, forming preliminary radial cuts or in-cuts, a common practice on bandsaws and stationary jigsaws, can be used with the saber saw (Figure 3-39). For example, if you need to cut a small half circle in the edge of a piece of stock, or wish to round off the end of a narrow board, you can "do the impossible" by making a series of cuts from the edge or end of the workpiece to the cut-line before starting to saw the arc. What happens then, is that pieces of waste fall away as you cut, thereby providing more room for the blade to maneuver. The wider the blade and the tighter the arc, the more in-cutting you must do.

3-39.   Sawing preliminary radial cuts or in-cuts will allow a blade to follow a curve it couldn't ordinarily do. The waste pieces fall away and so the blade has more room to turn.

When rounding an end, you can also get around a tight turn by making tangent cuts. Start sawing the arc and when the blade starts to bind, run the cut out to the edge of the stock. Then return to where you left off and repeat the procedure. You'll probably have to do this many times before the arc is complete.

You can saw gentle curves very accurately by letting the saw follow a clamped-on guide strip that you've shaped for the purpose (Figure 3-40). The critical factor is maintaining a constant tangent contact between the bearing surface of the guide and the edge of the baseplate. To put it another way, the distance from the blade's teeth to the guide must be constant throughout the pass.

It's an especially good procedure to follow when you need many similar pieces. You can extend the idea's usefulness by stacking pieces so you can cut several at a time.

Circles, whether you need a disc or are forming an opening through a panel, can be cut freehand, or the tool can be guided using a pivoting arrangement which will assure a uniform cut. Some edge guides are designed so they can also be used for this purpose (Figure 3-41). The fence of the accessory is slotted so a trammel point can be secured to serve as the center of the circle.

When the radius of the circle is beyond the capacity of the edge guide, or if your unit isn't designed for the purpose, you can easily custom design a pivot guide like the one being used in Figure 3-42. The pivot is a piece of thin metal which can be gripped in the slots normally used for the edge guide. The pivot end is bulked out so the hole for the pivot point, which is just a small nail, can be in line with the front of the teeth on the saw blade. The length of the guide is optional. In either case, the guide is adjusted so the distance from the pivot point to a tooth set in its direction is equal to the radius of the circle. This applies if the disc you are cutting is the part you need. When a circular opening in a workpiece is needed, then the dimension must be taken from a tooth on the opposite side of the blade—kerf on the outside of the line for a disc, on the inside for an opening.

To start the sawing you must make an opening for the blade, either by making a plunge cut (Figure 3-43), a technique we'll talk about in a bit, or by drilling a hole through the work. The entrance-hole idea is more convenient since it lets you get the saw established before setting up the pivot guide. When it doesn't interfere with appearance, the center of the entrance hole can be directly on the circumference. This way, positioning the blade directly on the cutline won't be a prob-

3-40.   Guide strips can be used for accurate sawing of gentle curves. The technique is most useful when you need many similar pieces. Stacking workpieces will make the job go faster.

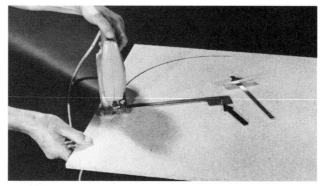

3-42.   You can make pivot guides using thin sheet metal or something similar so you can saw any size circle you wish. One end of the guide is wider so the pivot point, a small nail, can be in line with the front of the teeth on the blade.

3-41.   Edge guides, as we have said, are fine for guiding a saw through a circular cut, but they have limited capacity.

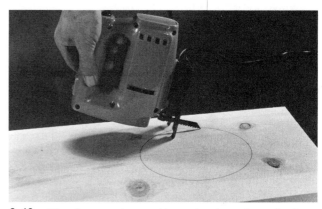

3-43.   The plunge cut is started by resting the tool very firmly at an angle on the forward edge of the baseplate. The angle must be extreme enough so the teeth will start to cut when the tool is switched on.

lem. Since plunge-cutting forms a straight kerf, it's best to use the idea when the disc is the waste piece.

After the saw's position is established, let the pivoting arrangement do the guiding. Move the tool slowly and steadily. Any blade can be used, but narrow ones will do a better job on small circles.

Plunge Cutting

Since one end of the saber-saw blade is free, the tool can be used to do internal cutting without the need of a lead-in cut from an edge of the stock, or the necessity of a starting hole for the blade (Figure 3-43).

The technique works this way. Place the tool at an angle so it rests on the forward edge of the baseplate. The angle must be judged so that some teeth on the blade will make contact with the work. A firm grip on the tool and sure contact between the baseplate and the work are critical. Turn on the motor and very slowly tilt the machine back to start sawing. It's necessary to avoid letting the initial contact be between the point of the blade and the work. If this happens, you'll feel like you're gripping a pogo stick—the tool will do nothing but hop about.

The starting cut is a surface groove. As you continue to tilt the tool back, the groove gets a bit longer and deeper and the blade finally penetrates (Figure 3-44). Keep the contact between the baseplate and the work very firm. If you allow the tool to move back, it will bounce off the back end of the groove. Also, letting the tool jiggle as you're going through the procedure can mar the surface of the work. To eliminate this possibility, start the cut by using a piece of thin scrap material as a buffer between the base plate and the work (Figure 3-45). The buffer can be any material that doesn't have a very slippery surface—even heavy cardboard will do.

Another way to provide firm bracing for the tool, and to keep it from moving about until the blade gets through, is to clamp a piece of scrap material to the work so the base plate can bear against it (Figure 3-46). When you attempt a plunge cut for the first time, do it in a waste area. After some practice you'll be able to accomplish it directly on a cutline.

Before proceeding with sawing, be sure the blade has penetrated sufficiently so the tool can seat solidly in its normal, fully-flat baseplate position (Figure 3-47). If the cutout is circular, then one continuous pass will complete the operation. There are several ways to go when the cutout has square corners. You can cut each side of a rectangle or square

3-44.   The blade starts to cut as you very slowly pivot the tool backward, until it finally penetrates the stock. Keep a very firm grip—don't force the blade.

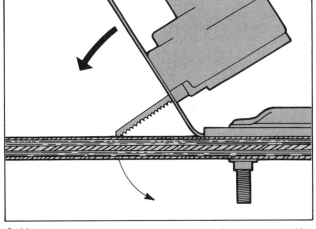

3-46.   Another method you can use to get a plunge cut started is to clamp a block to the work to act as a brace for the baseplate. It keeps the tool steady so you can start the cut accurately.

3-45.   You can use a scrap of thin material under the edge of the baseplate to avoid the possibility of marring the workpiece.

3-47.   After the blade has fully penetrated, sawing proceeds in normal fashion with the tool solidly on the baseplate.

3-48.   You can avoid having to repeat plunge cuts by working this way. Saw to an area where you can veer off and come back to the starting point to clean out the corner. Repeat the procedure for each corner.

3-49.   Guide blocks can be used for more accurate sawing with minimum fuss. The arm of the guide can be the full length of the cutting line. Position the guide to allow for the distance from the blade to the edge of the baseplate.

by starting with a plunge cut for each one. This can be bothersome, so since the piece being removed is usually scrap, it's more practical to procedure as shown in Figure 3-48. Make a partial cut and then veer off so you can circle back to clean out the corner. The job is finished by following a similar procedure for each corner.

When it's necessary to be perfectly accurate, you can use a guide block to control the sawing (Figure 3-49). The arms of the guide block can be longer than the one shown so the saw can be guided for the full length of the cut.

Entrance Holes

While the plunge cutting feature of the saber saw can provide a solution in some woodworking situations, it is not mandatory that you use it for all cutout work. In fact, it's often more practical and convenient to set up for the job by drilling a starting hole for the blade (Figure 3-50). The piece being cut out won't be marred to the point where it must be wasted if you locate the hole carefully, close to a cutline. Also, the diameter of the hole doesn't have to be greater than the width of the blade.

Many times, entrance holes can be part of the design (Figure 3-51). They can be located to provide nicely rounded corners or, in the case of some fancy scrollwork, anyplace in each of the waste areas. The point is, plunge cutting doesn't have to be considered the cure-all. It makes sense to preview cutout work and to use entrance holes where you can, either as part of the design or to make the job easier and faster to do.

Bevel Cuts

Bevel sawing is done by tilting the baseplate so the saw blade will be at the angle you need (Figure 3-52). Handle the tool as if you were doing a square cut but bear in mind that the cut is "thicker" because the blade is angled. This calls for the same feed-speed change you would make when going from, say, ¾" stock to 1½" stock.

Since more of the blade is in the cut and is more subject to twisting and binding, use the widest blade that will do the job. On thick material it pays to use a coarse blade, cutting

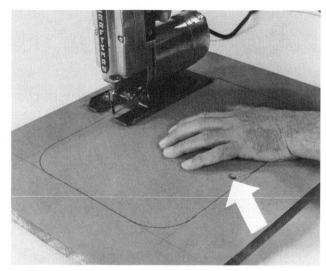

3-50.   It's not mandatory that you use the plunge-cutting technique for all internal cutting. Many times, it's more convenient to drill an entrance hole for the blade (arrow).

3-51.   Entrance holes, when accurately located, can become rounded corners. The system is flexible since the entrance holes can be as large as you wish.

3-52.   Bevel cutting doesn't differ too much from square cuts except that the blade, at an angle, has to get through more wood. So adjust feed-speed accordingly.

3-53.   A common metal-cutting saber saw blade is designed like a hacksaw blade and so can do any of the cutting that's possible with the hand tool. As with any blade, the cut must not be forced.

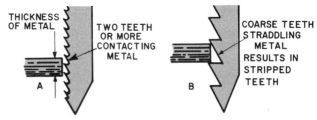

3-54.   The drawing demonstrates the rule of thumb for sawing metals. The thought applies particularly to thin materials.

3-55.   The most efficient way to saw sheet metal is to support it as shown or to sandwich it between thin sheets of plywood or hardboard. This keeps the metal firm and eliminates jagged edges.

3-56.   When you can't work the ideal way, be sure to hold the work very firmly and cut slowly. Toothless blades help do such work more easily.

just outside the line, and then make the edge more acceptable by sanding.

Bevel cutting can be done freehand but, like crosscutting and ripping, you'll work more accurately, especially on long cuts, if you use guides.

Sawing Metals

With the right metal-cutting blade installed in the tool and using a suitable speed, you can cut any metal that can be cut with a hacksaw blade (Figure 3-53). As we said in the beginning, the right blade is usually a wave-set type except when cutting do-it-yourself material that can be handled with regular wood cutting blades.

The saber lets you work faster than by hand and requires less effort. Capacity is also increased since you are not hindered by the frame on a conventional hacksaw. A point to remember is that as many teeth as possible should bear against the edge of the stock (Figure 3-54), so choose the blade accordingly. This material can sit between the teeth of a coarse blade, and this can result in stripping the teeth, bending or breaking the blade, and generally poor edges on the work. The rule, of course, doesn't apply to toothless, tungsten carbide blades. On thicker materials, you can use coarser blades so long as they are designed and tempered for metal work. Actually, it's good practice not to depend entirely on blades with tiny teeth since, on some materials, they can clog very quickly.

All workpieces must be firmly supported to eliminate vibration and so you can saw smoothly. The best way to cut thin sheet metal is to place it on some scrap wood or sandwich it between covers of thin plywood or hardboard (Figure 3-55). If you work this way, you'll get minimum vibration and the support pieces will prevent the blade from forming jagged edges. When it's not possible to work this way—you may be cutting rain gutters or downspouts—feed the tool very slowly to avoid distorting the metal (Figure 3-56). It's almost impossible to work this way without getting burrs on the cut edges, so some finishing with emery or steel wool is in order.

3-57. Thicker, more rigid sheet metal, doesn't require the support suggested for thin material, but be sure to use clamps to hold the material firmly. Keep the cut area clean of chips that might scratch the surface of the workpiece.

3-58. Keeping the workpiece firm leads to smoother, more accurate sawing. Gripping the work, especially small pieces, in a vice, is good practice.

You can work on thicker metals without providing support sheets so long as the work itself is suitably clamped (Figure 3-57). Be sure that the underside of the baseplate is smooth and clean to avoid marring the work. Also, keep the cut area clear of waste; chips can collect under the baseplate and cause scratches. Whenever possible, grip workpieces, especially small ones, in a vise (Figure 3-58).

When saber-sawing metals, especially heavy nonferrous materials, it pays to apply a grease stick lubricant to the blade as you work. Sometimes, wax will work. I've seen plumbers rub chalk on hacksaw blades. Anyway, the applications are meant to help the blade run cooler and to prevent the blade's teeth from becoming clogged with waste material.

Sawing Other Materials

Saber-sawing doesn't have to be confined to wood and metal. If something is sawable, this unique tool can perform. Usually, efficient sawing is a matter of the blade you use and how fast you move the tool. Figures 3-59 through 3-62 provide information on sawing other materials you might encounter in the shop or on location.

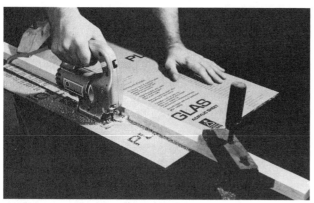

3-59. The only problem you might encounter when sawing materials like "Plexiglas" is heat build-up that can fuse waste in the kerf. The manufacturer of the material suggests using a blade with at least 14 teeth-per-inch. Keep the protective paper in place until all sawing has been done.

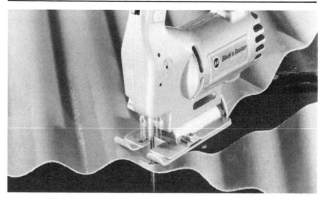

3-61. Fiberglass can be cut with almost any blade, but quick dulling can result. You can use a metal-cutting, wave-set blade or a toothless one when sawing is extensive. Be especially firm with your grip when sawing corrugated material.

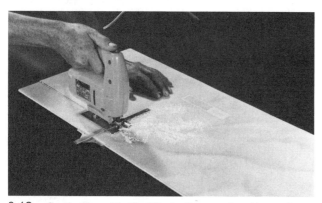

3-60. Synthetic marble like "Corian" cuts easily with wood-cutting blades but don't use coarse ones that might cause surface-chipping. Best results are with fine-tooth blades or toothless ones. In either case, the feed-speed should allow the blade to cut at its own pace.

3-62. Not much choice on tile and ceramics but to saw with a toothless blade. Be sure to provide firm support for the workpiece and to grip the tool securely—excessive vibration can cause the material to crack.

4. The Reciprocating Saw

There can be some confusion between the *reciprocating saw* and the *saber saw*, but it's in name only as you can see by comparing the representative tools shown in Figures 4-1 and 4-2. Some of the puzzlement results because of names used by manufacturers. Both tools are often called "Bayonet saws" or even "All-purpose saws", and for the reciprocating saw there are tags like "Tiger saw", "Blitz", "Recipro", "Super saw", "Cut saw", "Sawzall", or simply "Recip".

While there is a degree of overlap in function—each tool can work with rough, fast cutting blades or smoother, slower cutting blades—neither is a justifiable substitute for the other. Mechanically, the reciprocating saw is a more heavy-duty tool that can drive longer and tougher blades than those you can chuck in a saber saw.

The saber saw drives a blade that has a vertical sawing action. The blade on a reciprocating saw moves to and fro horizontally, longitudinally in line with the body of the tool. There are many times when the saber saw can be efficiently controlled with one hand. It will be a rare situation when you might feel free to control a reciprocating saw without both hands gripping firmly—which says something.

Carpenters will use the reciprocating saw for rough remodeling chores like cutting quickly through standing 2x4s or 2x6s, or even completely through an existing wall. A plumber will use it to cut holes or notches for pipes, or to cut through an installed pipe that must be replaced. An electrician finds it useful for shaping notches for wiring or for opening a wall to install an outlet box. All these chores, and others, are, of course, in the work-scope of home craftsmen. Add other chores like pruning heavy branches, cutting small logs for firewood, topping off fence posts, and so on, and you have a realistic view of the heavy-duty concept of a reciprocating saw.

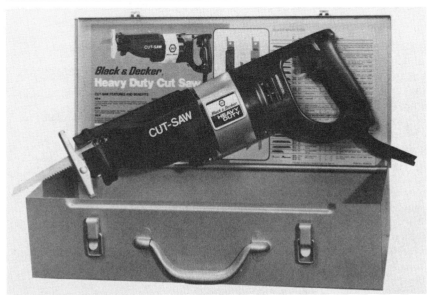

4-1. Any reciprocating saw is essentially a heavy-duty tool that can handle blades as long as 12″. When used with the correct blade, it will saw anything from soft, panel materials to heavy metals. Its blade, which cuts on the back stroke, moves to and fro in line with the body of the tool.

4-2. The saber saw, also a versatile machine, is not designed for the very rough work that can be accomplished with a reciprocating saw. There is some overlap in function, but neither is a complete substitute for the other.

An Overview

Reciprocating saws are available in single speed, two speeds, and variable speed models. On the average, a single speed model will operate at about 2000 strokes per minute (spm). With a two speed model you can operate in the areas of 1700 spm or 2400 spm. A variable speed unit has infinite speed settings starting at zero and ranging to about 2600 spm. These are general specifications; you will find some variations depending on the model and the manufacturer.

Having more than one speed is an advantage since you can adjust for compatibility with the blade you are using and the material being cut. For example, a slow speed for metal work and a higher speed for sawing wood and other relatively soft materials. Being able to adjust spm is a plus even when sawing wood since you can slow down a bit when hitting a particularly dense area or a knot.

Some of the tools are shaped so the front area provides for gripping by the left hand, or right hand as the case may be (Figure 4-3); others are equipped with auxiliary handles. Whatever the design, a two-hand grip that minimizes vibration and chatter and keeps the blade on the cutline should be standard practice.

The shoes (or sole plates) on some of the saws have a fixed position while others can swivel (Figure 4-4). Each has an advantage touted either by the manufacturer or a dedicated user. In general, a fixed base provides a firm brace-point for routine cutting, whereas one that swivels can make it easier to do plunge cutting. In either case, to make internal cuts without having to drill a starting hole for the blade, the tool is rested firmly on the shoe so the blade is clear of the work, then the tool is tilted, slowly, so the blade can start penetrating (Figure 4-5). A cautious initial contact is critical since being hasty will cause the tool to jump about. The blade will first form a groove which will deepen as you tilt the tool until the blade gets through the material. Plunge cutting is best done with the shortest, heaviest blade that is suitable for the work at hand.

The blade clamp on most reciprocating saws is adjustable so the blade can be situated to cut up or down, horizontally, or even at an angle. Setting a blade so its side is parallel to the body of the tool makes it possible to cut close to the base of a vertical surface (Figure 4-6)—handy, for example, in some phases of remodeling work.

The length of the blade stroke might be as little as 5/8" and as much as 1½" with the average being about 1". Longer blade strokes do more work more quickly and should be accompanied by greater horsepower.

Other features you can check for include a shoe that is adjustable in and out so you can, in effect, change the area of the blade that is working; thus, you don't have to discard a blade because an inch or two of its teeth are too dull to cut. Also, a guided air flow that helps keep the saw cool and clears waste from the cutting area is an asset.

As you might expect, electronics are affecting the design of modern reciprocating saws. Some have electronic speed controls. The unit shown in Figure 4-7 works with a microprocessor that provides feedback to the motor so that cutting power will be consistent under varying sawing conditions.

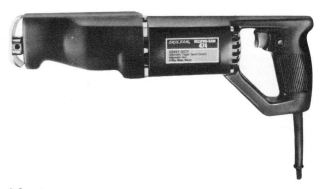

4-3.   Some of the units are shaped so the forward area of the casing is a grip area for the hand that is not holding the handle. Others may have an auxiliary handle. Whatever—most jobs call for a firm two-hand grip.

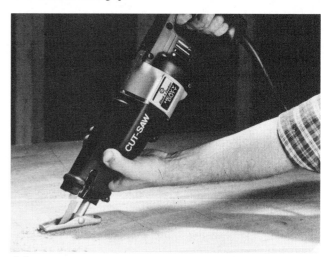

4-4.   The shoe, or sole plate, may have a swiveling action or it may be fixed. Whatever the design, it's there to provide a brace-point for the sawing operation. Keeping it firmly on the work throughout the pass will minimize vibration and chatter.

4-5.   Like the saber saw, the reciprocating saw can do plunge cutting—making internal cutouts without the need of a starting hole or a lead-in cut. It's critical that the initial blade-contact with the work be made very cautiously to avoid blade breakage or having the tool jump about.

Saw Blades

One of the secrets to getting the most out of a reciprocating saw or, for that matter, any sawing tool, is to make a study of the blades that can be used with it. Trying to do all things with one or two blades is like trying to get by with one or two screw-sizes for all wood connections. The chart in Figure 4-8 shows most of the blades that can be used with the saw and suggests the best application for each one. You'll note that even if your activities involve only wood there are particular designs for optimum results whether you are pruning a tree, doing remodeling work where you might encounter nails or plaster and metal lath, forming scroll-type components, and so on. The one, or the several blades that come with the tool are okay to get started with, but collecting an assortment is good practice and economical in the long run since you are

not likely to ruin a blade by using it on material it was not designed to cut.

Generally, when there is a choice of blades, it's wise to select the shortest one that will do the job.

Use Hints

Accept that the right way to work is with a firm, two-hand grip. Brace the shoe of the tool tightly against the work as you start to cut. Sometimes, for example, when encountering a tough knot in wood, you'll put less strain on yourself and the tool if you rock it a bit as you make the pass.

Be especially careful to determine in advance what is inside the wall when doing remodeling work that involves cutting through a wall covering or a partition. You don't want the saw to discover a water line or electrical wiring!

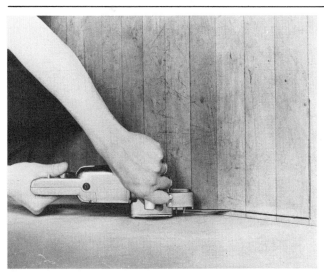

4-6. An adjustable blade-clamp mechanism that allows setting the blade on different planes is very handy. This can be a built-in feature or the manufacturer may offer an accessory that provides for the same setup.

4-7. As with all tools, electronic technology is affecting the design of reciprocating saws. A microprocessor "talks" to the motor and assures consistent cutting power regardless of the blade being used and the material being cut.

	LENGTH IN INCHES	TEETH PER INCH	RECOMMENDED USE
WOOD CUTTING			
	6 (Tapered)	6	General roughing-in wood
	9 (Tapered)	6	
	12 (Tapered)	6	
	4 (Scroll)	6	Premium quality scroll cutting hard wood, plywood, plastic, tile, asbestos
	6	6	

(Continued on next page)

	LENGTH IN INCHES	TEETH PER INCH	RECOMMENDED USE
ALL-PURPOSE CUTTING			
	6	6	Wood, plywood, insulation board, asbestos, all-purpose cutting
	6	10	
	6	18	Nail embedded wood, non-ferrous metals, plywood, insulation board, wood siding, all-purpose cutting
	3½	24	
	6	24	
SPECIAL PURPOSE CUTTING			
	6 (Flexible)	6	General roughing-in wood
	4 (Double Edge)	7	General roughing-in wood—thick plywood
	6	10	Plywoods, nail-embedded wood, heavy gauge (non-ferrous) metals
	12	10	Cutting nail-embedded wood in hard to reach areas
	12 (Flexible)	18	Opening crates, removing siding, cutting nail-embedded wood in hard to reach areas
	6	6	Plaster, including plaster with metal lath, plaster board
	4 (Armoredge)	14	Fiberglass and other abrasive materials
	6 (Armoredge)	14	
	4	Wavy Knife	Paper, corrugated cardboard, rubber, cork
	5 (Carbide)	6	Taper back carbide tip blade for cutting asphalt tile, plastics, sheet rock, plaster, and general wood cutting
	12	6	Pruning limbs, cutting green wood
METAL CUTTING HI-SPEED STEEL			
	3¼ (Scroll)	10	Heavy gauge ferrous and non-ferrous metals, cast aluminum, copper, brass, rubber, pressed wood, fiberglass
	6	10	Heavy gauge (non-ferrous) metals, bar and angle stock, cast aluminum, hard rubber, plastic, including laminates, pressed wood

(Continued on next page)

	LENGTH IN INCHES	TEETH PER INCH	RECOMMENDED USE
	3¼ (Scroll)	14	Heavy gauge ferrous and non-ferrous metals, cast aluminum, copper, brass, rubber, pressed wood, fiberglass
	6	14	Heavy gauge (non-ferrous) metals, band and angle stock, cast iron, sheet steel (over 18 ga.) hard rubber, pressed wood, fiberglass
	3¼ (Scroll)	18	Metal scroll, cast iron, bar and angle stock, galvanized pipe, tubing (over 18 ga.)
	4	18	Heavy gauge (non-ferrous) metals, bar and angle stock, galvanized pipe, tubing (over 18 ga.)
	6	18	Heavy gauge (non-ferrous) metals, bar and angle stock, cast iron, sheet aluminum
	3¼ (Scroll)	24	Metal scroll, stainless, cast iron, bar and angle stock, galvanized pipe, tubing (over 18 ga.)
	4	24	Sheet steel (under 18 ga.), galvanized pipe, tubing (under 18 ga.)
	6	24	
	4	32	Sheet steel (under 18 ga.), galvanized pipe, tubing (under 18 ga.)

4-8.   You don't have to own all these blades but an assortment that provides optimum results on the kind of work you do is good practice and a wise investment.

When making long straight cuts, say on plywood, you can work more accurately by moving the tool so its shoe bears against a guide strip clamped to the work. Don't try to turn corners with blades that are too wide for the job. If the narrowest blade you have won't do, use the relief cuts technique demonstrated in the chapter on saber saws.

Figures 4-9 through 4-14 show some typical applications for this versatile sawing tool.

4-9.   Combining a firm two-hand grip with good pressure down on the shoe will minimize vibration and lead to acceptable results. Often, on straight cuts, you can guide the tool along a clamped-on guide strip just as you would with a saber saw.

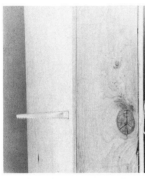

4-10.   Cutting through a full-thickness partition is no problem
for a reciprocating saw that is equipped with the proper blade. Be
sure you determine what is inside the wall before you start cutting.
Meeting a water line or electrical wiring can be an unpleasant
surprise!

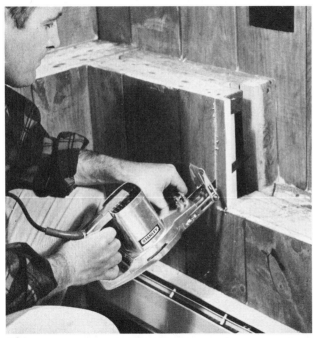

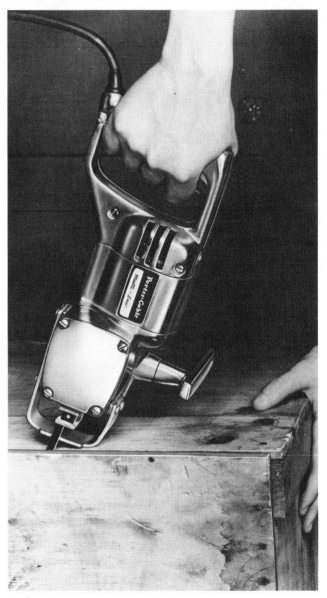

4-11.   Always use the shortest, heaviest blade that is adequate for
the job. If you are just sawing through a facing you don't want to
use a blade that is too long because it will tend to bounce against
the back area of the project. Don't forget to consider the stroke-
length of the tool when selecting a blade length.

4-12.   With the right kind of blade and the correct speed it won't
matter if you encounter an occasional nail. Many industrial firms
use a reciprocating saw to open crates with minimum fuss.

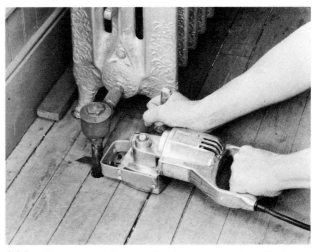

4-14.   Sawing through pipe or, for that matter, steel or aluminum or other metals, is routine. If the tool allows it, start such work at a slow speed and rev up to the point where the blade is cutting consistently. The cut should never be forced. Allow the blade to cut at its own pace.

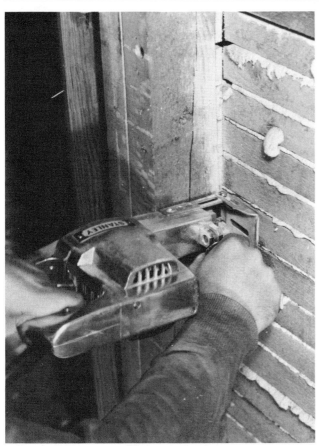

4-13.   Again, the right blade is the answer for getting easily through this stucco wall. Incidentally, you should not only know what is inside the wall, but also what is on the other side.

The Portable Electric Drill

5.

One of the most versatile power tools you can buy—actually a first choice on any list of practical power tool equipment—is the portable electric drill. The name "drill" doesn't tell the story, even though the tool is fantastic for drilling small or large holes accurately and with minimum effort. A more realistic picture, because of modern innovations and the myriad accessories that have become available for it, is of a lightweight, multipurpose shop you can hold in your hands. Alone, like many other electric tools, it can't do anything but spin its chuck, but add a suitable accessory and the unit serves efficiently as a drum or disc sander, grinder, polisher, screwdriver, flex-shaft machine, doweling jig, and more. It can also be used as a power source to drive specially designed units like a bandsaw, belt sander, even a small lathe. Place it in a stand and it will serve as a stationary drill press. The combination of portable drill and accessory isn't meant to be a substitute for the tool it imitates, however, the ideas do work.

Types, Sizes, Speeds

The mechanism of a portable drill is fairly simple (Figure 5-1). A motor drives a chuck which grips a cutting tool. In between motor and chuck is a system of gears that provides the correct torque and speed for what the drill is designed for. While this is the basic concept, there are other factors that are part of the picture; variable speed controls, double insulation, reversing switch, electronic features, and power.

Electric drill sizes you might be interested in are, ¼", ⅜", and ½". The size indicates the maximum tool-shank diameter that can be gripped by the chuck, not necessarily its drilling capacity. There are many cutting tools, like spade bits, that range up to 1½" and have ¼" shanks. Hole saws and the like can be used to form holes well over what you can accomplish with a drill bit but many of them have ¼" shanks and can be gripped in a small capacity drill. But it's not all roses. Complete freedom to use any cutting tool in any drill is another matter. The unit may not have the power or the efficient combination of power and speed to do the job.

The capacity of a drill can usually be judged by the manufacturer's specifications. The ¼" unit shown in Figure 5-2, with a speed range of 0-2000 rpm, is rated at 2.7 amps and can form ½" holes in hardwood and ¼" holes in steel. As the size of the drill increases so does its power, however, its top speed usually decreases. The ⅜" drill shown in Figure 5-3 is rated at 3.2 amps, has a speed range of 0-1200 rpm, and can drill ¾" holes in hardwood and ⅜" holes in steel. Move up to a

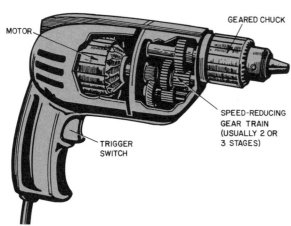

MOTOR

GEARED CHUCK

SPEED-REDUCING GEAR TRAIN (USUALLY 2 OR 3 STAGES)

TRIGGER SWITCH

5-1.   Basic mechanism of a portable electric drill. Engineering provides for a practical combination of power and speed.

5-2.   A ¼" drill, rated at 2.7 amp, provides speeds of 0-2000 rpm with capacities of ¼" in steel and ½" in hardwood. Other features include double insulation and a switch that can be pre-set at a desired speed.

½″ tool like the one in Figure 5-4, and you can drill ½″ holes in steel and 1″ holes in hardwood. This particular drill has an amp rating of 4.5 and a speed range of 0-850. Note that the size of the drill usually tells the maximum size hole it should be used for in steel, and that size doubles in hardwood.

The fact that speed decreases as power goes up tells something about good practice with electric drills. Jobs like drilling ½″ holes in steel (Figure 5-5) call for good power and low rpm. Of course, there is always some overlap in functions even among tools that are different sizes. You can occasionally use a "small" drill beyond its capacity for holes in steel by working in steps; start with a small bit and gradually increase bit-size which, by the way, is generally good practice with any drill. On the other hand, there's no reason why you can't use a "large" drill to form very small holes. Over-taxing the tool is what to avoid. If the tool gets too warm, or stalls, or its speed decreases drastically, you are asking too much.

Not too long ago when you selected a drill for its power or chuck capacity you got a single, compatible speed with it. The combination of size-capacity-speed made the unit ideal for a particular category of work. Such tools are still avail-

able, and they may even be a good choice if you require no-fuss performance for a particular application. However, the tool would be a compromise for general-purpose use. For example, it might be too fast for drilling in steel, too slow for small holes in wood.

The trigger-controlled variable speed feature that is available on drills of all sizes does away with the limitation of one speed and makes any drill a more versatile tool. Many times it's good practice to start work at a slow speed and gradually increase rpm until the cutter is working without strain. This variable speed feature also makes any drill an electric screwdriver, since choosing the right speed for such work is critical. Add a reversing feature, also generally available, and you can remove screws as well as drive them.

Electronic technology is making it easier to use a particular speed. The ⅜″ drill in Figure 5-6 has electronic analog feedback which maintains the desired speed under loaded conditions.

The ability to work anywhere, even without electricity, and being able to function without the fuss of a dangling cord has made the new cordless drills quite popular (Figure 5-7). I

5-3.   Generally, as the drill-size goes up power increases while top speed decreases. This ⅜″ unit has a 3.2 amp. rating and speeds of 0-1200 rpm. Its capacities are ⅜″ in steel and ¾″ in hardwood.

5-5.   Drill functions, regardless of the tool's speed and power, can overlap, but for heavy-duty work like drilling ½″ holes in steel, you can't substitute a small, light model for a husky unit like this ½″ model.

5-4.   This ½″ drill is reasonably light in weight (about 4½ lbs.), yet has the power to drill ½″ in steel and 1″ in hardwood. Variable speed ranges from 0-850 rpm. Extra handle allows a firm two-hand grip.

5-6.   New ⅜″ electronic drill features analog feedback which maintains desired speed under loaded conditions. Another feature is a powered chuck; no key is needed.

5-7.   Cordless tools are popular because of the freedom they provide; no cord from the tool, no extension line to worry about. Use them anywhere since they carry power with them.

5-8.   It's a good idea to have an extra power pack for a cordless tool; keep one charging while using the other. New chargers quickly bring batteries to full capacity.

5-9.   You have a choice with a "hammer drill". Use it conventionally, or add an impact action for faster hole-forming in materials like concrete and masonry.

find myself using a cordless drill, even in the shop, for many jobs I used to do with a plug-in portable. Much progress has been made in the design of cordless drills. The unit shown in Figure 5-8 has variable speeds, a reversing switch, a built-in torque control, and its battery can be recharged in a few hours. Most users buy an extra power pack to keep one battery charging while the other is used. That's a good idea.

Another innovation in electric drill design is the "hammer drill", a tool that drills like a drill but is also adjustable to provide an impact action. This adds a new term to electric drill nomenclature; bpm—which means *blows per minute*, an action that can be used alone or in combination with the routine rotary motion. These special concepts are given different names, like the "XTRA-TOOL" shown in Figure 5-9, but they all have similar advantages. Namely, modes that provide for routine drilling or hammer drilling or hammer-chiseling. The selection for the mode you wish to use is made by hand-turning a collar between the chuck and the forward end of the housing (Figure 5-10).

How can they help? Well, for one thing, if you do any kind of carving you can use the hammer mode with a gouge-chisel to do work like hollowing (Figure 5-11), or carving in

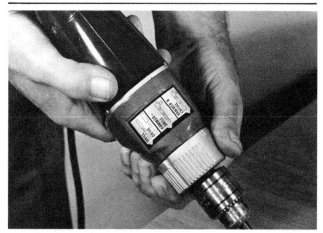

5-10.   Turning a collar lets you choose the action that is most efficient for the job at hand.

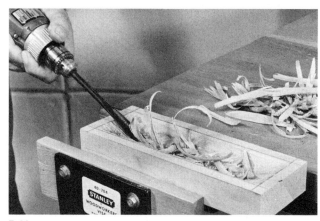

5-11.   Special chisels are available as accessories for the hammer drill. A gouge, used with the hammer mode, makes fast work of hollowing and similar chores.

the round, or bas-relief, much quicker and with less effort than required with the chisel and mallet technique.

Mount a butt chisel and you can use the hammer mode to form hinge mortises, clean out dadoes, or the cavities needed for tenons (Figure 5-12). Also on the practical side is combining the hammer and rotary actions when forming holes in concrete or masonry (Figure 5-13). I found I could drill three to five times faster when I added the impact mode.

Making a Choice

A ¼″ drill is a popular first choice but it may not always be the best one. This size drill may not have the power needed for some relatively heavy-duty work like using large hole saws or drilling in concrete. A ⅜″ unit with variable speeds might be the best *first* choice since it's huskier but can also do most of the lighter work ordinarily done with a smaller tool. Actually, since the price of electric drills is not out of line, you might think of having several if your work-load justifies it.

An adjustable speed control is a good feature. This is usually a small knob set into the trigger and turned in or out to provide a predetermined speed. Thus, you can do any

number of similar operations that require a particular rpm without reliance on finger control.

Double insulation makes sense since it provides additional safety barriers against a possible electric shock.

A reversing switch is recommended since it allows loosening fasteners, like screws, as well as driving them. Also, you can work more efficiently with accessories like sanding drums, wire brushes, and buffing wheels when you reverse direction of rotation. Doing this will often help these accessories last longer.

How the tool "feels" in your hand can be a selection factor. Some handles are placed centrally; others are more like a pistol grip. Heavy-duty drills, and even some lighter ones, might have an auxiliary handle that can be attached on either side and sometimes on top of the drill's body. This extra "hold" point is handy for tough drilling jobs.

Weight is a consideration and should be judged in terms of what you will use the tool for. It's logical that a powerful unit with greater capacity will be heavier than a unit with less capacity. Assuming all critical factors among an assortment of tools are similar, it's not illogical to base a choice on how the unit feels when you handle it.

Cutters That Form Holes

A rule to follow when choosing a hole cutter is that it should have a brad-type point, not the type of screw tip that is found on auger bits used in a hand brace (Figure 5-14). The screw tip is designed to pull the cutter into the work which is okay when using a hand tool but would require a specific rpm to match the pitch of the screw if used under power—a factor you can't coordinate when using a portable electric drill.

Twist drills are probably the most frequently used drill bits. This is probably because size-availability is so extreme, ranging from hair-thin bits to better than ½″, any of which can be chucked in a portable drill. Actually, the common twist drill, with a 59° cutting angle, is designed for drilling metal. It's okay to use them on wood, but should you have a

5-12.   A butt chisel is used to clean out drilled mortises, to make cavities for hinges, to clean out dadoes, and so on.

5-13.   Adding the hammer mode to the rotary action lets you drill much faster in masonry products—three to five times faster.

5-14.   Screw-point cutters like the auger on the right should not be used under power. The screw will take over feed-speed, which is something *you* should control.

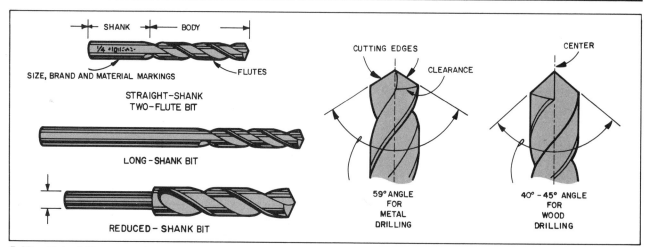

5-15. Twist drills are used for hole-forming in wood or metal, but they work most efficiently in the materials when the cutting edges have the angles shown here.

NUMBER SIZE DRILLS

NO.	SIZE OF DRILL IN INCHES	NO.	SIZE OF DRILL IN INCHES	NO.	SIZE OF DRILL IN INCHES	NO.	SIZE OF DRILL IN INCHES
1	.2280	21	.1590	41	.0960	61	.0390
2	.2210	22	.1570	42	.0935	62	.0380
3	.2130	23	.1540	43	.0890	63	.0370
4	.2090	24	.1520	44	.0860	64	.0360
5	.2055	25	.1495	45	.0820	65	.0350
6	.2040	26	.1470	46	.0810	66	.0330
7	.2010	27	.1440	47	.0785	67	.0320
8	.1990	28	.1405	48	.0760	68	.0310
9	.1960	29	.1360	49	.0730	69	.0292
10	.1935	30	.1285	50	.0700	70	.0280
11	.1910	31	.1200	51	.0670	71	.0260
12	.1890	32	.1160	52	.0635	72	.0250
13	.1850	33	.1130	53	.0595	73	.0240
14	.1820	34	.1110	54	.0550	74	.0225
15	.1800	35	.1100	55	.0520	75	.0210
16	.1770	36	.1065	56	.0465	76	.0200
17	.1730	37	.1040	57	.0430	77	.0180
18	.1695	38	.1015	58	.0420	78	.0160
19	.1660	39	.0995	59	.0410	79	.0145
20	.1610	40	.0980	60	.0400	80	.0135

LETTER SIZE DRILLS

A	0.234	H	0.266	O	0.316	V	0.377
B	0.238	I	0.272	P	0.323	W	0.386
C	0.242	J	0.277	Q	0.332	X	0.397
D	0.246	K	0.281	R	0.339	Y	0.404
E	0.250	L	0.290	S	0.348	Z	0.413
F	0.257	M	0.295	T	0.358		
G	0.261	N	0.302	U	0.368		

5-16. Decimal equivalents of number and letter size drills.

special wood-drilling chore that you'll repeat very often, it's a good idea to re-grind the point to an angle of 40° to 45° as shown in Figure 5-15.

Twist drills are available individually; however, it's more economical to buy them in sets and also equips you with bits for various jobs. Wire-gauge bits come in sets of sixty and are so numbered—#1 through #60. In a wire-gauge set you'll find bits that come close to drilling hair-size holes. A common set of fractional size bits will contain 29 units, starting at ¹⁄₁₆″ and increasing by a 64th of an inch up to ½″. Then there are letter size bits in sets of 26, identified by letters A through Z. The decimal equivalents of number size and letter size twist drills are shown in Figure 5-16.

Common twist drills are available in carbon or high-speed steel. Carbon steel is okay for drilling in wood and even in some soft metals, but for overall, durable performance in many materials, including steel, high-speed steel bits (identified as "H.S." or "H.S.S.") are a better choice even though they cost more.

Titanium-nitrade-coated bits have recently been introduced and are said to provide seven times longer life than conventional bits. The titanium bits can be used on tough materials like cast iron or stainless steel as well as on wood or plastics (Figure 5-17).

Using a nail to form a hole when you don't have exactly the right size drill bit is an idea you might occasionally find helpful (Figure 5-18). A practical application is forming pilot holes when nailing wood that tends to split. "Drill" with a smaller nail than those you will drive. The nail will do more burning than cutting, but it serves the purpose.

Spade Bits

Spade bits (Figure 5-19), sometimes called "wing" or "flat" bits, are available in various designs but all are meant for wood drilling under power. Although they do more scraping than cutting, they form clean, accurate holes when kept sharp and used correctly. An advantage is that they are available in sets that start at ⅛″ or ¼″ and range up to 1½″. Even if you

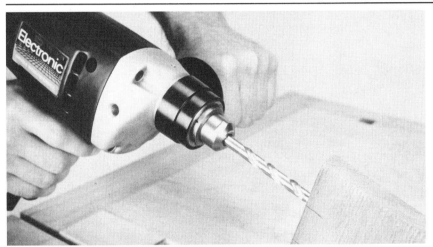

5-17. Titanium-nitrade-coated drill bits are newcomers, said to provide seven times longer life than high speed bits. They can be used on tough materials like cast iron and stainless steel in addition to wood and plastics.

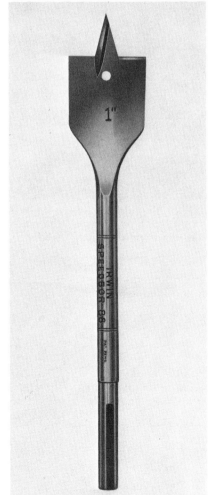

5-19. Good spade bits do a fine job of wood-drilling. Don't buy poor-quality ones, like the cheap sets often found in "bargain" bins.

5-18. Use a nail as a drill bit? It's a handy improvisation when you don't have the right size drill bit for the job. The nail compresses fibers instead of removing them, and it may burn a bit, but the idea works.

used them only for drilling oversize holes, they would be worth the cost.

The business end differs on various types. Although all have generous points, some cutting edges are winged while others are flat (Figure 5-20). The flat type produce flat-bottom holes which can be a useful feature in some areas of woodworking.

The long points help provide accuracy when starting a hole and make it easier to get started when drilling at an angle (Figure 5-21). The point, which you can embed by hand-turning the chuck, will set the cutter firmly before the hole starts to form.

Contrary to the good, general rule that advises drilling large holes at slow speeds, spade bits work best at higher rpm. Working at about 1500 rpm, even when drilling a 1½″ hole, is not out of line.

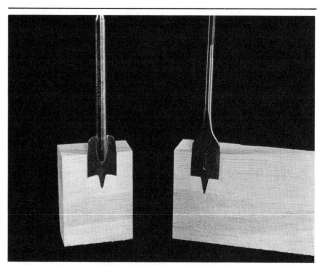

5-20.   All spade bits have nice, long points, but cutting edges may differ. This may not matter too much when drilling through holes, but affects the shape of the bottom when drilling blind holes.

5-21.   The long point on a spade bit is especially useful when drilling at an angle. The point penetrates enough to keep the bit from wandering when the cutting edge starts to work.

Hole Saws

Hole saws are used primarily to form holes larger than you can accomplish with conventional bits. Some, like those in Figure 5-22, have continuous saw teeth on the perimeter of a "cup" and come in specific sizes. Another design offers band-type saws, so it's possible to work with a single mandrel for different size holes (Figure 5-23). A third type, which can be fitted with wood or metal-cutting blades, has an adjust mechanism for setting the blades to a particular diameter (Figure 5-24). Since settings are infinite, you are not limited to specific size holes.

These cutters work hard and should be used with only enough feed pressure to keep them cutting. On the other hand, you'll do more burnishing than sawing if you try to be too gentle. Always start them at a very slow speed. Increase speed only to the point where the saw teeth are working efficiently. Although the tools cut cleanly and with minimum feathering when they break through, it's not a bad idea to use a back-up block (Figure 5-25).

Think of them as dual-purpose cutters; they form holes by removing a disc which, among other things, can be used as wheels for toys—the axle hole is already formed! An offbeat use is shown in Figure 5-26; overlapping, limited depth circles for a decorative effect. The pilot holes can be plugged with a matching or contrasting dowel.

5-22.   Specific-size hole saws are cup-like devices with continuous saw teeth. They mount on a mandrel that is gripped by the drill-chuck.

5-23.   This type of hole saw works with a single mandrel and an assortment of band-type blades. The saws lock into grooves in the mandrel—each saw a specific-size hole.

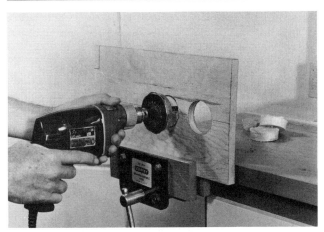

5-24. Another type hole-saw also has a single mandrel but works with individual metal or wood-cutting blades. Blade-diameter settings are infinite, so you can saw any size hole within the unit's capacity.

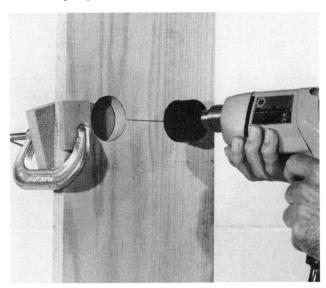

5-25. Hole saws cut pretty cleanly but if you wish to eliminate feathering completely when the saw breaks through, clamp a backup block behind the hole.

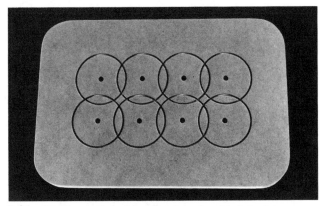

5-26. Drilling to limited depth and overlapping holes lets you use hole saws for some decorative work. Center holes can be plugged with matching or contrasting dowels.

Extension Bits

Conventional bits have limited depth capacity. Even with spade bits, which have long shanks, you can't drill deeper than four or five inches. Extension bits (Figure 5-27), which are made in several sizes, might provide a solution when you need an exceptionally deep hole or are making a project, like a lamp base (Figure 5-28). When doing jobs like this, it's best to drill from both ends. If you try going through completely from one end, the point of the bit might be influenced by grain direction and travel where it shouldn't.

It's also possible to buy extensions that can be used with conventional drilling tools (Figure 5-29). The advantage here is that they can be used with bits of different size so long as the shank on the bit can be gripped in the "chuck" of the extension.

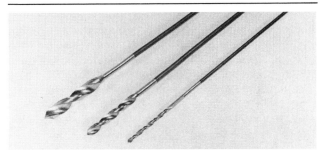

5-27. Extension bits are available in several practical sizes. These are ¼″, ⅜″ and ½″.

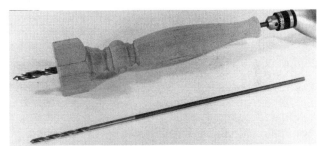

5-28. Forming a cord hole through a lamp base is a typical application for an extension bit. You'll work more accurately if you drill from both ends.

5-29. Extensions with a chuck-like device at one end are also available. These provide a long reach for conventional bits.

Always start extensions at a very slow speed and be sure the point is well seated before getting to operational rpm. These long cutters can "whip" if you allow them to run free.

Masonry Bits

Drilling in concrete or masonry calls for bits that have tungsten carbide cutting points and spiral-type flutes that carry waste from the hole (Figure 5-30). Like other bits, they are available individually or in sets; a typical set has ¼", 5/16", 3/8", and ½" sizes. Good results depend as much on the right combination of drill power and speed as on the bit. A light-duty ¼" drill is a poor choice. A heavy-duty 3/8", especially if it has variable speed is acceptable, but a husky ½" unit is best. As we mentioned before, a drill with an impact feature can make the work easier.

A slow speed and enough feed pressure to keep the bit cutting without overtaxing the tool is good, general practice. Using progressively larger bits helps considerably to get to the size hole you need. Using a small amount of water in the hole will minimize heat buildup. You'll find it easier to drill in materials like brick and cinder block and some flagstones than to drill in concrete, especially when the bit meets a particularly hard piece of aggregate. If the bit starts to do more rubbing than cutting, try cracking the aggregate by hammering with something like a length of drill rod.

Use the Chuck Key!

The key is designed to move the jaws of the chuck so they will bear firmly on the shank of the mounted tool (Figure 5-31). If you don't use the key (try to grip the tool by hand-holding the chuck and spinning the tool) the grip will not be secure enough. The bit may turn when running free but will stay put when working , while the chuck spins. Of course, remove the key before pressing the switch. It can be a harmful projectile. Be sure the shank of the tool is centered in the chuck. It *is* possible to grip it off-center. The jaws of the chuck should bear against any flats that might be on the shank of the bit.

Maybe a sign of things to come is the new portable electric drill shown in Figure 5-32. The tool has a power-driven, automatic chuck and doesn't require a chuck key to lock tools securely.

Operating Techniques

The more powerful the drill, the more torque there will be at the cutting end. Heavy, ½" drills are strong enough to spin you about should the cutting tool jam in the hole. To a lesser extent, this also applies to small units. They may not spin you about, but they can twist your hand. Maintaining a firm grip at all times is the way to avoid these hazards. When the work is small and the drilling chore is light, you might be able to secure the work with one hand and the drill with the other hand, so long as hand pressure is sufficient to keep the workpiece firmly down on a workbench or sawhorse. Holding the job in mid air and then applying the drill is not a good or safe practice. Whenever possible, secure the work to a stable surface with clamps or grip it in a vise. Most of the time, it makes sense to grip the drill with both hands, using any auxiliary handle that may be provided with the tool. This provides a safety factor in addition to helping you work more accurately.

5-31.   Always use the chuck key and then be sure to remove it. Center the bit in the chuck's jaws. If the shank has flats, let the jaws bear against them.

5-32.   New 3/8" drill has a power-driven chuck. You don't need a key to secure cutters.

5-30.   Tungsten-carbide-tipped bits are used for drilling concrete and masonry. Jobs like this are easier if you start with a small hole and enlarge it in stages.

The optimal drilling speed is something you will come to judge. You can control speed but there is no gauge to accurately pinpoint specific speeds through all the available ranges. Also, the free-running speed is not the load speed. Signs that call for an operational change in either rpm or feed pressure are—a cutter that jams, a cutter that spins without removing material, or an overheating tool. All factors assume, of course, that the cutting tool you are using is SHARP!

It's generally a good idea to use a piece of scrap as a backup to minimize the splintering that can occur when a bit breaks through a workpiece. This also applies to sheet metals which can buckle under drill pressure. Also, it's usually good practice, especially on metal, to drill "up" to the hole-size you need. This means starting with a pilot hole and enlarging it by stages.

Most accessories designed to be powered by an electric drill come with literature that, among other things, suggests an appropriate operating speed. Many times, the speed you *can* supply is a compromise. For example, shaping accessories are available for power drills, but conventional shaping is done at rpm of 10,000 and higher. Even so, you can do an acceptable job PROVIDING YOU USE CUTTERS DESIGNED FOR USE IN A PORTABLE DRILL. One way to compensate for lack of speed is to slow up on feed so, in effect, more cutting teeth will pass over a given area of the work. There are also safety considerations that have to do with speed. Turning large cutters at speeds they were not designed for can be dangerous. Always wear safety goggles, and a dust mask when one is needed.

Starting Accurately

A good way to spot a hole location is to use a square and a sharp, hard pencil to mark intersecting lines. To assure that the hole will start where it should, use an awl or a center punch to form an indent where the lines intersect (Figures 5-33, 5-34). A "center punch" has a sharper point than a

"prick punch" (Figure 5-35), and you can use this to advantage when hole locations in metal are critical. Make a slight indent with a center punch and then "broaden" it with a prick punch so the point of the bit will have a seat to start in.

Keep the drill vertical. This is critical if the hole is to be square to the work's surface. You can do this fairly accurately by aligning the drill with a square placed on the work, or you can make a guide block like the one shown in Figure 5-36.

5-34.   A punch can also be used to form the starting indent. Put the point where the lines intersect, then tilt the punch to vertical position and tap it with a hammer.

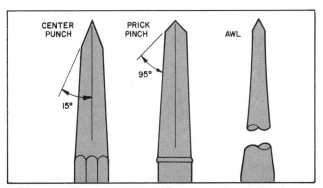

5-35.   Punches and awls have points with different shapes that should be maintained when they are sharpened.

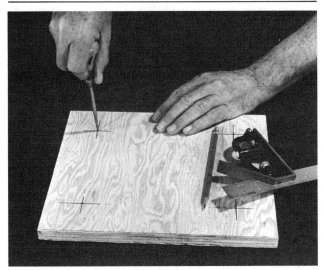

5-33.   Mark hole locations by drawing intersecting lines. Use an awl to form an indent so the bit can get started accurately.

5-36.   A guide block, which is marked for alignment with lines on the workpiece, assures that the hole will be perpendicular to the surface.

The block should be marked like the one in Figure 5-37 so it can be aligned with intersecting marks on the workpiece. Since the block can be used for various jobs, the hole through it shouldn't be more than ¹/₁₆″. Thus, it can be used for pilot holes in the work which you later enlarge to the right size.

A handy accessory that makes drilling at a 90° angle very easy when using a portable drill, is the Portalign "Drillguide" (Figure 5-38). This one application doesn't demonstrate the versatility of the attachment so we'll be seeing more of it as we go along.

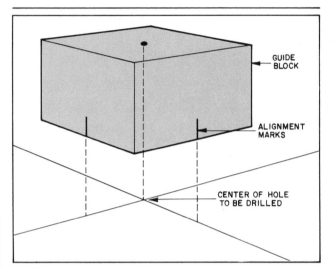

5-37.   Use hardwoods like maple or birch when making guide blocks. The guide-hole should be small to provide pilot holes in the work. Thus, the gauge can be used for various jobs.

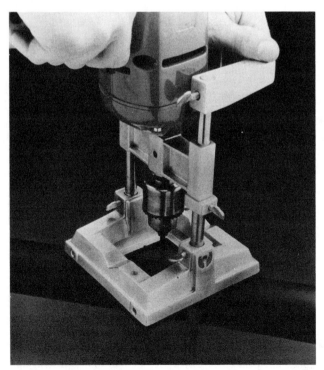

5-38.   The Portalign "Drillguide" is a handy accessory which, among others things, assures vertical-drilling accuracy.

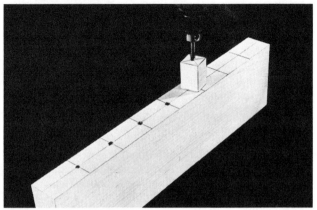

5-39.   You can drill to a specific depth by using a guide block that allows the bit to penetrate just so far.

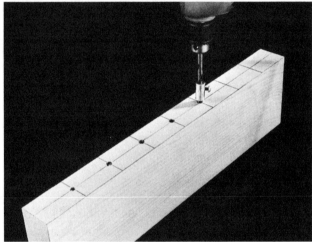

5-40.   A bushing, drilled and tapped for a set screw, is an adjustable hole-depth gauge that can be used on various drill-sizes. Two, one with a ¼″ hole and the other with a ½″ hole will serve for most work.

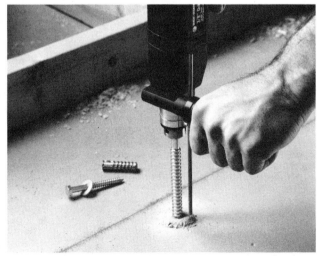

5-41.   Some manufacturers offer adjustable, depth-control accessories. Some may be used only on a specific product, so check before buying.

Drilling to a Specific Depth

Drilling to a specific depth, something you will need to do, for example, when forming holes for dowels, can be difficult without some sort of a depth gauge. The one shown in Figure 5-39 is simple but efficient. The gauge is made so its height allows the bit to penetrate just so far.

Another solution is to use a suitably-sized bushing which is drilled and tapped to receive a set screw (Figure 5-40). Since the gauge can be secured at any point on the bit, it can be used for various hole-depths.

A type of adjustable depth gauge which is offered as an accessory by some manufacturers is shown in Figure 5-41. Probably the easiest method of all to gauge drill penetration is simply to wrap several layers of masking tape around the bit so you'll know when to stop feeding.

Angular Drilling

Trying to judge a particular angle by eye is pretty rough. You can get some help by aligning the drill with a protractor, but to be precise it's best to work with a custom-made block that is clamped or tack-nailed to the workpiece (Figure 5-42). To make such a block, follow the steps shown in Figure 5-43. First, drill a hole through a block of wood that has parallel surfaces. Then saw off one end so the body will tilt to the angle you need. If you make the gauge correctly it can also serve to limit the bit's penetration.

The Portalign "Drillguide" may also be used for angular drilling (Figure 5-44). Since its base is vertically adjustable along the posts, the accessory can be braced to allow the drill to work at almost any angle. An adjustable stop, situated on one of the posts, allows you to control how far the bit will penetrate.

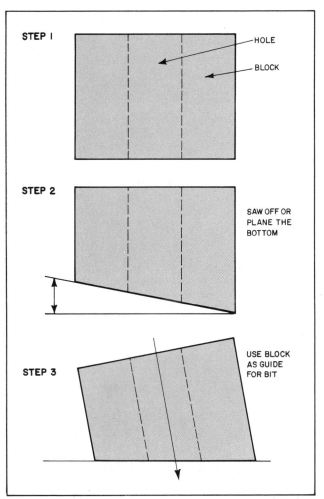

5-43.   One way to make an angular guide block. Shape the bottom of the block to the angle you need after drilling the guide-hole.

5-42.   For precise angular drilling, it's best to work with a custom-made guide block that can be tack-nailed or clamped to the work.

5-44.   The Portalign "Drillguide" may be used for angular drilling by raising the base so the drill can function in a tilted position. Adjustable stop is used to control hole-depth.

Center Drilling Jig

5-45.   A special jig that you make will allow center-drilling on stock edges regardless of the stock's thickness.

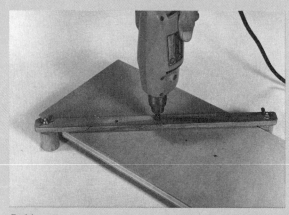

5-46.   The drilling jig can also be used to drill center holes on surfaces. You can increase the jig's capacity by making an extra, longer bar.

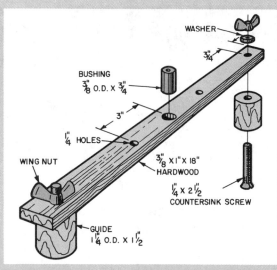

5-47.   Details of the center-drilling jig. It's a simple concept but take the time to make it accurately.

A Jig for Center Drilling

The center drilling jig will eliminate layout time while providing accuracy when it's necessary to drill in the center of a board or along its edge (Figures 5-45, 5-46). While it is simple in design, the project does require care in construction (Figure 5-47).

Make the bar first, drilling the holes exactly on the centerline. It's okay to use a bushing that is not the size shown, but be certain it's a press fit in the bar—or take the precaution of seating it with an epoxy. A ⅛″ hole will do for most jobs. The idea is to provide a pilot hole that you can enlarge if necessary. You can turn the guides yourself or make do by cutting sections from a large dowel, but be sure the hole for the bolt is centered. For more flexibility in the guide's placement, you can add additional holes in the hardwood bar.

Guide for Radial Holes

The guide shown in Figure 5-48 assures drilling accurate holes on a circumference. The guide is a strip of ⅛″-thick do-it-yourself aluminum, with ¹⁄₁₆″ holes spaced ½″ apart on a common centerline. A nail, at the center of the circle, is used in one hole so the guide can be pivoted to determine the correct radius at any point. When the holes must be spaced in a particular fashion, which is usual, start the job by marking diameters that indicate how the guide should be placed for each hole. The initial drilling provides pilot holes which can be enlarged to whatever size is needed.

The same guide, as demonstrated in Figure 5-49, can be used to drill equally-spaced holes. The points at each end of the guide are used to align it with a line marked on the work.

Drilling for Mortises and Slots

The major difference between a drilled mortise and one formed on a drill press with special mortising bits and chisels is that the drill-press version has square ends and the drilled version has round ends; there is no difference strength-wise.

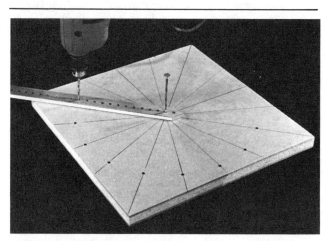

5-48.   An aluminum bar with accurately-drilled, equally-spaced holes is fine for drilling a series of holes on a circumference. Points on the bar are guides for aligning it with radial lines on the work.

To drill a mortise, select a bit whose diameter equals the width of the cavity and then drill overlapping holes on a common centerline (Figure 5-50). Drill end-holes first and then those in between, spacing them to remove as much waste as possible. Use brad point bits when you can since they permit more overlapping than twist drills.

When drilling is complete, clean out the remaining waste material with a sharp chisel (Figure 5-51). Note that the ends on the tenon are rounded.

Slots are formed in the same manner (Figure 5-52). If the slot needs to have square ends, use a file to clean out the end corners.

Drilling Holes for Wood Screws

In order for the fastener to have maximum holding power, there are two different diameter holes that should be drilled before driving a screw. One is the *body hole*, which equals the shank diameter of the screw, the other is the *lead hole*, which allows the screw to penetrate while providing enough material for the screw-threads to grip (Figure 5-53).

The holes can be formed individually using drill bits, in which case it's wise to drill the lead hole first and enlarge the top portion to body hole or you can do the work more easily and more accurately by using special cutters like those shown in Figures 5-54 and 5-55. Notice that some offer different features. One provides the essential holes and has the capability of countersinking (Figure 5-56) and, if you went deeper, would also form a counterbore.

Countersinking is needed so flathead screws can be driven flush. Notice in Figure 5-57 that a stop, which is available for the screw-hole forming tool, is used to control the bit's penetration. On hardwoods, countersink to the full depth of the screwhead. On softwoods, stay a bit on the minus side. The screw will pull flush as you finish driving. When you are driving very small screws, especially in softwood, you can simply make a straight starting hole with an awl. You might even find this possible to do on some hardwoods. Make a judgment after testing with one or two screws.

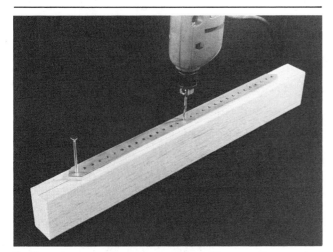

5-49. The same bar can be used for drilling equally spaced holes. Here too, the points on the bar are used to set it to a line on the work.

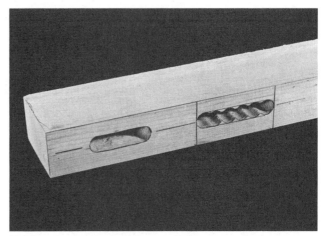

5-50. You can form mortises by drilling a series of overlapping holes. Drill the end holes first. You'll work more accurately if you use brad-point type bits.

5-51. The waste that remains is cleaned out with a sharp chisel. Note that the ends on the tenon have been rounded to conform to the shape of the mortise.

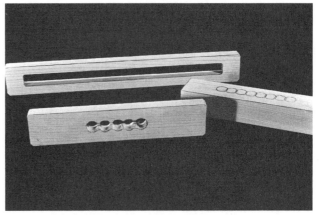

5-52. The overlapping holes technique also serves to form slots. Finish with a file if the slot must have square ends.

HOLE SIZES FOR WOOD SCREWS

SCREW NO.	SHANK DIAM.	LENGTHS AVAILABLE	LEAD HOLES	
			HARDWOOD	SOFTWOOD
0	.060"	¼"-⅜"	70 (1/32)	75 (1/64)
1	.073"	¼"-½"	66 (1/32)	71 (1/32)
2	.086"	¼"-¾"	56 (3/64)	65 (1/32)
3	.099"	¼"-1"	54 (1/16)	58 (3/64)
4	.112"	¼"-1½"	52 (1/16)	55 (3/64)
5	.125"	⅜"-1½"	49 (5/64)	53 (1/16)
6	.138"	⅜"-2½"	47 (5/64)	52 (1/16)
7	.151"	⅜"-2½"	44 (3/32)	51 (1/16)
8	.164"	⅜"-3"	40 (3/32)	48 (5/64)
9	.177"	½"-3"	37 (7/64)	45 (5/64)
10	.190"	½"-3½"	33 (7/64)	43 (3/32)
11	.203"	⅝"-3½"	29 (⅛)	40 (3/32)
12	.216"	⅝"-4"	25 (⅛)	38 (7/64)
14	.242"	¾"-5"	14 (3/16)	32 (7/64)
16	.268"	1"-5"	10 (3/16)	29 (9/64)
18	.294"	1¼"-5"	6 (13/64)	26 (9/64)
20	.320"	1½"-5"	3 (7/32)	19 (11/64)
24	.372"	3"-5"	1 (¼)	15 (3/16)

5-53.   Chart tells what size holes are needed when drilling for wood screws. Providing the holes is the right way to go if you wish to drive screws with minimum effort and have them hold with maximum grip.

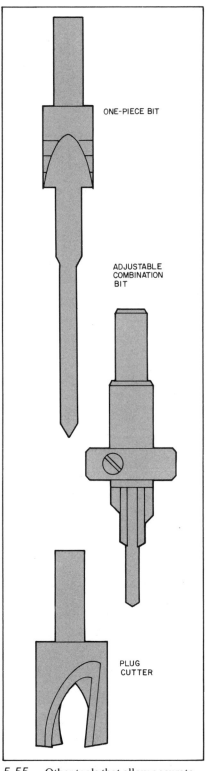

5-55.   Other tools that allow accurate drilling of holes for screws with minimum fuss. The bottom cutter is used to make plugs that are used in counterbored holes. They are useful because you can cut plugs from any species of wood you choose.

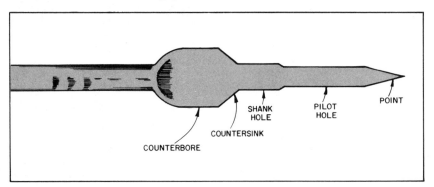

5-54.   A typical screw-hole former. Whether you countersink and then add a counterbore depends on how deep you drill.

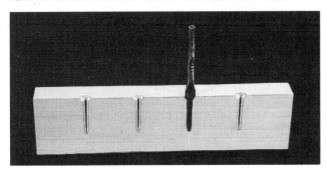

5-56.   Cross-section of holes drilled for screws shows what a neat job the special cutter can do. The cutters should be purchased in sets, since each is designed for a particular size screw.

5-57.   Some sets come with an adjustable stop, or one can be purchased as an accessory. The stop makes it easy to control hole-depth for either countersinking or counterboring.

Counterboring is required when you wish to set the fastener head below the surface, which is usually done so the fastener can be concealed with a wood plug (Figure 5-58). The counterbore is no more than a shallow hole sized to suit the head of the screw or bolt or whatever. When you wish to use a particular size plug, it's okay to form the counterbore with a conventional drilling tool like a spade bit or brad-point bit and then use a screw-hole forming tool or regular bits to do the shank and pilot holes.

Counterbored holes can be filled with dowels, plugs you cut yourself, or with plugs or buttons that you buy and use as-is (Figure 5-59). Both types are set in place with glue. The plugs are sanded flush—the buttons are used to provide a decorative detail.

When power-driving screws, use the slowest speed that will keep the screw turning and a screwdriver-bit that will fit snugly in the screwhead slot (Figure 5-60). It's wise to have an assortment of screwdriver-bits in various sizes and types on hand.

Drilling for Dowels

A common use for dowels is as reinforcement in wood connections. They are often used in edge-to-edge, end-to-edge joints, miter joints, and so on. Since the dowels must fit into matching holes, accuracy in layout and in drilling is essential. Dowel Centers (Figure 5-61) are often used to mark the location of mating holes after the first ones have been drilled. The centers are placed in holes drilled in one

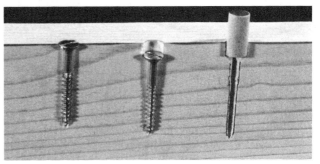

5-58.   Lengths of dowel are often used to fill counterbored holes, but store-bought dowels are not always accurate and they are not available in many wood species. It's best to make your own by using plug cutters.

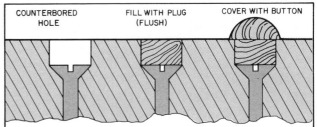

5-59.   Plugs and buttons, which you buy ready-made, can be used to fill counterbored holes. The plugs are sanded flush, the buttons are used to provide a decorative detail. Both are glued in place.

5-60.   Use a slow speed when driving or removing screws. The screwdriver bit should fit snugly in the screwhead slot, which is why it's wise to have several sizes on hand.

5-61.   Dowel centers, placed in holes in one piece, mark hole locations in the mating piece when the two parts are pressed together.

piece and then the two pieces are pressed together so the points on the centers mark the spots where the holes are required in the second piece. These items are available in sets that include ¼″, ⁵⁄₁₆″, ⅜″, and ½″ sizes.

A doweling jig can be a big help when drilling holes in boards that will be edge-joined to form a wide panel. The one being used in Figure 5-62 can grip material as wide as 4″. Its revolving turret has holes that allow the use of ³⁄₁₆″ through ½″ drill bits. To work accurately, clamp the boards to be drilled surface-to-surface and mark the hole locations across all edges using a square. Index lines on the turret make it easy to line up the hole with the mark on the work.

An offbeat use for the jig is shown in Figure 5-63. Round or square stock is placed between V-blocks and then secured with the screw-clamp of the jig. The idea can be a big help when you need to drill concentric holes.

A fairly new "how to drill for dowels" idea is the Haddon Wood Joiner Kit which includes the materials shown in Figure 5-64. The tool, actually a very precise template, has 72 holes that are positioned so that one row of holes will center on boards of various width. The joiner, as it's called, is positioned on the edge of one board (Figure 5-65) and holes are drilled, spaced according to the holes you select. Stop collars on the bits, which are supplied, limit the drilling depth. Then the operation is repeated on the second board using the other side of the joiner (Figure 5-66). This is a rather quickie presentation of the jig but it's pretty much how it works. It can also be used to drill holes in mitered edges (Figure 5-67) and for face-doweling work.

Figures 5-68 through 5-71 show how to use dowels to reinforce various wood connections.

5-62.   Doweling jig, clamped to the work's edge, provides a guide for drilling centered, perpendicular holes. Revolving turret has holes for various size bits. The tool can grip stock up to 4″ thick.

5-63.   Using it as a guide for drilling concentric holes is an off-beat use for the doweling jig. Round or square stock is gripped between V-blocks.

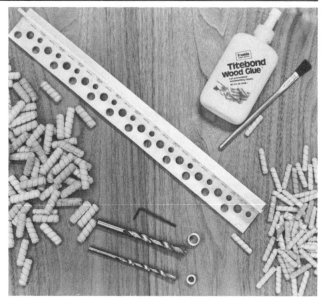

5-64.   Hadden Joiner Kit includes materials shown here. You can get started on edge-to-edge joints right off.

5-65.   The joiner is clamped to the edge of one board and holes are drilled with spacing determined by the holes you select.

5-66.   The second step is done with the other side of the joiner clamped to the second board. Adjustable stop collars are provided so you can drill all holes to the same depth.

5-67.   The Hadden tool can also be used to drill dowel holes in miter cuts. The system is fairly simple and can be used on stock of various thicknesses.

Reinforcing Joints with Dowels

5-68.   Miter joints can be reinforced by drilling a through hole and then gluing in a dowel. Use a longer dowel than necessary so you can trim it and sand it flush after the glue dries.

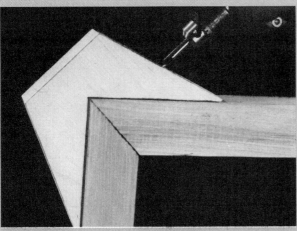

5-69.   A pre-drilled, V-shaped guide will let you drill accurately through the miter joint.

5-70.   Dowels can be used to reinforce the joint between a drawer front and its sides. Drill the first hole and then insert a dowel to keep the pieces aligned for the remaining holes.

5-71.   Use a dowel this way to reinforce a finger lap joint. Drill the hole after the parts have been assembled.

The Drill as a Sander

Among the most practical sanding accessories for the portable drill are sanding drums like the one shown in Figure 5-72. They are available in diameters as small as ½″ and as large as 3″ or more. Most will have ¼″ shanks but oversize ones may have ⅜″ or even ½″ shanks. The tools are rubber cylinders that grip, or release, abrasive sleeves when a nut at the free end of the shank is tightened or loosened. They are available individually or in sets of various diameters. A typical assortment contains four or five sizes ranging from ½″ to 1½″.

The abrasive sleeves come in various grits with common designations being "fine", "medium", and "coarse". The texture of the sandpaper has some bearing on the most efficient speed to use. Generally, 1000 to 1500 rpm is okay for coarse paper, while higher speeds can be used with finer grits.

In all cases, bear in mind that the abrasive particles are cutting tools and you must give them a chance to work. Excessive pressure against the piece being sanded does more harm than good and can even distort the cylinder on which the sleeves are mounted. Other harmful effects are— premature wear of the abrasive, burning the sleeve or the work, and sanded edges that are irregular.

One of the major uses for sanding drums is smoothing curved edges and the inside edges of cutouts (Figures 5-73, 5-74). Good control of the tool is necessary for the sanded edge to be square to surfaces. A light touch and a continuous feed are basic techniques. If you don't keep the drum moving, you'll form indents in the work-edge. The workpiece should be held firmly. It's wise to clamp small parts to a benchtop or to grip them in a vise.

You can arrange to apply the work to the tool rather than the tool to the work by mounting the drill on a stand, which is a common portable drill accessory (Figure 5-75). Secure the stand to a plywood base or, so it will be more portable, attach it to a block of wood so it can be gripped in a vise when needed. Go a bit further by duplicating the setup shown in Figure 5-76 and you will have more assurance that the sanded edge will be square. The support piece, with a hole through it for the drum, has a base-cleat so it can be clamped in place or attached with screws. Be sure it's a sturdy attachment and that the angle between the support plate and the surface of the drum is 90°.

The drill can also be used like a stationary disc sander when you mount it as shown in Figure 5-77. Discs are usually available in rubber and designed for use while hand-holding the drill. The jig idea works best with a rigid disc. If you can't find a suitable one, or if you prefer, you can make several of your own by following the specifications in Figure 5-78. Be sure you install the table and situate the drill so the angle between the disc and the table is 90°. Always apply the work to the "down" side of the disc (Figure 5-79). If the drill has a reverse mode, you can choose to work on the left- or the right-hand side of the table.

Another practical sanding accessory for the portable drill is the "Sand-O-Flex" product shown in Figure 5-80. The abrasive strips are backed by cushioning brushes which make them conform to various configurations or force them into corners and even small openings. As the abrasive wears,

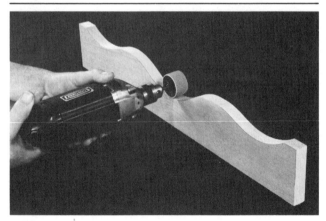

5-73.   Smoothing irregular edges is a job you can do very quickly with a drum sander. Keep the drum moving to avoid indenting the edge. Keep the drill horizontal throughout the pass.

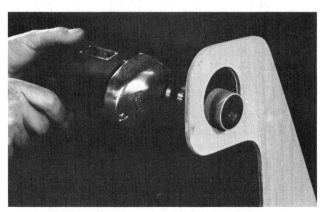

5-74.   Drum sanding is especially useful for smoothing internal cutouts. It's best to hold small workpieces in a vise, or to clamp them.

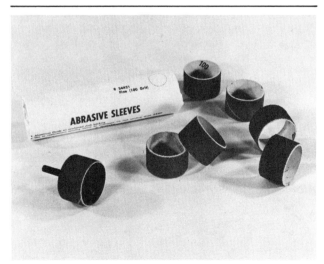

5-72.   Drum sanders can be used very efficiently with a portable drill. It's best to buy them in sets and to have a nice supply of sleeves in various grits on hand.

5-75.   Secure the drill to a stand and you can apply the work to the tool instead of the reverse. The stand can be attached to a plywood base or to a block of wood that can be gripped in a vise when needed.

5-76.   Add a support piece that has a hole the drum can pass through and you have more assurance that the sanded edge will be square to surfaces. Be sure the angle between the drum-surface and the support-face is 90°.

5-77.   Use a table like this with a stand-mounted drill and you have a small but efficient disc sander. You can buy discs or make your own by following the suggestions in the next illustration.

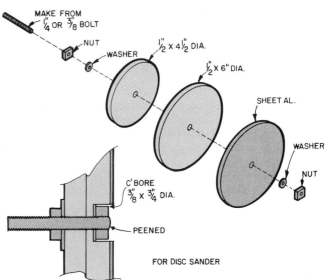

5-78.   How to make your own sanding discs. Make several so you can have various sandpaper grits ready to go.

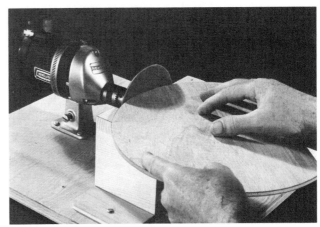

5-79.   Always apply the work to the "down" side of the disc. This would be on the left side of the table if the disc is turning counterclockwise when you face it.

5-80.   "Sand-O-Flex" wheel has brush-backed sanding strips that let you smooth contours or get into tight areas. Worn strips are cut off and "renewed" by turning the tool's index knob.

the ends are cut off and fresh strips are exposed by turning the index knob on the unit. Here too, you can sand by hand-holding the drill or apply the workpiece by securing the drill on a stand (Figure 5-81).

Other Abrading Tools

For heavy stock removal, you can consider various types of rotary rasps, examples of which are pictured in Figure 5-82. The "Surform" product, shown in Figure 5-83, cuts in one direction with hundreds of preset, hardened steel teeth, each of which works like a miniature chisel. The teeth work hard to remove a lot of material but they are spaced so that they resist clogging. Like a sanding drum, the tool should be used with only enough pressure to keep the teeth cutting. A continuous feed is necessary to keep the cutter from indenting a workedge. Unless the project calls for a less-than-smooth edge, rasping should be followed by sanding.

The smaller rotary rasps are available in various shapes and sizes so, with several in stock, you can select one that's just right for the job at hand. I use them to get into corners and areas where other tools won't fit, and for fun jobs like carving in the round (Figure 5-84). These too, are not really "smoothers", so if you need a slick-to-the-touch finish follow rasping with sanding.

A cheese-grater-type disc rasp (Figure 5-85), is a simple concept that does some surprising work. It cuts fast and doesn't clog, but, on the other hand, it doesn't produce a ready-to-stain finish. I use it to round off edges and corners quickly and for preliminary surfacing on rough stock (Figure 5-86). The disc is not as rigid as a steel plate so it must be applied carefully to avoid distorting it. Light pressure is wise; bear down too heavily on the disc and it will tend to stall or try to travel like a wheel.

Wire Brushes

There are many types of wire brushes available. Like other abrasives they are designated as "fine", "medium", and "coarse" which essentially tells the gauge of the wire they are made of. Some are complete units, mounted on a shank that can be gripped in a chuck, others are designed for mounting on a separate arbor (Figure 5-87).

When you mount one, especially a new one, hold it away from you and allow it to run free for a bit to be sure no loose wires are thrown your way. Always wear safety goggles! The speed to use will depend on the type of wheel and the job. Most of the time, the literature that comes with the tool will warn of a maximum operating speed. To be safe, and to work efficiently, start wire-brushing jobs at a slow speed and increase rpm to the point where the unit is doing what you wish.

Coarse brushes do a good job of removing rust or dirt from metals, while fine ones can be used to create a satin finish (Figures 5-88, 5-89). Usually, it's best to make parallel, overlapping strokes, but there are options, especially if you are trying for a decorative effect.

Either a fine or coarse wheel can be used on certain wood to create a sculptured, 3-D effect (Figure 5-90). The

5-81.   This unique sanding tool can also be used with a stand-mounted drill. Be careful when smoothing small pieces; your fingers, as well as the wood can be sanded.

5-82.   Rotary rasps and the "Surform" drum at the right will remove stock quickly but they are not "smoothers".

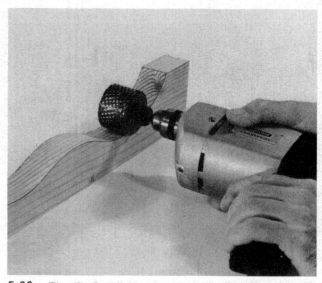

5-83.   The "Surform" drum has hundreds of small, sharp teeth that work like tiny chisels. It cuts only in one direction. Keep it moving—try to work so you cut *with* the grain of the wood.

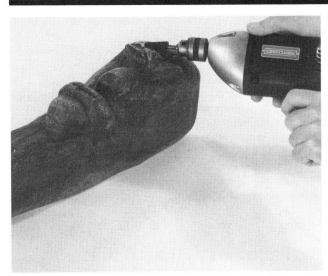

5-84.   Rotary rasps are great for getting into tight places and for carving operations. If you want a smooth finish, you'll have to do some sanding after rasping.

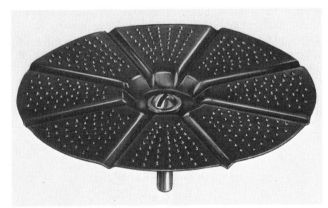

5-85.   Disc rasp has cheese-grater-type teeth that cut fast without clogging.

5-86.   The disc rasp is helpful for, among other things, preliminary surfacing of rough stock. Keep a firm grip on the drill and move the disc slowly. Excessive pressure will do more harm than good—the drill may stall and the disc might "walk".

5-87.   Wire brushes are available as "cups" with built-in shanks, or as wheels with center holes so they can be mounted on arbors. Safety goggles, as always, are a must.

5-88.   A coarse-grit wire brush can be used to remove rust or dirt from metals. Use overlapping strokes. Move the drill so cutting is done against the wheel's rotation. Keep a firm grip to prevent the wheel from walking.

5-89.   A fine-grit brush can be used to put a satin finish on soft metals. Strokes can be parallel or haphazard, depending on the effect you want.

5-90.　A wire brush will create a sculptured, 3-D effect on wood. The treatment is especially effective on wood with hard and soft grain areas, like fir. Use a coarse wheel to start with, a fine wheel to finish.

5-91.　Some of the stands that are available for portable drills include a guard that is mounted as shown here. Use it for all abrading operations but don't let it lull you into neglecting safety goggles.

5-92.　Add a table that can function somewhat like the tool rest on a bench grinder. It serves as support for workpieces and also covers more of the wheel.

treatment is more effective on wood that has areas of hard and soft grain, like fir plywood or lumber.

Some holders available as accessories for portable drills include an adjustable guard so a wire brush can be used (Figure 5-91). This is a nice way to work on small pieces that require cleaning or polishing. Be sure you don't abrade your fingers along with the work; a possibility you can help avoid by wearing tight fitting gloves. If what you are working on is very small, grip it with pliers so your fingers can't come close. Figure 5-92 shows an example of a tool-rest table that you can add to the setup.

If the drill has a reversing feature, use it occasionally to reverse a wire wheel's direction of rotation. This will bring new, sharper points on the end of the wires into play, and will prevent the wires from taking a set in one direction.

The Portable Drill as a Drill Press

Many portable drill users who don't care to add a stationary drill press to their shop equipment but want some of the accuracy and convenience such a tool can provide, buy one of the many stands that allow a portable drill to be used in similar fashion. Most manufacturers offer one as an accessory —Skil, Wen, Sears, Black & Decker, Montgomery Ward, Rockwell all have one. Some will take *any* drill, others are designed specifically for one product, so check if you decide to buy one.

Some of the units are basic, being a post and stand combination, with a vertically adjustable drill holder, and a feed handle with a spring-action return (Figure 5-93). Others

5-93.　Most manufacturers who sell drills also offer a stand that allows drill-press functions. Some are designed for a single product, so check before buying.

(Figure 5-94) are a bit more sophisticated and come closer to imitating the functions of a drill press. The addition of a work table and extra features allows operations like those shown in Figures 5-95 and 5-96.

In no way can the portable-and-stand combination downgrade the stationary tool, but for many workshop chores it can serve as a substitute. You'll find that many jobs you've done by hand-holding the drill are easier and more accurate using a stand-mounted drill (Figures 5-97, 5-98). I feel that the portable-and-stand combination should be viewed on its own merits. It can be an asset to any shop regardless of the existing complement of tools. You can use it as-is, or extend its versatility by improvising setups and by dressing it up with some homemade jigs.

5-96.   Being able to turn the drill holder 90° allows a horizontal mode.

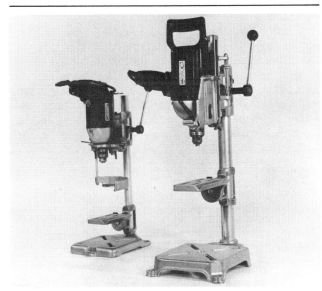

5-94.   Some stands are more sophisticated than others. These examples are closer to drill-press design since they include a work table in addition to the base. They might even include a guard (Left).

5-97.   It's more convenient to use accessories like hole cutters when the drill is mounted in a stand. Use a backup block under the work, and a clamp to keep the work secure. This stand is mounted on cleats to provide room under the base for clamping.

5-95.   The table may have a V-slot which is handy when drilling radial holes through round stock or tubing.

5-98.   Use a drill-press vise or another adequate holder when working on small pieces and when drilling or countersinking metal. Often, it's also necessary to clamp the vise. This photo doesn't show it, but stands should be bolted or screwed to a firm surface.

5-99.　The drill/stand combination is completely portable so you can use it like this to drill perfectly square-to-the-surface holes in standing posts, beams, joists, or whatever.

A novel but practical application is demonstrated in Figure 5-99. Say you must drill squarely through a post or column or beam; by clamping the stand to the work, as shown, you will assure that the hole will be perpendicular to the work-surface. The base of the stand can be clamped under the work or, assuming the base has a center hole, on top of it.

You can come closer to a true drill-press mode with stands that do not have a worktable by making a special base like the one in Figure 5-100. This allows the base of the stand to be used as a worktable. You can increase capacity between chuck and table by substituting a length of tubing or pipe that has the same diameter as the original post. If the base—now the table—flexes under drill pressure, brace under its front edge with a block of wood. The drawing in Figure 5-101 suggests how a new base can be made.

Another modification that provides even greater flexibility is shown in Figure 5-102. Here, galvanized pipe and fittings are used in place of the original base and post. Now the unit can be used in horizontal mode and, by adding the table and guides that are detailed in Figure 5-103, it becomes practical for quite a few chores that are normally done on a drill press. Figures 5-104 through 5-108 show how the table and guides can be situated, and demonstrate a few applications for the setup.

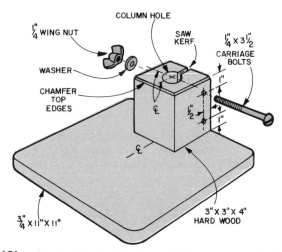

5-101.　Construction details of a special base you can make for a drill stand.

5-100.　Make a special base and the original base can be used as a work table. For more capacity, you can substitute some heavy tubing or pipe for the original column.

5-102.　Add even more flexibility by making a completely new column module. Actually, the only original part you use is the drill holder.

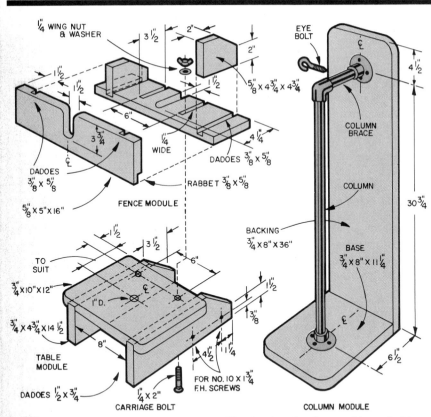

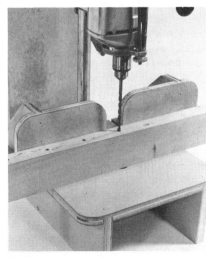

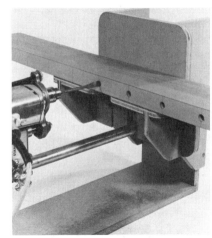

5-103. How to make a new column module. The drawing also shows guides and tables that are used with it.

5-106. The fence can be used as a guide when it's necessary to drill a series of holes on a common centerline.

5-107. Place the unit on its "back" and you have a horizontal boring machine.

5-108. The eye bolt shown in the drawing is there so the drill's cord can be held out of the way.

5-104. Stand the unit on end, add the table and you have the drill-press mode.

5-105. The fence is attached to the table with bolts and wing nuts so it is adjustable in relation to the centerline of the drill.

Drilling Metal

Twist drills are the most common tools used for forming holes in metal. While there are some similarities between drilling wood and drilling metal, there are *major* differences you should be aware of. While it might be possible to drill a good-size hole in wood in one operation, it's not a good idea to do so in metal. The practical procedure, for accuracy *and* safety, is to start with a small hole and get to the size you need by enlarging the hole in stages.

Metal drilling can develop considerable twisting action, and the bit can snag when it starts to break through. Therefore, the work must be securely clamped to a firm surface or gripped in a vise. There are several types of holding devices—usually called "drill-press vises"—that are handy for holding work, especially small pieces, securely (Figure 5-109). The faces of the units are usually V-cut or extra pieces with the same configuration are supplied so you can use them to grip round stock as well as straight pieces. The bases of the units are designed so they can be bolted or clamped to the drill-press table. You can provide the same extra security when working with a portable drill by locking the unit to a bench top or to a hefty block of wood that you can then grip in a bench vise.

Always start the drilling operation by marking the hole location with a punch (Figure 5-110). If you don't do this, the bit will probably move off the mark when you start the drill. Always start at a very low speed; gradually increase speed, but only to the point where the bit consistently cuts away material. A good combination of speed and feed pressure will curl a ribbon of metal out of the hole. Being too gentle won't accomplish anything but dull the bit since it will be doing more rubbing than cutting.

The best way to drill thin, sheet material is to sandwich it between pieces of scrap wood (Figure 5-111) or, at least, clamp or tape it so it lays flat on a backing block. If you work without these precautions, the bit will start to snag right off, the hole will have considerable burrs, and it may be anything but round.

An interesting and practical operation—not a drilling chore—that I use when working with small tubing is shown in Figure 5-112. Instead of turning the cutter, let a stand-mounted drill spin the tubing. The idea, of course, is most useful when you need many pieces. In fact, when many pieces of the same length are required you can use the jig setup shown in Figure 5-113. An L-shaped block clamped to the vise serves as a gauge while the tubing cutter is gripped by the jaws of the vise. In both cases, the knob of the cutter is turned while the drill spins the tubing at a fairly low speed.

5-111.   The best way to drill clean, burr-free holes in sheet metal is to sandwich it between scrap pieces.

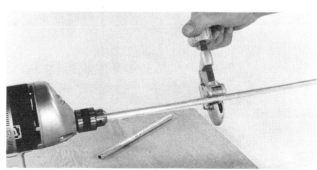

5-112.   Not a drilling job, but the idea may come in handy, especially when you have many pieces of tubing to cut. The knob of the cutter is turned slowly while the drill rotates the tubing.

5-109.   Vises like these are designed for use on a drill press but they are also very practical for use when working with a portable drill. The V-blocks, with clamps used for holding round stock, are usually sold as separate units.

5-110.   Always start a metal drilling operation by indenting the hole location with a punch. In this automatic punch, a heavy spring impels the point when the top cap is pressed down.

5-113.   When you need many similar pieces you can clamp the cutter in a vise and use an L-shaped gauge to determine the length of the cutoffs.

A Selection of Special Accessories

The portable electric drill, on its own, isn't more than a power-source. What can be gripped in its chuck, whether for drilling or doing other shop and home chores, is what makes it such a versatile tool. The following illustrations and captions describe some of the accessories I have used with favorable results. They make the portable drill more than a drilling tool.

The Drill as a Lathe
Figures 5-114 through 5-116.

5-114.   A Leichtung "kit" supplies all the necessary components needed to use a drill as a lathe. "Headstock", "tailstock", and tool rest clamp to the edge of a workbench while the drill, through a special bushing, drives the spur center. End parts are situated to accommodate the length of the mounted workpiece.

5-115.   The drill sits at the headstock end and connects to drivers by means of a shaft and ball bearing bushing. What you can do with the lathe depends on the drill you use. A heavy-duty, ⅜″ drill with variable speeds is recommended.

5-116.   A faceplate is included in the kit. Always be sure that components are firmly clamped. Check them while working to be sure that vibration hasn't caused them to loosen.

As a Sander/Grinder
Figure 5-117.

5-117.   With the Hirsh sander/grinder, you use a portable drill to turn a disc to which you can attach conventional or wet-or-dry abrasive sheets. The unit can be used for conventional disc sanding and as a sharpening tool. A water tray and brush assembly, under the table, carries moisture to the disc so sharpening can be done with minimum heat buildup. The unit provides a tilting table and a small miter gauge.

As a Water Pump
Figure 5-118.

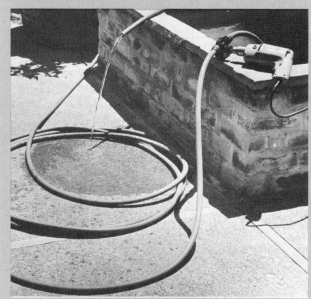

5-118.   Hand-size drill pump works impressively. It can be used with any garden hose to move 200 gallons per hour. Results are best when the drill turns at about 2000 rpm. The intake hose should not be longer than ten feet but the outlet hose can be as long as one hundred feet. The unit that is shown is a Black & Decker product. It's a good idea to wear rubber boots and gloves when using electricity near water.

As a Drill Saw
Figure 5-120.

5-120.   With "drill saws" you drill through to the cutter section of the tool and then cut in any direction you please. Thus you can form odd-shaped holes, do some scroll work, shape curves, and so on. Another typical use is enlarging existing holes. Metal as well as wood-cutting units are available.

For Right-Angle Drilling
Figure 5-119.

5-119.   Right-angle drilling is a boon when working in tight places. A special accessory that makes such an application easy is generally available. Most of them can be used with any drill.

For Mixing Paint
Figure 5-121.

5-121.   Tools that make it easy to mix paint to the correct consistency come in various forms. Be sure the mixer is in the paint before you turn on the drill—and—that the drill is stopped before removing the tool. Use a slow speed so you don't churn paint out of the container.

As an Earth Auger
Figure 5-122.

5-122.   Jisco earth augers form 1¼″ holes quickly in all kinds of soil. They are available in 18″ long units for use with a ¼″ or larger drill, and in a 24″ long model that should be used with at least a ⅜″ drill. The augers are handy for jobs like deep root fertilizing and watering of trees and shrubs, and for drilling holes near foundations for insecticide treatment.

For Shaping
Figures 5-123 through 5-126.

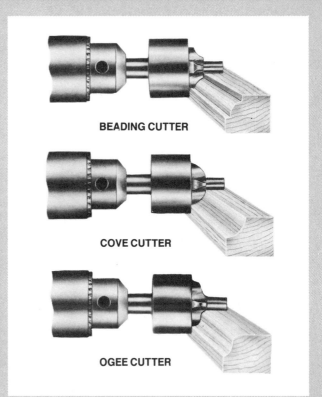

BEADING CUTTER

COVE CUTTER

OGEE CUTTER

5-124.   Examples of shapes available for use in a portable drill.

5-123.   Special bits are available that allow some amount of shaping with a portable drill. It's best to move the cutter very slowly and to use the drill's highest speed. The work should be held in a vise or firmly clamped. Keep a good grip on the drill and maintain it in a horizontal position through the pass.

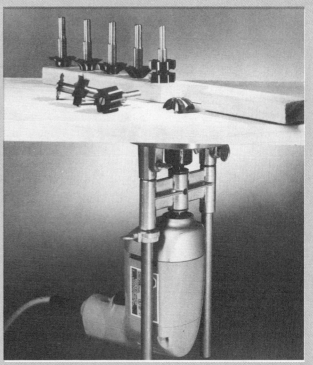

5-125.   Portalign offers special, low speed shaper bits which can be used together with their "Drillguide". The guide is mounted under a platform that has been drilled so the cutters can pass through. A clamped, straight strip of wood with a notch in it serves as a fence.

For a Special Kind of Sanding
Figure 5-127.

5-126.   The shaper bits are available in various profiles. Nine cutting edges and a fairly large diameter for higher rpm speed, is what enables the bits to make acceptable cuts at low speeds. They are not meant to be used freehand.

5-127.   Sears kit for sanding or polishing round components includes a special attachment, sandpaper strips, and a polishing strap. It can be used with 1/4" or 3/8" portable electric drills.

6. The Portable Router

If you associate the saber saw with a jigsaw or band-saw, a portable drill with a drill press, or a cutoff saw with a table saw or radial arm saw, then you'll view the portable router as a close relative of the stationary shaper. Too often though, the router—and the shaper too—is limited by the user to forming decorative edges on furniture components, which is like using a saw only for crosscutting. The router is as practical a power tool as you can find. Professional woodworkers see it as a first-choice tool for many of the operations required for classic wood joints. It can often make the difference between amateurish and professional projects.

For example, the dovetail joint, a hallmark of well-designed and constructed furniture, is easily within the scope of a beginner when the router is used together with a dovetail jig. With a jig, dovetails can be formed about as quickly and easily as a dado or rabbet joint, and they will be precise. Some of the jigs are for equally spaced, through dovetails, while more sophisticated units allow variable spacing, whether you are forming through or half-blind dovetails. The point is, you

don't have to be an expert to use them, but they provide expert results.

With appropriate cutters, the router is used to form spline joints, mortise and tenon connections, rabbets, dadoes, half-laps, the mating shapes needed for a drop-leaf table, and it does them with impressive ease and speed.

The router can be used freehand with accessories you buy, jigs you make, or with templates. Often, template cutting and freehand work are combined. The drawer fronts on the little Spanish chest in Figure 6-1 are an example; outlines were cut using a template, rough texturing was done freehand.

The router is basically a simple tool, consisting of a motor with a cutter-gripping device at one end, and a base that holds the motor erect and allows vertical adjustment to control depth-of-cut (Figure 6-2). Alone, like a portable drill, it can't do anything but whir. However, have an assortment of router bits, jigs, and a selection of accessories (some of which are briefly described in Figure 6-3) on hand and the tool will be one of the most-used in your shop.

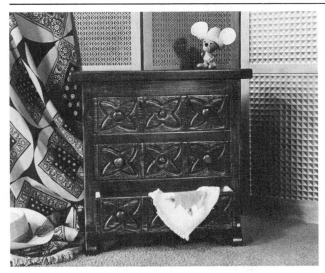

6-1. The router is used for esthetics as well as practical purposes. The carved drawer fronts and all the joints required to put this little Spanish-style chest together were done with a portable router.

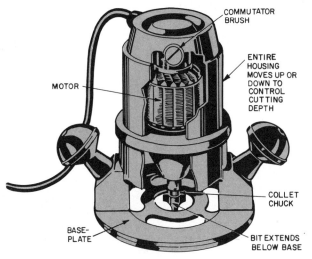

6-2. Basic construction of a router. Features not shown are things like double insulation, placement of switch, and possible electronic controls.

A QUICK LOOK AT PORTABLE ROUTER ACCESSORIES

ACCESSORY	REMARKS
ROUTER BITS	Many types available either for joinery or decorative work—may be high-speed steel, solid tungsten carbide or carbide-tipped—most designs available with integral or ball bearing pilots.
DOVETAIL TEMPLATES	Devices that allow quick and accurate forming of various types of dovetail joints—some permit user to space joints to suit—used with dovetail bits.
SPECIAL TABLES	For mounting a portable router so it can be like a shaper—usually equipped with adjustable fences and guard.
HINGE MORTISING TEMPLATE KITS	Adjustable templates on a clamp that secures to edge of door—quick and accurate method of routing mortises for hinges.
PLANER ATTACHMENT	Allows the use of a router as a portable plane not available for all makes of portable routers.
EDGE GUIDE	Used when making cuts parallel to an edge—sometimes supplied with the tool.
CIRCLE-CUTTING GUIDE	Used for forming circular grooves or cutting discs—EDGE GUIDE and CIRCLE-CUTTING GUIDE often available as combination tool.
TEMPLATE GUIDES	Attach to router's base—typical application is pattern routing—needed when working with dovetail templates.
LAMINATE TRIMMING BITS	Special cutters for trimming of plastic laminates and wood veneers—usually carbide-tipped—some routers require a special base or attachment for such applications.
BIT SHARPENER	Unit attaches to router base and works with router motor—grinding wheel is secured in router collet—special guides assure accurate work.
LETTER AND NUMBER GUIDES	Special templates for routing house numbers, nameplates, and so on—available in various sizes—usually with template guides.
PANTOGRAPH	Router duplicates illustrations, letters, and numbers that are traced with a stylus—some units allow enlarging or reducing the pattern.
DOOR AND PANEL KITS	Adjustable guides and templates for decorative grooving of doors, panels, and drawer fronts.
EDGE-CRAFTER*	For decorative edging of round or oval frames and piecrust-type table tops—used with a router table.
ROUTER-RECREATOR*	Allows router to duplicate 3-dimensional objects as well as letters or numbers.
ROUTER-CRAFTER*	Lathe-type accessory for forming decorative furniture legs and posts.
WOOD THREADER**	For cutting threads in any species of hard or soft wood—matching taps available.
BOWL CRAFTER*	Used with router for "turning" a variety of projects such as bowls, goblets, plates, and boxes with fitted lids.

*Sears (Craftsman) product   **Beall Tool Company

6-3.   The router is one of the power tools that can perform beyond its basic function because of the host of accessories that are available for it.

Types, Sizes, Speeds

While the basic function of the portable router is fairly standard, manufacturers have specific ideas about how the product should look, where the on-off switch should be placed, and how the handles should be formed. Many times, you'll find a variety of shapes in a single catalog. So there are about as many to choose from as there are designs of automobiles. Those pictured in Figure 6-4 don't begin to tell the story but do show something of the various tool profiles.

All units provide for a two-hand grip. This may be matching knobs, a pair of upright handles, or a combination of knob and pistol grip (Figure 6-5). Some have the switch at the top of the motor, others incorporate it in one of the handles (Figures 6-5, 6-6). An advantage of the latter design is that you can have your hands in place and the tool in position before using the switch. A disadvantage is that there must be an extra length of cord between the motor and the handle.

Routers have split-collet type chucks which tighten around the shank of a bit when a threaded lock nut is turned. This is often accomplished with a pair of wrenches, one used on the motor shaft, the other on the lock nut. Some units have a built-in motor shaft locking mechanism which can be a convenience since you need only one wrench to tighten the collet.

Routers, especially light-duty ones, may be designed for a single collet, say, one that will grip bits with ¼″ shanks. More rugged routers might take a ⅜″ or even a ½″ collet, or be so designed that they can handle collets of different sizes. It's logical to assume that the horsepower of the tool must go up along with increases in collet size. In general, a one-collet router grips only one shank-size. A router with interchangeable collets is more versatile, not only because it will probably have more horsepower and can do more work, faster, but because it can also grip a greater number of cutters, including some that are specialized production units.

The plunge router is a newcomer, in our country anyway, which has some advantages over conventional designs (Figure 6-7). For one thing, you can start internal cuts like those needed for stopped dadoes, mortises, and many types of carving, with the router sitting firmly on the work.

6-5.   D-shaped handle on this 1¼ hp router has a built-in trigger switch, which is a convenience on many operations. The 10 lb. tool turns at 22,000 rpm and can be used with a ⅜″ or ¼″ collet.

6-6.   Weight usually goes up along with horsepower. This 1½ hp unit weighs 14 lbs and turns at 23,000 rpm. Standard collet size is ½″, but it can be used with ¼″ size as well.

6-4.   Router designs are as varied as the number that are available. Whatever the profile, handle placement, and so on, they all turn at high speeds.

6-7.   This 1½ hp plunge router has an electronic depth of cut readout which reads in inches or centimeters. It has a built-in work light and a spindle lock so only one wrench is required to secure bits.

Then you can lower the bit to a depth you read off on a scale or to a depth you have previously established by a control on the tool. Without the plunge capability, the router has to be held at an angle and then slowly tilted downward until the bit has penetrated and the router's base is firmly settled. It works, but it's inconvenient and somewhat more difficult to get the cut started accurately. Regular, straight-shank bits can be used for plunge cutting but when you need to go completely through the work, it's best to work with a plunge-cutting bit which has a cutting point that works something like a drill bit.

All routers operate at high speeds, somewhere between about 15,000 and 30,000 rpm, which is why they cut so smoothly. You might think that horsepower should increase with speed, but it doesn't work that way. Many light routers turn just as fast as heavy ones. More horsepower allows for deeper or heavier cuts.

Generally, among tools of equal horsepower, the faster turning one will cut more smoothly because of a greater percentage of cuts along a given distance. It's just a theory, and it also assumes that the feed-speed—how fast the tool is moved—is exactly the same. Which brings up a point; if the tool with fewer rpm's is moved more slowly than the faster turning one, it can provide just as many cuts per inch.

Router horsepower can start at about ½ and range up to better than 3 (Figures 6-8 and 6-9). One thing that does go up along with horsepower is weight. A ¾ hp model might weigh less than 4 lbs, while a big 3 hp unit can be as heavy as 18 lbs. Weight, along with what you anticipate using the router for, is a factor to consider when deciding which router to purchase. A 1 hp or 1½ hp tool that weighs 7 or 8 lbs will be fine for general woodworking. It's a size and weight that's pretty popular even in commercial woodworking shops. If you need to do really heavy-duty work, like plunging and

cutting through a 1½" pad to get duplicate pieces, then you should think of one of the big fellows. After you know something of what can be done with a router, you may be tempted to have more than one size.

Electronic technology is starting to affect the design of portable routers. The router in Figure 6-10 has many of the good features of conventional routers but also contains an electronic microprocessor which maintains the set speed under loaded conditions. It also monitors how fast you move the tool and signals when you are cutting too fast or too slow. You can preset the unit's speed to be compatible with the hardness of the material and the size of the cutter you are working with. It's nice to know that no matter how sophisticated tools become they will still need a human hand to guide them.

Another type of router is called a "trimmer" or "laminate trimmer" (Figure 6-11). Such units are usually light in weight—4 lbs and under—and turn at top speeds, usually in the area of 30,000 rpm. The units are compact and lack handles since they are designed for one-hand control. Their primary purpose is trimming plastic laminates and similar materials but they are often used for freehand carving and other router chores that require a light touch.

Router Bits

Router bits are what make the router, and you can find exactly the right one for forming anything from classic molding to merely rounding off an edge, and from making complicated joint forms to merely doing a rabbet cut. Some catalogs have page after page of cutters. Those shown in Figure 6-12 are just a sampling, but it's a selection that I feel is very practical for general woodworking.

6-8.   Double insulated, 3 hp tool can be preset for specific-depth plunge cuts. It turns at 23,000 rpm and can be used with ½", ⅜", and ¼" collets.

6-9.   Black & Decker claims that this 3½ hp electronic router is the most powerful unit on the market. It can be used at 20,000 rpm for working in wood and other light materials, or at 16,000 rpm for harder materials like aluminum and plexiglass.

6-10. Router with electronic microprocessor does about everything but guide itself. It maintains the set speed under loaded conditions, monitors the feed rate, and a panel lets you select speed depending on material hardness and cutter size. Speed range is 11,000 to 25,000 rpm.

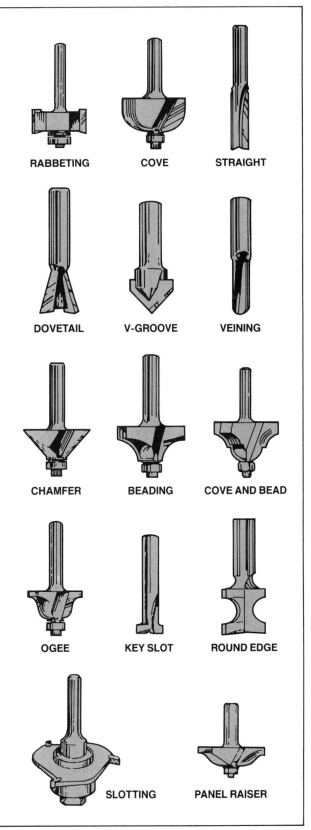

RABBETING   COVE   STRAIGHT

DOVETAIL   V-GROOVE   VEINING

CHAMFER   BEADING   COVE AND BEAD

OGEE   KEY SLOT   ROUND EDGE

SLOTTING   PANEL RAISER

6-11. Trimmer is compact and light for one-hand control but has the power to do what it must. This unit has an offset drive spindle which allows laminate trimming in-and-out of 90° corners. Flat top, found on many routers, permits "up-right" bit changes.

6-12. A sampling of typical router bits. Hundreds of shapes and sizes are available.

CUTTING DIAMETER	NO. OF FLUTES	LENGTH OF CUTTING EDGE	SHANK DIAMETER	OVERALL LENGTH
1/16	1	5/16	1/4	1 1/2
1/8	1	3/8	1/4	1 1/2
1/8	2	3/8	1/4	1 1/2
5/32	1	5/8	1/4	1 1/2
5/32	2	5/8	1/4	1 1/2
3/16	1	1/2	1/4	1 1/2
3/16	2	1/2	1/4	1 1/2
3/16	2	5/8	1/4	2
7/32	1	3/4	1/4	2
7/32	2	3/4	1/4	2
1/4	1	3/4	1/4	2
1/4	2	3/4	1/4	2
1/4	1	1	1/4	2 1/2
1/4	2	1	1/4	2 1/2
1/4	2	1	1/4	3
1/4	1	1	1/4	3
1/4	2	3/4	1/2	3
1/4	2	1	1/2	3
5/16	2	1	1/2	3
5/16	1	1	5/16	2 1/2
5/16	2	1	5/16	2 1/2
3/8	2	1	3/8	2 1/2
3/8	2	1	1/2	3
3/8	2	1 1/4	1/2	3 1/4
1/2	2	1	1/2	3
1/2	2	1 1/4	1/2	3
1/2	2	1 1/2	1/2	3 1/2

6-13.   The number of bits available is affected by sizes in each category as well as different shapes. This chart, from a Freud catalog, illustrates this point.

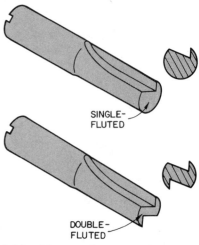

SINGLE-FLUTED

DOUBLE-FLUTED

6-14.   The more flutes, or cutting edges, on a bit, the smoother it will perform simply because it makes more cuts per revolution.

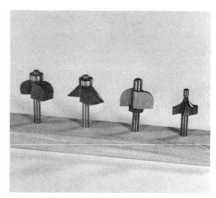

6-15.   Examples of bit styles. The two on the left have tungsten-carbide cutters and ball bearing pilots. The next one is an arbor on which various cutters can be mounted. The last is an all-steel unit with integral pilot.

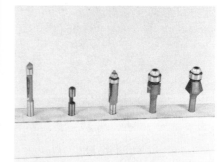

6-16.   Bits like this are designed primarily for laminate trimming. The pointed one is used for plunging. All are designed so the cutting circle matches the diameter of the pilot. The one on the right produces a beveled edge instead of a square one.

Not only are bits offered in an impressive variety of shapes, but in each category you'll find modifications of forms and different sizes. The information about straight bits in Figure 6-13, taken from a Freud catalog, makes the point. It may seem confusing, but it's actually a help, since by careful selection you will have a bit that is right for the tool you have and for the bulk of the work you do. Incidentally, double flute bits will cut smoother than single flute bits (Figure 6-14), simply because they make twice as many cuts per revolution.

Good router bits come in three varieties—high-speed steel, high-speed steel with tungsten-carbide cutting edges, and solid-tungsten carbide (Figures 6-15 and 6-16). Bit styles include one-piece units with integral pilots, units with ball-bearing pilots that are secured with screws so they can be replaced or exchanged for a different diameter, drill-point types that can penetrate through a workpiece, and arbor-type designs that are primarily a shaft and pilot between which you can secure various cutters (Figure 6-17). There are also slotting cutters which need to be mounted on an arbor (Figure 6-18), and which come in sizes to cut kerfs ranging from 1/16" to 1/4". Ball-bearing pilots of various diameters are available for the arbors so you can choose one to provide the kerf-depth you need. Slotting cutters are regularly used to form the groove that is required to install T-molding in the edge of a counter, but there is no reason why they can't also form, for example, grooves for splines when joining boards edge-to-edge.

Tungsten-carbide bits can cost three times as much as their all-steel counterparts, but they are smoother cutters and will stay sharp for much longer periods especially if they are used frequently on tough or abrasive materials (Figure 6-19). For some jobs, like trimming plastic laminates, a tungsten carbide tip is mandatory for optimum results and long cutting life. This doesn't mean you should completely avoid all-steel bits. Those of good quality will do a good job. In general, if you have a constant need for a bit, tungsten carbide is a good idea. If you don't spend all your time with a router in your hands, then high-speed steel will do nicely.

Remember that tungsten carbide, while tough, is also brittle. You can't bang them about or store them carelessly, not if you wish to maintain nick-free cutting edges.

The pilot on a router bit, whether it's an integral, smooth shank or an attached ball bearing, rides against the edge of a workpiece to guide the router and to control the width of the cut. The fixed pilot turns just as fast as the cutting edges of the bit and so can create friction that results in burn marks on the wood. A ball-bearing pilot turns freely, rotating only as you move the tool, so there is no friction to cause burn marks.

Whichever is being used, the pilot must be kept firmly against the work edge throughout the pass, and there must be sufficient bearing surface between pilot and work (Figure 6-20). It's also critical for the work edge to be perfectly smooth and free of imperfections. The pilot will faithfully follow any bump or crevice—and guide the cutter to duplicate it.

Some new cutters, not necessarily with strange profiles but requiring non-conventional router-use methods, have

6-17.   With arbor types, a single shaft is used with a variety of cutters.

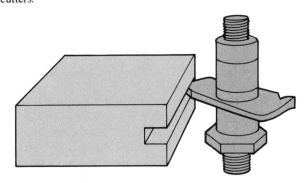

6-18.   Slotting cutters are used with arbors. While offered primarily for the grooves needed to install T-moldings on counter edges, they can be used for spline grooves as well.

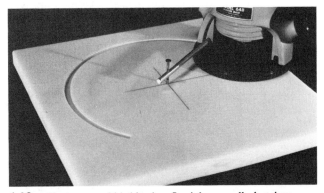

6-19.   Tungsten-carbide bits do a fine job generally, but they are especially efficient when used on hard, abrasive materials like "Corian". Guide here, is simply a length of rod with a hole for the nail that serves as the pivot.

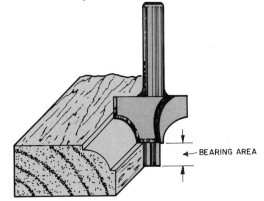

6-20.   Always be certain that there is sufficient bearing surface between the work edge and the pilot. If the cut is too deep to allow this, clamp a second piece under the work to "thicken" the edge.

been introduced. The Sears "Crown Molding Kit", shown in Figure 6-21, is one of them. The kit includes bits for V-grooves, end coves, beading and chamfering, cove box (which is tungsten carbide), and an arbor with pilots. Each bit forms part of a pattern so that when the sequence of cuts shown in Figure 6-22 is followed, the end result is a standard molding form, or an exclusive profile that you create. The advantage of the kit has to do with the difficulty in finding moldings to match the wood used for a furniture project or a wall paneling installation. With the cutters, you can produce moldings on any wood species.

With a kit of cutters called "The Door Shop", produced by Zac Products, you can use a portable router for the stile, rail, and panel-edge shapes required to make professional paneled doors (Figure 6-23). The illustrations in Figure 6-24 show, briefly, how the cutters are used. The bits have ½" shanks so you know they must be used with a heavy-duty router.

However, there is a catch. The bits are not used in conventional fashion, that is, by hand-holding the router. Instead, the router must be used in stationary shaper fashion. This can be accomplished by mounting the tool under a surface that will serve as a worktable, plus using a clamped-on strip of wood to work as a fence. Many manufacturers offer special stands so the router can be used like a shaper (Figure 6-25). This is much better than a makeshift improvisation, especially since the setup can also be used with conventional router bits. Later in the book, we'll provide construction details so you can make your own router/shaper stand.

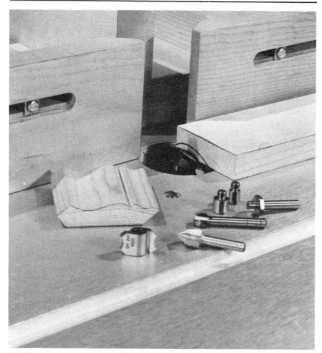

6-21.   Crown Molding Kit includes all the bits needed to produce standard molding forms. The advantage is that you can produce moldings on any wood species. Cutters like these *must* be used in a router/shaper setup.

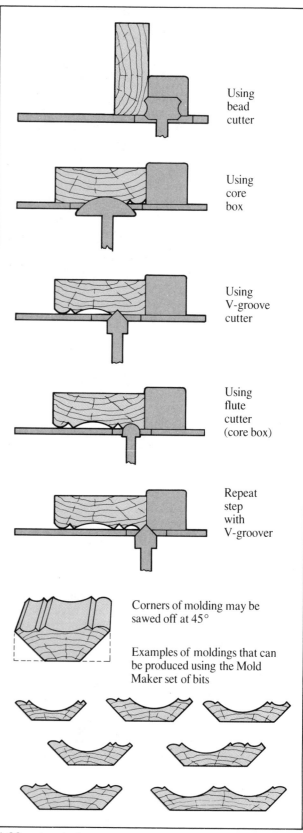

Using bead cutter

Using core box

Using V-groove cutter

Using flute cutter (core box)

Repeat step with V-groover

Corners of molding may be sawed off at 45°

Examples of moldings that can be produced using the Mold Maker set of bits

6-22.   A typical sequence of steps to follow when using the mold maker set of bits. Many design variations are possible.

6-23.   The router, with special bits and mounted in a stand, can be used to make all the cuts that are required to produce professional, paneled doors.

The Router at Work

If you take a bird's eye view of the router, you will see that the motor rotation, and thus the direction of cut, is in a clockwise direction. Basic practice is to move the router so the cutter tends to pull itself into the work. If, for example, you are shaping an edge, the feed direction, how you move the router, is from left to right. If you reverse this, the bit has the freedom to run along the edge like a wheel. It might occasionally be necessary to reverse the feed direction, but a greater degree of control is needed to keep the router firm and to avoid rough edges. Freehand carving or hollowing a project like a tray or bowl, when the tool is moved in various directions, are examples of reversing feed direction. The answer is to keep a very firm grip on the tool but, actually, this applies to any router operation, even fairly simple ones like shaping a straight edge (Figure 6-26).

You'll get the smoothest cuts when you move the router so the bit is cutting *with* the grain of the wood. When this isn't possible, as is often the case, move the router more slowly than you normally do. When working on four edges of a workpiece, do the end-grain cuts first. This is because some feathering and even some splintering may occur where the cutter leaves the work. The final passes, made parallel to the grain, will remove any imperfections.

Feed speed and depth of cut go hand in hand, although it's not farfetched to say that the slower the feed, the smoother the cut will be regardless of its depth. But you must

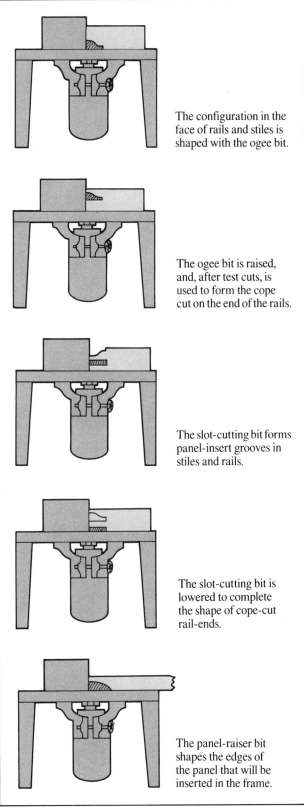

The configuration in the face of rails and stiles is shaped with the ogee bit.

The ogee bit is raised, and, after test cuts, is used to form the cope cut on the end of the rails.

The slot-cutting bit forms panel-insert grooves in stiles and rails.

The slot-cutting bit is lowered to complete the shape of cope-cut rail-ends.

The panel-raiser bit shapes the edges of the panel that will be inserted in the frame.

6-24.   This is a quick look at how the bits in the set called "The Door Shop" are used. A very detailed instruction booklet comes with the cutters.

6-25.   A table like this sets the router up for stationary shaper operations. This particular one can also be used with a saber saw.

6-26.   Let the router get to full speed before you contact the work. Use a two-hand grip and keep the tool moving steadily. Wear safety goggles even if the router has a chip deflector.

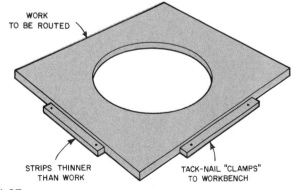

WORK
TO BE ROUTED

STRIPS THINNER
THAN WORK

TACK-NAIL "CLAMPS"
TO WORKBENCH

6-27.   It's important to secure workpieces with clamps, or in a vise, or with weights. One way to secure small pieces is to frame them with thinner, tack-nailed strips.

keep the cutter *working*. Generally, the more wood being removed, the slower the feed should be. Feeding too fast or cutting too deep will tax the motor and reduce its efficiency. This will be apparent from the sound of the motor, if nothing else. Feeding too slowly will not accomplish much and may result in burning the wood, even drawing the temper from the cutting tool. At the correct "load", which has to be a combination of feed-speed and cut, the tool will maintain a uniform speed without overheating, the cut will be smooth, and there will be no burn marks.

The more powerful the tool you are using, the faster you can feed and the deeper you can cut. Final judgments, guided by the equipment being used, have to be made by the operator. If it's obvious that the tool is struggling to make a particular cut, decrease the depth of cut for the first pass and then repeat the pass after adjusting the bit to get the full cut you need. You might even do this more than once—it's a way to use a light-duty unit for a heavy-duty operation.

Work security is important. By assuring that the project will remain still, you automatically eliminate one factor that leads to rough cuts and you contribute to your own safety. On large components, say you are shaping the edges of a plywood panel, and on assembled projects, the movement problem is minimized. But many times, routing is required on small parts prior to final assembly. In my own shop I keep a heavy piece of steel on the workbench for just such applications. This is used as a weight to keep the part firm as I apply the router. If this isn't practical, or doesn't do the job, I often use tack-nailed strips of wood around the piece which act as a frame to hold it firm (Figure 6-27). Clamps and a vise are also means of gripping pieces so they can't move when you work on them.

Be prepared for the jolt, caused by the starting torque of the motor, that occurs when you flick the switch. A firm grip will keep the router where it should be. Allow the tool to attain full speed before applying it. Don't have the cutter in contact with the work when you first turn it on. Let the tool come to a full stop after a cut before you set it down on its side. Never hold the machine, or rest it, so that the cutter is pointing toward you.

Follow the instructions concerning bit security that come with the tool. Bits must be tight in the collets. Placing them so the collet grips less of the shank than it should, in order to get more depth of cut, is not a good idea. If you have never used a portable router, be an apprentice for a bit. Make some light cuts on scrap stock. Use wood like pine and maple so you can judge the different cutting characteristics. Get the "feel" of the tool. Always wear safety goggles!

Straight Cuts

Straight cutting can be done by allowing the pilot on the bit to guide the router or by moving the router along a guide-strip that is tack-nailed or clamped to the work (Figure 6-28). The guide strip must have a smooth, straight edge and should be fairly stiff, especially if the cut is a long one. The direction of feed is from left to right, and you may either push or pull the tool—a decision that is based primarily on operational convenience. Whichever way you work, it's necessary to exert some lateral force as well, in order to keep the router base snug against the guide throughout the pass. There are times when a guide strip is good to use even if the bit has a pilot, especially if you are working on hard wood. The guide will allow you to minimize the pressure you must exert to keep the pilot in contact with the work edge, thereby reducing the possibility of friction burns.

Straight cuts on an edge or away from an edge, can also be done with an edge guide, a router accessory which, if not supplied with the tool, can be purchased as an 'extra'. Figure 6-29 shows a typical unit being used to guide the router through a groove-cut, which is actually a dado that is cut parallel to the wood grain. Always be sure that the work edge against which the guide will bear is smooth and straight.

A point to remember when making cuts on work edges is that you can often vary the results you get from a single cutter by using different depth-of-cut and width-of-cut settings. This applies whether you are using a shaped cutter or a straight-shank bit.

Since straight cutting is a routine, often-used router application, it pays to make some clamp guides like those shown in Figure 6-30. Then you won't have to improvise or search for wood-strips that are right for the job. Construction details for some that I use are shown in Figure 6-31. Note that the guide may have a fixed length or can be adjustable if you form a slot in the bar. Use a fairly stiff wood; something like straight-grain fir.

The clamp guide can be used whether you are working on or away from a work edge as demonstrated by the rabbet and dado cuts shown in Figure 6-32. Forming a dado or a rabbet that is wider than the largest diameter bit you have is just a matter of making more passes after the clamp guide has been repositioned (Figure 6-33).

The router is often used to make decorative surface cuts (Figure 6-34). This is just a matter of using a particular bit and controlling the depth of the cut. Straight cuts are accomplished with a guide. Some techniques for guiding the router for curved lines will be shown later.

6-29. Edge guides that come with the router or are available as accessories are used this way. The cut may be on the edge of the work or away from it. The edge the guide bears against must be smooth and straight.

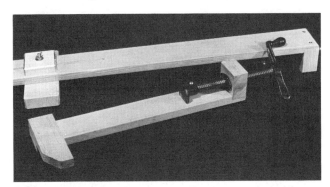

6-30. Clamp guides that you can make are very practical for straight router cuts.

6-28. A tack-nailed or clamped strip of wood is a good guide to use for long, straight cuts. The tool may be pushed or pulled so long as it is moved from left to right.

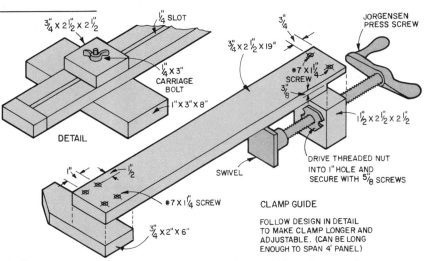

6-31. This is how the clamp guides are made. It's a good idea to have one for use on boards of standard, maximum width (11¼″), and another, adjustable one for various stock widths.

6-32.   The clamp guide can be used whether the router is working on an edge or away from it. Here, it has been used to guide the router through a rabbet cut and a dado.

6-33.   Repeat passes produce a rabbet, or a dado, that must be wider than you can form by making one pass with the largest cutter you have.

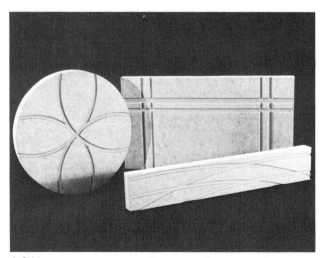

6-34.   Decorative surface cuts are made by using particular bits and limiting depth of cut. A "veining" bit, which forms round bottom grooves, is often used for this kind of work.

Circles and Curves

Shaping the edge of curved pieces doesn't differ from shaping a straight edge, except that the bit, unless special techniques are employed, must have a pilot. A method that solves the problem of keeping the router flat on the work is demonstrated in Figure 6-35. The scrap piece that remains after the workpiece has been sawed to shape is positioned to provide outboard support for the tool. The idea is practical for straight as well as curved cuts.

The router is a super tool to use for forming perfect circular grooves or for producing uniform discs or rings, providing it is used with a circle guide (Figure 6-36). Most manufacturers have a version of such an accessory; some might even provide one with the router. In a few cases, the edge guide that is available is designed so it can also be used as a circle guide. In any case, the technique is simply a matter

6-35.   Shaping irregular edges is done in routine fashion but always with a piloted bit. Using the cutoff, as shown here, will keep the tool horizontal throughout the pass. Use the same technique on straight cuts.

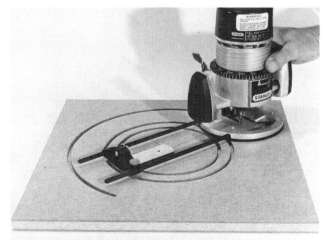

6-36.   Some edge guides do double duty. They can guide the router through a circular as well as a straight cut.

of moving the router about a pivot point that is established with the guide.

One of the problems with commercial circle guides is that they have a limited capacity. To do more, or simply to avoid having to buy one, you can make your own along the lines shown in Figure 6-37. Yours will be exclusive for the router you own since the holding ring must be just right for the router's base. If you have routers with bases of different diameters, various holding rings can be provided and held in place with short screws.

To use the jig, determine the radius of the circle you need and then drive a nail through a hole in the bar that will provide it. Then, move the router so it is guided by the jig (Figure 6-38). Normal feed direction for the router will be in a clockwise direction. The jig, as I've made it, will form circles up to 36″ in diameter.

Circle guides can be used to form rings or discs (Figure 6-39). An extra precaution is needed here. Since the cutter must pass through the material, clamp or tack-nail the work to a backup piece. If the stock is thick, and the router doesn't have the power for a one-pass operation, get through by adjusting the bit extension for each of any number of passes you must make. Proceed in routine fashion when cutting a disc; for rings, make the inside cut first. When you need many similar pieces, you can pad materials and cut through them all at once.

A "gadget" you can make that will serve as a circle guide and also as a trammel tool is shown in Figure 6-40. One head is mounted when the project is used as a circle guide for the router; two heads are used for layout work. The advantage of such a tool when used as a circle guide is that the distance between the pivot and the bit is infinitely variable.

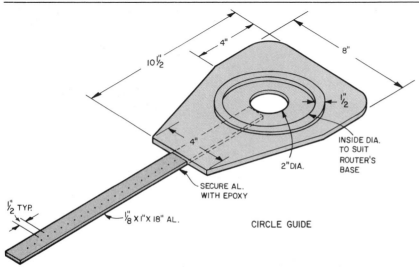

6-37. A circle guide that you can make. The holding ring must suit the router's base. If you have several routers, you can provide rings with different inside diameters, attaching them to the jig with screws as you need them.

6-39. Forming precise rings or discs is routine when you work with a circle guide. A backup piece is needed since the cutter must penetrate through the workpiece.

6-38. The circle guide that you make will have more capacity than a commercial one. The one I use, which you can duplicate, has a 36″ diameter capacity. A longer bar would increase the capacity.

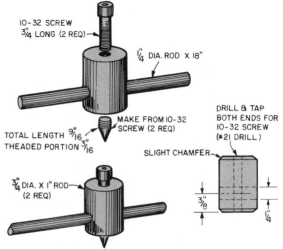

6-40. How to make a tool that can be used as a trammel for marking arcs and circles, and as a circle guide for the router.

Working with Templates

By using a template—or a "pattern" if you prefer—the router can be guided along fairly complicated lines or used to make as many similar pieces as you need. To be used in this fashion, the router's base must be equipped with template guides like those shown in Figure 6-41. This particular type of guide is not interchangeable with all routers, so be sure you buy those that work with the tool, or tools, you own. The guides provide what is essentially a sleeve through which the cutter passes (Figure 6-42). The router is moved while keeping the sleeve in constant contact with the edge of the template. Since the wall of the sleeve has thickness, the cutter will be held away from the pattern's edge by that distance. This may not be critical on some jobs, but when it is, you simply compensate by making the template larger or smaller, as the case may be. For example, the template for an inside circle would be sized to suit the radius of the circle you need *plus* the thickness of the sleeve's wall. The reverse would be true if you were cutting a disc.

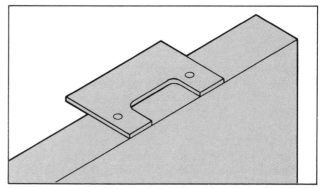

6-43.   Templates can be as simple as this one, which was shaped to guide the router through a hinge mortise.

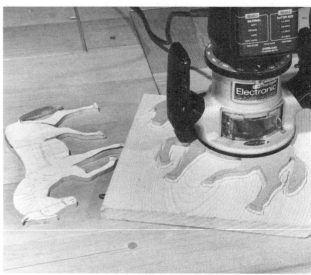

6-44.   Use the smallest straight, or veining bit you have when working with more complicated templates like this horse profile. A tiny bit lets you get into confined areas.

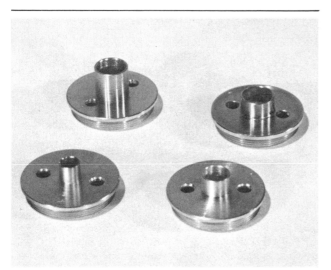

6-41.   Template guides, used in the router's base, are designed for bits of different diameter. One design can't be used with all routers so be sure to buy those that are right for the tool you own.

6-45.   The groove for the horse carving was filled with plastic aluminum. There are other ways to go—use the router freehand to recess the figure, or to raise it by cutting away material on the outside.

6-42.   The router bit passes through the sleeve of the template guide. The sleeve, riding against the edge of the template, guides the cutting.

Templates can be fairly simple, like the one in Figure 6-43 which is used to guide a router through a mortise for a hinge, or they can be quite complicated, involving many twists and turns like the one in Figures 6-44 and 6-45. On jobs like this, you should use the smallest diameter veining or straight-shank bit that the router can handle so you can get as close as possible into tight corners. For jobs like the hinge mortise, you should work with a fairly large straight-shank bit. Some hinges are made so they will fit the round corners left by the bit. If not, the corners can be cleaned out with a chisel.

Commercial router templates, especially those that are designed for incising decorative patterns on doors, are used in many cabinet shops. One of them, the "Wing Router Template", consists of lengths of tubing and special fittings so a guide system for the router can be organized to suit the project. Various templates can be added to the assembly for incising designs like those shown in Figure 6-46.

Such products might not be the kind of tool for every home shop, but by improvising you can achieve similar results. Figure 6-47 demonstrates how guide pieces of various shapes can be tack-nailed to a component and used as a template. The design that results is shown in Figure 6-48. The possible variations are limitless; the end results depend entirely on how you construct the template (Figure 6-49). Often, a single template can be used to create designs that are more advanced than the template itself. The idea is to preview the design you want and then to place the template

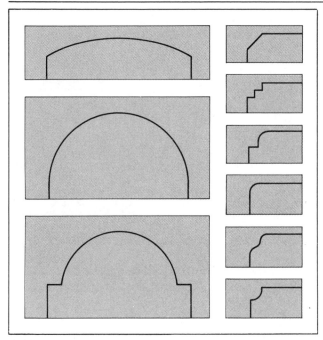

6-46. Various guide patterns are used with the "Wing Router Template" to produce decorative grooves like these. Work like this is very common on cabinet doors.

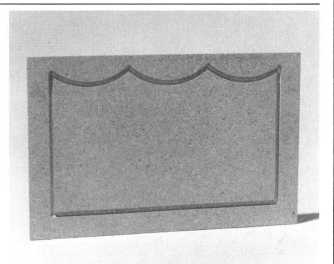

6-48. The template shown in Figure 6-47 was used to produce this grooved decoration.

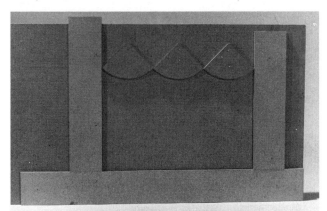

6-47. Templates can simply be pieces of specially shaped wood or hardboard that are tack-nailed or clamped to the project. Holes left by tack-nailing can be filled with wood dough.

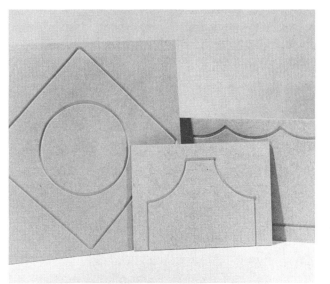

6-49. You can create a template to produce just about any kind of design. Once made, the template can be used to produce any number of similar pieces.

appropriately for each of the cuts (Figures 6-50 and 6-51). Tack-nailing does leave small holes in the project but they are easily concealed with wood dough. When possible, of course, use clamps to hold the parts of the template.

Grooves for tambour doors are usually formed with a router (Figure 6-52). Since the grooves must be perfectly aligned in top and bottom case members, it is necessary to work with an accurate template and to be precise when attaching the template to the mating pieces. Note, in Figure 6-53, that the template is designed so the grooves will "run out" at the back edge of the components. This allows the tambours to be inserted from the rear after the case members have been assembled. It's more convenient than having to put the doors in place *during* assembly.

Special Router Bases

The diameter of bases on routers is fine for most work but there are times when it is difficult to keep the router level because the base isn't large enough to span across support areas. Typical situations are hollowing jobs on trays or bowls or boxes. The practical solution is to make a long, auxiliary base that substitutes for the regular one (Figure 6-54). The homemade bases can be any shape or size and they will fit the router as they should if you use the original base as a pattern for drilling the center hole and those needed for the screws

6-52.   The grooves that are required for tambour doors are usually formed with a router.

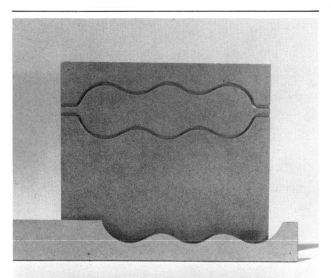

6-50.   Often, a single template can be used as a multi-form guide. It's just a question of repositioning the template for each of the cuts you need.

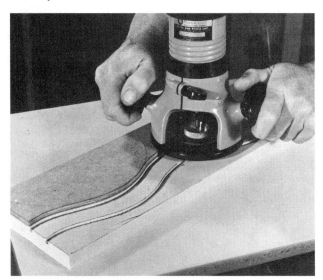

6-51.   The single template idea also works for jobs like forming a series of "parallel" irregular grooves. Accuracy depends on how carefully you set the template for each of the cuts.

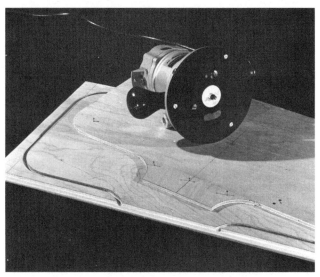

6-53.   A carefully made template is used for the grooves needed for the tambour. Note that the grooves "run out". This is so the doors can be inserted from the rear of the project after it has been assembled.

(Figure 6-55). The screwheads will have to be set flush in counterbored holes.

It's also possible to use a special base when the job requires a template guide. It's just a matter of seating the guide in the auxiliary base so its bottom surface will be flush (Figures 6-56 and 6-57). This calls for a slight counterbore on the perimeter of the through hole. You can accomplish this with the router itself by making a template with a suitably-sized hole. It can also be done with hole saws, using one to go just deep enough for the counterbore, and a second one to form the through hole.

One of the problems with regular router bases and those you might make is that they don't provide as much visibility as you might like. A solution is to make see-through bases using a material like "Lexan", a shatterproof, scratch resistant plastic.

Router Joinery

The more familiar you become with the portable router, the more impressed you will be with its versatility. You will find, for example, that you will use it more and more for precise joint constructions. By using particular bits, sometimes with special techniques or jigs, you can master any of the connections that are shown in Figure 6-58.

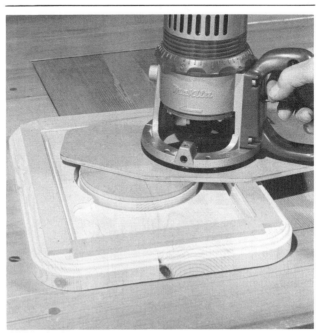

6-56. Many hollowing, and similar jobs, are done by working with templates. Any auxiliary base that is used must be fitted with a template guide (Figure 6-57).

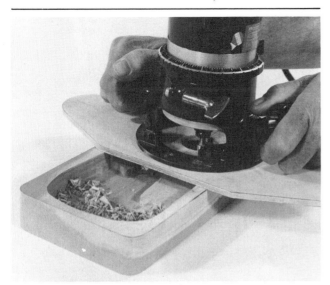

6-54. Auxiliary bases are used for jobs like hollowing when the regular base isn't big enough to span across supporting edges.

6-55. One-quarter-thick hardboard is a good material for auxiliary bases. Use the original base as a pattern for the center hole and for the holes for attachment screws. See-through bases can be made by using "Lexan", a tough, plastic material.

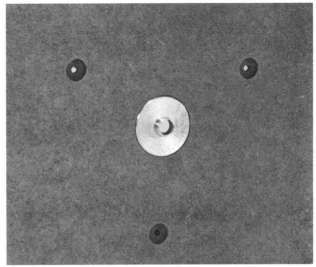

6-57. The template guide must be set flush in the special base. This calls for a slight counterbore on the perimeter of the through hole.

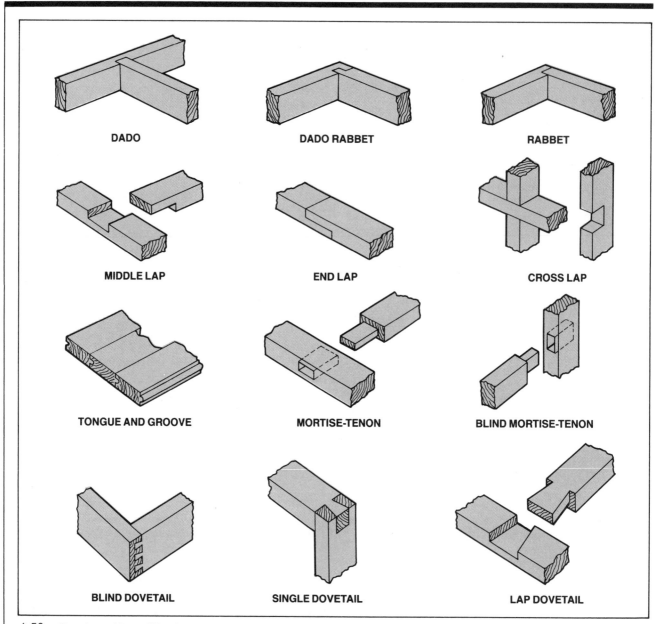

DADO **DADO RABBET** **RABBET**

MIDDLE LAP **END LAP** **CROSS LAP**

TONGUE AND GROOVE **MORTISE-TENON** **BLIND MORTISE-TENON**

BLIND DOVETAIL **SINGLE DOVETAIL** **LAP DOVETAIL**

6-58.   By using guides and jigs that you make or buy, you can form all these joints with a portable router.

6-59.   Rabbets and dadoes (or grooves) are done best by moving the router along a guide strip. When possible, use a bit with a diameter that matches the thickness of the piece that will be inserted in the cut.

6-60.   "Stopped" dadoes or rabbets are cuts that start and end away from the work edge. Stop blocks, clamped to the guide, control the length of the cut. Plunge routers make jobs like this easier to do.

Dadoes and rabbets, which are used so often in woodworking, are probably the easiest to do, requiring only that you guide the tool accurately along a straight line. This can be accomplished with an edge guide, but for more flexibility in router placement it's best to work with a clamp guide (Figure 6-59). How wide the cut will be depends on the bit you use. Cuts beyond the capacity of a particular bit, can be widened by repositioning the guide and cutting again. How deep you can cut in a single pass depends on the hardness of the material and the power of the tool. Usually, the depth of a rabbet or dado is about one half the thickness of the stock.

The appearance of a rabbet or dado isn't too pretty when viewed from the front after assembly, but you can get around this when the project calls for it, by making "stopped" cuts like those in Figure 6-60. The cut is started away from the edge of the work, and its length is controlled by stop blocks that are secured to the guide with clamps. The cut is started with the router at an angle so the cutter clears the work. Then it is tilted down until it rests fully on its base. This is an operation where you can see the advantage of a plunge router—the cutter can be lowered into the work with the tool firmly seated to begin with.

The router does a fine job of forming both parts of a tongue and groove joint (Figure 6-61). You can clamp the work between scrap pieces when you feel you need extra support for the router. The router, situated so it will cut in the center of the work edge, can be guided with an edge guide (Figure 6-62). To be sure that the groove will be centered, make a second pass with the edge guide bearing against the opposite edge of the work. To form the mating part, use a similar setup and make a pass on each edge of the stock to leave the projection which is the tongue. In this case, you will be cutting into the scrap pieces as well as the work. When making many parts, the one set of scrap pieces can be used for all of them.

One way to form a round-end mortise is shown in Figure 6-63. An L-shaped guide block, situated so the bit will cut along the center of the stock, is secured directly to the router's base. The cut is started with the router tilted like it is in the photograph. Here too, is an example of where a plunge router can be handy. If you form slots in the L-shaped guide instead of just drilling attachment holes, it will have some adjustment capability so you will be able to use it on stock of different thicknesses.

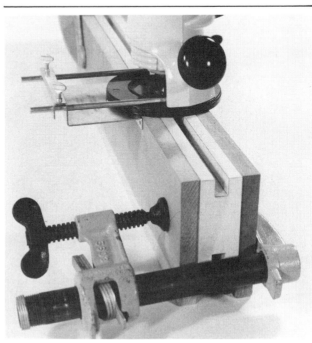

6-62. Forming a groove by controlling the router with an edge guide. The extra, clamped-on pieces provide more support surface for the tool.

6-61. On a tongue and groove joint, the groove is formed in a single pass; the tongue requires a pass on each edge of the stock.

6-63. Round-end mortises can also be formed with an edge guide, or you can work with an L-shaped guide that you make. When the guide is slotted, it can be adjusted for use on stock of different thicknesses.

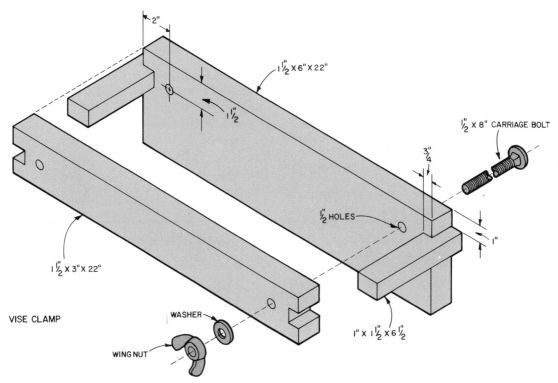

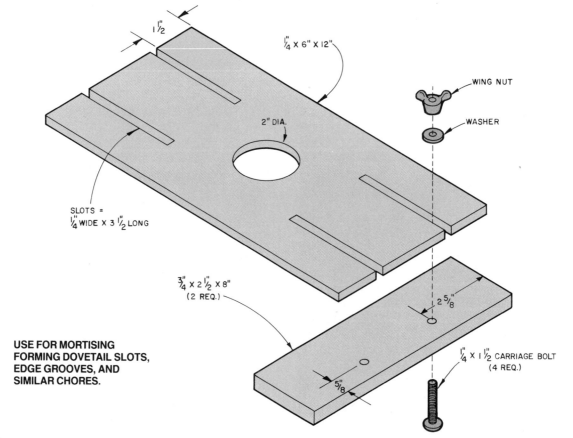

6-64.   How to make a vise clamp. Use a hardwood like maple or birch.

6-65.   A special, adjustable base lets you guide the router accurately for many types of joint cuts.

In my own shop, I use custom-built jigs for jobs like mortising and forming edge-grooves whether they are simple or dovetailed. One jig is the vise clamp detailed in Figure 6-64, the other is an adjustable, auxiliary base (Figure 6-65). For mortising, the work is gripped between the jaws of the vise clamp and the assembly is then secured in a bench vise. Forming the mortises begins after the work has been marked to show the position and the length of the cuts (Figure 6-66).

The adjustable side-guides of the auxiliary base are secured so that the cut will conform with the layout that is on the workpiece (Figure 6-67). You can form mortises that are centered or off-center, depending on how you situate the left- and right-hand side-guides.

Tenons to match the mortise can be formed with a router by following the ideas shown in Figures 6-68 and 6-69. First, select a block of wood that is wide enough to supply the number of rails you need. Don't forget to allow for the kerf-waste when the block is sawed into individual pieces. Then, working with a clamp guide and a large straight bit in the router, make as many passes as it takes to establish the length of the tenon. This is done on both sides of the stock, with depth-of-cut established to produce the correct tenon-thickness.

The second step, after individual pieces have been sawed from the block, is to flip them on edge and assemble them in a clamp guide (Figure 6-69), or directly in a bench vise. Then use the router to finish trimming the tenons which, like the first step, requires cutting on both surfaces. Since the mortise has round ends and the tenons have square ends, you will have to dress one or the other. Either use a narrow chisel to square the ends of the mortise, or round off the end of the tenon to suit the mortise.

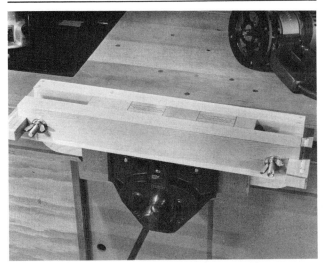

6-66.   A mortising operation starts by gripping the work in the vise clamp and marking it so you'll know where to start and end the cuts.

6-68.   First step when forming tenons. Work on a piece of wood that's wide enough to supply the number of rails you need. Use a large, straight bit and make as many passes as it takes to reach the tenon's length. Cuts are made on both edges.

6-67.   The slides on the special base can be adjusted so the bit will cut on the center of the edge or, if you choose, away from it.

6-69.   The pieces ripped from the original block are placed on edge and secured in a clamp guide. Then the router is used to finish forming the tenons. Depth of cut must be precise for both of the operations required to produce tenons.

Mortises for splines that are used to reinforce miter joints can also be formed by using the vise clamp/adjustable base technique (Figure 6-70). It's just a matter of situating the pieces in the vise clamp so the mitered ends will be on a horizontal plane. Be careful with layout and depth of cut. If the mortise is too long or too deep, the cutter will pass through the material. Splines should be a slip-fit, with a length that is a fraction less than two times the depth of the mortise (Figure 6-71). The same also applies to tenons. If they must be forced into the mortise and if they don't allow some room for glue, they can split the mating piece.

Figures 6-72 and 6-73 show how the special jigs are used to guide the router through straight or dovetail grooves in stock edges. The vise clamp is also a practical way to secure narrow pieces for edge-shaping (Figure 6-74).

6-72.   Accurate grooves in stock edges can be cut by gripping the work in the vise clamp. You can be certain that the groove will be centered if you make a second pass after reversing the position of the router.

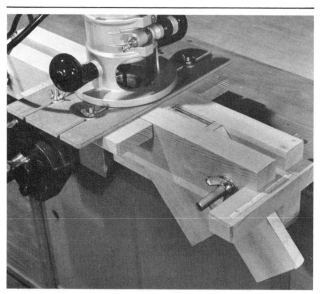

6-70.   Mortises can also be formed in miter cuts. It's just a matter of situating the pieces correctly in the vise clamp.

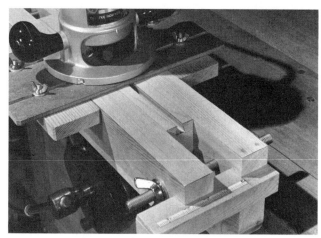

6-73.   Work the same way to provide dovetail grooves. To shape the tongue for the groove or the pin for the dovetail, grip the work between scrap pieces. Then make cuts on both edges of the material.

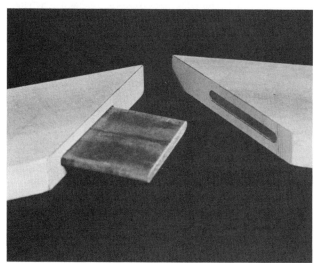

6-71.   The spline for the miter joint is shaped to suit the round ends of the mortises. It should slip easily into the cuts and be a bit shorter than the combined depth of the mortises.

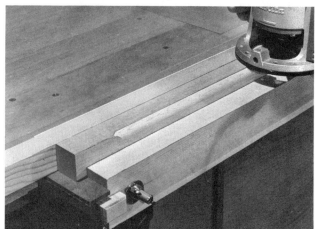

6-74.   Another use for the vise clamp is gripping narrow pieces securely. Scrap pieces can be added if you need more support for the router.

Dovetails

The router, turning a dovetail bit, and used with ingenious jigs that you buy, makes you an instant dovetail expert. The application is one of the router operations that impresses everyone. In a short time, even a rank beginner can produce classic, quality joints like the one shown in Figure 6-75. It's just a matter of acquiring the jig—a finger template goes with it—and then being careful about following the instructions. A common jig design, offered by many manufacturers, provides for holding two pieces of wood (for example, the front and side of a drawer) in correct position. The router, fitted with a template guide, follows the shape of the fingers (Figure 6-76). Since the shapes are cut simultaneously in both members, they fit precisely. The only "problem" with this jig design is that you are limited to uniformly spaced dovetails of a particular size and pattern.

The Leigh jigs that are shown in Figures 6-77 and 6-78, are more advanced designs which allow some originality in the appearance of the dovetail joint. They can be used for through or half blind dovetails (Figure 6-79), but the operator has the option of deciding how many connections there should be in the joint and how they should be spaced (Figure 6-80). This is an advantage. While small, equally spaced, hidden dovetails are perfectly fine for drawer joints, it is often more estheticly pleasing to have dovetails that appear larger and which are spaced creatively on case work, or any project where the joint is exposed.

Being able to choose spacing is possible on the Leigh jigs because of individual template fingers which are locked along a slide bar in the position you opt for. Cutting techniques differ in that the parts of the joint are formed separately. Also, pin pieces with the fingers set up as shown in

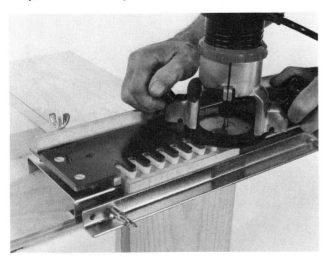

6-75.   The router, used with special jigs, makes you an almost instant dovetail expert. You do have to learn to use the jigs correctly, but that doesn't require much time.

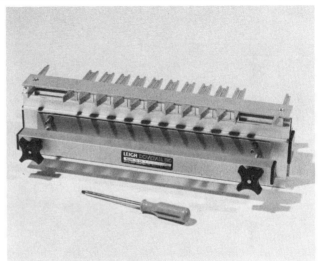

6-77.   One of the Leigh dovetail jigs lets you work on stock up to 12″ wide.

6-76.   A common dovetail jig grips both parts of the joint. The router, moved around a finger template, cuts both parts of the joint. You can't miss if you use the jig correctly.

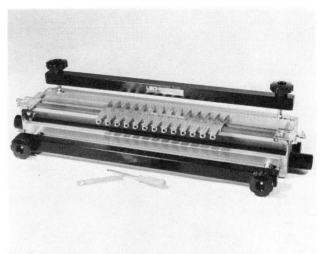

6-78.   A more advanced model will take stock up to 24″ wide. The advantage with both units is that you are not limited to uniformly spaced dovetails.

Capabilities of Leigh Jigs

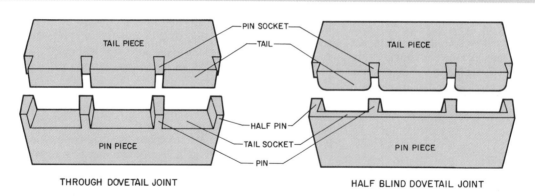

THROUGH DOVETAIL JOINT

HALF BLIND DOVETAIL JOINT

6-79.   The Leigh jig can be organized for through or half blind dovetails.

6-80.   Being able to choose dovetail spacing, whether they are through or half blind, can make projects appear more customized.

6-82.   The mating part of the joint is formed with a dovetail bit after the position of the guide fingers has been reversed.

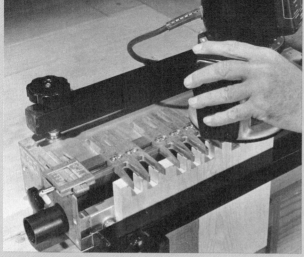

6-81.   The jigs have clamp bars that hold the stock firmly under the adjustable guide fingers. The fingers are adjusted by moving them along a slide bar. Pins are formed with a straight bit.

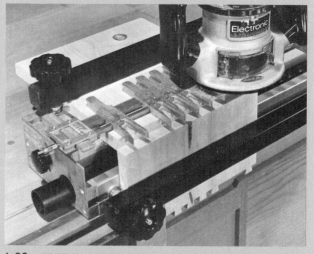

6-83.   Half blind cutting is done with the work in horizontal position. The Leigh jigs require some study time but the design freedom they provide is worth it. Large jig has an adjustable tube which can be connected to the hose of a vacuum cleaner.

Figure 6-81 are formed with a straight bit, while the tail pieces with the finger assembly flipped over (Figure 6-82) are formed with a dovetail cutting bit. It takes a little getting used to but the system is anything but complicated. Once you have spaced the fingers on the slide bar, the same setup is used to cut both parts of the joint.

Pin pieces for a half blind dovetail are done with the workpiece clamped in horizontal position under the template fingers (Figure 6-83). If you are really into dovetail work and are using a Leigh jig, it pays to work with two routers, one with a dovetail bit, the other a straight bit. A very detailed instruction book comes with the jigs. Read it carefully and then do some experimental dovetailing on scrap stock.

Routing Plastic Laminates

Any router can be used to trim plastic laminates. One way is to substitute a special base for the regular one. The trimmer base is essentially a guidance system, usually with a ball bearing "pilot" that lets you move the router along an edge while the cutter, preferably tungsten carbide, trims the sur-face laminate flush with the edge of the workpiece. The critical step is adjusting the guide so the cut will be accurate.

Another way to work, which doesn't require a special accessory, is simply to work with router bits that are specifically designed for such cutting (Figure 6-84). Some have integral pilots, others have a ball bearing, but whatever, they are made so the diameters of the pilot and the cutter are exactly alike. Thus, doing perfect trimming is merely a matter of moving the router along the work edge (Figure 6-85). Be careful to hold the router in correct position throughout the pass. Any accidental tilting will mar the work.

For perfect butt joints, improvise a setup like the one shown in Figure 6-86. Both pieces, after they have been carefully aligned and clamped, are cut at the same time. The edges will be smooth and will mate perfectly. Simultaneous cutting can also be done to assure a perfect connection for miter joints (Figure 6-87). The workpieces are taped face-to-face and then clamped at a 45° angle with a strip that also serves to guide the tool. The straight-shank, tungsten-carbide bit passes through a groove in the plywood jig.

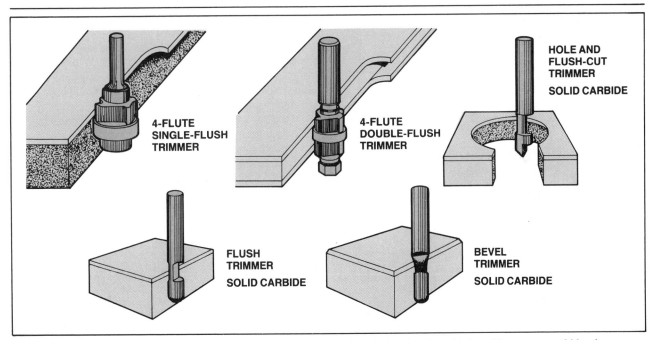

4-FLUTE SINGLE-FLUSH TRIMMER

4-FLUTE DOUBLE-FLUSH TRIMMER

HOLE AND FLUSH-CUT TRIMMER
SOLID CARBIDE

FLUSH TRIMMER
SOLID CARBIDE

BEVEL TRIMMER
SOLID CARBIDE

6-84. Laminate trimming bits come in a variety of styles. Some are solid carbide, others have blades with tungsten-carbide edges.

6-85. Trimmer bits are designed so the diameter of the pilot and the cutting circle of the blades are exactly alike. The part being trimmed will be perfectly flush with the work's edge.

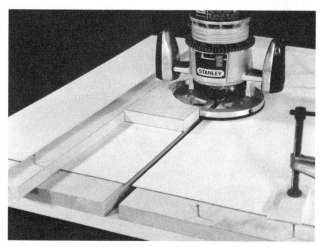

6-86.   A setup like this will let you cut edges so they will form perfect butt joints. The parts must be carefully aligned to begin with.

6-87.   You can use a similar idea to get perfect edges for miter joints. Be sure to situate the pieces at the correct angle.

The Router as a Shaper

The router can provide many of the advantages of a stationary shaper as long as it is mounted, inverted, to the underside of a stand that you buy or make. Many manufacturers offer stands that are similar to the one in Figure 6-88. Some are designed to take most any router, while others can be used only with a specific product. What all of them provide, in addition to the stand, is individually adjustable fences so depth of cut can be controlled and so they can be organized to provide support for workpieces whether you are making a partial cut or one that removes the entire edge of the stock—which is exactly the way a stationary shaper is used. The fences are set in line for a cut like shaping a top edge of a workpiece. When the cut is deeper, in essence one that reduces the width of the work, the outfeed fence is placed forward of the infeed fence an amount equal to the stock that is removed so that the work will have support after it has passed the cutter.

How much you can do with a router/shaper stand depends on the tool you use. A heavy-duty router, especially one that can be used with ½″ shank bits, is recommended, although not essential. Much depends on the kind of work you will demand from the unit.

Making your own shaper table has some advantages. You can decide how large a table you want. When the unit is designed as a floor model you can use it anywhere without having to worry about bolting it down, and you'll have room to install storage drawers.

One that I made for myself, and which gets considerable use in my shop, is shown in Figure 6-89. It has large fences that are individually adjustable to or fro and which can also be moved laterally to minimize the opening around cutters. It is equipped with two guards, one for fence work, the other for freehand shaping against fulcrum pins; a technique that is used when the shape of the work doesn't allow it to be guided by a fence.

6-88.   Stands are available so a portable router can be used like a stationary shaper. The idea makes the router even more versatile.

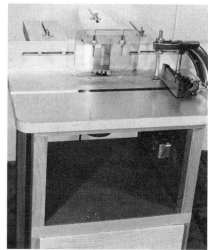

6-89.   A router/shaper stand that you can make. It features heavy-duty, individually adjustable fences, an aluminum clad work surface, and guards.

6-90. The stand has its own on-off switch so you don't have to keep reaching under the table to use the one on the router. Don't let the router keep running unnecessarily.

The only custom aspect of the stand is the recess on the underside of the table to suit the router's base. You may also have to cut a groove to accommodate a D-shaped router handle. Allow the router to run only when you are cutting. That's why the outside on-off switch is included; it makes turning on and shutting down easy (Figure 6-90). There is little point in letting those tiny ball bearings in the tool run at high speeds unnecessarily. Another point, since the tool is used in an inverted position, it might catch more waste than usual. Check occasionally—remove waste with a blower or small brush.

Figures 6-91 through 6-94 show a few, typical router/shaper stand operations. Construction details and a materials list for a stand you can make are shown in Figures 6-95 through 6-97.

Typical Router/Shaper Operations

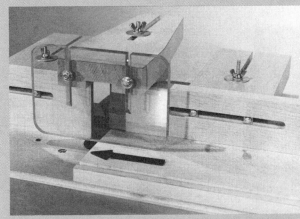

6-91. Straight shaping is done by moving the work along the fences in the direction indicated by the arrow. Keep the fences in line for partial cuts—offset the outfeed fence when the entire edge of the stock is removed. Use the guard!

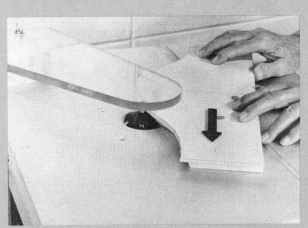

6-93. Work edges that can't be guided with a fence can be shaped freehand. Always use the fulcrum pins for bracing the work. Don't work on narrow pieces. Keep your hands away from the cutting area.

6-92. Always use a miter gauge when edge-shaping narrow pieces. Make the slot in the table to suit a miter gauge you have or one that you buy. (Guard removed for clarity.)

6-94. Freehand work MUST BE DONE WITH PILOTED BITS. Arrow indicates the fulcrum pin against which the work is braced before it is moved to contact the cutter. Use the guard!

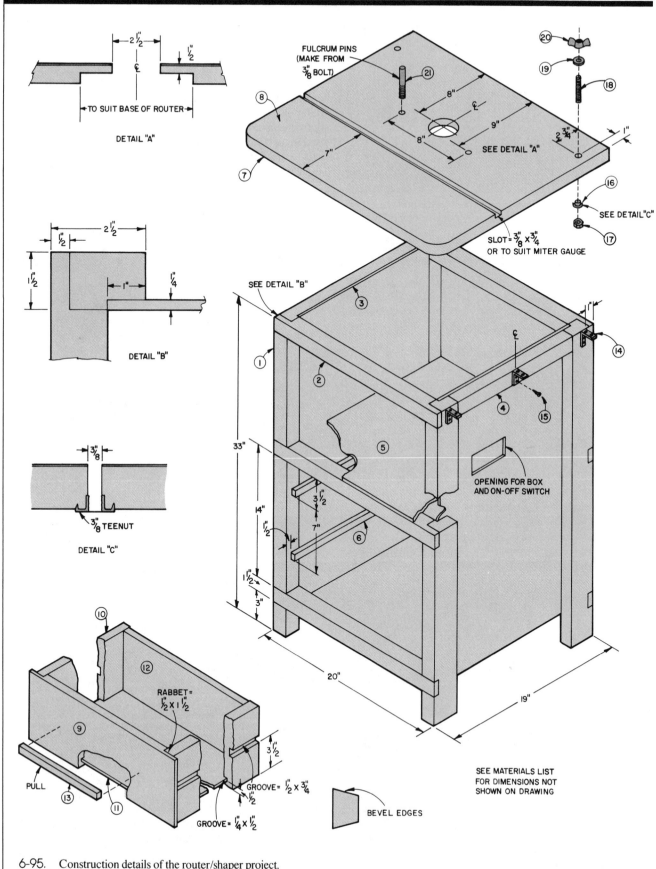

6-95. Construction details of the router/shaper project.

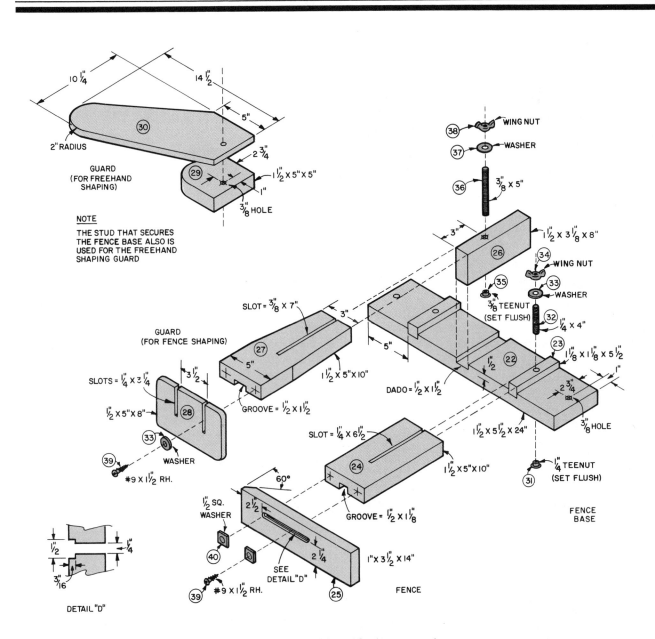

6-96.   These details show the parts required for the fence assembly and for the two guards.

MATERIALS LIST FOR ROUTER-SHAPER TABLE

KEY	PART	NO. PCS.	SIZE	MATERIAL
1	Leg	4	1½" x 2½" x 33"	Fir
2	Rail	6	1½" x 1½" x 20"	Fir
3	Side	2	¼" x 16" x 20"	Hardboard
4	Brace	2	1¼" x 1½" x 14"	Fir
5	Shelf	1	¼" x 17" x 19"	Hardboard
6	Guide	4	½" x ¾" x 18½"	Fir
7	Table	1	1⅛" x 21" x 24"	(See note)
8	Cover	1	.025" x 21" x 24"	(See note)

(Continued on next page)

KEY	PART	NO. PCS.	SIZE	MATERIAL
MATERIALS LIST FOR ROUTER-SHAPER TABLE				
DRAWER				
9	Front	2	¾" x 7" x 18"	Pine
10	Side	4	¾" x 7" x 17½"	Pine
11	Bottom	2	¼" x 16" x 17½"	Hardboard
12	Back	2	¾" x 6" x 15¼"	Pine
13	Pull	2	½" x ¾" x 10"	Pine
HARDWARE				
14	Connector	6	½" x 1½" x 1½"	Metal angles
15	Screws	24	#8 x 1"	Roundhead
16		4	⅜"	Teenut
17		2	⅜"	Nut
18	Stud	2	⅜" x 4"	Threaded rod
19		2	⅜"	Fender washer
20		2	⅜"	Wing nut
21	Fulcrum pin	2	⅜" x 2¾"	Make from bolt
FENCE ASSEMBLY				
22	Base	1	1½" x 5½" x 24"	Fir
23	Guide	2	1⅛" x 1⅛" x 5½"	Fir
24	Fence support	2	1½" x 5" x 10"	Fir
25	Fence	2 (L/R)	1" x 3½" x 14"	Fir
26	Guard guide	1	1½" x 3⅛" x 8"	Fir
27	Guard support	1	1½" x 5" x 10"	Fir
28	Shield	1	½" x 5" x 8"	"Lexan"
FREEHAND SHAPING GUARD				
29	Height block	1	1½" x 5" x 5"	Fir
30	Shield	1	½" x 10¼" x 14½"	"Lexan"
HARDWARE				
31		2	¼"	Teenut
32	Stud	2	¼" x 4"	Threaded rod
33		4	¼"	Fender washer
34		2	¼"	Wing nut
35		1	⅜"	Teenut
36	Stud	1	⅜" x 5"	Threaded rod
37		1	⅜"	Fender washer
38		1	⅜"	Wing nut
39		6	#9 x 1½"	Roundhead screw
40		4	½" x ½"	Sq. washer

Notes: Table (#7) made from ready-made glued-up pine slab.

Cover (#8) Wilsonart's aluminum "decorative metal" or do-it-yourself aluminum.

Hardwood like maple or birch can be substituted for fir.

6-97. Materials list for the router/shaper stand.

Some Special Accessories

The portable router continues to become more and more versatile. There are a host of practical accessories for it in addition to those already shown, and it's logical to accept that more will be introduced. The following illustrations and captions describe some that have been tested with impressive results. All of them are supplied with detailed use-instructions, so you should have no problem getting the most out of them —unless you choose to just plunge ahead, which isn't a wise thing to do.

As a Power Plane
Figure 6-98.

6-98.   When the router is fitted with a special cutter that may have straight or spirally shaped cutting blades, and mounted in a special holder, it becomes a super tool for smoothing edges or reducing stock widths. Many of the jobs done with a hand plane can be done with a router that is equipped with a planer attachment. Such accessories are not interchangeable. To get a match, always purchase the accessory from the manufacturer of the router.

As a Lathe Tool
Figure 6-99.

6-99.   The router, when used with a special "contraption" called a "Router-Crafter" (Sears), can be used, for one thing, to shape table and chair legs in round or square stock up to 3" square and 36" long. It's a unique concept, and getting good results isn't difficult. The uses include lathe-type turning, forming flutes and beads, forming spirals or diamond shapes on round stock, and forming shapes by using templates. Since you can use various bits in the router, the effects you can create in any of the tool's modes is virtually unlimited.

As a Bowl Former
Figures 6-100, 6-101.

6-100.   The "Bowl-Crafter" turns a router into an efficient tool for making an almost unlimited variety of bowl-shaped projects. The accessory has its own motor-driven head-stock to turn the mounted workpiece. As the workpiece turns, the router-driven bit does the cutting. The accessory can be used with any router that has a 6" diameter base.

6-101.   Typical projects that you can "turn out" with the "Bowl-Crafter". The initial preparation of the turning blank has a lot to do with the final appearance of the project.

As a Wood Threader
Figure 6-102.

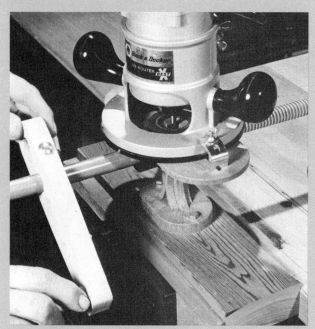

6-102.   A router, any router, can be used to form threads in wood when it is used with an accessory called the "Beall Wood Threader". The router is clamped to a device that can be fitted with various inserts to suit different size dowels or round stock. A special cutter in the router cuts the threads as the work, guided by an indexing device, is turned.

As an Edge Crafter
Figures 6-103, 6-104.

6-103.   To cut, or to edge-shape, uniform or wave-shaped edges, you can work with a router/shaper stand accessory that is called an "Edge-Crafter". The system can be used on round or oval solid parts or frames up to 30″ in diameter.

6-104.   A set of guide templates is provided with the "Edge-Crafter", but you can also make your own.

As a 3-D Carver
Figures 6-105 through 6-107.

6-105.   With a tool called "Router-Recreator" you can carve 3-D figures up to 8″ tall, and do sign plaques, even do some work on spindles. The router motor and a stylus are mounted on a carriage that can move laterally and to and fro.

6-106.   The stylus, following the shape and contours of the model, guides the router bit through the cuts it must make. An adjustable, counter-balancing weight at the rear of the carriage, makes it easier to move the router about.

6-107. You can make signs or form house numbers with the "Router-Recreator". The stylus can follow stencils or ready-made letters or numbers, or any shaped piece whose outline you wish to duplicate.

The "Mill-Route"
Figures 6-108, 6-109.

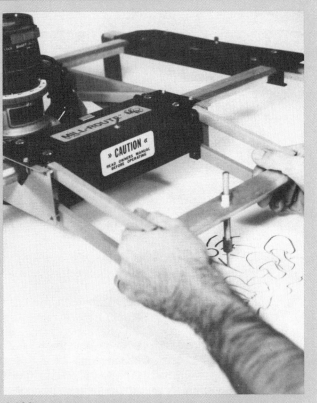

6-109. With the "Mill-Route", the router will duplicate any design that you draw or buy. This is a good way to create templates that you first draw on paper. The 3-D carving is possible since the router can be moved in all three dimensions.

For Sign Making
Figure 6-110.

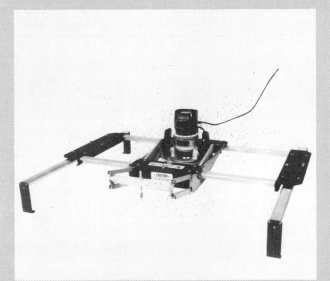

6-108. The "Mill-Route" combines features ordinarily available with a pantograph and milling machine. The router is mounted on a platform which glides easily in any direction on rails. It is also adjustable vertically about 3½". The router always remains parallel to the working surface.

6-110. A layout kit that can be used to produce letters and numbers 2″, 3″, and 4″ high is offered by Dremel, manufacturer of a hand grinder that is often used for light-duty routing, which we'll talk about in a later chapter. The kit includes templates in Old English, Script, and Block styles.

7. The Portable Belt Sander

O f all woodworking chores, the one we most likely want to get through as quickly and efficiently as possible, is sanding—whether it is getting a new project to the point where finishing coats can be applied, or preparing an existing project for a new look. Portable electric tools like the belt sander and the pad sander provide the means of achieving professional results with minimum fuss and effort.

There are two words that can be used to describe the belt sander—tough and fast. It's a super tool for rapid, heavy stock removal. Getting an even, smooth surface on a slab that you can use as a bench or table is one of the impressive belt-sander applications (Figure 7-1). It is often used to strip old paint or varnish, and with a proper choice of abrasive belt, you can use it on non-wood materials like plaster, slate, plastics, marble, and metals. But it's more than a smoothing tool. For example, you will find yourself using it for jobs like removing a smidgen of material from the edge of a door so it will close properly, forming a bevel on a door's edge, or removing excess material on a wood connection. Many times, a joint is deliberately cut so one part will extend more than it should; a rabbet for example, is often cut wider than necessary and the belt sander is used to sand the projection

perfectly flush after the parts have been assembled. Other joints that are treated in similar fashion are the through mortise and dovetails. Dowels used to hide screws or to reinforce joints are quickly sanded flush with a belt sander.

Some manufacturers offer accessories so the portable belt sander can be secured in an upright or horizontal position and used as a stationary unit.

Types, Sizes, Speeds

The belt sander drives a continuous loop of coated abrasive over drums or "pulleys", as they are sometimes called, that are located at each end of the machine. One drum, at the rear of the tool, is powered by the motor, usually through a system of reduction gears. The second drum, spring-loaded so it can provide correct belt tension, runs free and has a slight, adjustable swivel action that is used to keep the belt tracking correctly over the drums (Figure 7-2). This has been a manual operation, but some modern units like the one in Figure 7-3 incorporate a system that automatically keeps the belt tracking correctly. It's quite a nice feature since tracking usually requires some attention while the tool is working.

All of the abrasive belt works, of course, but the area that actually contacts the work is determined by the size of

7-1.   The belt sander is a workhorse. It removes a lot of material quickly so it is a popular choice for preliminary work on slabs and rough lumber, but it should not be discounted as a "smoother."

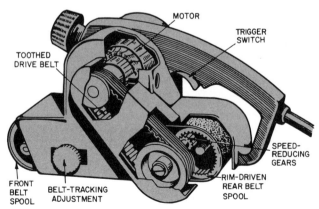

7-2.   The belt-sander motor powers the rear drum through a reduction drive. The front drum is "free", but is used for tracking the belt and to keep the belt taut.

the platen or "shoe" on the bottom of the tool (Figure 7-4). This is usually 3″ or 4″ wide, but platen width is not the only consideration. A 4″ x 4″ platen doesn't provide much more contact surface than one measuring 3″ x 5″, but many users find that the broader surface makes the tool easier to control, especially on wide, flat surfaces.

The size of the tool may be expressed in terms of belt width or belt width plus length. The physical size, weight, and power of the tool usually increase along with increases in belt size. The 3″ x 18″ belt-size unit in Figure 7-3 weighs 6 lbs and is rated at 3.3 amps. The 4″ x 21¾″ belt-size unit in Figure 7-5 weighs almost 11 lbs and is driven by a 9 amp motor that

develops 1⅛ horsepower. Also, notice the difference in grip controls. You might use a one-hand grip for some work with the lighter one, but it's not likely that you would try it with the big fellow. The larger unit is designed so that it can be used in a stationary mode by inverting it and clamping it securely to a bench top (Figure 7-6).

The majority of belt sanders, especially large ones, are equipped with dust collection systems or designed so one can be added (Figures 7-7, 7-8). Even though the systems might do a good job, it is still good practice to use a dust mask for extra protection. Dust collection bags should be emptied frequently since a stuffed one will reduce the efficiency of the

7-3.   Compact tool drives the belt at 700 surface feet per minute (sfpm). It provides an impressive amount of sanding surface despite its small size. Design allows a one-handed operation but an assist knob can be used for extra control.

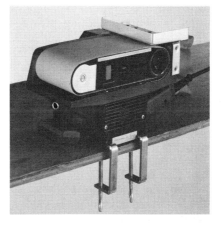

7-6.   The tool is turned upside down and secured with clamps. Accessory kits for the clamps and a combination guide are available.

7-4.   The area of the belt that actually contacts the work is determined by the size of the platen. On most belt sanders the width of the platen is 3″ or 4″.

7-7.   This 10 lb sander turns a 3″ x 21″ belt at 1300 sfpm. The tool is rated at 6.5 amps. A vacuum dust pickup system is standard equipment.

7-5.   Heavy-duty, 1⅛ hp unit drives a 4″-wide belt 1400 sfpm. The tool comes with a dust collection system and features automatic belt tracking. Figure 7-6 shows how it can be inverted and used as a stationary tool.

7-8.   Many belt sanders, like this 3″ x 21″ example, are double insulated. Operators should wear a dust mask even when the tool has a dust collection system.

tool. Clean the bag whenever you change from wood sanding to metal work. Sparks from metal can cause fires in wood dust.

Belt sander speeds are listed in surface feet per minute (SFPM), with the range starting at about 600 sfpm and going up to better than 1500 sfpm. The faster the speed, the faster you can sand, but the speed itself has nothing to do with the quality of the tool or even its capability. A coarse-grit belt moving at high speed will remove stock fastest especially when working across the grain. A fine-grit abrasive can cause burning and can clog quickly when working at a very high speed, but this can be controlled with light feed pressure and taking the time to clean the belt as you work. Any single speed will be a compromise when you consider the variety of jobs a tool can do, but wise tool-handling provides compensation.

Making a Choice

What you plan to use the belt sander for should be a major determining factor when choosing one to buy. A rugged, heavy-duty machine will speed up chores like evening and smoothing large surfaces (Figure 7-9). It will be easier to keep the tool from tilting and gouging the work if it has a broad platen, but it will be a tiresome handful when you use it on vertical surfaces or, possibly, overhead.

On some jobs it will be convenient if you can work up against a vertical surface. For example, you might be sanding a floor or smoothing a shelf and wish to work flush to the wall (Figure 7-10). Many models are shaped to allow for this application, so, if it's important to you, check for projections on the open side of the machine that might prevent such use.

Check to see what is involved in changing the belt and adjusting the drum for correct tracking. Will it be much of a chore to keep the tool properly lubricated? Does it have or will it take a dust bag? Check the balance, the "feel" of the tool, before deciding. If the features of several meet your standards, the more comfortable one might be for you.

Adjustments

Unless the tool has automatic tracking, the idler drum at the front of the machine is adjusted for both belt tension and belt tracking. Abrasive belts are marked with an arrow on their uncoated sides which indicates correct direction of rotation. This is necessary so the seam in the belt will not snag on workpieces. The rotation is clockwise so, when you mount a belt, be sure the arrow points accordingly.

Decreasing the distance between the drums allows you to slip a belt into place. In most cases, this is accomplished by standing the tool on its front drum and pushing down firmly until the drum is locked firmly in a retracted position. After the belt is slipped over the drums a lever, or some similar device, is used to release the front one (Figure 7-11). This pulls the belt taut between the drums to provide necessary tension.

Correct tracking guides the belt in a perfectly straight line over both drums. Any lateral motion would allow the belt to slip off the free end of the drums or to move in the opposite direction where it would rub against the machine's casing. A

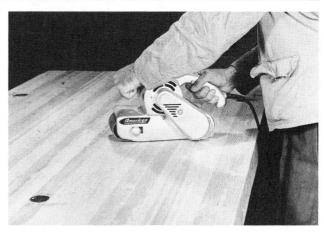

7-9. A rugged, heavy-duty tool, turning at high speed, makes it easy to even and smooth down large areas. Many operators find that it is easier to keep the tool from tilting when it has a broad platen.

7-10. Many models are designed so they can be used flush against a vertical surface. Here, even the dust bag doesn't interfere.

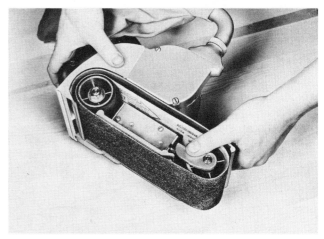

7-11. Belt mounting is accomplished by decreasing the distance between the drums. It's easy to place the belt when the front drum is locked in a retracted position. Spring-pressure causes the drum to snap forward to provide belt tension.

knob on the side of the tool is used to control the angle of the front drum (Figure 7-12). After the belt is mounted and tensioned, turn the tracking knob one way or the other until the front drum appears correct. Then, observe the results as you quickly turn the tool on and off. Make a slight adjustment, if necessary, and turn the tool on and off again. Make a final adjustment with the belt continuing to run.

Tracking is correct when the outboard edge of the belt is in line with the outboard rim on the drums. Tracking may have to be adjusted after you have used the sander a bit and the belt takes a set. This is normal and simply requires an additional touch of the adjustment knob. On the other hand, if tracking requires constant attention return the tool for repair.

Some sanders have a traction block mounted inside the casing at the rear of the idler drum. The block protects the machine against abrasion due to poor tracking. The inboard edge of the belt should parallel to the block. The belt may touch the block, but must not sand into it.

Using the Belt Sander

If you place a belt sander on a surface and then turn it on, the belt will work like the treads on a tractor. The tool will try to get away from you or pull you along with it, but it won't do any sanding. So a primary rule is to grip the tool securely and start it before making contact with the work. Initial contact must be with the platen flat on the work. Only part of the belt will work if the tool is tilted, and the gouges that result will be difficult to remove. Keeping the sander moving is another important rule; hold it in one spot and you'll have a dent the size of the platen.

Generally, the sander should be moved in long strokes run parallel to the wood grain, working to and fro and moving the tool so you overlap the strokes a bit. If the stroke direction is oblique instead of in-line, you will, in effect, be doing cross-grain sanding which is an acceptable technique at times but not to be used when you are sanding to smooth a surface for finishing coats. Cross-grain lines might not be seen under paint, but even slight ones become very apparent after an application of stain.

The major feature of the belt sander is its straight-line action which makes it easy to sand parallel to the wood grain, and this procedure is what always produces best results. It's even advisable to sand *with* the grain whenever possible since working against the grain can raise a nap which requires more sanding to eliminate. This basic rule can be ignored when you wish to remove a lot of material quickly. Then, working against the grain or across it is the way to go.

Keep the platen flat on the work at all times and don't bear down on the tool more than is necessary to keep the sandpaper cutting (Figure 7-13). Most of the time, the weight of the tool alone will provide adequate feed pressure. Forcing won't accomplish much and can interfere with correct belt tracking. Turn the sander off after you have broken contact with the work and don't set it down until the belt has come to a stop.

Keep the sander on the same plane when you come off the end of the work. Allowing it to tilt will form a ramp or will round off the end of the workpiece (Figure 7-14). Another error to avoid is lifting the tool before the stroke is complete.

7-13.   Normally, the weight of the tool is enough for good contact between the abrasive belt and the work. Maintain a firm grip—keep the tool flat and moving.

7-12.   Manual tracking is done by turning a knob on the side of the tool. This alters the angle of the front drum so the belt can move left or right until tracking is correct.

7-14.   Keep the tool level when you come off the work. Letting it tilt, like this, will form a ramp on the work or round off its edge. Turn the machine off after it is free of the workpiece. Let the belt stop before you set the tool down.

Remember that the sander, especially when coarse-grit belts are used, removes material quickly. So be cautious when sanding veneers or plywood (Figure 7-15). It isn't difficult to sand right through surface plies. This is especially important when working on fancy hardwood plywood where surface veneers might be quite thin.

Keeping Work Secure

Just as the belt sander can travel like a tractor and take off on its own unless you hold and guide it with firmness, it can grip pieces of wood and throw them back at the operator. Anytime you are sanding material that is not heavy enough to stay put on its own, or is not attached to something solid, secure the job to a bench top or across sawhorses by using clamps or weights, or even by tack-nailing in waste areas. When the part is small, you can secure it by bracing it against a backup strip that is clamped or tack-nailed to a solid surface (Figure 7-16). The backup, of course, must be thinner than the stock thickness.

7-15.   Sanding veneers of plywood calls for careful handling. It's not difficult for a belt sander to get through a tin ply.

7-16.   Small pieces can be braced securely by backing them against a strip of wood that is tack-nailed or clamped in place. Never try to hand-hold small work.

Some types of clamps, like the "Tru-Grip" model shown in Figure 7-17, do nicely as work holders since they have back-to-back jaws—one set grips a solid surface, the others secure the work. Even very small pieces can be belt-sanded safely if you improvise a means of keeping them secure. A typical jig, designed to hold discs, is shown in Figure 7-18. The hook prevents the sander from throwing the work, while a cleat braces the jig against the edge of a bench.

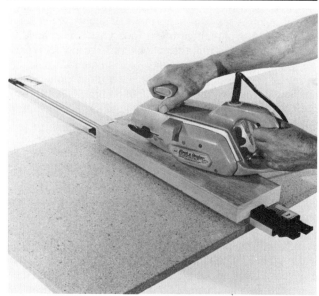

7-17.   Clamps that have back-to-back jaws are useful for gripping workpieces. With this design, one set of jaws grips a solid surface while the other set holds the work.

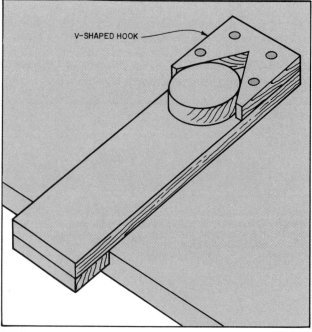

7-18.   You can make special holders to secure small or odd-shaped pieces. A V-hook can be used for square as well as round pieces.

Cross-Grain Work

The cross-grain sanding technique is used to remove material quickly. Moving the sander directly across the grain removes material fastest, but you can also use an angular stroke direction. The method is best for jobs like smoothing down edge-to-edge assemblies that you plan to use as a bench or table top, removing the roughness from a tree slab so it can be used as a bench or coffee table, or doing the initial work that removes roughness from unplaned lumber (Figure 7-19). In all cases, the cross-grain work is a preliminary step. Straight-line passes done with finer grits of abrasive must follow in order to eliminate the scratches that will be on the project. Actually, any sanding will leave scratches or grooves. The idea is to reduce them to the point where they can't be felt and are not visible.

Sanding Edges

You can sand edges with a belt sander but the work requires careful handling of the tool in order to keep the platen flat on the work. The narrower the work, the more difficult this is to do. When there are many pieces to do, they can be clamped together as a pad (Figure 7-20). All the edges will be smoothed, with little danger of tilting the tool since the assembly is sanded as if it were a solid block of wood. The method is applicable in other ways. If, for example, you need to sand curved or pointed ends of fence pickets, clamp a dozen or so as a pad and sand them all at the same time.

When it's necessary to sand a single edge and square-ness of the edge is critical, you can try one of the systems shown in Figures 7-21 and 7-22. The idea is to broaden the work edge to provide more bearing surface for the sander.

7-20.   It's easier to sand edges when you have many similar pieces to do. Clamping them in a pad lets you work as if you were sanding a solid block. Note the backup strip.

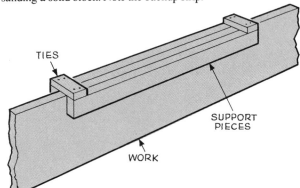

7-21.   Adding extra pieces to broaden the work surface is one way to go when you must sand a single edge. The extra strips can be clamped in place or secured with ties.

7-19.   Cross-grain sanding on rough lumber and the like is usually a preliminary step. In-line sanding with a finer-grit belt is required to bring the piece to acceptable smoothness.

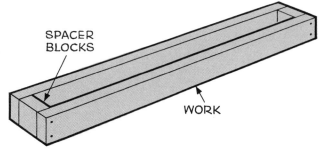

7-22.   Another way to sand a single edge is to make an assembly with an extra support piece. These precautions are necessary only when it is critical for the sanded edge to be square.

Special Stands

Special stands that allow the belt sander to be used vertically or horizontally in stationary fashion are available as accessories. Most resemble the sketch in Figure 7-23. If you buy one, be sure it is right for the tool you own. Actually, it wouldn't be difficult to make one by imitating the design in the sketch and improvising a means of securing the tool. If you add a groove to the support surface (Figure 7-24), you'll add miter gauge capability to the setup. A later chapter that provides information for constructing a "Sander Shop", shows how you can secure a portable belt sander—and a pad sander—for stationary use.

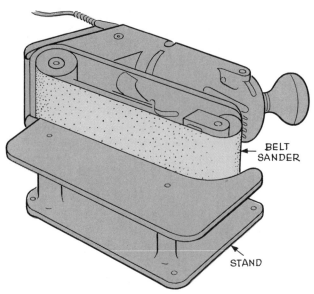

7-23.   Stands, similar to this, are available as accessories—or you can make your own. We'll discuss this use later in the book.

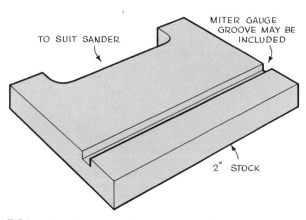

7-24.   Forming a groove in the support surface of an accessory stand that you make will allow the use of a miter gauge. This can be handy when you must sand the ends of narrow pieces.

Removing Old Finishes

Make the first passes with an open-coat abrasive. Select a grit in relation to the thickness of the finish. Thin coatings like lacquer and similar materials don't require very coarse-grit abrasives. You especially want to stay away from coarse grits if the project is made of plywood (Figure 7-25).

Thick coatings of paint, some of which can be softened by the belt's action, will quickly clog even tough, open-coat abrasive belts. In such situations, you can save considerable energy and even some money by removing the bulk of the finish with a heat gun and scrapers or with a solvent that is designed for the purpose. Then, for final touches, you can use a sanding machine.

Generally, it's best to work so you are pulling the sander toward you. Start strokes from the end of the project that is farthest from you, so you will be moving the tool from abraded areas back into painted ones. In most cases, this technique seems to help prevent quick belt clogging. Nevertheless, examine the belt frequently. Keep it as clean as possible by working on it with a stiff brush or an eraser-type product that is made for the purpose. (Further information on abrasives and their use can be found in Appendix 4).

7-25.   The belt sander is often used to remove old finishes, but the applications can be overdone. For example, to remove heavy paint coatings, it's best to start with a heat gun and scrapers or a solvent. Then use the sander for the finishing touches.

The Portable Pad Sander

8.

The pad sander backs up the abrasive paper with a "soft" material, unlike the belt sander which has a hard platen. It's often called a "finishing sander"; this is a clue to one of the tool's major functions—producing a satin-like surface on many materials before they are coated, and putting a mirror-like gleam on projects after they have been covered with varnish or lacquer or shellac. Often, the sander is used *between* applications of finishing coats, and even to smooth paint jobs.

It might seem that the pad sander is only a light-touch tool, but don't judge it so; it's no sissy. While it should not be used for jobs that can be done better and faster with a belt sander or a hand plane, it does have some heavy-duty capabilities. The kind of hard work you can do with it depends, to some extent, on the type of pad sander you have. A unit that is not much more than palm-size (Figure 8-1) can't be expected to work as fast as a huskier version like the one in Figure 8-2. For one thing, the larger tool has a lot more sanding area.

It's a mistake to assume that the pad sander is just a time saver and a convenient substitute for elbow grease. It's possible to produce fine finishes by hand, but extreme care is required in addition to hard work. The broad, flat pad on the powered sander makes it possible to maintain an even, level, abrasive-to-work contact that is difficult to imitate with fingers.

Types, Sizes, Speeds

Pad sanders operate with the type of mechanism shown in Figure 8-3. The motor, through a unique drive system, causes the pad to move in one of two ways—to and fro in short,

8-1. One-hand, palm-size pad sander is light and easy to handle and can sand flush into corners. It's a super smoothing tool but can be used with many abrasive grits so its use should not be confined merely to finishing chores.

8-2. Larger pad sanders have impressive amounts of sanding area. Units of this type usually have an orbital motion or can be switched from orbital to straight-line action. Being able to work either way is a help on many sanding chores.

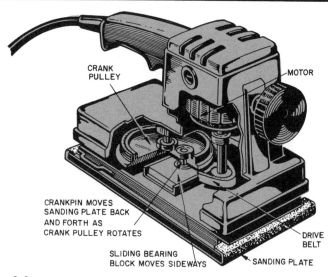

8-3.   Mechanism inside a pad sander converts the motor's rotary motion into an orbital or straight-line action. Many modern pad sanders are double insulated.

CRANK PULLEY

MOTOR

CRANKPIN MOVES SANDING PLATE BACK AND FORTH AS CRANK PULLEY ROTATES

SLIDING BEARING BLOCK MOVES SIDEWAYS

DRIVE BELT

SANDING PLATE

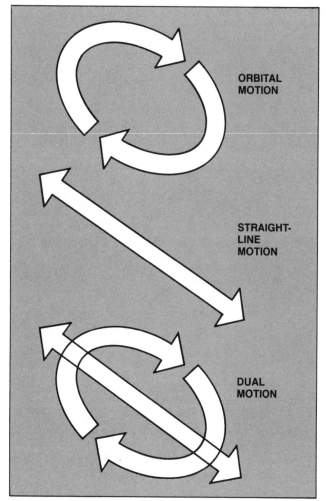

ORBITAL MOTION

STRAIGHT-LINE MOTION

DUAL MOTION

8-4.   Typical pad-sander actions. Getting from orbital to straight-line on tools that offer both modes is just a matter of moving a lever.

straight-line strokes, or orbicularly so abrasive grits move in very tiny circles. Some dual-action models offer a choice of both motions—you use a switch or a lever to choose whether the sander will work in an oscillating or orbital mode (Figure 8-4).

In general, orbital sanding works faster and is a little better suited to heavier stock removal because cutting is both 'with' and 'across' the grain. Straight-line sanding is slower, but when done with the grain, produces impressively smooth, swirl-free results. In practice, however, the difference between finishes produced by one action or the other can only be seen with a microscope. One reason is that modern orbital sanders have high speeds and move the sandpaper in tiny circles so that swirl marks are kept to a minimum. In this respect,

8-5.   Palm-grip sander delivers 13,000, $\frac{1}{16}$" orbits per minute. The unit works with quarter-size sheets of sandpaper, which you can buy or cut from standard sheets.

8-6.   Unique feature of this sander is that it can be used with 4" or 5" square diameter pads. The 1.8 amp, 12,000 orbits per minute tool weighs only 2.4 lbs.

consider the one-handed, palm-grip unit shown in Figure 8-5. It delivers 13,000, $\frac{1}{16}$" orbits per minute. Actually, most pad sanders available today will be orbital or provide a dual action.

Palm-grip sanders are popular because they are powerful, yet light in weight so they can be handled for long periods of time with less operator fatigue. The sander in Figure 8-6, operates at 12,000 orbits per minute (OPM) with a 1.8 amp motor, yet weighs only 2.4 lbs. A unique feature of this tool is that it can be equipped with 4" or 5" diameter pads.

The size of the sanding pad, which is the actual area of contact between the abrasive and the work, is an indication of the amount of work a sander can do. Obviously, the larger the pad the more area it will cover at one time. Pad sizes will vary and, usually, tool weight, size, and horsepower will increase along with greater abrasive area. The double insulated, heavy duty, 4 amp model in Figure 8-7 works with a full half-sheet (4½" x 9¼") of standard-size sandpaper.

The size of the sanding sheet the tool can work with is something to consider. If the sheet size is odd, you'll always have to buy directly from the manufacturer or put up with some waste when cutting pieces from standard sheets. Usually though, the tool is designed to eliminate this annoyance.

Some pad sanders are designed to minimize, if not eliminate, the amount of sawdust that escapes into the air. Usually, this is accomplished by enclosing the pad area in a skirt, and providing a collection bag (Figure 8-8).

A new and interesting concept is an air driven, oscillating sander that can be powered by a canister-type vacuum cleaner (Figure 8-9). The unit offers dust-free sanding and, since it doesn't have an electric motor, weighs only about 1½ lbs. The revolutions of the eccentric turbine wheel that creates the movement of the sanding pad can be adjusted with a top-mounted air-flow control. A self-adhesive polishing pad can be used in place of sandpaper so the unit serves as a polisher for automobiles or furniture (Figure 8-10).

8-7. Large pad sanders like this double-insulated unit accept half sheets of standard size sandpaper. Sanding area of about 42 square inches does a lot of work, fast. Levers at each end are for gripping sandpaper.

8-9. Air driven, oscillating sander can be powered by a vacuum cleaner. Unique, eccentric turbine system drives the pad and also collects sawdust. An air-flow control lets the operator control sanding speed.

8-8. Enclosed pad and a collection bag scoop up most of the sawdust. Like all sanders, the trigger switch may be locked in the "on" position, which facilitates using the tool for extended periods.

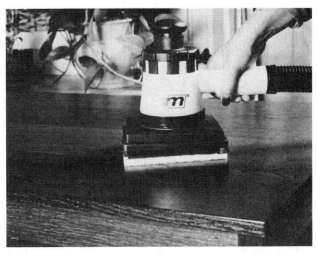

8-10. By using a special, self-adhesive pad which is supplied with the tool, the air-powered sander can be used for polishing jobs on furniture or automobiles.

Mounting the Sandpaper

In order for a pad sander to work efficiently, abrasive sheets must lie flat and be held taut over the entire area of the pad. If the paper is loose, it won't move with the pad and the amount of sanding it will do, if any, will be minimal. A loose paper is also prone to wrinkles and tearing.

Paper-mounting systems vary from tool to tool. A common method provides spring-loaded clamps at each end of the pad. The paper is gripped by one clamp and then pulled taut and slipped under the second one (Figure 8-11). The paper must be correct in width and length. The paper that comes with the machine will be perfect; it's a good idea to make a matching cardboard template that you can use as a guide when cutting your own replacements. Some manufacturers offer self-adhesive sheets (Figure 8-12). They can be used even though the sander has a clamping system. They are also convenient to have when you need to temporarily change to a different sanding grit. You just stick them on to the paper that is already attached, and then remove them when the current phase of the job is done.

The Pad

All sanders are equipped with a soft pad of felt or some similar material that provides the right flexibility for average work (Figure 8-13). On some materials, like fir with its hard-and-soft-grain characteristics, a soft pad can create depressions between hard-grain areas. In such cases, a hard pad will provide a more efficient backing for the paper since it will span across hard-grain areas. You can provide a hard pad with a piece of thin hardboard that is placed between the original pad and the paper. Slim brads of suitable length can be used to hold the new pad in place, or you can mount the hard pad in place of the original one (Figure 8-14). If you use brads, be sure they are set flush or slightly below the bearing surface of the pad.

8-11.   Abrasive sheets are held, in some way, at both ends of the pad. Be sure to follow manufacturer's instructions. It's critical for the sheet to be flat and taut over the entire pad area.

8-13.   The soft pad with which the sander is equipped is fine for general applications. Most of the time, the weight of the sander supplies enough pressure for the tool to work efficiently. Keep the tool moving.

8-12.   Cut-to-size, self-adhesive sandpaper sheets are available. They will adhere directly to the pad or to a sheet that is already mounted. Remove this type of paper once a job is done. The adhesive can take a 'set'.

8-14.   You can make a hard pad by using a piece of ⅛"-thick hardboard. Mount the new pad with short brads directly to the felt, or substitute it for the original pad. In either case, the fasteners must flush or be a bit below the surface of the hardboard.

Conversely, a pad that is thicker (softer) than the one provided can be more efficient when working on curves and cylinders, even on moldings. This type of pad might be offered as an accessory, but you can improvise with pieces cut from an old rug, sponge, or foam rubber. How soft the pad should be will depend on the curves that need sanding. With thicker pads, you must provide longer sheets of sandpaper.

Felt pads can become disfigured and even acquire a smooth patina after extended use. Very bad ones should be replaced, but you can often extend the life of one simply by moving it across a sheet of 60 or 80-grit sandpaper.

A common accessory for pad sanders is a polishing pad. It can be handy to have when you are involved in polishing and waxing chores.

The Pad Sander at Work

How the tool is handled depends to a considerable extent on its design. Palm-grip type sanders are always held with one hand, whereas other types offer options (Figures 8-15— 8-17). The extra knob or handle on some units is there mostly so you can provide more control, not so you can 'muscle' the tool to do more work, faster. In some situations, like sanding vertical surfaces, the extra knob provides handling convenience. In most cases, when you are doing routine work on flat, horizontal surfaces, the weight of the tool is about all that's needed for efficient sanding. Too much pressure can harm the tool and leave scratches that you have to remove with more sanding.

Sanding goes faster, but leaves a rougher finish when you move the machine across the grain. Working with the grain is slower, but the work will be smoother (Figure 8-18). It's normal procedure when much sanding is required, to start with cross-grain sanding and then, after changing to a finer grit of sandpaper, finish with with-the-grain strokes. General advice is to start with a coarse-grit paper and work down to the grit that produces the finish you want, but judgments should be made depending on the condition of the work. There is little point in starting with a coarse-grit paper when the work is already reasonably smooth.

8-16.   Larger sanders can also be controlled with one hand, but if you push down, the abrasive sheet will not lay flat on the work surface. Use the hand only for guiding the tool.

8-17.   The extra knob on large sanders permits a two-hand grip, but for more control on rough work, not so you can bear down heavily. It's always best to make several light passes over an area instead of a single heavy one.

8-15.   Palm-grip sanders are designed for one-hand operation. They are super tools for producing satin-like finishes, whether working on raw wood or applied finishes.

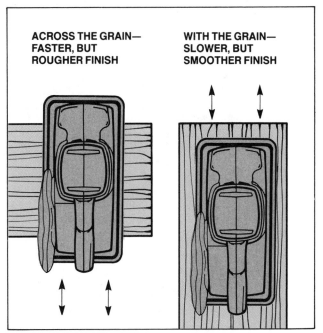

ACROSS THE GRAIN— FASTER, BUT ROUGHER FINISH

WITH THE GRAIN— SLOWER, BUT SMOOTHER FINISH

8-18.   Work across the grain only when you wish to remove a lot of material quickly. Always finish the job by making passes that parallel the wood grain.

No matter what the action of the sander, it's usually best to finish sanding jobs by using strokes that parallel the wood grain. If you overlap the strokes by as much as 75%, you'll be sure to get good coverage.

Pad sanders allow working into corners or flush against a vertical surface or edge (Figure 8-19). This applies whether you are sanding a vertical or horizontal surface. It's usually the 'open' side of the sander that you can bring to bear against an obstruction, but the sanding action being used can also affect how you should work. Anyway, you'll know when you are wrong because the contact between the tool and the obstruction will cause excessive vibration and noise.

Sanding Edges

When sanding edges, a two-hand grip helps to keep the tool level so you don't round off corners. If you apply too much pressure, the pad will 'bend' over corners and you'll have a convex edge instead of a square one. Edge sanding isn't difficult to do freehand, but when squareness is critical, you can use some of the ideas that were explained in the chapter on the belt sander. Pieces can be clamped together and sanded as if they were a solid block. Bearing surface for the sander can be increased when sanding a single edge by adding side strips, and so on. The object is to provide enough work surface so it will be easier to keep the sander on a level plane.

Keeping Work Firm

If you are working on a small part, and it is not secured in some way, it will probably move along with the action of the tool and sanding will be nil. Unless the workpiece is substantial enough to stay put on its own it should be secured to something solid with clamps or gripped in a vise (Figure 8-20). A fixed workpiece allows you to concentrate on controlling the sander.

In some situations, especially when odd-shaped parts are involved, it pays to work as shown in Figure 8-21. An extra piece of wood, which can be the waste that remained after the work was shaped, is clamped along with what must be sanded. This technique helps in two ways—it provides good tool support, which is nice especially when using a large machine, and it assures that the work edge will be flat.

8-20.   Keeping the work still is essential for good sanding results. If you don't use very light pressure, and keep the tool level when sanding edges, you may get a convex edge instead of a flat one.

8-19.   Pad sanders can be used in corners and flush to obstructions. It's usually the open side of an oscillating sander that can be used this way. Either side can be used if the sander has a straight-line action.

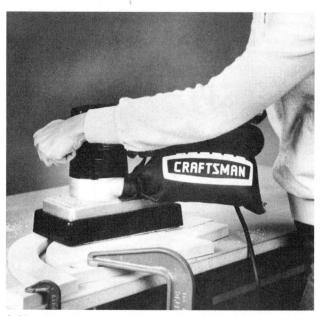

8-21.   Clamping scrap pieces together with the work is a means of keeping a sander on a level plane. It's an especially good way to go when the part being sanded is narrow.

As a Sharpener

A pad sander will never replace an efficient grinder or honing machine, but when it is fitted with a hard pad and a very fine emery paper, it can be used to do touch-up work on butt or lathe chisels, plane blades, knives, and the like (Figure 8-22). This is not a grinding operation—it's not suggested that you use this technique to *renew* edges, but it's a handy way to maintain the keenness of cutting edges. Apply the tool very carefully so you don't cut into the abrasive or the pad.

Sanding Finish Coats

A pad sander is a fine tool to use to smooth surfaces between applications of finishing coats, and to even add a subtle patina to final coats of lacquer, enamel, shellac, varnish, or whatever. How you work on the final application will depend on the material involved and the gloss, or lack of it, you want. A common procedure is to use a ready-made 'rubbing compound'; a standard material that is available in auto-supply stores and many hardware stores.

The compound, which feels like a very fine powder, is sprinkled over the work surface and then gone over with the sander using a piece of carpeting in place of the regular pad and paper. Burlap may also be used, and it is often possible to use the material simply by wrapping it tightly about the base of the machine and gripping it tightly with one hand as you use your other hand to move the tool about.

For a superfine finish on furniture, you can do wet sanding with a silicon-carbide, superfine-grit, waterproof paper mounted on the sander. There are many lubricants you can use for wet sanding, but many professionals still adhere to the clean water and soap combination. The technique involves rubbing the abrasive paper with ordinary hand soap and wetting the work surface with a sponge.

Another mixture often used by professional finishers is a combination of 'pumice' or 'rottenstone' and a light or heavy oil. Often, just a light oil and a very fine emery paper will produce a finish you like. Even though most modern tools are double insulated, it's wise to take extra precautions when work involves electricity and liquids. Wearing tight-fitting rubber gloves and insulated shop shoes is one way to work carefully.

Applying a wax finish is fairly straightforward. Apply the wax by hand, spreading it uniformly in a thin coat. Then make a pad of cheesecloth or some similar material and place the sander in the center of it. Apply just enough pressure on the sander to allow its action to move the cloth pad.

8-22.   A sander that is equipped with a hard pad and very fine emery paper can be used to maintain edges on various cutting tools. Don't use this technique to *reshape* edges; that's a job for a grinder.

9. Portable Disc Sanders and Polishers

Portable disc sanders and polishers belong in the category of abrasive tools, but their functions are often misunderstood and unappreciated. While there is overlap in the functions of various sanding machines, those that use a disc to do the work have distinctive features and special applications. They are not substitutes for pad or belt sanders anymore than the latter tools can replace disc-drivers. Overall, as far as use and even appearance are concerned, it is the word 'disc' that supplies the clue to the major distinctions.

There are various types of tools in this category and some confusion can result. For example, one tool that is designed for sanding can have a twin that is best used for polishing. The units shown in Figures 9-1 and 9-2 have the same specifications except for one critical factor. The disc *sander* has a no-load speed of 4000 rpm; the disc *polisher* turns at 2000 rpm. Polishers operate at speeds that are less than sanders require for efficient abrading.

The names of the tools may include 'disc sander', 'disc polisher', 'disc sander/polisher', or 'disc sander/grinder'. A combination sander/polisher (Figure 9-3) may offer a choice of speeds or it may have a single speed, in which case the speed would probably favor the polishing mode. This is logical since too much speed when polishing or buffing can cause burn marks.

Newcomers among disc polishers, simply called 'polishers' or 'buffer/polishers', offer unique work-actions. The one shown in Figure 9-4 has a random orbit action which, in a sense, simulates the motion of hand polishing. Another unit will have an elliptical action, also intended to move the pad about as you would move a cloth with your hand. These tools, which are strictly for polishing, may have two speeds; a low one, in the area of 1700 to 1900 rpm for applying wax, and a high one that might range from 1900 to 2400 rpm, for buffing and polishing.

The sander/grinder (Figure 9-5) is always a heavy-duty tool. Speeds are generally high, running in the area of 5000 to 6000 rpm, and they have workhorse motors—one, two, even three horsepower is not unusual. Accessories for these units, in addition to abrasive discs and grinding wheels, include

9-1.   This 7″ disc sander works at speeds of 4000 rpm and can do a variety of finishing jobs on wood or metal. The size of the tool is stated in terms of the diameter of the backup pad it is equipped with.

9-2.   This 7″ disc *polisher* has the same specifications as the disc *sander,* but there is a critical difference. Its speed is 2000 rpm as opposed to the sander's 4000 rpm. Typically, both tools have built-in lock buttons, which is a convenience for continuous use.

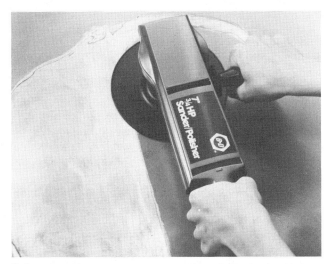

9-3. This 7″ unit is used as a sander when the backup pad is covered with an abrasive sheet or as a polisher when the pad is covered with a bonnet. Single choice speed is 2400 rpm.

9-4. This 8″, random-orbit disc polisher is designed to simulate the motion of hand polishing. The ¾ hp motor provides ample power for waxing and polishing tasks. This two-speed tool has a high speed of 2400 rpm and a low speed of 1950 rpm.

9-5. The disc sander/grinder is always a heavy-duty tool that will stand up under the kind of continuous work that is characteristic of automobile repair shops.

items like cup wheels and wire brushes. This is the kind of tool that is found in welding shops, auto-body repair and remodeling garages, and so on—any place where heavy-duty sanding and grinding are continuing, routine chores (Figure 9-6).

Offset and In-Line Designs

The in-line design looks pretty much like a portable drill. The weight of the motor is near to or directly over the center of the disc. The control handles are in positions that will be familiar to you if you have done any portable drill work at all.

A right-angle bend is the major feature of offset versions. Since these tools usually have a longer body, your hands will be more widely separated; one on the main handle of the tool, the other on an auxiliary knob, or handle, as the case may be. Most of the time one hand will guide the tool while the other exerts as much pressure as is needed for the tool to work. Favoring a light feed pressure is usually much better than forcing the tool. Abrasive discs are cutting tools and, like saw blades, should not be pushed beyond what they were designed for.

Longer tools provide more reach, which can be helpful under certain conditions. For example, it's easier to reach the center of the top of an automobile with an offset polisher.

Choosing a particular design has a lot to do with personal preference. Considering the work these tools are specifically designed to do, the offset is often preferred, even though for average jobs the in-line tool will probably feel more comfortable for most people. It seems easier to let the weight of the tool supply pressure to the pad. With an offset, a lot of the tool's weight is between your right hand and the working end of the machine. This pretty much dictates that your left hand supply any pressure that is needed above what is naturally available simply by resting the abrasive disc on the work. Of course, that's not a good idea with any of the tools. The disc is a wheel and will move in circles unless you keep it where it should be working.

Controlling an offset isn't more difficult than handling an in-line unit. You just adapt to a new handling technique and soon become at ease with the tool.

9-6. The roughness of this much-used welding table was no match for a sander/grinder. Jobs like this can throw off sparks and a lot of metal particles, so work should be done in a clean area. Safety goggles—with all sanding operations—are a must!

Using a Disc Sander

Like the belt sander, a disc sander is an abrading workhorse. In many situations, like doing preliminary smoothing work on rough lumber, a disc rotating a coarse-grit paper will remove stock faster than a belt sander (Figure 9-7). But there is a catch. Because the sanding action is circular, which means consistent cross-grain cutting, a disc can't do as smooth a job as a belt or pad sander. Of course, it just isn't designed for that purpose. It does star on first-step work on soft or hard woods, 'taking down' and feathering filled dents on automobile bodies, refinishing metal surfaces, removing old paint, and even, with the correct abrasive, smoothing stone or concrete.

To get to a fine finish on rough stock, you can start with a disc sander and then complete the job with a belt or pad sander. Since you can mount sandpaper of various grits on a disc sander, it's often possible to go directly to pad sanding after the disc-tool has done its job. Less critical surface preparation, like exterior paint jobs, may require nothing but the disc, especially if you use one of the new foam backup pads with a fine paper. Overall, it's wise to remember that the disc has a rotary action which is essentially cross-grain sanding.

A particular handling technique is necessary for efficient portable disc sanding. Never place the disc flat on the work and always keep it moving. If you let the disc make full contact and keep it in one place, you will do nothing but cut concentric grooves. Also, since a lot of the waste will not be thrown off, the abrasive paper will clog very quickly (Figure 9-8).

A primary rule is to tilt the machine a bit and to apply just enough pressure to bend the rubber backup pad (Figure 9-9). Quite often just the weight of the tool will be sufficient to do the job. You can judge if additional pressure is required by how the work is going, but never force the tool to the point where the speed of the disc's rotation is drastically reduced.

9-7.   A disc sander is probably the fastest stock remover of all sanding tools, but since the circular cutting action is primarily across the grain, the work will have to be smoothed with a belt or pad sander.

9-9.   Using only part of the disc, and keeping the tool moving, is the most efficient way to use a disc sander. A light touch is always better than a forced one.

9-8.   Working with the abrasive disc flat on the work will create concentric grooves and will clog the paper very quickly, especially if you don't keep the tool moving. This technique is not good practice.

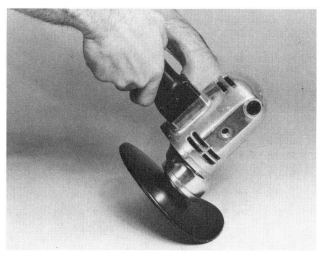

9-10.   The tool must be tilted so only part of the disc will be used, but an extreme angle will limit sanding to the disc's edge and this will result in more 'grooving' than smoothing.

Tilting the tool too much is almost as bad as not tilting it at all since only a small part of the disc will make contact and this will do more circular grooving than sanding (Figure 9-10). In any case, the excess tilt doesn't take maximum advantage of the abrasive disc. The general rule for efficient operation is to keep the machine positioned so that about one quarter to one third of the abrasive surface is in constant contact with the work (Figures 9-11, 9-12).

Other rules to follow are—turn on the motor and let the disc come to full speed before you make contact with the work and keep the tool moving constantly. A haphazard feed pattern might be acceptable at times, but it is generally incorrect. It's best to work with sweeping, straight-line, over-lapping strokes. Even with a disc sander, you'll get optimum results by working parallel to grain lines when you are doing the final strokes.

Open-coat abrasive paper is recommended for general use; it's essential when you are removing an existing finish.

Coarser grades of sandpaper will rough out material very quickly. Finer grades won't cut as fast but will produce smoother finishes. Generally, coarse grades should be used on hardwoods, at least to begin with, whereas finer grades are better when sanding softwoods.

When using a disc sander to clean a metal surface, say the table on a saw (Figure 9-13), always use a tender touch and a very fine emery paper. The tool should just 'whisper' over the material. Finishing the job with a pad sander is a good idea.

Replace the abrasive disc when it is dull or has become clogged and glazed with paint. You can try to renew clogged discs by using one of the methods suggested in the Appendix dealing with abrasives, but if the attempt isn't successful, discard the disc. There are times when you can get more from a worn disc by using it in place of a new disc of finer grit. It's also true that a worn disc, so long as it isn't completely shot, will produce a smoother finish than you can get with a new disc of the same grit number.

When doing extended sanding, use a brush or even a vacuum cleaner to remove loose grit, paint particles, or any waste material. This will lengthen the life of the abrasive and will prevent scratches that can be caused by foreign material that is stuck between grains of abrasive.

When sanding existing finishes you may find that a high sanding speed may soften the material being removed—especially if it is paint—and cause the disc to clog very quickly. When this happens, and assuming the tool allows it, switch to a lower speed; this will reduce heat buildup. If the precautions you take don't lead to an acceptable procedure, it might be best to remove the bulk of the material by working with scrapers or solvents made for the purpose.

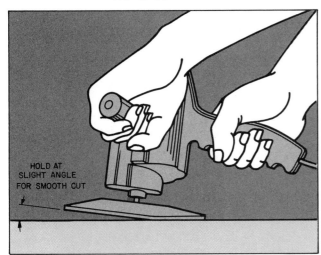

9-11.   The correct tool-tilt will allow much of the abrasive disc to work without causing gouging problems.

HOLD AT SLIGHT ANGLE FOR SMOOTH CUT

9-12.   Hold the tool so about one quarter to one third of the abrasive will contact the work. Position yourself so waste will be thrown away from you.

9-13.   Nowhere is the tender-touch technique more advisable than when you are smoothing or cleaning a tool's table-surface. Use a very fine emery paper—finish with a pad sander.

Stationary Mounting

Some manufacturers offer a special stand as an accessory so the tool can be secured and used in stationary fashion. If not, or if you choose, you can create the same kind of setup for an offset or in-line tool by making a jig (Figure 9-14).

Another improvisation that can be very handy when using an in-line tool for waxing and buffing floors is shown in Figure 9-15. This idea works best when the tool has auxiliary-handle mounting holes on each side. Then it's easy to mount and secure the yoke.

Polishing

A disc polisher, or disc sander/polisher, can be as handy around the house as it is in the shop. Getting a smooth, glossy surface on a car, walls and floors, and furniture becomes an almost-pleasant chore when you can do it with power.

When polishing, tool handling doesn't differ too much from disc sanding except that, with the tool's backup pad covered with a suitable bonnet, it's okay to rest the bonnet flat on the work surface, at least at the start of the job. You can end with the tool tilted some, using only part of the bonnet in smooth, sweeping stokes. If you have a two-speed tool, you should, of course, switch to the low, polishing speed.

Hold the tool firmly but operate with an easy, free motion. It's never necessary to bear down on the tool; its weight alone will supply as much pressure as is needed for good polishing results.

Keep the tool moving. Use long, sweeping motions in a back-and-forth, overlapping pattern that covers the work. Working with a circular or spiral pattern usually leaves visible swirl marks.

Be sure to read the instructions on the container of wax or polish you use. Some materials must be buffed while in a damp state; others must be allowed to dry. Use polishes, compounds, or wax that are designed for machine application. Some that are intended for application by hand will quickly mat a powered polishing pad and can result in smears and even burn marks on the work.

When working on vertical surfaces, it's more convenient to start at the top and work down. Dust and film from completed sections will be cleaned away as you move downward. On horizontal surfaces, start at the point furthest away from you so you won't be dragging the tool's power cord over finished areas.

Pads and buffs used on a machine polisher will become clogged or gummed up after they have been used a while. They can often be renewed with a thorough wash in soapy water and a rinse in clear water. Shake off as much of the water as possible and then spin them dry by mounting them on the tool. A lamb's wool bonnet can be treated in similar fashion and left to dry completely while still on the rubber backup pad. This will minimize shrinkage of the bonnet.

Don't forget to wear safety goggles. Buffing and polishing chores can spew out small, harmful projectiles just as disc sanding can.

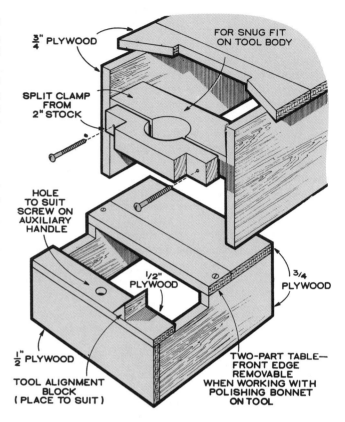

9-14.   You can use designs like this to organize an offset tool (top) or an in-line tool (bottom) for stationary use. Plywood can be used for all parts except the split clamp. Make the clamps from 2″-thick solid stock with the holes sized to suit your machine.

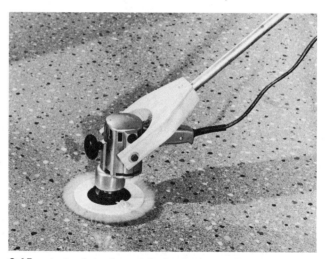

9-15.   A pivoting yoke, attached to the tool like this, will make it much easier to use a disc polisher on floors. The handle can be a length of aluminum tubing or heavy dowel. The opening in the yoke must be sized to suit the tool. Use bolts through holes in the yoke and into the tool's side-handle holes.

10. Portable Power Planes

Any woodworking chore that can be done with various types of hand planes, including rabbeting planes, can be done faster, even better, with a portable electric plane. Actually, these tools will also accomplish many of the jobs normally done on a jointer (some are called planer/jointers) or with a planer blade that is mounted on a table saw or radial arm saw.

Many of the tools are real huskies, with an impressive depth of cut and the ability to smooth wide swaths in wood (Figure 10-1). Others, like the block plane shown in Figure 10-2, while no less capable, are handled with a more tender touch. Being able to remove as much as ⅛″ of wood in a single pass, as some of the tools can do, *is* impressive, but to me, the products are intriguing because of how easily they can accomplish the *minimum* cut. Planing off see-through shavings is no chore for any of them.

Such control, for example, makes it less likely that you will make a costly or unsightly error when fitting house or cabinet doors. This applies especially at the top or bottom of the door where you are shaving end grain on the stiles. The minimum cut, plus the high rpm of the tool's cutters, do such jobs with negligible feathering and with far less chance of splitting.

Actually, you have a choice of how you equip yourself for power planing. The *power plane* is a tool in itself. It owns a built-in motor and removable cutter which might have the spiral configuration shown in Figure 10-3, or a cutterhead with replaceable blades, something like the arrangement found in jointers. The tool works in single-purpose fashion. It's a *planer*.

The *plane attachment* is an accessory for a portable router. When the router is fitted in the accessory and equipped with a special cutter, it becomes a portable electric plane. A major difference between the true plane and the router/plane is that the former will usually have (not always) a top-side motor, whereas the power source for the other hangs outboard. This calls for a little more control to keep the tool level when planing edges. A fact to consider when

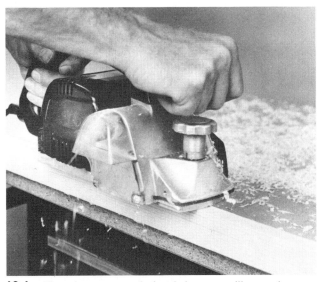

10-1.   If you have ever used a hand plane you will appreciate how a portable power plane lets you do similar chores much faster and with considerably less effort.

10-2.   Block plane is 'palm size' and can be handled with a more delicate touch than is required with heavier versions, but it's no sissy. Cutting width is 1¹³/₁₆″. Spiral-type cutter turns at 21,000 rpm.

making a choice is this: With a power plane, you can do surfacing beyond the tool's maximum width of cut by making repeat, overlapping passes. You can't work that way with an attachment or, for that matter, with a power plane whose design permits working only on edges.

Types, Sizes, Speeds

One feature all the modern planers have in common is speed: most work in the area of 20,000 rpm. It's interesting, and also makes a point, that while there are differences in how wide a tool can cut, the difference in depth of cut between a "large" tool and a "small" one is rarely extreme. The block plane that was shown in Figure 10-2 has a depth-cut of 1/64″, whereas the larger, more powerful tool in Figure 10-4 has a maximum cut-depth of 3/32″.

There are more noticeable differences in width of cut. All the planers can cut across the narrow edge of 2″-thick stock (which actually measures 1½″). Some can plane across the wide edge of a 2x4 (which has a real dimension of 3½″). The average range is about 3″ to 3¼″. If you plan to use a plane a lot for dressing rough lumber and for reducing stock thickness, then width of cut can be an important factor, since a greater cut-width will require fewer passes to get across wide stock. If your work will be mostly on stock and door edges, and it usually is, then the cut-width factor becomes less important.

Some of the tools have adjustable edge-guides as standard equipment, others do not, but can be equipped the same way with optional accessories (Figures 10-5, 10-6). Adjustable edge guides are important since they allow organizing the tool for accurate beveling and chamfering.

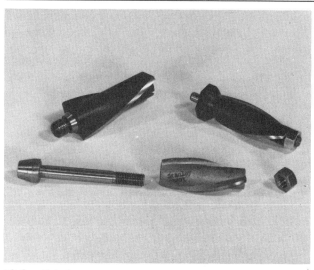

10-3.   Spiral-type cutters are common on many portable electric planes. Some units have jointer-type cutterheads with replaceable knives. It's critical to keep cutting edges keen no matter what the design.

10-5.   This 3″ plane is equipped with reversible, double-edged carbide blades. Combination edge and bevel guide can be adjusted up to 45°. Interesting feature is a V-groove in the footplate which makes it easier to do chamfering jobs.

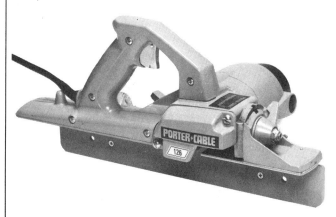

10-4.   "Porta-Plane" is rated at 7 amps and has a cutter speed of 22,000 rpm. It can remove 3/32″ of material in a single pass on stock up to 2 13/32″ wide. All planers have a depth of cut adjustment so you are not confined to a single cut-depth.

10-6.   This 3¼″ product has a maximum depth of cut of 1/64″ but can cut rabbets up to 9/16″ deep. The 3 amp motor drives the cutterhead at 20,000 rpm. Like many other models, the unit is double insulated.

The unit shown in Figure 10-7 can be converted into a benchtop jointer by means of a special stand. Most planers can be used for rabbet cutting, but the maximum depth of cut for such work will vary from tool to tool.

Planing with Power

Be sure to strictly follow the alignment procedures that are outlined in the manual that comes with the tool. The horizontal plane of the rear shoe *must* be tangent to the cutting circle. The fence, when one is used, must be at a right angle to the shoe at the zero setting. If these relationships are not provided for correctly, and maintained, you'll get bevels instead of square cuts, and will probably create gouges in the work edge (Figure 10-8).

The secret to good work is controlled, uniform pressure down on the tool throughout the pass. Use both hands; one on the main handle of the tool, the other up front (Figure 10-9). Start cuts by placing the front shoe on the work and applying downward pressure with the hand that's up front. As the cutter engages, apply downward pressure equally with both hands. This can change toward the end of the cut. You can relieve the left-hand pressure and exert more with the right hand. The idea is to keep the tool on an even keel. It's also a good idea to let up a bit on feed-speed as you near the end of the cut to minimize chipping and feathering that can occur as the cutter leaves the work.

Chipping and feathering will occur to a greater degree when planing across end grain and when working on plywood (Figure 10-10). Two methods you can use to completely eliminate these negative possibilities are shown in Figure 10-11. Clamp a scrap piece to the end of the work so it instead of the work will take the abuse, or do the planing on a piece that is slightly oversize, and then saw its end off. You're more likely to get a lot of splintering at the end of the cut when planing across end grain on lumber, but here too, a scrap block clamped to the work as shown in Figure 10-12 will provide a solution.

10-8.   Gouges in the work can be the result of poor tool handling or misalignment. Some feathering or splintering is usual at the end of a cross-grain cut, but can be eliminated by following particular techniques.

10-9.   Secret to good work is controlled pressure down on the tool throughout the pass. Some tools have a thumb indent up front for a comfortable, non-slip grip.

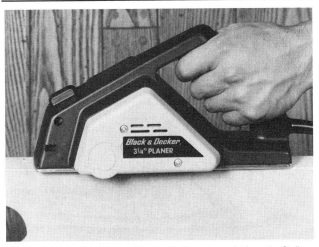

10-7.   Lightweight unit still has a 3¼″ cutting width and a ⁵⁄₁₆″ rabbeting depth. The ⅖ hp motor turns the cutter at 19,000 rpm. It features double-edge throwaway blades that are easy to replace and a stand that converts it into a benchtop 'jointer'.

10-10.   Flaws like this will occur on plywood regardless of whether the planer is moved across or parallel to the grain of the surface veneer. They can be minimized by making extremely light cuts, or eliminated by using one of the methods shown in Figure 10-11.

10-11. To eliminate end-flaws, clamp on a scrap block to take the abuse, or work on an oversize piece so you can trim off the bad end.

10-12. Use the clamped block idea when planing end grain on lumber. The precaution isn't needed when planing with the grain on stock edges.

10-13. Bevels or chamfers are done by adjusting the fence to the angle you need. Be sure to keep the fence snug against the side of the work. Chamfers can be accomplished in one pass, but full bevels require repeat strokes.

You can move the tool faster on material like pine than you can on hardwoods. The idea is to adjust the feed speed in relation to the material so the blades will cut consistently but without overloading the motor. On the other hand, you can't be overcautious. Feeding too slowly can cause premature wear on the cutter and can even cause burn marks on lumber or plywood.

The wise general rule is to take it easy with depth of cut. Results are usually better when you accomplish a cut in two passes, even though the tool has the power and the depth of cut to do the chore in a single pass.

If you are working on an uneven edge—one that is slightly wavy—draw a pencil line from end to end on the stock so you can isolate the high spots. Plane this down first before you make full-length passes.

Bevels and chamfers are not more difficult than square cuts. Adjust the guide fence to the angle you need and proceed in normal fashion. A slight chamfer can be accomplished in one pass, but full bevels require multiple passes (Figure 10-13). Full bevels are wider cuts than square ones so it's usually better to slow up a bit on feed-speed.

Always try to feed the tool so it will cut *with* the grain of the wood. When planing four edges, or two adjacent ones, make the cross-grain cuts first. The final with-the-grain cuts will remove any imperfections that occur at the end of the first passes.

Rabbeting

To form a rabbet, you must organize the planer so that only a limited length of the cutter does the work. Some units incorporate a means of accomplishing this. The unit shown in Figure 10-14 has an L-shaped cut machined in the right side of the front shoe. This cut is held firmly against the side of the

10-14. Rabbets are formed by regulating how far across the board the cutter will extend. This determines the width of the rabbet. Adjustable angle on this tool is set to gauge the depth of the cut.

board while the rabbet is being formed. The rabbeting plate, which is just a metal angle, is secured at a particular height to judge the depth of the rabbet cut. In any case, and since correct procedures can differ from tool to tool, a wise operator follows the instructions that are supplied by the manufacturer.

You can improvise to some extent, but it's something to do only when the tool isn't equipped for the job. One way is shown in Figure 10-15. A block of wood secured to the tool's fence acts as a width-of-cut control as the planer forms the rabbet (Figure 10-16). The width of the wood block determines the working length of the cutter.

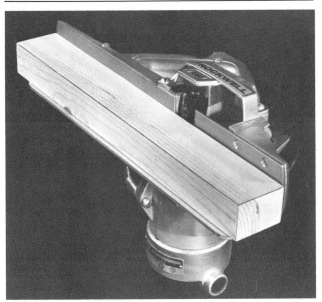

10-15.   Lacking other means, you can do rabbeting by attaching a strip of wood to the tool's fence.

10-16.   The thickness of the wood-strip determines how far across the board the cutter will extend. Keep the strip snug against the side of the work throughout the pass.

Another idea is shown in Figure 10-17. Here, the guide is L-shaped and slotted so it can be moved across the base of the tool. Thus, it is adjustable for rabbets of various widths. It is assumed that the design of the planer will allow this type of guide to be attached securely and without interfering with the tool's mechanism.

Making a Jointer Jig

The jig that is shown in Figure 10-18, and detailed in Figure 10-19, allows a planer to be used somewhat like a stationary jointer. There are too many planers around of different shapes and sizes for one jig to be right for all of them, so a little, or maybe a lot of modification is in order. The jig that was photographed was designed around a Stanley router/plane that's been a friend in my shop for many years. The jig has a block to support the motor and a channel that can be tightened with a C-clamp to secure the plane's handle (Figure 10-20).

A spring-loaded guard lets work pass over the cutter and returns automatically to cover the cutter after the pass is complete—just like a real jointer (Figure 10-21).

Planing Safely

While the openings around cutters are minimal, the cutters are always exposed. So make it a habit to keep your hands topside. Turn the motor off at the end of a cut and allow the cutter to stop turning before you set the tool down. Never touch the cutters for any reason while the tool is plugged in. Always let the motor come to full speed before starting a cut.

Keep the cutters sharp; this contributes to better work and to safety. Most manufacturers offer special sharpening devices. Owning one of these devices, and using it as often as necessary, is a good idea.

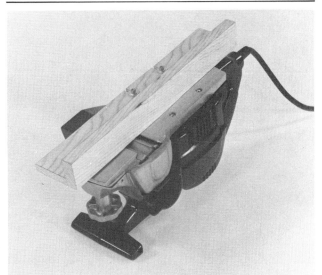

10-17.   Whether you can use an adjustable L-shaped guide like this one will depend on the design of the tool. You must be able to attach the guide securely to the base of the tool. Always check the owner's manual to see if, and how, rabbeting can be accomplished without improvising.

Jointer Jig

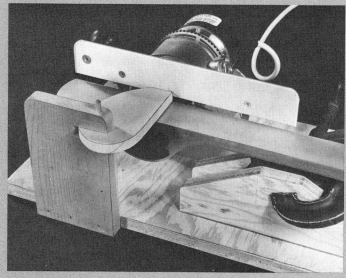

10-20.   The jointer jig is more adaptable to a planer that has an outboard power source. The wood block supports the motor, while the handle of the tool is gripped in the plywood channel.

10-18.   A jointer jig lets you use a portable planer in stationary fashion. This prototype was made for a Stanley router with a planer attachment.

10-21.   Jointing is done as it would be on a stationary machine. Keep the work snug against the fence and firmly down on the planer's base throughout the pass. The spring-loaded guard moves aside during the pass, then returns to cover the cutter when the pass is complete.

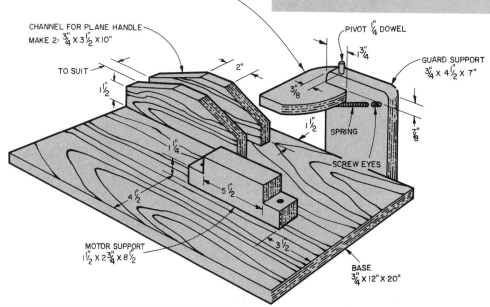

10-19.   Construction details of the jointer jig. It's not likely that the dimensions given here will be exactly right for the tool you own, but the concept is simply to provide a sturdy setting for an inverted planer.

11. Hand Grinders and Flexible Shafts

From woodworker to metalsmith, diemaker to auto mechanic, dentist to podiatrist, the handful of speed and power known as the hand grinder can be a most helpful power tool. Quite often, its real capabilities are not appreciated, probably because its small size creates an image of delicate precision and very light-duty applications. Paradoxically, these qualities in themselves are enough justification for rating the hand grinder as an important shop tool. A touch with a hand grinder will often add a customized look to an otherwise routinely finished project. It can take over where other tools leave off, and it can get into places where other tools can't reach.

Like the router, the hand grinder is essentially an encased motor driving a spindle that has a device at its free end for gripping the shaft of various grinding, shaping, sanding, polishing, and sawing tools (Figure 11-1). It's often called a "hobby" tool, but this is misleading. For one thing, those that are available today are much improved in terms of power and durability. For another, there are a wide range of designs available. Not all hand grinders are "palm" size; those that are recommended for use by automobile mechanics, for tool and die shops, as tool post grinders, and so on, are comparatively husky fellows. Weights of small ones might be listed in ounces, while the big ones are called out in pounds.

A clue to the tool's power might be found in the size of shanks its chuck can grip, and even in the design of the chuck. A tool that is designed to grip cutters with a 1/8″ shank doesn't need the same power that is required of another tool that can run cutters with 1/4″ shanks (Figures 11-2 and 11-3).

In application, the tools should be visualized as high-speed power sources that will drive an endless assortment of abrasive wheels, brushes, buffs, sanding drums, drill bits, saws, and discs. They can be used for machining jobs on most any material, and also drill, cut, smooth, and polish. You can use these tools to shape or sand wood or metal, and they can also be used on plastics, and to mark steel or glass. Often they enter the area of sharpening, engraving, and routing. You can drill holes with them that would be difficult to do with a conventional drill. Therefore, the term "grinder" does not fully describe the tool. What you can accomplish with one depends pretty much on what you lock in the chuck.

You will find that most of the heavy-duty tools are called "die grinders". This doesn't mean that they can't be used with

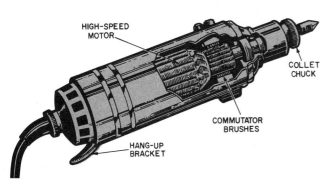

11-1.   The hand grinder has a simple concept—a motor drives a spindle which has a gripping device at its free end to secure various types of cutting and abrading tools.

HIGH-SPEED MOTOR

COLLET CHUCK

COMMUTATOR BRUSHES

HANG-UP BRACKET

11-2.   Power, speed, and chuck designs can differ from tool to tool. This unit has a conventional 3-jaw chuck which is tightened with a key to secure cutters. Speed is 18,000 rpm; chuck capacity is 1/4″.

11-3.　Many high-speed grinders employ a collet-style chuck to grip tool shanks. A wrench is used to turn a nut that squeezes the collet about the shank of the tool. This tool has variable speeds of 5,000 to 28,000 rpm. Note the combination router base and edge guide.

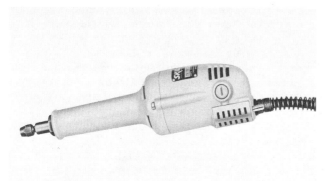

11-4.　Heavy-duty tools like this one are often called "die grinders". Speeds on various models can range from 4,500 to 20,000 rpm. Some can develop as much as 2 hp, yet they can weigh under 3 lbs.

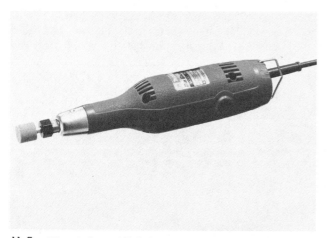

11-5.　Die grinders, while being powerful enough to do what they must, can be deceptively slim. This example has a 2 amp rating, a 25,000 rpm speed, and a standard collet size of ¼". It can also be used with an optional ⅛" collet.

small-shank cutters. Those shown in Figures 11-4 and 11-5 will work with either a ¼" or ⅛" collet chuck. Often various size chucks are supplied with the tool, and chucks other than the standard ones are available as accessories.

Speeds

The one feature that most hand grinders have in common is high speed. Speeds of 20,000, 25,000, or even 30,000 rpm are not rare. This points out an important fact as far as tool-use is concerned. Speed does the job, not feed pressure. This is the reverse of electric drill use, tools with comparatively low speeds but with high torque. For example, feed pressure is required if a drill bit, for example, is to form a hole. Generally, hand grinders are high speed, low torque tools. It's a rare situation when you must apply any kind of pressure to get a job done. High speed, plus the cutter mounted in the chuck, does the job.

While high speed is generally the rule with hand grinder operations, some new models are designed to provide various speeds, or have an infinitely variable speed control. This is usually a small, numbered dial; each number indicating, approximately, a particular speed. With some models, you can add an external speed control like the benchtop unit shown in Figure 11-6. Other types of speed controls can be operated with a convenient foot switch.

Operations you might want to do at lower speeds include polishing, using wire brushes, or maybe even drum sanding.

Cutting Tools

The word "cutters" is used in a general sense to encompass all items that can be locked in the chuck of the tool (Figure 11-7). Generally, any cutter that has a shank that is larger than ⅛" is meant for bigger, heavier grinders. When making choices there really is no problem though, since the maximum size of the collet, or collets, that can be used with a tool determines maximum shank-size on cutters.

Cutters are either mounted or unmounted. The mounted ones have the cutter permanently attached to the shaft or they are one-piece units. When the cutter is worn, the unit is discarded. Incidentally, dentists use similar tools in their high speed "machines" but accept minimum use, hopefully, in order to save you discomfort. These partially used cutters are not so dull that they can't be used on wood and metal in a home shop. So, you might ask your friendly dentist to pass over his discards. If what he gives you won't cut wood, change to another dentist!

Unmounted cutters are locked on a special fixture that is called a *mandrel*. This is a shaft with a device at one end for gripping the cutter. The lock-on arrangement may be a small nut and bolt, a straight or tapered length of screw thread, or a flathead screw that is turned into a threaded hole in the end of the shaft. Typical accessories that are designed for mounting on a mandrel are felt wheels for polishing, small buffs, rubber polishers, and small, steel saws.

In most cases, brushes are permanently mounted and are available in various sizes and materials. Steel wire, brass wire, nylon, and bristle are very common. Soft brushes are

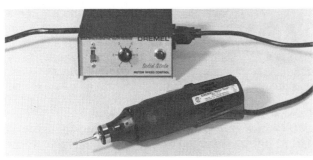

11-6.   Hand grinders may have a single speed, variable speed with a built-in control, or speeds that can be controlled with a unit placed between the power source and the tool. Controls, like this one, may be benchtop units, or they may be operated with a foot switch.

CUTTERS FOR CARVING, ROUTING, MILLING, ENGRAVING

STEEL AND BRISTLE BRUSHES

GRINDING WHEELS FOR SHAPING AND SHARPENING

SANDING, POLISHING, AND SAW DISKS

DRUM SANDER   MINIATURE DRILL BITS

11-7.   Typical categories of cutters that can be used in a hand grinder pretty much tell the story of the variety of jobs the tool can be used for.

used for cleaning operations on soft materials, while hard ones do similar operations on denser materials. Hard brushes can also be used to produce a decorative brushed effect on soft metal surfaces. Mild abrasive compounds like rottenstone, very fine emery powder, or even ordinary household scouring powders can be used with the brushes.

Steel saws can be used to cut wood, some soft metals, and plastics. Hard abrasive discs (sometimes called saws) are good for cutting or slotting nonferrous and ferrous metals and for many operations that are required on stones used in lapidary work.

Drum sanders are miniatures of those used in a drill press or with a portable drill. The diameter of a rubber drum is increased or decreased by means of a screw so that abrasive sleeves can be mounted or replaced. Hard, mounted abrasive wheels are available in an endless variety of sizes, shapes, grades, and grains.

As you can tell from the types of cutters available for hand grinders, dust and thrown off waste are part-and-parcel of most operations. So, safety goggles and a dust mask should be a standard uniform.

Most grinders use a collet to grip the shank of the cutting tool, and it's important to use the correct one. If you don't the cutter will not be as secure as it must be. The owner's manual that comes with the tool will tell the range of shank sizes a particular collet will grip. For example, a ⅛″ collet will grip shank sizes from ³⁄₃₂″ up to ⅛″; a ¹⁄₁₆″ collet will take shanks from ¹⁄₆₄″ to ¹⁄₁₆″. There are also adapter chucks that are used with the standard collet for gripping very tiny (#60—#80) drill bits.

Make a Storage Chest

The hand grinder, or a machine that is specifically designed to drive a flexible shaft, can be considered a small workshop in itself. Because the numerous cutting tools and other accessories that go along with a grinder are usually small, easy to damage, or lose it pays to make a special case to house the equipment.

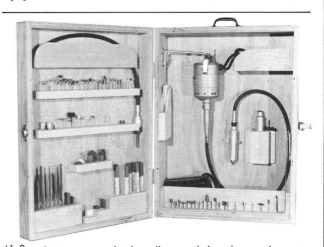

11-8.   A storage case that is easily moved about is a good way to house and protect a hand grinder "workshop". This one is arranged for a motor/flex shaft combination but its interior can be modified to suit your own equipment.

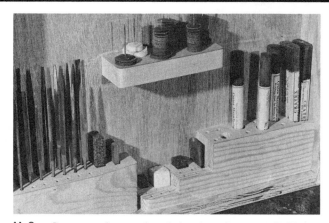

11-9.   Cutters can be stored on shelves in various ways. Drill holes for shafted tools; use blunted nails for wheels that have center holes. Note the provisions made for needle files and abrasive sticks.

The case shown in Figure 11-8 was designed for a flex-shaft tool, but its interior can be easily organized to accommodate just a hand grinder or both types of tools. The important thing is to lay out all the equipment you have and to design the case specifically for each piece, to leave room for items you'll probably add. Making the case as a closed box and then slicing off the lid on a table saw or with a handsaw is a good way to assure an accurate fit.

Note in Figure 11-9 that the cutters are stored on shelves that are drilled to receive the tool shanks. This system works very well for mounted cutters. For unmounted units, drive slim nails up through the bottom of the shelves. Be sure to dull the points on the nails.

The overall size of the case (Figure 11-10) is 7½" x 17½" x 22½". These dimensions can be increased a few inches without making the case unwieldy. Install a handle at the top and a latch to keep it closed; then you can tote it about for any work you must do outside the shop.

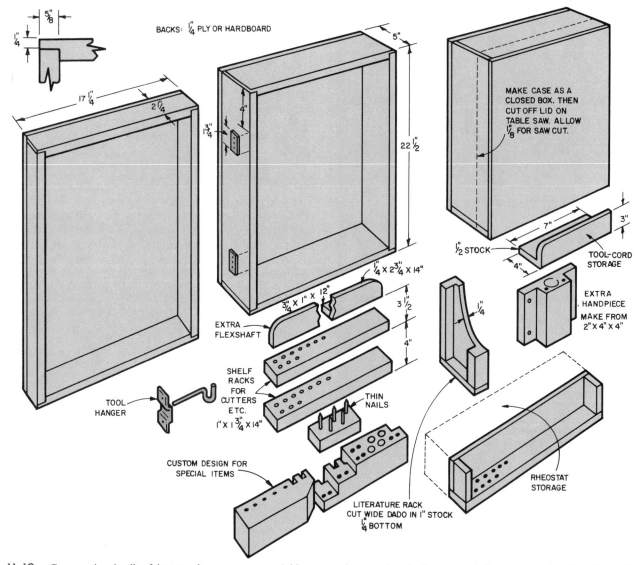

11-10.   Construction details of the tote-about storage case. Add a screen-door type handle for transportation, and a latch to keep it closed.

The Hand Grinder at Work

Always rely on the speed of the tool to do the work. A tool that is running at 24,000 rpm and is driving a cutter that has sixteen cutting edges, is actually making 384,000 cuts every minute. That kind of cutting speed requires only the slightest feed pressure; just enough to keep the cutter in contact with the work. Folks who aren't familiar with hand grinders will often apply enough feed pressure to stall the tool or to seriously reduce its speed. Then feed pressure is reduced to allow the rpm to build up again and, unfortunately, the procedure is repeated. This is bad practice. It doesn't improve the quality of the work, and it can do considerable harm to the tool.

If the tool gets hot, or if there is excessive decrease in speed, it's almost certain that you are forcing the cut; allowing flutes to become clogged and preventing cutting edges from working as they should. Choose the right style of cutter and the right cutter shape for the job you must do, then use a touch that is just enough pressure to keep the cutter working. This practice leads to maximum tool efficiency, and respectable work quality.

Work that is large enough to stay put on its own, or that can be gripped securely in one hand while the other hand manipulates the tool, can be worked on in a freehand manner. Establish one important rule—don't position a hand that is holding the work so that it is in line with the cutter. Then, if the cutter slips from where it should be, it won't cut more than the work.

It's best to grip small work in a vise or to clamp it to a bench top. A handscrew clamp, with cardboard or some similar protective layer used when necessary between the work and the clamp jaws, makes a good "vise" for holding workpieces.

Most of the time, the hand grinder is gripped in one hand, but there is no law to prevent you from using two hands when the operation makes it advisable. Often, it's possible to work more precisely if you grip at the shaft end of the tool with the fingers of one hand and "palm" the other end of the tool in your other hand.

Cutters are so small and take such tiny bites that it's possible to move against the grain without dire results. Even so, to minimize the sanding chores that might still have to be done, make final strokes *with* the grain of the wood.

Particular cutters are often used to leave a textured surface on projects, especially in-the-round or bas-relief carvings. Finishing such work with a fine, soft brush, will remove sharp ridges and clean away tenacious waste particles. A hard brush, steel or brass, will remove soft wood from between hard grain areas on certain woods and create a sculptured effect.

Tool Holders

Because of the variety of accessory holders that are available commercially, and others that you can make, the grinder does not have to be limited to hand-held use. For example, a swivel-type base to which the grinder can be attached allows positioning the tool in an attitude that is most convenient for the work being done (Figure 11-11).

Some stands allow the grinder to be used in combination with other tools. Team it with a lathe or a drill press, for instance, and it functions as a precision milling, grinding, or routing accessory that can do many jobs normally possible only with larger, more costly machines.

There are stands, including the drill-press version shown in Figure 11-12, that allow a hand grinder to be used like a stationary tool. It may be held vertically, horizontally, tipped at an angle, or even inverted for use as a miniature shaper. With the tool in a rigid position, you can apply the work to the cutter as you would with any stationary tool, and this often guarantees precision that is difficult to duplicate when working freehand. It isn't difficult to create a stand for a hand grinder when a particular one isn't available as an accessory for the tool you own.

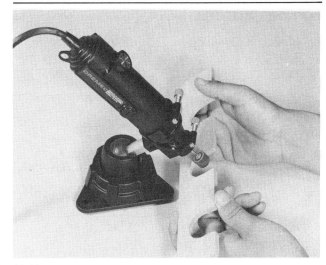

11-11.   There are many types of tool holders available for hand grinders. This swivel-type base provides a lot of flexibility.

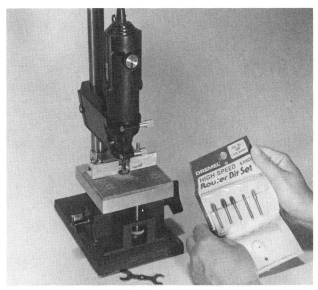

11-12.   Accessories like this one let the grinder be used as a miniature drill press. The table on the drill-press accessory is used for routing operations.

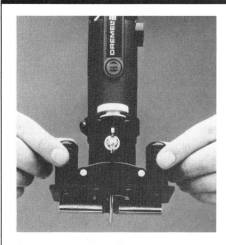

11-13. Special base holds the grinder in vertical position so you can use it for freehand or controlled routing. An adjustable fence is part of this particular unit.

Hand-Grinder Routing

The small hand grinder is not about to rival the big jobs that can be done with a regular portable router, but on a small-job basis it can match a big fellow almost function for function. In fact, for many techniques, particularly in light-cut applications such as inlay or marquetry work, the palm-size tool can be more convenient to use while still doing an exemplary job.

For some hand grinders, especially the Dremel "Moto-Tool", accessories are available that are specially designed so the tool can function as a miniature router-shaper that will do some surprising things in a woodworking shop. The accessories are light and neat, easy to attach and handle, and are used pretty much like conventional router bases. Adjustments are provided for depth of cut, and the accessory may include an edge guide (Figure 11-13).

Routing with the Hand Grinder

11-14. With the grinder mounted in the router base, and the fence (edge guide) attached, the tool can be used for accurate parallel-to-edge cuts.

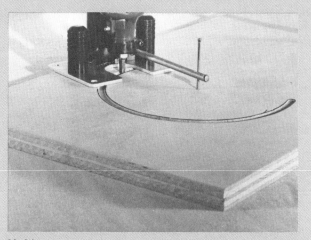

11-16. A single rod, with a hole through it for a pivot pin, guides the grinder through accurate circular cuts. Accomplish deep cuts by making repeat passes. A slow feed is the answer to quality results.

11-15. The same setup can be used for cuts in stock edges. Always move the router so the cutter moves into the work. This is usually from left to right.

11-17. With just the base, the grinder can be used for free-hand routing. Keep a firm grip since cutting will be done in various directions.

With the grinder mounted in the special base/edge guide combination, you can make straight cuts parallel to an edge like those shown in Figures 11-14 and 11-15. Maximum distance between the fence and the cutter isn't startling, but when it proves limiting you can substitute longer rods for those that are supplied, or you can remove the edge guide and work with a tack-nailed or clamped guide strip as you would with a conventional router.

If you use just one rod, an extra-long one if necessary, you can guide the grinder through perfect circular cuts, again, just as you would with a larger router (Figure 11-16). Work with just the base and you have good control for chores like bas-relief carving (figure 11-17).

The palm-size tool does have limitations. Don't expect to form full-size bead-and-cove or drop-leaf table edges on 1″ stock. Much can be done beyond the full profile shape of the cutter itself, by making repeat passes to deepen or widen cuts, or by using different cutters on the same edge to create an original profile. Some practical applications for the tool when it is fitted with a router base include mortising for hinges and strike plates, raising or incising letters or numbers, inletting for escutcheons, and so on.

How fast you can move the tool and how deep you can cut in a single pass depends on the hardness of the material. In any case, feed must never be so fast or so hard that the tool tends to stall, or that the tool or the cutter get too hot.

As a Shaper

The basic difference between the hand grinder as a router and its use as a shaper, is that in the latter mode the tool is inverted and attached to the underside of a work-support table with flathead screws that thread into holes in the router-base attachment (Figure 11-18). Projects like this can be complicated or as simple as the one shown, but they must be sturdy. Glue blocks, which can't be seen in the photograph and which are not shown in the drawing (Figure 11-19), will reinforce the connection between the top of the project and its legs.

When the grinder is used upside down, its rotation, in a sense, is reversed. Always feed the stock *against* the cutter's direction of rotation. Depth-of-cut, which should never be extreme, is adjusted as it would be normally. Take it easy with feed-speed. As always, don't force the cut. It's bad practice to push hard enough for the tool to slow up excessively.

Other ideas for stands or tables you can make for a hand grinder are illustrated in Figure 11-20 and 11-21.

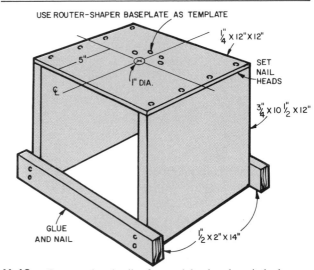

11-19. Construction details of a stand that lets the grinder be used as a shaper. Add glue blocks to reinforce the connection between the work surface and the legs.

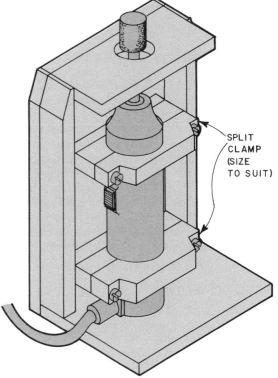

11-20. A stand like this can be made to hold a grinder in a vertical position.

11-18. An easy-to-make stand converts the grinder into a shaper. A strip of wood with a true edge is used as a fence. Always move the work *against* the cutters' direction of rotation.

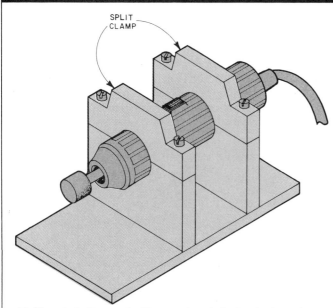

11-21.   A similar stand will secure the grinder in a horizontal position. Keep the stands secure by clamping them to a solid surface.

Make a Swivel Jig

The unusual fixture that is detailed in Figure 11-22 allows the grinder to be rotated or swung in an arc so it can be used to form decorative cuts like the samples shown in Figure 11-23. The jig is designed so it can be secured to projects that are already assembled, or to components prior to assembly. Take your time when making it; it does require careful work to avoid extra play in either of the actions. The hole in the stand, with a shoulder for the indexer to rest on, can be formed accurately on a drill press, or by using a template-guided router. The indexer plate can be formed in similar fashion. Be sure its outside diameter fits precisely in the hole that is in the stand. Actually, it's best to cut the indexer a bit oversize and then sand it for a perfect fit: it should turn, but without wobble. The swivel collar pivots on pins that pass through the indexing plate (Figure 11-24). Its dimensions, as given in the construction drawing, even its shape, must be checked against the hand grinder you plan to use. Shaping it is a fairly straightforward lathe job, but it also may be made by boring the center hole and then using a coping saw, followed by sanding, to shape its perimeter. Note that two versions of the collar are suggested. One has to be a tight fit for the grinder; the other, which is slotted so it will work something like a split clamp, is tightened with a hose clamp.

Freehand Work

Much work with a hand grinder is done without an attachment or special gadget to guide the tool. Here, more than ever, a wise choice of cutter and a light touch are critical. Keep a firm grip on the tool to keep the cutter working where you want it to. If you are too casual, the cutter will try to move like a wheel. Some typical freehand applications are demonstrated in Figures 11-25 through 11-29.

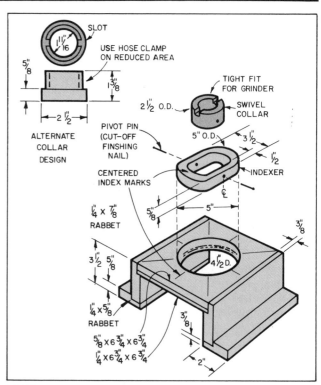

11-22.   How to make a swivel jig. Careful construction is necessary for the unit to work accurately.

11-23.   A sampling of cuts that were made by using a hand grinder in a swivel jig.

11-24.   The swivel jig allows the grinder to be rotated or swung in an arc. Use repeat passes when you want deep cuts. The jig can be used on components or on projects that are already assembled.

Typical Freehand Applications

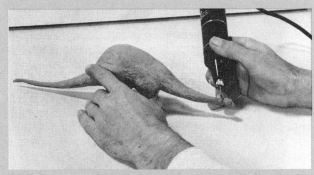

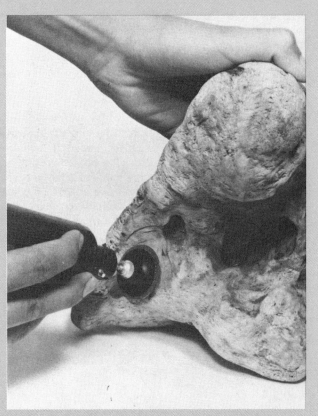

11-25.   A light touch and wise cutter selection leads to quality work when carving. Keep a firm grip but allow the cutter to work at its own pace.

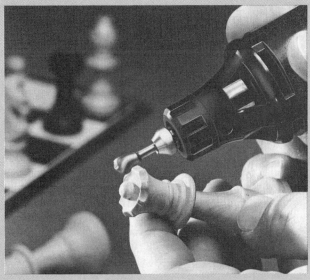

11-26.   Often, the shape of the cutter is enough to produce the form you need. Be careful when hand-holding pieces that you don't inadvertently advance to a finger.

11-28.   The grinder can be used with very small brushes and abrading units so it is easy to get into crevices and tight corners. A lot of driftwood sculpture is smoothed or textured with a hand grinder.

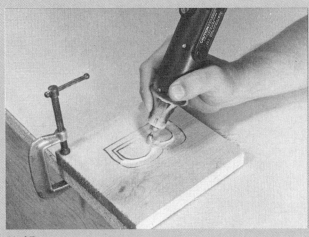

11-27.   It's a good idea to keep small workpieces clamped whenever possible. A light touch doesn't mean that you don't have to grip the tool firmly. If you are too cautious, the cutter will try to move like a wheel.

11-29.   The hand grinder will not replace the portable drill but it can be used to drill small holes. Some hand grinders will take an auxiliary chuck that can grip bits as small as #80.

As a Sharpener

Most any tool in the shop or in the house can be ground or honed with a hand grinder so long as the grinder is fitted with the correct abrasive. Aluminum oxide wheel points are available in many shapes and sizes so it's not difficult to choose one that is right for a particular job. Mostly, the grinder serves best as a touch up tool or as a honer. Removing a lot of metal, necessary when forming a new edge, is best done on a bench grinder.

Many times, the success of a sharpening job depends entirely on the choice of grinding point or wheel. For example, a point with the correct shape will quickly clean out the gullets on a circular saw blade, or redo the teeth of a chain saw. Accessories that guide you through a perfect job when renewing or sharpening the cutting teeth of a chain saw are available (Figures 11-30 and 11-31).

11-30.   Dremel offers a "Chainsaver" chain saw sharpening kit that does such work with speed and precision.

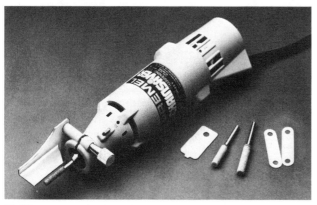

11-31.   The chain saw sharpening kit includes aluminum oxide grinding wheels, spacers, and guides so you can organize to sharpen various types of chain.

Aluminum oxide wheel points will wear and can change shape when they have been used for a while. It's a good idea to touch the turning wheel to a "dressing stone" occasionally to return it to original form. This treatment will also remove grit that tends to clog the pores of abrasive wheels.

Tips on Plastics

Plastics are either *thermosetting* or *thermoplastic*. "Bakelite", "Marblette", and "Plaskon" are trade names of the former type. "Lucite", "Plexiglas", and "Acrylite" are trade names of the latter type. Once the first type has set, it will not become pliable again. The second type becomes pliable when a correct amount of heat is applied.

Thermoplastics will soften if you generate enough heat with the cutter. The gummy result can quickly clog the tool and even cause a drill bit to be cemented in the hole you are trying to drill. The answer is to work with light touches and frequent retractions of drill or cutter to minimize heat build-up. When possible, use coarser fluted cutters than you would use on wood or metal. Check the cutter frequently for signs of gumming and when it occurs stop working long enough for things to cool down. Clean the cutters with a small, stiff brush. Often, plastic chips that have cooled on the cutter can be flicked off with a splinter of wood.

Flexible Shafts

A flexible shaft is a pliant extension between a power source and the cutter, or whatever you are working with. The power source can be a drill press, a motor, a type of hand grinder, a special power unit designed for the purpose (Figure 11-32), or even a portable electric drill (Figure 11-33). With a flexible shaft, assuming that its free end is equipped with a suitable chuck, you can grip any cutter that is operable in a hand grinder, and work as if your fingers were a drill chuck powered by a motor in your shoulder. That is not too unrealistic a picture of what a flexible shaft setup is. The torque and the rpm of whatever power source you choose nestle in the palm of your hand, and the dexterity in your fingers, wrist, and elbow directs the power exactly to where you wish to apply it.

11-32.   Foredom power unit is designed especially to drive flexible shafts. Advantage of a motor-and-shaft combination is that they are tuned to work together for maximum efficiency.

When applicable, a flex shaft allows you to work without the limitations imposed by the rigidity of a solid, straight-line shaft, like when using cutters in a portable drill, a drill press, or even a hand grinder.

A flex shaft can be used with the delicate touch of a surgeon or the muscle of a steel worker. It's not the talents of these people we're talking about, but the fact that they must work with different equipment. To be delicate or tough, efficiently, you must make a wise choice of power source and shaft. The two go together—many high-hp power tools will provide a lot more torque than slim flexible shafts are designed to take.

The Right Core Size

Jobs requiring delicate precision are accomplished more with speed than with power. On the other hand, chores like heavy sanding, weld-grinding, and so on depend more on torque than on high speed. Most of the time, you can judge the type of work a flex shaft can be used for by the size, even the shape, of the end on which chucks are mounted (Figure 11-34). If it can take a heavy, 3-jaw chuck or an arbor on which large buffs, wire brushes, grinding wheels, and the like can be mounted it's certain to be a heavy-duty tool (Figures 11-35 and 11-36). Most of the time, light-duty shafts will have collet-type chucks, but there are exceptions (Figures 11-37 and 11-38).

Overall, small-core shafts are made for high speed (as much as 35,000 rpm) and a light touch; large-core units are designed for jobs that require heavy pressure.

The core size is the diameter of the shaft itself, not its casing. However, it's reasonable to assume that the larger the casing, the larger the core.

A large core can be as much as 5/16″, or up to 1/2″ in diameter. Small-core units can start at diameters as small as 1/16″. A 3/16″ core is probably the maximum size for chores that require extreme flexibility and control more than power. A 1/4″ or 5/16″ core is fine for general, light-duty applications in areas of polishing, buffing, and grinding. For heavy sanding, heavy grinding, and such, a core that is at least 3/8″ in diameter is not out of line.

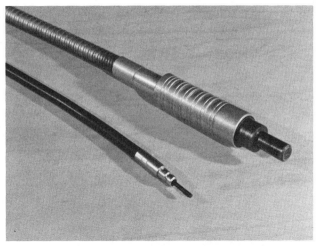

11-34.   The tool-holding end of a flex shaft, in addition to its core size, can indicate what it was designed to do. Generally, slim shafts are for high speed and a light touch, whereas others, like the one on the right, will hold up under a lot of power and heavy feed pressure.

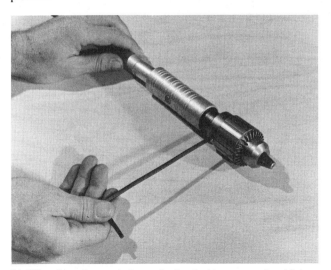

11-35.   Some heavy shafts can be fitted with a conventional 3-jaw chuck that can grip tools with 1/2″ shanks.

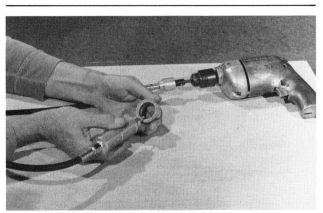

11-33.   You can operate a flex shaft with a portable drill but the disadvantages might be—speeds that are too low, and torque that is too high.

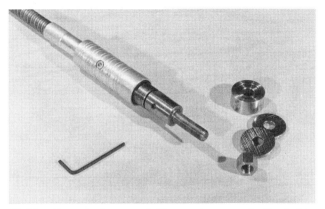

11-36.   Some shafts are made like an arbor, or can be fitted with one, so that accessories like grinding wheels and large wire brushes can be placed between washers and secured with a nut.

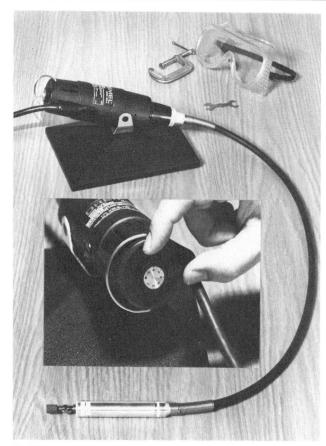

11-37.   Dremel's new "Moto-Flex" tool uses collets to grip cutting tools. It comes with a ⅛″ collet, but ¹⁄₃₂″, ¹⁄₁₆″, and ³⁄₃₂″ sizes are available as accessories. The tool has a built-in variable speed control with a range of 7,500 to 25,000 rpm.

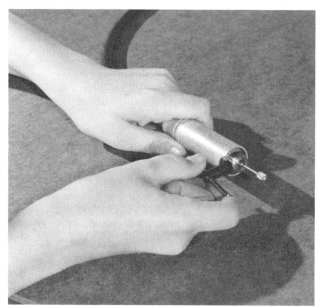

11-38.   Key-type chuck handpieces are available for some units—this one, for the Foredom line of flex shafts. An adjustable chuck can be more flexible since it can grip any shank size up to its maximum capacity.

All flex shafts are composed of a core, which turns, and a casing, which doesn't. The casing may be a hose-like affair, or a spirally wound steel tube that resembles the type of armored cable often used in electrical work. In quality units, the core, regardless of whether it is large or small, is made of spirally wound, directionally alternating layers of steel wire. The "pitch" of the final layer of wire determines in which direction the shaft should turn.

The most common pitch allows the use of common motors and shop tools as power sources. But since shaft cores are sometimes made with unusual pitches, this feature should be checked before the shaft is used.

The Rotation Rule

Literature that comes with the tool, and , usually, an arrow on the casing, will tell you the shaft's correct direction of rotation. Failure to comply can result in unwinding the core wires, especially under heavy-torque conditions. It's possible to ignore the rule, but to do it safely requires a technical decision that must be based on loading the unit to no more than half its power rating. This type of information may not be available to you and, even if it were, the limits would be difficult to establish in a home shop. Therefore, adhere to the one-direction-of-rotation rule.

Shaft Ends

The coupling end of larger units is usually designed for locking directly to a motor shaft, but the size of the coupling is not always a good indication of the power requirements. For example, a 72″ x ½″ core shaft may fit ½″ or ⅝″ motor shafts and be rated for 1 hp. A 50″ x ⅜″ core shaft may fit the same motor shafts but may have a capacity rating of only ½ hp. These particular specifications are used as examples because both shafts were purchased from the same store. A full load from the more powerful motor applied to the smaller shaft, even though it fits on the motor spindle, can cause problems. The point is—always be sure to check the capacity of the shaft in terms of the horsepower it can handle.

In Use

One of the major rules is not to overload. This is especially important when driving a slim shaft with drill-press, or lathe, or even portable drill power. The available torque may be far beyond the capacity of the shaft. In other words, let the shaft decide the capacity, not the power source.

The tool-mounting end of many large shafts is a straight, threaded spindle fitted with flanges and a lock nut. This spindle design allows mounting of any accessory that has a center hole of suitable size. It's also possible to use conventional chucks that screw onto the threaded spindle so you can mount shafted tools like drill bits, drum sanders, and the like.

Use special care when driving grinding wheels, wire brushes, and similar tools; protect yourself by adding accessory wheel guards. These safety devices cover most of the wheel and some have a handle that lets you grip more firmly. An auxiliary handle is a good idea on all jobs that are done with a heavy-duty shaft (Figure 11-39). Safety goggles, of course, are always a must.

The maximum size of wheels that can be used on a shaft will be listed in the literature that is supplied with the tool. Some ½″ shafts can be used with 6″ wheels, but I think it's better to stay with 4″ wheels on any of the big shafts. When you work with small shafts, say a ⅛″ core, the maximum wheel diameter should be about 1″. Acceptable speeds are determined by efficiency and safety. A safe speed for a 6″ wheel might range from 4,000 to 4,500 rpm, but this is not something you must determine for yourself. Maximum rpms are printed on the flanges of wheels. You need only to read them and obey them.

Very Small Shafts

Slim shafts can be individual units that you operate with various power sources, or they might be sophisticated motor/shaft combinations like the one shown in Figure 11-40. Some units have built-in variable speed controls, which can be handy even though the majority of work done with a slim shaft requires high speed.

When the tool itself is not equipped to provide different speeds, check to see if the manufacturer offers an auxiliary unit—a hand-, or foot-controlled rheostat—that is used between power source and tool to control speed. When high speed and a light touch are required for the job, you may be disappointed if you are powering an individual shaft with a drill press or similar power source—the speed won't be there. It will *always* be available on the coordinated motor/shaft combinations. Some workers make do with a motor salvaged from an old sewing machine or some other high-speed universal motor.

A possible solution when you want more speed than a power source can provide, is to get a special handpiece with a planetary drive which automatically increases the speed at the handpiece to two and one half times the input speed. Thus, for example, if you are driving a shaft 5,000 rpm, you'll get 12,500 rpm at the handpiece. The Foredom unit shown in Figure 11-41 can run as high as 35,000 rpm and can be equipped with collets to take shafts with ¹⁄₁₆″ to ¼″ diameters.

What to Buy

Your interests should, of course, influence your choice of equipment. For example, if your major interests involve work like welding, cleaning, and patching dents in automobiles, applying a satin finish to metals or a sculptured texture to large wood panels, then a heavy-duty shaft, organized with its own motor, is the best way to go. Many such units are available mounted on a roll-around pedestal which makes them more convenient to use. The illustrations in Figures 11-42 to 11-45 show how you can make one.

If most of your work will be in areas like carving in various materials, engraving, glass etching, gunsmithing, model building, jewelry making or polishing, and so on, then a slim shaft or, preferably, a motor/shaft combination is a good choice.

The cutters, wheels, special chucks, and drill bits shown in Figure 11-46 represent what can be done with a slim, flexible shaft.

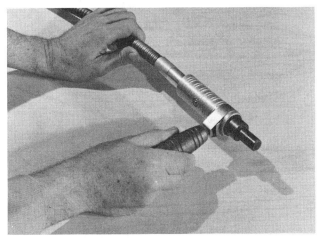

11-39.   If a heavy-duty flex shaft does not have an integral auxiliary handle, check to see if one is available as an accessory. The extra grip helps you do better work and adds a safety factor.

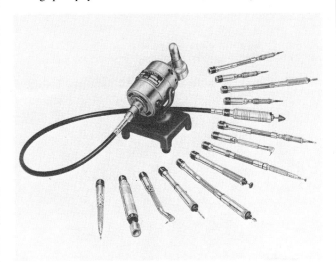

11-40.   The Foredom power-source-flex shaft combination is a super tool that can be used with any of the handpieces shown here. Some of the handpieces themselves have flexible sections.

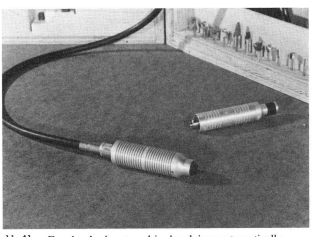

11-41.   Foredom's planetary drive handpiece automatically increases the source speed by 2½ times. The unit can run as high as 35,000 rpm and will take shaft sizes from ¹⁄₁₆″ to ¼″.

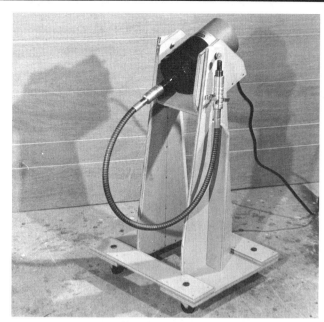

11-42.   Roll-about pedestal that you can make for heavy-duty motor/shaft combinations is always ready to work, anywhere.

11-43.   The motor I use with this setup has its own variable speed control. The pedestal adds convenience to many operations since it eliminates motor-placement problems.

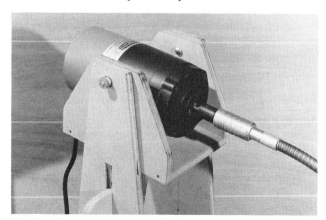

11-44.   The motor, with a conventional motor-mount base, is secured in a cradle that swivels on bolts that pass through the project's vertical components. The swivel action can be stopped by securing the nuts on the bolts.

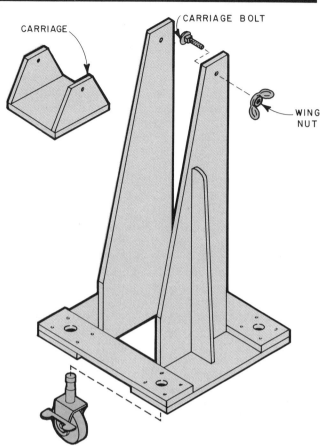

11-45.   Construction details of the roll-around pedestal. Use heavy-duty casters, preferably those that have a locking lever.

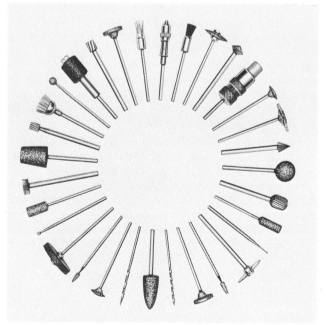

11-46.   A slim flexible shaft can be used with all these accessories, and more. Special chucks available for some units let you mount cutters with shanks that are too small to be gripped by a standard collet or chuck.

12. Some Other Interesting Tools

There are more power tools, stationary as well as portable, "than meet the eye". Beyond the assortment that is considered basic for most shops, there are tools that are used infrequently. This is a general statement and will be opposed by those who use a particular tool which they consider a necessity. It certainly doesn't apply to the electric screwdriver or electric stapling gun, tools whose current popularity is justified.

All tools should be considered in the light of your personal needs, and this applies to fundamental equipment as well as borderline tools. The person who is distraught when not playing golf, but might have use for a portable saw once or twice a year, might be better off renting instead of buying one.

The following illustrations show some tools that were not covered in previous chapters, but which are practical and can be considered as permanent acquisitions, or tools to rent when needed.

Electric Screwdrivers

Electric screwdrivers (Figures 12-1 and 12-2) are essentially a low-speed, high-torque tool. They are available in cordless models, which makes them convenient to use anywhere, or as conventional plug-in units. All can be used with slotted or Phillips type bits, and are reversible so screws can be removed as well as driven. Some are more powerful, and the clue is what can be gripped in the chuck. A tool with a $\frac{3}{8}''$ chuck has to have more horsepower than one with a $\frac{1}{4}''$ chuck.

A built-in clutch is a good feature since it causes the driver to slip once the screw is "home". This prevents damage to the screw or work surface since the bit will not slip off the screwhead. The clutches on some units can be set to provide the correct torque for the fastener being used. Check to see if accessories that can be used to drive or remove nuts and bolts, as well as screws, are available.

12-1.   Cordless screwdriver is neat and easy to use. Low-speed, high-torque tool reverses so it can remove screws as well as drive them.

12-2.   Electric screwdrivers are made with various shapes. This one resembles a pistol-grip type electric drill. They are also available as conventional plug-in units.

Electric Handsaw

The "Wellsaw" (Figure 12-3) looks something like a hand-saw, but it cuts with power. Sawing occurs both coming and going and moves at 8,000 cutting-strokes per minute. The tool can be equipped with 8" or 16" blades and there are enough blade designs so working on various materials is not a problem.

The tool is very popular with home builders and remodelers since it can saw heavy or light materials, even through walls. Landscapers use it for pruning and, as examples of its versatility, it's used by butchers, farmers, paper manufacturers, crate builders, and others.

It is not a difficult tool to use and has built-in safety features like a blade that stops in less than 1½ seconds, and a blower that clears chips from the work line.

Portable Bandsaw

This is not a tool you will find in every home workshop but it is a type you will find in rental shops. The portable, metal cutting bandsaw (Figure 12-4) is appreciated by folks who are planning for a house foundation and have a lot of reinforcement bars to cut, and others who are usually or temporarily involved in working with bar stock, angle iron, pipe, and so on. These tools have plenty of power for heavy metal cutting and often offer a choice of speeds (in feet per minute) so an efficient one can be selected for the job at hand. The tools are limited in cut-off length, but it's what they can get through that counts. Capacities can be 3¼" to 3¾" in round stock, and 3¼" by better than 4" in rectangular material.

The tool has everything needed for efficient operation—planetary gearing system for power directly to the endless blade, adjustable blade guides and tensioning knob, and an assortment of available blades. An accessory is a stand/vise combination so the unit can be used in stationary fashion.

Slim-Belt Sander/Grinder

Black & Decker calls the product shown in Figures 12-5 and 12-6 the "Powerfile". It is a unique tool in that it can drive

12-4.   Portable bandsaw is a metal-cutting tool that gets quickly through round or rectangular stock. Saw blade is a loop, just like those on stationary tools.

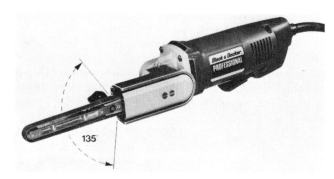

12-5.   Unique tool works with narrow, endless belts for sanding, grinding, and polishing. Different size, interchangeable arms are available. Pivoting arm can be locked in any position through a 135° arc.

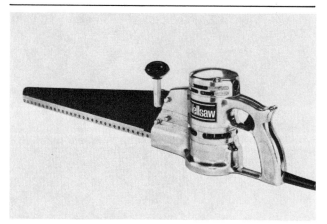

12-3.   "Wellsaw" works like a handsaw, but is electrically powered to deliver 8,000, 1⅛" strokes per minute. The replaceable blades are designed to cut on both stroke directions. Blades are available for cutting wood, paper, bone, and other materials.

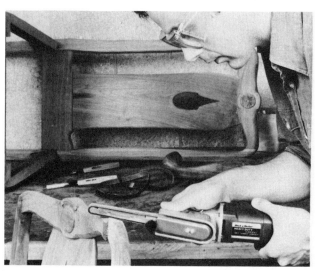

12-6.   The "Powerfile" can get into tight places and can work on many intricate contours.

endless, abrasive belts as narrow as ¼″ and polishing pads as narrow as ⅛″. Add to this interchangeable arms of various lengths and a sanding head that rotates through a 135° arc, and you can visualize how handy the tool can be for filing, deburring, sanding, and polishing in tight places and on odd-shaped surfaces. In many situations it does jobs that can't be accomplished with a conventional sander or grinder. The tool is less than 17″ long and weighs about 4 lbs.

Slim-Belt Belt Sander

The product shown in Figure 12-7 is a 1⅛″ x 21″ belt sander that is designed for excellent maneuverability when doing close quarter work. The front pulley is exposed so you can even get into tight, inside curves. Its removable side handle can be locked in at various angles so you can place hands in positions that are most suitable for the job. Accessory belts are available in seven grit sizes.

Powered Metal Shears

Cutting a few lengths of sheet metal with a good pair of hand shears is no problem, but when you have a lot more to do you can speed the work and do it more easily and more accurately with electric sheet metal cutters (Figures 12-8 and 12-9). Power, which determines the maximum metal-gauge units can get through, differs from tool to tool, but most are fairly light in weight and are designed for one-hand use. It's easier to get good results with these tools if you provide adequate support for the work near the cutline.

Electric Staplers and Nail Guns

You can appreciate the difference between a hand stapler and an electric one on jobs like installing ceiling tiles (Figure 12-10), vapor barriers, carpeting, and weather stripping. Most can be used with staples of various sizes and designs so the right choice can be made for the material being fastened. Many jobs that are usually done with brads or tacks can be done faster and more efficiently with a powered stapler.

12-8.   Electric shear can get through 10-gauge mild steel and up to 12-gauge stainless steel. The blades have four cutting edges: turning the cutter 90° brings a new, sharp edge into play.

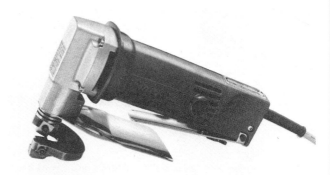

12-9.   This electric shear has a scrap guide to protect the operator's hand. Capacities of the double insulated tool are: up to 16 gauge in mild steel and 18 gauge in stainless steel.

12-7.   Sander works with 1⅛″ x 21″ belts and can be used on a wide variety of surfaces and materials. The compact tool weighs about 4 lbs and has a belt speed of 3,280 feet per minute.

12-10.   The electric staple gun will drive staples cleanly and to full depth as fast as you can pull the trigger. It's a wonder tool for jobs like installing ceiling tiles, but it has other practical uses, like recovering chair seats, attaching weather stripping, and covering valances with fabric.

The electric nail gun (Figure 12-11) looks like a stapling machine, but it drives 1 1/32″ nails with enough power to sink them completely in hard oak. Eliminating having to hold a nail and driving it with a hammer makes installing paneling, assembling picture frames, attaching moldings and edge bandings, and many other chores a lot easier to do. The tool is more accurate than the human hand. Press the trigger with the tool resting solidly on the work and the nail is driven perfectly straight in one quick stroke. It can only drive the nails that are made for it, but when they are suitable, the possibility of whacking a thumb instead of a nail is eliminated, and that's nice.

Vacuum Cleaner

A shop-type vacuum cleaner (Figure 12-12) is as handy in the house or on the patio as it is in the shop. A shop broom and a bench brush, while needed, can't compare with the efficiency of a powered unit. Many portable tools, and stationary ones, are designed to accept the hose of such a unit. Thus, sawdust and wood chips can be collected as the work goes on. Overall, a vacuum cleaner can keep you healthier and safer when you are in a workshop environment.

Power Hone

A power hone (Figure 12-13) is actually a stationary tool but it can help you work better and safer with power tools, and hand tools as well. Many of the units have accessories that hold tools correctly so you are sure to maintain the efficient cutting edge. A power hone is handy for tools used in the house as well as shop tools. It will keep keen edges on knives, scissors, and similar items.

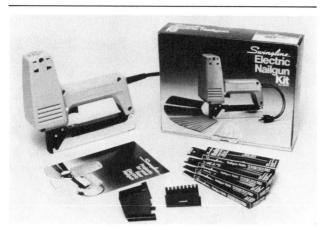

12-11.   The electric nail gun drives nails of a particular size with speed and accuracy. You just hold the tool firmly on the work and press the trigger.

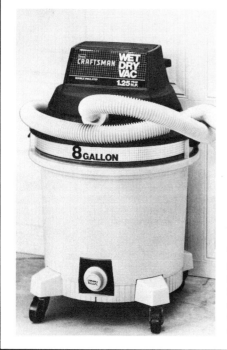

12-12.   The "prosaic" vacuum cleaner is an important shop tool. Like this one, many are designed to pick up virtually any dry or wet debris.

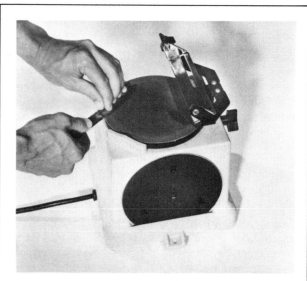

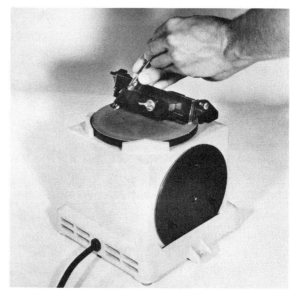

12-13.   With a power hone you can quickly learn to do a professional job of sharpening shop and house tools.

Bench Grinder

The bench grinder (Figure 12-14) is also a stationary tool, but like the power hone, it helps you work better and safer because it lets you maintain keen edges on cutting tools with minimum effort. Actually, the bench grinder and the power hone are good companions. The hone takes over after cutting edges have been reshaped or renewed on the grinder.

Paint Stripper

The electric paint stripper is an effective alternative to caustic chemicals that have unpleasant odors and leave a messy, liquid goo to clean up. The concept of the stripper is simple—

it blasts out super hot air that heats painted surfaces so the old coating can be quickly removed with a scraper (Figure 12-15). The tool has other uses, like drying surfaces, softening floor tiles and adhesives for easy replacement, and shrinking electrical tubing that is used to cover wire connections.

Glue/Caulker Gun

Electric glue guns (Figure 12-16) are handy because they can be used on wood and non-wood materials like cloth, paper, plastics, and leather. When the correct "stick" is placed in the gun, it becomes an easy-to-use caulking tool. The secret to using the glue gun is to work fast. The stick adhesive is a hot liquid when it leaves the gun but it cools pretty rapidly, so parts should be pressed together as quickly as possible. Use the tools carefully, since the nozzle end of the gun and the glue itself are quite hot.

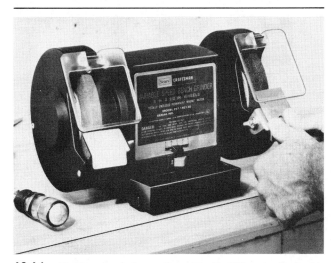

12-14.   The bench grinder can be used with different grit wheels so it can be used for sharpening as well as grinding. Tools like this are often used to drive buffs and wire wheels, so having variable speeds can be an asset. This unit has speeds ranging from 0 to 3,800 rpm.

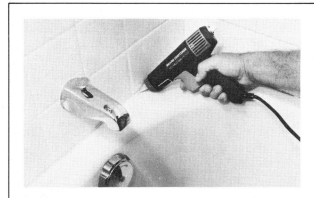

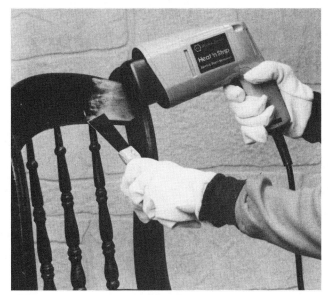

12-15.   The nuisance job of removing old paint becomes less of a chore when a heat gun is used to soften the coating enough so it can be scraped off easily.

12-16.   An electric "gun" that can be used with different "ammunition" can serve for caulking as well as gluing.

Chain Saw

The chain saw is a super tool for sawing logs (Figure 12-17), so its popularity has grown together with interest in wood burning stoves. It is not a tool to treat lightly even though modern ones have built-in safety features that were lacking in earlier models. Even so, the instructions that come with the tool should be followed to the letter. If you should ever rent one, be sure to ask for the original instruction manual.

Actually, the tool is used for more than cutting firewood. They get through heavy beams, fence posts, and the like quickly. You have probably read articles about chain-saw sculptors. Some manufacturers, like Stihl, provide accessories so the saw can be converted for jobs like hedge trimming and brush removal (Figures 12-18 and 12-19).

Chain saws are available as gasoline-powered or electrically-powered units.

12-18.   Some chain saws have accessories so they can be used for more than sawing. A hedge trimmer is one of them.

12-17.   The chain saw is noted as a fine tool for cutting firewood, but it has other uses. For example, experts can use the front end of the chain to shape mortises in heavy timbers. The wise user wears safety goggles, a hard hat, steel-toed shoes, and ear plugs or some other hearing protector.

12-19.   In addition to the hedge trimmer, the motor of the Stihl chain saw can be attached to a unit that allows cutting heavy grass, weeds, and unwanted shrubbery.

How To Make Stationary Work Stations For Portable Tools

13.

Your portable belt and pad sander—and drill—can be harnessed and used as stationary tools if you make the work station described in this chapter. It's not a difficult project and it doesn't limit the tools to a particular mode. Detaching the tools is easy so you can quickly put them back into service as portables. It's like having your cake and eating it too. You can mount all the tools when there are a variety of sanding chores to do, or you can work with just the one that is most suitable for a particular job.

All the sanders are secured to pivoting platforms and thus can be used in a vertical or horizontal position as shown in Figures 13-1 and 13-2. The drill provides rotary-sanding capability. It can be used to drive a variety of sanding drums or a disc that you can make or buy. The saber saw was an afterthought on my part and is optional. If you include it, be sure to have a blade mounted *only* when doing a sawing job.

I designed the prototype sanding station around good-size tools: a Sears Craftsman 4″ belt sander and a 4½″ x 9⅛″ pad sander. Thus, the pivoting mounting plates on which the tools are secured should be large enough for any brand tool.

The heart of my tool-mounting system is a yoke into which you slip the tool's handgrip, and a pipe strap bent to fit over the grip's projecting top. I lined all straps and yokes with self-adhesive weather stripping but did not allow for its thickness when forming and sizing them. That ensured a snug mounting for the tools and minimum vibration. Tool levelers—blocks of wood sized for the job and weather stripped—complete the mounting system (Figures 13-3 through 13-5).

13-1.   The sander "shop" provides for a belt and pad sander, and a drill that is used to drive disc or drums sanders. The saber saw is optional, but including it involves little extra work.

13-2.   The belt and pad sanders are mounted on hinged plates so they can be used in vertical or horizontal positions. In either case, locking-bolts hold the tools securely and minimize vibration. The drawers provide storage for accessories used with the shop and for abrasive materials.

13-3.   This is the system used for mounting the pad sander. The arrow indicates a support block that is sized so the sander will be held in a level position.

13-4.   Pipe clamps, lined with self-adhesive weather stripping, grip the sander securely. Weather stripping is also used to line the top edges of yokes and other support pieces.

13-5.   Mounting arrangement for the belt sander is similar to the one used for the pad sander. In both cases, some customizing is necessary to suit the handle arrangement and the shape of the tools you will use.

Constructing the Shop

Construction details for the body of the shop, mounting plates, accessories, and guides are shown in Figures 13-6 through 13-8. Saw the legs (# 1 in Figure 13-6) to size, then form the 2¼″ x 10¾″ notch that is required in the top rear of each leg. Be sure the legs are perfect triplets, then begin the assembly by adding the two frame pieces and the back brace. Cut the tool supports and the short leg to size and secure them in place with glue and #10 x 1½″ flathead wood screws. Also, nail through the back brace into the front edges of the tool supports. The drawings don't show them, but there are many areas where you can add some glue blocks for additional rigidity.

Add the drawer guides and then construct the drawers. The materials list (Figure 13-6) calls out exact sizes so you might wish to reduce the width of the drawers by ¹/₁₆″ or so to avoid binding. Anyway, doing this part of the job before the top is added makes it easier to be sure the drawers will work smoothly. Bore 1½″-diameter finger holes through the drawer fronts instead of adding knobs.

Make the Top

Cut the piece to overall size and, before forming the openings for the sanders, use a table saw or a portable router to shape the miter-gauge groove and the drill-accessory positioning groove. Use a saber saw to form the relief for the drill's handle, the opening for the junction box, and the open areas for the sanders.

If you decide to include a saber saw, use a router to form the recess for it in the underside of the bench top. The recess is included so the saw blade will have more projection when the saber saw is mounted. Drill a ¼″ or ⁵/₁₆″ hole for the saw blade, then use the saw to form the blade's access slot. The saw clamps should work for most any saber saw, but check the dimensions against the tool you own just to be sure. The idea is to allow the saw to slip into place merely by loosening the clamp locking screws.

Add the top by coating the top edges of the base assembly with glue and then driving 6d finishing nails, spaced three to four inches apart. Set the nailheads, and fill the cavities with wood dough.

Tilting Mounts for Sanders

Cut the sander-mounting plates and then mark them for the hinge positions. Clamp a strip of wood on the marked line so you can position the hinges accurately, then attach them to the plate. Put the plate on the tool support, then drive the screws for the second leaf of the hinge. Work carefully to be sure the plate is parallel with the shop's work surface. Add the height strip, which should be just thick enough to compensate for the hinge thickness (Figure 13-9).

Swing the plate to the vertical position and drill the two holes for the locking bolts that thread into T-Nuts in the underside of the tool supports. Follow this procedure for all locking bolts and T-Nuts. Drill a ⅛″ pilot hole and then enlarge it to ¼″. Enlarge the end of the hole into which the T-Nut is pressed to ⁵/₁₆″. The T-Nuts do not have to be set flush, but be sure to use the pronged type. Drill the hole for the

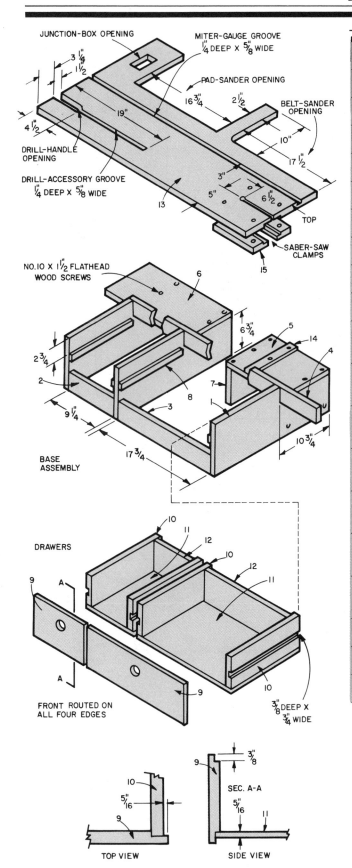

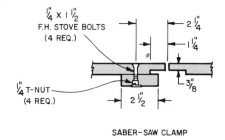

MATERIALS LIST		
KEY	QTY.	NAME AND SIZE
1	3	Legs ¾" x 9" x 24"
2	1	Frame ¾" x 3" x 9¼"
3	1	Frame ¾" x 3" x 17¾"
4	1	Brace ¾" x 2¼" x 37¼"
5	1	Tool Support ¾" x 10" x 12¼"
6	1	Tool Support ¾" x 10" x 16"
7	1	Leg ¾" x 6¾" x 10"
8	4	Guides ⅜" x ¾" x 13"
9	1	Large Drawer Front ¾" x 6½" x 18⅜"
9	1	Small Drawer Front ¾" x 6½" x 9⅞"
10	4	Large/Small Drawer Sides ¾" x 5 9/16" x 12¾"
11	1	Large Drawer Bottom ¼" x 12¾" x 17¾"
11	1	Small Drawer Bottom ¼" x 9¼" x 12¾"
12	1	Large Drawer Back ¾" x 5½" x 16¼"
12	1	Small Drawer Back ¾" x 5½" x 7¾"
13	1	Top ¾" x 24" x 42"
14	2	Height Block 5/16" x 1½" x 10"
15	2	Saw Clamps ¾" x 2½" x 8"

13-6. Construction details for the base cabinet of the sander shop. The key in the materials list is the number that identifies the part.

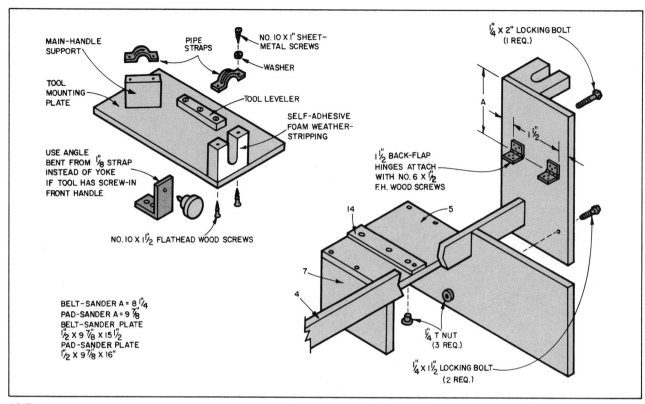

13-7. Details of hinged tool-plates and a typical system for securing the sanders.

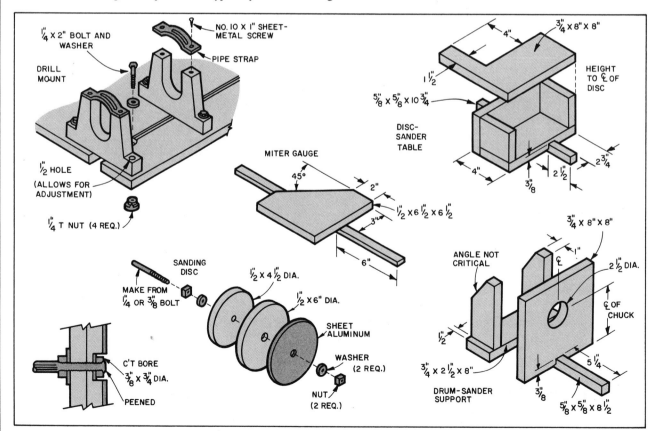

13-8. These are accessories and guides that are used with the sander shop. Upper left detail shows one way to secure a portable drill.

bolt that secures the plate in horizontal position *after* the sander has been mounted.

Mounting the Sanders

Check the detail in Figure 13-7 that shows a typical mounting arrangement. It is very important for the tool to be level and positioned so most of its abrasive surface is above the bench top and perpendicular to it.

Make the yoke first, cutting it longer than necessary and then reducing its height to suit the tool. After the yoke is set, cut the support for the tool's main handle and place it to suit the tool. Pipe straps do a good job of securing the tools but they will have to be modified to fit. Most of the time, it's just a question of tapping them with a hammer to flatten the arc a bit. The straps should bear down enough to keep the tools secure. Be especially careful with the pad sander since it will cause more vibration than the belt sander.

The final step is to secure the tool and then to size the tool leveler so its height and position will be exactly right for the tool. Be sure the tool's vent holes will not be covered.

Adding the Drill

The simplest way to add the drill is to buy and bolt on a commercial accessory to hold it. I prefer the yoke-mounting method because it holds the drill more securely (Figure 13-10). It will be easy to draw the patterns for the yokes if you work with a contour gauge. Otherwise, fold a sheet of heavy paper and, by snip-and-see, work out a half-contour. Be sure that the yokes will hold the drill so the horizontal centerline of the chuck will be parallel to the project's work surface. The oversize holes for the locking bolts allow for lateral adjustment.

Accessories

The accessories, detailed in Figure 13-8, are mostly for sanding jobs done with the drill. Adjust the height of the disc-sander table so its surface will be on or slightly above the centerline of the sanding disc. The centerline of the hole in the drum-sander support must match with the centerline of the chuck.

Use a ¼″ or ⅜″ bolt as an arbor for the sanding disc. Cut the bolt to leave a threaded portion that is exactly the right length for the item to be mounted. Peen the free end heavily to secure the nut so the disc can safely rotate in either direction (with reversible drill). Attach the aluminum sheet-metal cover with contact cement.

The miter gauge is used with the sanders and can be used to guide pieces that have square or miter-cut ends.

In General

It is important to work carefully through all phases of construction, especially when mounting the tools. Taking ten minutes to do a five minute job will pay off.

Use a good, cabinet-grade birch or maple plywood. Sand all parts smooth before doing assembly work, then sand once more when the job is complete. Finish with two or three coats of sanding sealer, sanding between applications, and after the final one. Apply paste wax, rubbed to a polish, to all work surfaces.

I used a single combination switch/outlet, and I think it's a good idea for you to do the same. You will be able to plug in just one tool at a time. Thus, you won't accidentally or forgetfully, start a tool while another is running.

Some typical chores that can be done on the sanding station are shown in Figures 13-11 through 13-22.

13-9.   The thickness of the height strip—on the right—should equal the thickness of the hinge when it is in closed position.

13-10.   The yoke-mounting method for the drill provides good security. The bearing areas of the yokes, and the pipe clamps should be lined with weather stripping. Holes for the screws that secure the yokes are oversize so there is some freedom for lateral adjustment of the drill.

Typical Chores on the Sander Shop

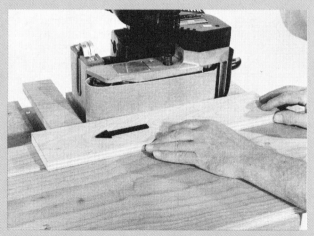

13-11.   Edge sanding on the belt sander is done by moving the work against the belt's direction of rotation, as indicated by the arrow. The belt will tend to move the work back, so keep a firm grip. Don't stand in line with the workpiece.

13-14.   Use the open end of the belt sander to smooth inside curves.

13-12.   You can do end-sanding on some good-size workpieces when the belt sander is locked in vertical position. You can sand miter cuts the same way.

13-15.   Stationary pad sander is especially useful when you want a super-smooth finish on stock that is too small to hand-hold safely. Move the work slowly across the abrasive. Note the combination switch/outlet that is used for all tools.

13-13.   When using the belt sander in horizontal position to smooth miter cuts, keep the miter gauge on the right side of the tool. Hold or clamp it securely to counter the belt's tendency to move the work.

13-16.   Use the pad sander in vertical position to smooth the rounded end of a workpiece. Being able to apply the work to the tool, in this fashion, ensures a square edge.

Typical Chores on the Sander Shop (cont'd.)

13-17.   Miter-cut pieces can also be smoothed on the pad sander. The miter gauge, that you make, is reversible, so it can be used for left- or right-hand cuts.

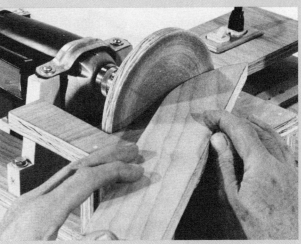

13-20.   Custom-made, 6″-diameter sanding disc works well with a variable-speed, reversing drill and the accessory sanding table. Always apply the work to the "down" side of the disc.

13-18.   The drill can be used to drive drum sanders, or buffers and polishers. DON'T use it to turn a grinding wheel. Always wear safety goggles and a dust mask.

13-21.   The sanding table can also be used with drum sanders. This is one of 3M's new drum types. The surface of the table should be at or a bit above the centerline of the drill chuck.

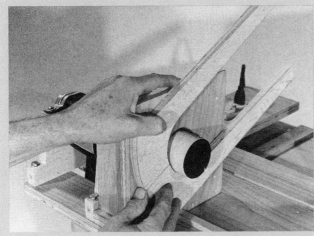

13-19.   The advantage of working with the drum-sander support is that it ensures that sanded edges will be square to workpiece's surfaces.

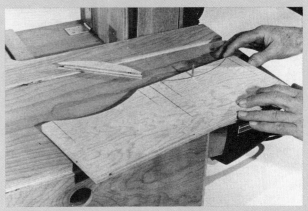

13-22.   The saber saw is not a replacement for a jigsaw, but it can be quite handy for many sawing jobs. Don't leave a saw blade in the tool when it is not being used. With a scroller-type saw, turn the control handle 180°; with a conventional saw, mount the blade backwards.

An All-Purpose Table for Portable Tools

You can't beat the convenience of using portable tools in work situations where it's more practical to apply the tool to the job, but the reverse is also true. Quite often it is easier to work more precisely when the tool is stationary and the work is brought to it. With a multipurpose table, that you can build, you can quickly convert portable tools to stationary-tool use (Figure 13-23).

Even though I included a portable saw in the unit, it is an *optional feature* because the guard on the saw will move to the underside of the table during crosscutting and ripping operations and return to cover the blade when the pass is complete, but there will be no over-guard *during* the cut. If you eliminate the cutoff saw, the project can still be used for drilling, sanding, saber sawing, and shaping. If you include the saw, always work so your hands never come near the blade. Adjust the projection of the saw blade so it barely pokes through the surface of the stock.

Picture the project as a sturdy box with a hinged top that has a cutout in it to receive "plates" to which portable tools are secured (Figures 13-24 and 13-25). The large 23″ x 23½″ surface provides a lot of work-support area. The project itself can be considered portable since it can be placed on a workbench, or even on a pair of sawhorses that are spanned with a sheet of thick plywood. It can also be supported on a stand that you make or buy. The system of interchangeable inserts provides the mounting arrangement for each of the portable tools.

Construction details for the main table and the accessories that are used with it, are shown in Figures 13-26 through 13-31. Most of the work involved in making the project can be accomplished with portable tools. Form dadoes with a cutoff saw by setting the blade projection to the required depth and then making a series of overlapping passes to achieve the width of the dado. A straightedge, clamped to the work, will guide the saw to assure parallel cuts. It's best to make the shoulder cuts first and then clean out the waste that remains between them. If you prefer, a chisel instead of a saw can be used for the last step.

For slots, drill a series of overlapping holes and then remove waste with a file or chisel. Another method is to drill end-holes for the slot and then cut between them with a saber saw. Large, internal cutouts can be done by just using the saber saw.

13-24.   The top of the table pivots on two ¼″ bolts so it's easy to mount any tool that won't fit through the table opening from above. The strip of wood is just a prop to hold the table top up.

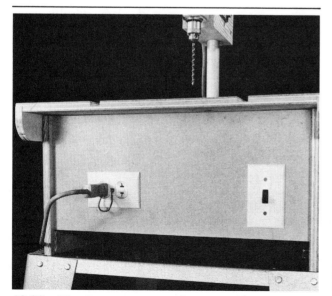

13-23.   The all-purpose table I made is mounted on its own steel stand. The outlet is wired so it's controlled by the on-off switch. Tool switches are locked in the "on" position, and the cords are plugged into the outlet. Thus, tool activity is controlled with the switch in the table.

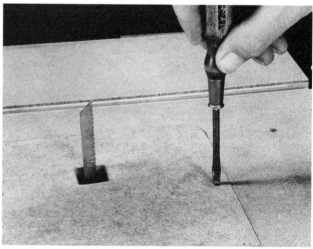

13-25.   Tool mounting-plates can be secured with flathead screws. Be sure to set them flush so they don't interfere with workpieces.

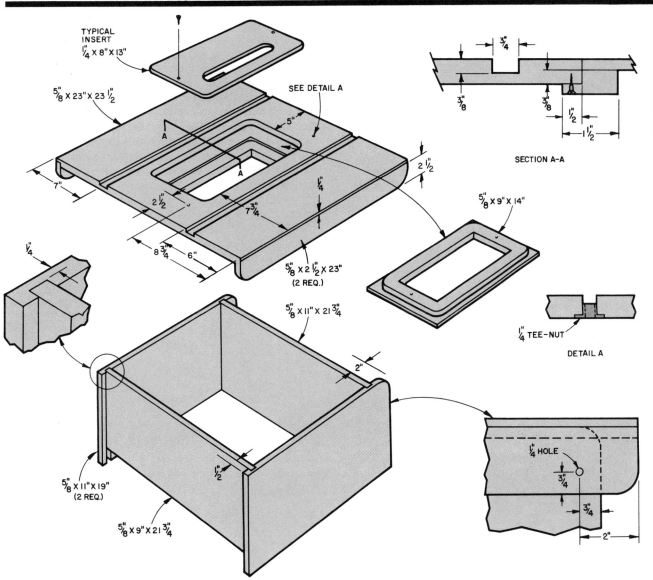

13-26.   Construction details of the basic table. A hardboard veneered plywood is a good choice for material since it can take abuse and will hold up for a long time.

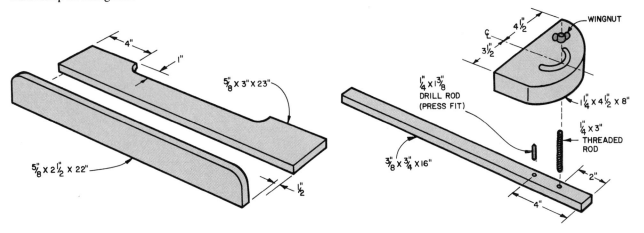

13-27.   An easy-to-make rip fence is held in place with clamps during use.

13-28.   You can make a miter gauge like this or use one that is already on hand.

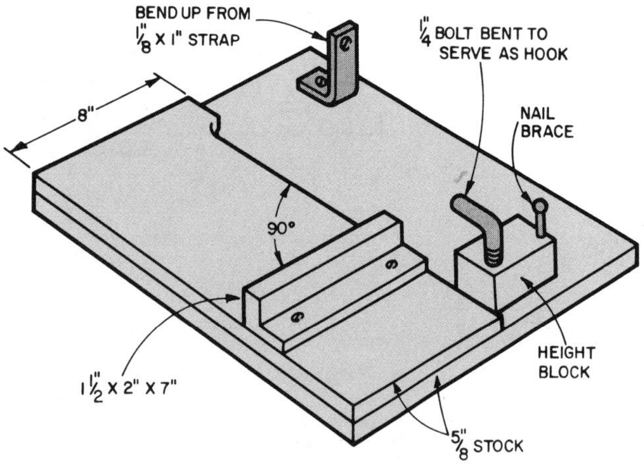
BEND UP FROM 1/8 X 1" STRAP
1/4" BOLT BENT TO SERVE AS HOOK
NAIL BRACE
8"
90°
HEIGHT BLOCK
1 1/2 X 2" X 7"
5/8" STOCK

13-29. The belt sander has a mounting of its own, but an insert can be attached to the underside so the assembly can be fitted easily to the table. The raised work surface follows the belt's contour for sanding curves. The steel angle and the L-shaped hold-down, which you can make from a 1/4" bolt, will work with belt sanders that have a removable front knob. You may have to modify the arrangement a bit to suit the tool you own.

Work carefully to be sure that the dadoes in the table top will be parallel to the table opening and to the sides of the table. These grooves will be guides for the miter gauge. The accuracy of the finished project relates strongly to the care you use when making it. Since the end result can be a lifetime tool, it pays to take extra time to make it correctly.

First, make and assemble all parts for the main table, then go on to the accessories and the inserts required for the tools. Make a separate insert (mounting plate) for each tool you plan to use, adapting it to accommodate the specific tool. Except for the drill, tools are mounted on the underside of the inserts with holes through their baseplates.

Sand all surfaces before and after assembly, then apply several coats of sanding sealer, sanding between coats and after the last one. The last finishing step is an application of paste wax, rubbed to a polish.

Typical applications of the tools and some construction hints are shown in Figures 13-32 through 13-44.

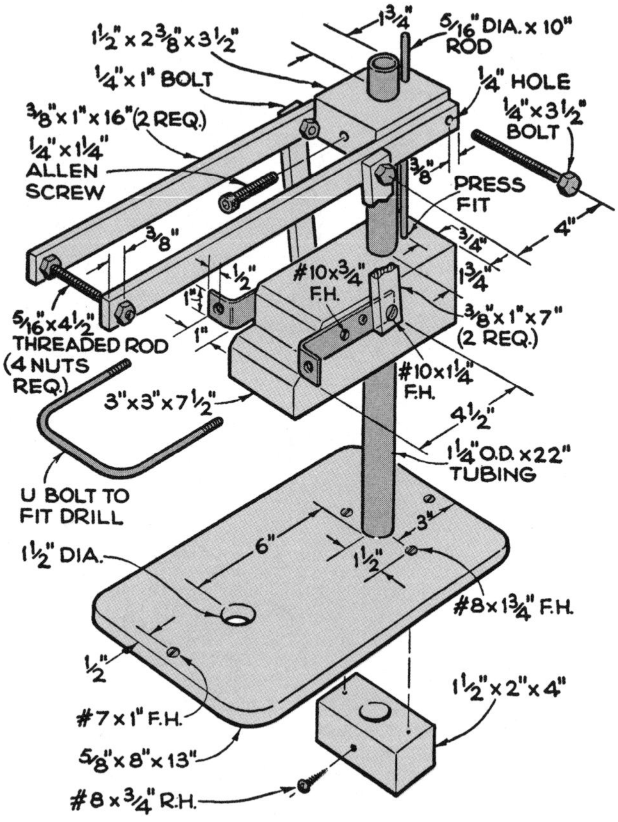
1 1/2" x 2 3/8" x 3 1/2"
1/4" x 1" BOLT
3/8" x 1" x 16" (2 REQ.)
1/4" x 1 1/4" ALLEN SCREW
1 3/4"
5/16" DIA. x 10" ROD
1/4" HOLE
1/4" x 3 1/2" BOLT
3/8"
PRESS FIT
4"
3/4"
1 3/4"
#10 x 3/4" F.H.
3/8" x 1" x 7" (2 REQ.)
#10 x 1 1/4" F.H.
4 1/2"
5/16" x 4 1/2" THREADED ROD (4 NUTS REQ.)
3" x 3" x 7 1/2"
1 1/4" O.D. x 22" TUBING
U BOLT TO FIT DRILL
1 1/2" DIA.
6"
3"
1 1/2"
#8 x 1 3/4" F.H.
1/2"
#7 x 1" F.H.
1 1/2" x 2" x 4"
5/8" x 8" x 13"
#8 x 3/4" R.H.

13-30. Construction details of the drill press. If you can't find a U-bolt that will work with the portable drill you use, you can make a special one by bending a length of threaded rod. Make the hole in the mounting block so the column fits it tightly. If you wish to avoid making this unit, you can probably substitute a ready-made stand.

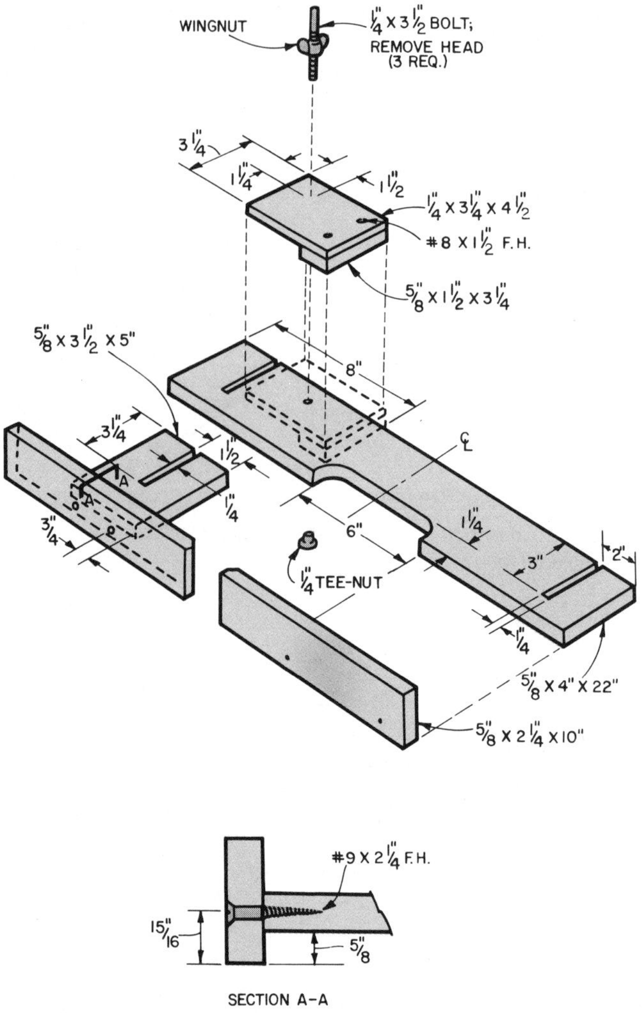
WINGNUT
1/4" X 3 1/2" BOLT; REMOVE HEAD (3 REQ.)
3 1/4
1 1/4
1 1/2
1/4 X 3 1/4 X 4 1/2
#8 X 1 1/2 F.H.
5/8 X 1 1/2 X 3 1/4
5/8 X 3 1/2 X 5
8"
℄
3 1/4
1/2
1/4
3/4
6"
1 1/4
1/4 TEE-NUT
3"
2"
1/4
5/8 X 4" X 22"
5/8 X 2 1/4 X 10"
#9 X 2 1/4 F.H.
15/16
5/8
SECTION A–A

13-31. How to make the adjustable fences that are needed for the router/shaper setup.

Typical Applications and Construction Tips

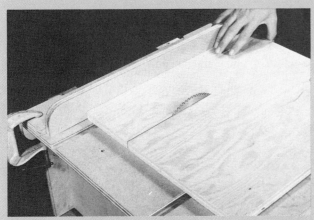

13-32.   The rip fence, if you have installed a saw, is used by setting it parallel to the saw blade and clamping it in place. Keep hands well away from the blade. For clarity, the projection of the saw blade is higher than it should be. In practice, the blade should barely poke through the surface of the material.

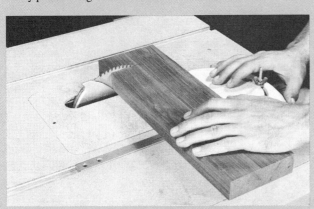

13-33.   Crosscutting is done by using the miter gauge. Note that the guard on the saw is pushed below the table as the pass is made. It will return to cover the blade when the pass is complete. Obey the safety rules if you decide to include a saw in the project.

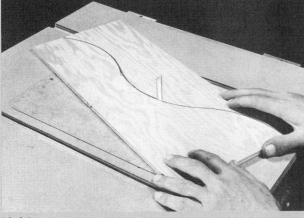

13-34.   The table on the project supplies ample work-support area. Since saber-saw blades are chucked only at one end, you must feed the work slowly to avoid twisting the blade off the cut-line.

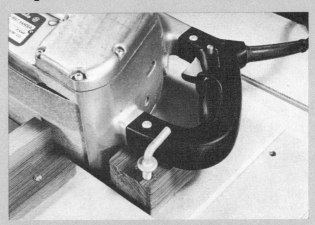

13-35.   If the belt sander is shaped somewhat like this one, you can rest the main handle on a height block and secure it with an L-shaped bolt. Install a T-Nut in the underside of the height block for the bolt.

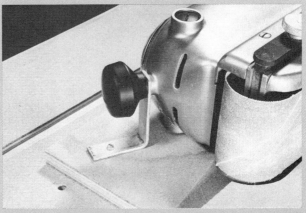

13-36.   A belt sander that has a removable auxiliary knob can be secured at the front end by using a metal angle. You can make the angle by bending a length of 1/8" strap steel.

13-37.   The "stationary" belt sander makes it easy to do end-sanding on narrow pieces. The backup holds the workpiece in correct position and keeps it from moving. When sanding edges, move the work against the belt's direction of rotation. Hold the work firmly, since the belt's rotation will oppose the direction in which you move the workpiece.

(Continued on next page)

Typical Applications and Construction Tips (cont'd.)

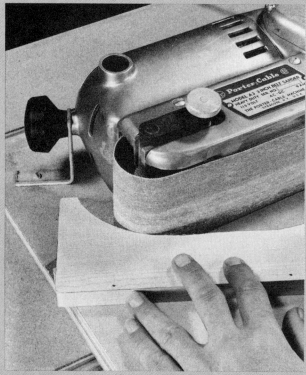

13-38.   The forward end of the sander is open, so it can be used like a drum sander to smooth inside curves.

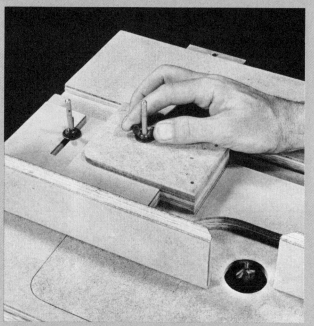

13-40.   The outfeed fence of the router/shaper arrangement is adjusted so its bearing surface is on the same plane as the infeed fence, or ahead of it. Its position depends on the kind of cut being performed. In any case, its place is secured by means of a wing nut on a stud that screws into a T-Nut that is in the underside of the table.

13-39.   Router/shaper setup, with individually adjustable fences, imitates a conventional shaper. Depth-of-cut adjustments are made by moving the router vertically as is normally done. The width of the cut is controlled with fence adjustments. The router is attached to the underside of a mounting plate which has an opening for the bit.

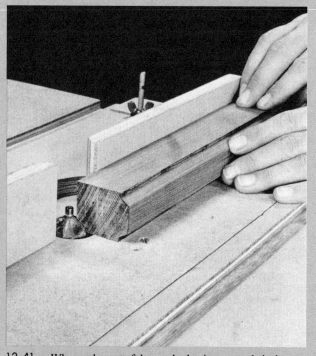

13-41.   When only part of the workedge is removed, the bearing surfaces of the infeed and outfeed fences are set on the same plane. The cutter, because the router is in inverted position, is rotating counterclockwise—so the work must be fed from right to left.

Typical Applications and Construction Tips (cont'd.)

13-42. When the cut removes the entire edge of the stock, the outfeed fence is set forward of the infeed fence to provide support for the workpiece after it has passed the cutter. The outfeed fence is positioned forward of the infeed fence a distance that equals the mount of material that is removed.

13-44. The drill press design may have to be modified in some details to fit your drill, but the basic concept will work for most models. Shape the front end of the drill mounting block to fit the case of your particular tool. Use a U-bolt that you buy or make to secure the drill to the mounting block. Careful construction will assure that the drill bits will travel parallel to the column. If necessary, use shims between the drill case and the mounting block. The bolts in the linkage should be just tight enough to keep the drill from sliding down under its own weight.

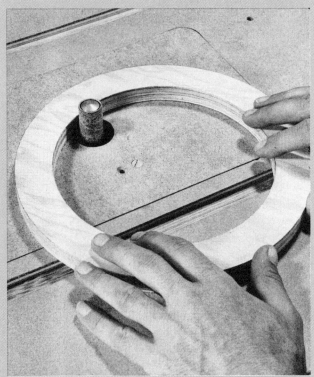

13-43. You can mount a small drum sander in the router when it is used in the router/shaper mode, but feed pressure must be *very* light since router speed is excessive for this application.

APPENDIX

1. Lumber

Lumber is the staple of almost every handyman, woodworker, or craftsman. The term refers to 'solid' wood—boards cut from a tree, dried, and perhaps planed or treated chemically, but not processed in any other way. You might think that this would be a simple subject, but it's not. There are a wide variety of woods, several different ways to saw a tree, and dozens of variations in grain, density, and strength. Because of this, it takes a bit of study to 'know your lumber'.

The information in this section will help you to select the type of lumber you need for a job. First, there is a list of terms that apply to lumber—this will help you understand the many details you must consider when working with lumber. There is a brief description of the hardwoods and softwoods that are commonly available. You may never have the need to work with many of these woods, but you'll find the information useful in making a selection. There is a simple description of how lumber is graded, how to calculate the 'board feet' in a board, and the common methods for sawing a log. If you do much carpentry, there's information on how to choose lumber for the various parts of a job. Finally, there are instructions on how to interpret the 'lumber marks' you find on most boards.

Lumber Terms to Know

ACTUAL SIZE   As opposed to "nominal size"—the size of a piece of wood after it is reduced by surfacing. For example, a 2 x 4 will be 1½″ thick and 3½″ wide—length will be what you order.

AIR-DRIED   Moisture content is reduced to a specific percentage by stacking wood so air can circulate around it. When the work is done correctly and sufficient time is allowed, air-dried wood is as good as material that has been kiln-dried.

BATTEN   Usually, a slim, narrow strip of wood used to cover a vertical joint between boards. Often used synonymously with "cleat."

BIRD'S-EYE   A small figure resembling the eye of a bird. Can be found on various woods but usually associated with maple. Sugar maple has more of it than other species.

BLEEDING   When soluble salts or resins cause blemishes in or on a painted surface. Resinous woods like pine should be sealed before finishing, especially over knots.

BLEMISH   Has to do with the appearance of wood. Imperfections that are not attractive but do not affect the utility of the material.

BLUE STAIN   A blemish that can be caused by fungi in lumber that has yet to be seasoned. Stains can be grayish or bluish. Blue stain does not affect the strength of the material.

BOW   A type of warp. A board will describe an arc, lengthwise, instead of being flat.

BS   Means "both sides."

BURL   Actually an abnormality. A growth, often dome-shaped, which can be sliced to make beautiful veneer. Large but slabs are often used as table tops.

CLEAT   A strip of wood that is used to support a shelf or similar project. A strip attached to an existing wall to provide a base for hooks. Used across the back of several pieces of lumber to hold them on a similar plane and to help prevent warping.

CLEAR HEART   A fine grade of wood cut from the heart of the tree. In redwood, clear heart means there will be no visible defects on one face of the wood.

CLOSE GRAIN   Wood that has very small and closely spaced pores. Usually, such wood does not require a filler before finishing. "Fine textured" is also used to describe the condition.

CROOK   A distortion that combines a bowed surface and a bowed edge. Also, the distortion might simply be a bowed edge.

CUP   A distortion across the width of a board. Surface is concave instead of flat.

DEFECT An imperfection in wood that can affect its strength or durability.

DELAMINATE A separation of plies in a laminated material like plywood—this can happen if an interior grade of plywood is used outdoors or in areas high in moisture.

DRY ROT Wood-rotting fungi require considerable moisture for growth so the term is used loosely. Wood contaminated by dry rot can be crushed to a powder.

FAS Means first and seconds.

FIGURE Patterns produced by annual growth rings and by irregular coloration. Deviations from normal grain structure such as knots and rays contribute to figure design.

FLITCH A term applied to a log that has been sawed on two or four sides. It is ready for additional cutting, but can be used as is as rough timber.

GRAIN Generally, the pattern described by the fibers in wood. Affected by how a log is sawed into lumber.

GREEN Lumber which has not gone through a drying schedule.

GROWTH RINGS A layer of wood, sometimes bark, which occurs during one growing season. Counting the rings can tell the age of the tree. Close-grained woods and stronger woods come from trees that have narrow growth rings.

HARDBOARD A man-made material composed of compressed wood fibers. Standard panels are brownish and have one textured surface. Panels with embossed surfaces or with tough, baked-on finishes are available. Uses include furniture components, siding, and inside wall covers.

HARDWOOD Botanically, wood produced by deciduous trees. Usually, but not always, harder and denser than "softwoods."

HEARTWOOD From central areas of trees. Usually darker than other areas and in some species more decay and insect resistant than sapwood.

HONEYCOMB A condition caused by a fungus that leaves small, white pockets in the wood. It does not affect the strength of the material.

KILN-DRIED Lumber whose moisture content has been reduced to a specific percentage by placing it in a heated chamber for a particular length of time. Temperature and humidity are closely controlled during the procedure.

KERF The cut made by a saw blade. When the blade has set teeth, the kerf will be wider than the gauge of the blade.

KNOT Caused (mainly) by the connections between the trunk and branches of a tree. "Tight" knots are firmly fixed and can add to the appearance of wood. For example, knotty pine is used effectively in furniture and for wall paneling.

LATH A slim, narrow strip of lumber, usually rough, that was widely used as the base for plaster walls. Today, steel mesh and special sheets of gypsum are used instead. These materials are also called "lath."

LINEAR FOOT Actual length of lumber and wood products regardless of thickness or width.

LOUVER One or a set of strips set at an angle, usually in horizontal fashion. Used in doors, shutters, and similar projects. A louvered fence will have larger boards set vertically.

LUMBER The material cut from logs to a size and shape that is usable by woodworkers.

MEDULLARY RAYS Bands of cells that radiate from the center of the tree. They are most prominent in lumber cut from trees like oak and beech.

MILLWORK Covers lumber and wood materials that have been fabricated to a particular shape or assembly; for example, doors and windows.

MOLDING Shaped pieces that can be decorative or structural. There are many varieties: quarter and half round, cove, crown, picture, cornice, and base-cap. Often, its use identifies the shape.

NOMINAL SIZE The size of lumber before it is surfaced. The nominal size of a 2 x 4 would be 2″ by 4″ or more. After surfacing it would be 1½″ x 3½″.

OPEN-GRAIN Wood that has rather large, open pores that usually require filling before finishing. Oak is an example.

ORDERING SEQUENCE How to list dimensions when ordering lumber—thickness in inches by width in inches by length in feet. Use nominal size for thickness and width.

PANELING Usually, wall coverings that can be plywood or composition material. Solid lumber used as a wall covering is often called paneling.

PARTICLEBOARD Panels made of wood chips, flakes, or particles that are bonded together under pressure. Available in 4′ x 8′ sheets and in various thicknesses. Can be used for furniture components, substructure for plastic laminates, and floor underlayment.

PATINA The color and the feel that wood can acquire with age.

PECK Can be a pitted area or a channel in wood. Usually found in cedar ("pecky cedar").

PITCH STREAK An accumulation of resin that forms a very obvious streak.

PITH A soft core that can be found in the center of a tree or limb. Lumber that contains much of it should not be used for structural purposes.

PLAIN-SAWED An economical method of sawing a log into lumber. Cuts are made tangent to the growth rings. Surface grain pattern displays conspicuous growth rings.

PLY A layer in an assembly composed of laminated pieces.

PLYWOOD A material made by bonding together an odd number of veneers with the grain of adjoining plies running at right angles. Grain direction of surface veneers usually follows the long dimension of the panel. Sometimes made by bonding surface veneers to a solid core. Fancy plywood panels are made of the most rare, exotic woods.

POCKET Actually a crack that appears between growth rings. Often contains pitch.

PRESSURE TREATED   Lumber subjected to a vacuum process that forces preservatives deep into the cells of the wood. The material withstands attack by rot and insects and has become very popular for decks, porches, or any project that will be exposed to the elements. Also used in soil-contact situations.

QUARTERS   A thickness term often used when ordering hardwoods—4/4 means four quarters or one inch, 5/4 means one and one quarter inches, and so on.

QUARTER-SAWED   Lumber sawed from a log that was first cut into quarter sections. The line of cut runs from the center toward the bark, and is parallel to the radius of the quarter section. Grain pattern generally runs in straight lines.

RANDOM LENGTH   Quantity of lumber made up of pieces of various lengths.

RWL   Quantity of lumber made up of pieces of no specific width or length.

SAPWOOD   Those areas of wood that are next to the bark and which are actively involved in the life processes of the tree. Usually lighter in color than heartwood. It can be just as strong as heartwood but can be more susceptible to decay.

SELECT   Lumber that has been carefully selected for appearance.

SHEATHING   An underlayment placed over framework of walls and roofs before finish material is added. Can be plywood or composition material.

SIDING   The final material that covers exterior walls of buildings. Many varieties including plywood, boards, hardboard, and shaped pieces such as "bevel siding."

SLABS   The first pieces cut from a log. Usually processed for use other than lumber.

SOFTWOOD   Botanically, lumber that is cut from evergreen trees. For example, wood from pine or spruce is softwood. The term should not always be taken literally; yellow pine (a softwood) is much harder than basswood (a hardwood).

SQUARE   A quantity of material. A square of shakes will cover 100 square feet of a roof.

STUD   A piece of wood of standard dimensions that is the vertical component in wall structures.

SUBFLOOR   The base for finish flooring. Various types of plywood are made for the purpose.

SUMMERWOOD   A part of annual growth rings that form during the latter part of the growth period. This part of the wood is usually denser and stronger than springwood.

S1S   Surfaced one side.

S2S   Surfaced two sides.

S3S   Surfaced three sides.

S4S   Surfaced four sides.

VENEER   Thin sheets of wood that can run from 1/100 to ¼″ thick. "Rotary cut" veneer is formed in a special lathe by rotating a log against the edge of a knife. "Sawed" veneer is produced by simple sawing. "Sliced" veneer is made by moving a log or flitch against a knife.

WIND   A distortion, actually an obvious twist that runs from end to end in a board. A board in wind is difficult to salvage.

WHITE POCKET   A blemish caused by a fungus disease. Sometimes called "white speck." It detracts from the wood's appearance but doesn't affect its strength.

Notes on Popular Woods

AFRICAN CHERRY (MAKORI)   African hardwood which is generally pale red with darker red lines. Often used in furniture, it's strong and easy to work.

AFRICAN MAHOGANY   A hardwood with tones that range from reddish brown to pink. It can be found as the surface veneer of fancy plywood and is a respectable furniture material. Not a true mahogany.

AFRICAN TEAK (IROKO)   A brown wood with yellow bands that follow a zigzag pattern. It has a fine texture and can be found in paneling and furniture. Africans often use it for carving and for making bowls.

AFRORMOSIA   A heavy hardwood somewhat like teak. Generally brownish with streaks that are yellowish-brown. Tough enough to be used for ship decking, but is also used for paneling and furniture.

AGBA   The wood is easy to work, has a pale brown tone, and is very close in appearance to African mahogany. Source is West Africa.

ALDER (RED)   Its use is generally limited to plywood and to reinforcement components in furniture. Tones range from brown to white. Source is the Pacific Northwest.

AMARANTH (PURPLEHEART)   A hardwood of Central America that changes from brown to purple after it is cut. Available in boards and veneers.

AMBOYNA   Interesting wood from the East Indies that is generally rosy red with tiny knots that resemble bird's eyes. Often used for inlay work.

ASH   A tough, heavy wood with a prominent figure. Sapwood is white, other areas can be brown with a grayish tone. Popular for furniture. Takes abuse so it is often used for handles and projects like baseball bats.

ASPEN (POPLAR)   Aspen used in furniture is usually cut from the crotch of the tree. The wood from the cottonwood (an aspen) is used to make boxes. Most species in this category produce wood that is considered inferior and weak.

AVODIRE (AFRICAN SATINWOOD)   A strong, lightweight wood with a clean grain and a golden yellow color.

Can be surfaced to a high polish. Available as lumber and veneers. Very popular for marquetry.

BASSWOOD   One of the hardwoods that is actually quite soft and light. The wood is white, has little grain, is very easy to work but is weak. It's used for crates and boxes, general millwork, and as a core in panels. The "linden", a basswood, is popular for landscaping and shade.

BEECH   A heavy wood that is strong and durable. One of the woods easily bent by steaming. Often used for food containers and woodenware since it doesn't impart odor or taste. Available as lumber or veneer.

BIRCH   Many species, most common being the yellow birch and the sweet birch. The woods have a close grain and are hard and heavy. There are many applications, among them, cabinetmaking, millwork, furniture, and paneling. Available as lumber or veneer.

BOXWOOD   A heavy, hard wood that is not too difficult to work. Uses include tool handles, small combs, backs of bushes, and similar items. Popular for lathe turning, carving, and for inlay and marquetry. The color is generally a yellowish white.

BUTTERNUT   Characteristics are so similar to the American black walnut that it is often called "white walnut;" the difference is in the latter's lighter color. The wood is soft, close grained, and easy to work with all types of tools. Used for paneling, cabinetwork, and furniture.

CEDAR (RED)   This is the aromatic wood that is often used in closets and chests. Generally red in color with a thin layer of white sapwood. Today, manufacturers use material with many knots simply because clear stock is hard to come by. The wood from other varieties of cedars is suitable for fences, poles, shingles and shakes, and furniture. Heartwood is resistant to decay.

CHERRY   A naturally beautiful hardwood that takes a fine polish. Can be worked fairly well with all types of tools and is a popular choice for furniture, cabinets, and paneling. Available as lumber or veneer.

CHESTNUT   Difficult to find today because of chestnut blight which has almost entirely exterminated the species. Might find some as "wormy chestnut," the result of insects eating the tree after it has been killed by the blight.

COCOBOLO   An oily wood that doesn't take to gluing, but colors are intriguing and the wood is often used for turnings. One must be careful about dust from this wood; it can produce an effect similar to ivy poisoning.

EBONY   Most varieties produce wood that is heavy, black, and very durable. Takes a good polish and can be used in cabinetwork, inlaying, and turning. Piano keys and tool handles are often made of it.

ELM (ENGLISH)   The wood is used in cabinetry and for decorative touches. Hard to find except as a manufactured veneer. Importing of logs no longer allowed because of elm disease.

FIR (DOUGLAS)   A "hard" softwood used extensively as structural components in house building and as veneers in plywood. Works easily with power tools but not so with hand tools. Has areas of hard and soft grain; not the best wood for painting.

GUM   Color runs from brown to gray. Often called "spotted" gum because whitish bark contains differently colored spots. Sometimes used as a substitute for satinwood. Grain is erratic; occasionally, highly figured areas are sought after for paneling.

HEMLOCK   An important commercial wood used extensively in construction. Much of western hemlock is used for quality paper and newsprint.

HICKORY   Color is generally brownish. Combination of strength, hardness, toughness, and stiffness make it very suitable for tool handles, agricultural implements, and lawn furniture.

HOLLY (AMERICAN)   Wood is white, light, and practically grainless. Small amounts are made into veneers and lumber. Leaves and berries are important to industries that manufacture holiday sprays and wreaths.

KOA   Hawaiian Islands exclusive; dugout canoes were made from large trees. Resonant qualities of the wood make it exceptional for musical instruments. Has interesting fiddleback figure and takes a fine finish. Can be used in furniture and paneling.

LACEWOOD   Wood has striking figures with colors that range from pink to reddish-brown. Craftspeople like it for cabinetwork when they seek an unusual appearance. An import, often sold here as "silk oak" or "selena."

LARCH   A soft wood that is hard and strong and that has generally straight, uniform grain. It is used in construction, sometimes in the manufacture of lesser quality furniture. Other uses are poles, railroad ties, pulp for fiberboard, and paper.

LAUREL (CALIFORNIA)   Noted for highly figured veneers that take an excellent polish. Used in panels and furniture. Much prized for turning into bowls, trays, candlesticks, and the like.

MAHOGANY   Many species available. Much admired and used for cabinetwork, furniture, paneling, and boat building. Generally reddish brown with nice figuring; is reasonably close grained and easy to work with power or hand tools.

MAPLE   Hard maple is valuable for paneling, flooring, furniture, cabinetwork, veneers, and more. Wood is strong, close grained with generally straight grain, but can be highly figured. Figures sought after for cabinetwork and furniture are "curly," "bird's eye," and "wavy."

MYRTLE   Wood is hard and strong with interesting colors ranging from golden brown to yellowish green. Burls are often used for veneers. A fine wood for lathe enthusiasts.

OAK   Many varieties. Both white oak and red oak produce strong, tough woods, but the white, having a better appearance, is used more for furniture, paneling, trim, and flooring.

Red oak is often found in flooring but it's not completely ignored for other uses.

PADOUK   Some of its wood has a brilliant red color so it is often called "vermilion." Many craftspeople enjoy using it for furniture, musical instruments, and for turnings.

PEAR WOOD   Generally pink in color with light cream background shadings. A good deal of it is used in marquetry for reproducing flesh colors. European pear wood is used for veneers.

PECAN   A species of hickory with reddish brown wood with occasional dark streaks. Wood is hard and heavy. Some of it is made into veneers for furniture. The tree is more popular for its nuts than its wood.

PINE (YELLOW)   Many species; in the "yellow" category which covers "longleaf," "shortleaf," "loblolly," and slash, the wood is yellowish, heavy, and hard. It has good strength and is used in construction and plywoods. Not the easiest wood to work with.

PINE (WHITE)   Generally, this category covers "ponderosa," "sugar," "eastern white," and "western white." There are very slight differences, although the eastern white is often the choice for cabinetry and general carpentry. It is light in color and has a straight, close grain. Easy to work and can be stained or painted without problems.

REDWOOD   The magic wood, growing in a limited area along the pacific coast of the U.S., thought by indians to be immortal because of their long life. Grows to great size; one tree produced 344,000 board feet of lumber. The wood is soft, light, and generally reddish brown. Heartwood is decay and insect resistant. Burls are much sought after for table tops and veneers. Popular material for outdoor projects like planters, decks, and furniture. More than half the redwood lumber is in the form of planks, joists, and beams used in house construction. It is also used for siding and paneling.

ROSEWOOD (BRAZILIAN)   Colors range from cream to brown to black streaks. Once used in the production of superior pianos. Takes a smooth and high polish. Veneers are often for decorative touches and inlays in cabinetwork.

SPRUCE   Many varieties. Much of the wood is valued as pulp for paper. The commercial value of the blue spruce is in landscaping. Most of the wood has a lot of strength in relation to its weight and is used extensively in construction. White spruce is used for interior finishing, for furniture, and for oars and canoe paddles.

SYCAMORE   A moderately heavy hardwood, reddish brown in color. Available as lumber or veneers. It's tough enough to be used in butcher blocks. Much of it goes into railroad ties and fence posts.

TEAK   A very durable wood used extensively for paneling, furniture, shipbuilding, and flooring. Available as lumber or veneers. Dimensional stability is excellent. The wood can vary in color from straw-like tones to deep browns, sometimes with black streaks. It can have an oily surface and may feel sticky when first cut.

WALNUT (BLACK)   One of the most desirable native U.S. woods. Many excellent working qualities in addition to its inherent beauty. Butts, crotches, burls, fiddleback, leaf, and stripes are some of the forms available in veneers. The tree is also appreciated for its food value, the black walnuts we eat.

Pointers on Wood Grading

Softwood

Select Grades

A   Flaws are difficult to find; suitable for natural finishes and staining.

B   This grade is also suitable for natural finishes but it does contain a few, small, visible defects.

C   Contains defects but they will be hidden if the project is to be painted.

D   Will contain defects similar to those in grade "C" but more of them. Another grade that can be selected for painted projects.

Common Grades

1   A sound material that will contain tight knots and limited number of blemishes. It should be free of decay, checks, and splits.

2   Can have defects such as end-checks, loose knots, and some blemishes and discoloration. It should not have splits or distortions like warp.

3   Usually used as a construction lumber of medium quality. Can contain various types of defects some of which should be cut out before the material is used.

4   A construction lumber of low quality. Can contain many defects, even open knot holes.

5   Lowest quality material. It can be used as a filler but much of it will be waste.

Structural Grades

CONSTRUCTION   This is the best quality structural material.

STANDARD   Very similar to "construction" but will have defects.

UTILITY   Structural material but of poor quality. Useable, but should be reinforced with additional components or by increasing number of pieces used.

ECONOMY   The lowest quality structural material.

(Continued on next page)

Pointers on Wood Grading (cont'd.)

Grades for Hardwood Lumber

FIRSTS   The top of the line for super cabinet making. Should be over 90% clear on both sides.

SECONDS   A good choice for most cabinetwork. Should be at least 80% clear on both sides.

FIRSTS AND SECONDS   Combines "firsts" and "seconds" but should contain a minimum of 20% "firsts."

SELECTS   A good material for cabinetwork but some culling may have to be done. One side is ungraded but the other should be at least 90% clear.

1 COMMON   Often used for interior and less demanding cabinetwork. One side should be at least 65% clear.

2 COMMON   Often used for paneling and flooring. One side should be about 50% clear. Sometimes used for painted projects.

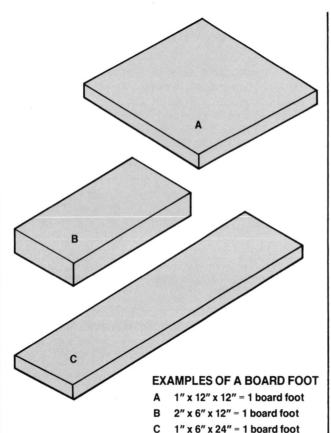

EXAMPLES OF A BOARD FOOT

A   1″ x 12″ x 12″ = 1 board foot
B   2″ x 6″ x 12″ = 1 board foot
C   1″ x 6″ x 24″ = 1 board foot

To Find Number of Board Feet in Any Piece of Wood, Use Following Formula:

$$\frac{T \times W \times L}{12} = \text{board feet}$$

T = thickness in inches
W = width in inches
L = length in feet

Examples:

(A   4″ x 24″ x 12′)

$$\frac{4 \times 24 \times 12}{12} = 96 \text{ board feet}$$

(A   1″ x 12″ x 18′)

$$\frac{1 \times 12 \times 18}{12} = 18 \text{ board feet}$$

Cross Section of a Tree

You can learn much about wood by studying a cross section of a tree. The size of the inner cores (pith and heartwood) increase each year as the tree's diameter grows. There is a lot of difference between heartwood lumber and material cut from outer areas of summer and spring growth. For one thing, heartwood is generally closer grained and harder. In some species, like redwood, it is the section of the tree that is resistant to insect damage. How and from what areas boards are cut determines such things as grain pattern and warpage characteristics.

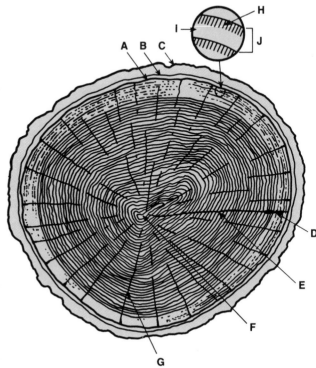

A.   CAMBIAL ZONE
B.   INNER BARK
C.   OUTER BARK
D.   SAP WOOD
E.   HEARTWOOD
F.   PITH
G.   VASCULAR RAY
H.   LATEWOOD
I.   EARLYWOOD
J.   ANNUAL RING

Common Methods of Sawing Logs

Economical method called "plain-sawed" for hardwoods; "flat-grained" for softwoods. Sawing is done lengthwise, tangent to the growth rings. This method results in the greatest amount of lumber with minimum waste. The grain pattern on the surface of the sawed material is the common "U" or "V" shape; annual rings are very apparent.

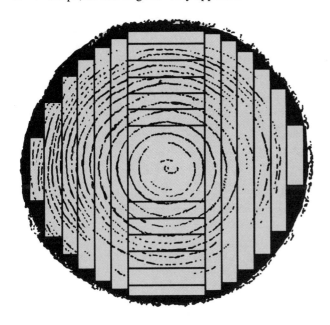

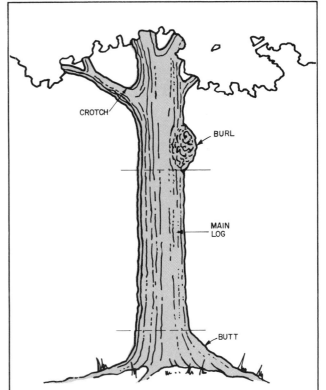

Various areas of a tree lend themselves to particular applications. Lumber, of course, comes from the bulk of the tree. Because of exotic configurations, the burl, butt, and crotch areas are usually formed into veneers.

This method is called "quarter-sawed" for hardwood; "edge-grained" for softwood. Boards are sliced from quarter sections of a log with cuts running parallel to the radius of the sections. Advantages include figure beauty and less danger of warping. Grain pattern is generally straight lines running parallel to the long dimension. Lumber produced this way is more costly.

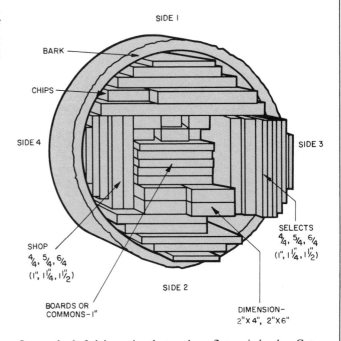

One method of plain sawing that produces flat-grain lumber. Cuts are made on four sides of the log leaving a solid, center timber for a particular purpose, or which can be reduced further as shown.

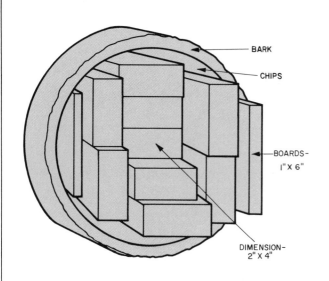

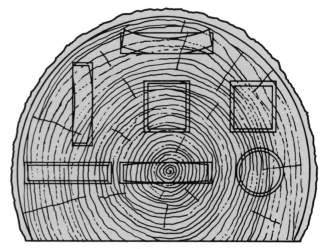

A typical method of sawing lumber from small logs.

Shrinkage factors are determined by the area from which the material is cut. This affects the warpage characteristics of the boards.

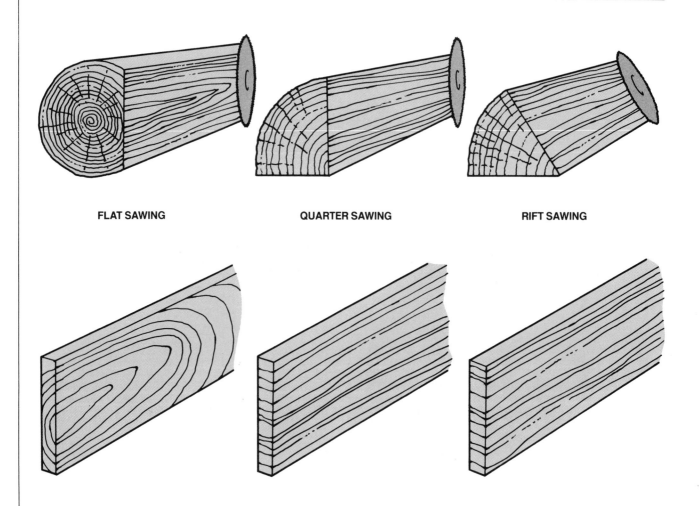

FLAT SAWING   **QUARTER SAWING**   **RIFT SAWING**

Grain patterns that result from different kinds of sawing.

WOOD DISTORTIONS (WARPAGE)

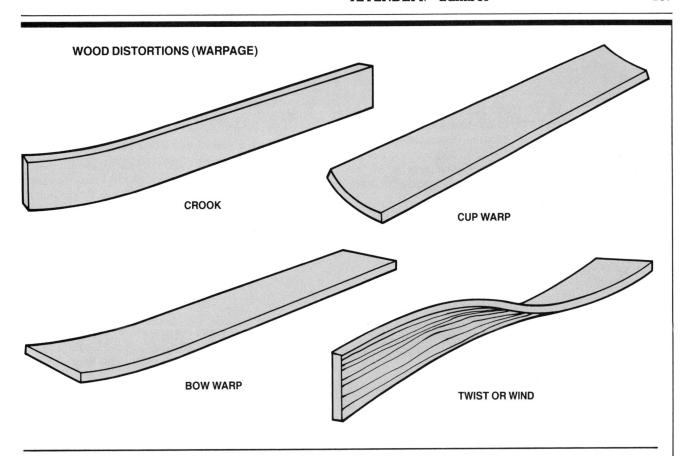

CROOK

CUP WARP

BOW WARP

TWIST OR WIND

TYPICAL LUMBER PRODUCT CLASSIFICATIONS		
MATERIAL	**THICKNESS**	**WIDTH**
Board lumber	1″	2″ or more
Light framing	2″- 4″	2″- 4″
Studs	2″- 4″	2″- 6″
Structural light framing	2″- 4″	2″- 4″
Beams and stringers	5″ and more	More than 2″ greater than thickness
Posts and timbers	5″ and more	Not more than 2″ greater than thickness
Decking	2″- 4″	4″ and more
Siding	Shaped pieces—precut pieces—dimension at butt edge = thickness	
Moldings	Shaped pieces—purchased by linear foot	

Note: Lumber lengths usually start at 6 feet—increase in multiples of 2 feet.
Lumber materials ordered in sequence of thickness, width, and length.
Examples: 1″ x 6″ x 8′ ; 2″ x 8″ x 10′

Lumber Marks

These marks are applicable to all western lumber species graded under the supervision of the Western Wood Products Association.

A WWPA grade stamp on a piece of lumber indicates its assigned grade, species or species combination, moisture condition at time of surfacing, the mill of origin and may also give other useful information. At buyers' request, mills authorized to use WWPA grade stamps will grademark the lumber they ship. Included are nearly a dozen commercially important western lumber species.

This is the official Association certification mark. It denotes that the product was graded under WWPA supervision. The symbol is registered with the U.S. Patent Office and may be used only when authorized by the Western Wood Products Association.

12

Each mill is assigned a permanent number. Some mills are identified by mill name or abbreviation instead of by mill number.

2 COM

This is an example of an official grade name abbreviation, in this case 2 Common Boards as described in the WWPA 1970 Grading Rules. Its appearance in a grade mark identifies the grade of a piece of lumber.

This is a species mark identifying the tree species from which the lumber is sawn, in this case Douglas Fir.

S-DRY
MC 15
S-GRN

These marks denote the moisture content of the lumber when manufactured. "S-DRY" indicates a moisture content not exceeding 19 percent. "MC 15" indicates a moisture content not exceeding 15 percent. "S-GRN" indicates that the moisture content exceeded 19 percent.

When an Inspection Certificate issued by the Western Wood Products Association is required on a shipment of lumber and specific grade marks are not used, the stock is identified by an imprint of the Association mark and the number of the shipping mill or inspector.

Note: All of the above components may appear in various combinations in the official grade stamps.

Courtesy of Western Wood Products Association.

How to Read Lumber Marks

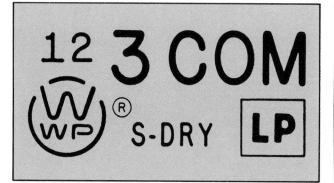

12	Identifies mill
3 COM	Identifies grade
LP	Identifies species (lodgepole pine)
S-DRY	Moisture content not over 19%

12	Identifies mill
C&BTR SEL	Grade—selects and finish
SP	Sugar pine
MC 15	Moisture content not over 15%

RELATIVE CHARACTERISTICS OF SOME POPULAR WOODS						
SPECIES	HARDNESS	WEIGHT	STRENGTH	GRAIN	GLUING QUALITY	NAILING QUALITY
Ash	High	High	Medium	Open	Medium	Medium
Basswood	Low	Low	Low	Medium	High	High
Beech	High	High	Medium	Medium	Low	Low
Birch	High	High	High	Close	Medium	Low
Cherry	High	Medium	Medium	Medium	High	Medium
Gum	Medium	Medium	Medium	Medium	High	High
Hickory	High	High	High	Open	High	Low
Mahogany	Medium	High	Medium	Open	High	Medium
Maple	High	High	High	Close	Medium	Low
Oak	High	High	High	Open	High	High
Pine	Low	Low	Low	Close	High	High
Poplar	Low	Low	Low	Open	High	High
Redwood	Low	Low	Medium	Medium	High	Medium
Walnut	High	Medium	Medium	Medium	High	Medium

LUMBER SIZES			
WHAT YOU ASK FOR	ACTUAL SIZE	WHAT YOU ASK FOR	ACTUAL SIZE
1 x 2	¾ x 1½	2 x 4	1½ x 3½
1 x 3	¾ x 2½	2 x 6	1½ x 5½
1 x 4	¾ x 3½	2 x 8	1½ x 7¼
1 x 5	¾ x 4½	2 x 10	1½ x 9¼
1 x 6	¾ x 5½	2 x 12	1½ x 11¼
1 x 8	¾ x 7¼	3 x 4	2½ x 3½
1 x 10	¾ x 9¼	4 x 4	3½ x 3½
1 x 12	¾ x 11¼	4 x 6	3½ x 5½
2 x 2	1½ x 1½	6 x 6	5½ x 5½
2 x 3	1½ x 2½	8 x 8	7½ x 7½

BOARD FOOT CONTENT IN COMMON LUMBER SIZES									
IN INCHES		BOARD LENGTH (IN FEET)							
THICK	WIDTH	10	12	14	16	18	20	22	24
1	2	1.666	2	2.333	2.666	3.0	3.333	3.666	4
1	3	2.5	3	3.5	4.0	4.5	5.0	5.5	6
1	4	3.333	4	4.666	5.333	6.0	6.666	7.333	8
1	5	4.167	5	5.833	6.666	7.5	8.333	9.167	10
1	6	5.0	6	7.0	8.0	9.0	10.0	11.0	12
1	7	5.833	7	8.167	9.333	10.5	11.666	12.833	14
1	8	6.666	8	9.333	10.666	12.0	13.333	14.666	16
1	9	7.5	9	10.5	12.0	13.5	15.0	16.5	18
1	10	8.333	10	11.666	13.333	15.0	16.666	18.333	20
1	12	10.0	12	14.0	16.0	18.0	20.0	22.0	24
1	14	11.666	14	16.333	18.666	21.0	23.333	25.666	28
1	16	13.333	16	18.666	21.333	24.0	26.666	29.333	32
2	2	3.333	4	4.666	5.333	6.0	6.666	7.333	8
2	3	5.0	6	7.0	8.0	9.0	10.0	11.0	12
2	4	6.666	8	9.333	10.666	12.0	13.333	14.666	16
2	6	10.0	12	14.0	16.0	18.0	20.0	22.0	24
2	8	13.333	16	18.666	21.333	24.0	26.666	29.333	32
2	9	15.0	18	21.0	24.0	27.0	30.0	33.0	36
2	10	16.666	20	23.333	26.666	30.0	33.333	36.666	40
2	12	20.0	24	28.0	32.0	36.0	40.0	44.0	48

APPENDIX

2.

Panel Materials

The first panel materials—plywood—began to appear in the last half of the nineteenth century. The manufacture of plywood was made possible by the development of new wood saws, glues, and processing equipment. With continued development, manufacturers introduced more and better varieties of panel materials—hardboard, particleboard, waferboard, strand board, and plywood for many different purposes.

The information in this section will help you to understand the different panel materials that are commonly available and how to best use them. You'll find that although the materials here are grouped under the same general heading, they are very different. With most of the materials, there are a list of terms that apply to just a single material. Materials differ in relative strength, durability, how they take paints, stains, and finishes, and how they may be worked and joined—all of this is discussed. Materials are also graded and classed and specified differently. With each type of panel material, there may be many variations for different applications—interior and exterior, underlayment, fire-retardant, etc. All the common variations are explained, and there are instructions for how to tell one variation from the next.

Waferboard

Waferboard was designed as a structural-use panel, but because it is easy to work with and has a distinctive appearance, its applications have been broadened to include a host of home craft projects. The material has become popular for wall paneling and other uses that include doors or door paneling, fencing, outdoor sheds and farm structures, and decorative inside projects.

Standard panel size is 4' x 8'—thicknesses range from ¼" through ¾".

The panels are made by compressing wafer-like pieces of wood that are bonded with phenolic resin. The wafers can differ in size and thickness, and they can be assembled randomly or in a particular direction. Sometimes the wafers are arranged in layers that relate to their size and thickness.

The panels can be stained, painted, or finished in natural fashion. Semi-transparent stains will provide color while allowing wafer grain and other natural characteristics to show through. When light colors are used, it's recommended that the stain be an oil-based type to guard against discoloration that can happen because of water-soluble compounds (extractives) in the wood.

The material can be covered with either oil- or water-base paints. Most times it's best to use a primer or undercoat before the final finish, but do a test on a scrap piece if the color you wish to apply is very dark. It's possible that a single coat may do.

Varnishes and oils may be used for a natural finish. Two coats of clear, penetrating sealer with a light sanding between coats and after the final coat will produce an attractive finish that is easily maintained. Use a sealer before applying a varnish finish.

The attractive wood texture of Waferwood adapts to "non-structural" applications such as these kitchen cabinets. Other uses include wall paneling, basic furniture, shelving, and storage projects.

Various wood species are used in the manufacture of Waferboard, but aspen (a soft-grain hardwood), is used most often. Logs are debarked and then cut into lengths that are easy to handle.

Large, generally paper-thin wafers are produced by moving the log against a set of razor-like knives that are attached to a rotating surface. The wafers are then dried, separated from waste, and sorted by size.

After wafers are mixed with phenolic resin and assembled on mats, they are fed into a hydraulic press where heat and pressure forms them into solid wood panels.

Particleboard

Particleboard is a man-made panel that may be composed of various wood materials such as flakes, chips, splinters, various selected mill wastes, or even sawdust. The materials are combined with a bonding agent and put through the same type of heat and pressure procedure as waferboard. This results in hard-surfaced panels that may be used as is or as core material for various types of surface veneers. The bonding agent that is used and the particular manufacturing procedures determine the density of the panel and whether it is suitable for exterior applications.

Common panel six is 4' x 8'—readily available thicknesses range from ¼" to ¾". In addition to paneling, the material is available as, for example, bull-nosed stair treads ready for covering with carpeting, or resilient flooring. It is often used as a core for doors and as vinyl-wrapped jambs and molding. The fact that it is flat, smooth, and stable makes it an ideal substrate for countertops and similar projects. Kitchen cabinet manufacturers use particleboard for backs, sides, shelves, and front panels. The construction industry finds it a good material for floor underlayment.

Particleboard is very abrasive, so sawing should be done with a tungsten carbide-toothed blade; a metal-cutting blade when saber sawing. Use tungsten carbide bits when shaping the material with a router.

The material can be finished in various ways—left natural, stained, painted, or varnished. Painting, unless you are using panels that were factory-prepared for the purpose, calls for application of sanding sealer with special attention paid to edges, before final coats. Filling can be eliminated if you wish to achieve a textured effect.

Use oil-based instead of water-based material for staining. Stains can be overcoated with finish like varnish, or such materials can be used alone for a natural finish.

Edges are usually more absorbent and "rougher" than surfaces and need more attention. They can be made smooth with applications of wood paste or, as is common, covered with strips of wood, veneer, or molding. Edges are often covered with special metal moldings when the material is used as a substrate for countertops.

Particleboard Terms

DENSITY   This tells the weight of a panel per cubic foot and has an influence on its strength. Lightweight projects can be constructed with low-density particleboard. Panel strength is also affected by board composition and construction.

TYPE 1   Interior-use panel made with a urea-formaldehyde binder.

TYPE 2   Phenolic resin is used as a binder. Panels are *resistant* to moisture and heat.

CLASS   The product's overall specifications.

MODULUS OF ELASTICITY   Measure of resistance to deflection under load. Generally, it indicates the stiffness of a panel.

MODULUS OF RUPTURE   The measure of a load that is needed to cause a break in a panel. PSI = pounds of load pressure per square inch.

INTERNAL BOND   A measure of the strength of the bond between the individual particles that compose the pane. Tested by measuring the force panel faces will withstand before failure occurs.

SCREW HOLDING   How well does a screw hold? Tests indicate the force required to pull out a No. 10, type A sheet metal screw from the face and edge of a panel.

LINEAR EXPANSION   A measurement of average dimensional changes that can be caused by atmospheric or environmental humidity.

Note: Specifications are stamped on panels, usually in three letter/number symbols. Examples: 1-B-1, 1-A-2. The first symbol (a number) tells the *type*, which bonding adhesive was used. The second symbol indicates density. The third symbol is an overall classification and, in a sense, indicates the actual strength of the panel.

Panels with lower internal bonds are more flexible. This is important when considering the length of span between supports. Generally, denser particleboard is more rigid and can support greater loads without failure. When in doubt it is wise to test, use what the shelf must hold as the test load. This will reveal whether intermediate supports are necessary.

PARTICLEBOARD SPECIFICATIONS								
TYPE	DENSITY	CLASS	MODULUS OF RUPTURE (PSI)	MODULUS OF ELASTICITY (PSI)	INTERNAL BOND (PSI)	LINEAR EXPANSION (%)	SCREW FACE LBS.	HOLDING EDGE LBS.
1*	A	1	2,400	350,000	200	.55	450	
1*	A	2	3,400	350,000	140	.55		
1*	B	1	1,600	250,000	70	.35	225	160
1*	B	2	2,400	400,000	60	.30	225	200
1*	C	1	800	150,000	20	.30	125	
1*	C	2	1,400	250,000	30	.30	175	
2**	A	1	2,400	350,000	125	.55	450	
2**	A	2	3,400	500,000	400	.55	500	350
2**	B	1	1,800	250,000	65	.35	225	160
2**	B	2	2,500	450,000	60	.25	250	200

*Interior applications—generally bonded with urea-formaldehyde resin.
**Interior and exterior applications—moisture and heat-resistant binders, generally phenolic resin.

A = High density (at least 50 lbs./cu. ft.).
B = Medium density (between 37 and 50 lbs./cu. ft.).
C = Low density (37 lbs./cu. ft. and under).

Courtesy of National Particleboard Association

PARTICULAR TYPES OF PARTICLEBOARD		
TYPE	**DESCRIPTION**	**TYPICAL USES**
CORE	Basic material of various densities and properties	Laminated components, furniture, casework, doors, paneling
VENEERED	Corestock overlaid with wood veneer or other material. Ready for use.	Cabinetwork, panels, furniture, dividers, wainscots
OVERLAID	Veneered with fiber sheets or material like hardboard and plastic laminates	Paneling, countertops, furniture, doors, cabinetwork
FILLED	Material that has been surface filled and sanded	For projects to be painted
EXTERIOR	Treated with special bonding materials	Exterior applications but material is not waterproof
UNDERCOATED OR PRIMED	Painted base coat applied by manufacturer. Available in exterior or interior types	For products that will be painted
UNDERLAYMENT	Panels that are specifically engineered as a substrate	Common application is underlayment for carpeting and other finish flooring
FIRE-RETARDANT	Particles are treated with special fire-retardant materials	Used where required by building codes
TOXIC-TREATED	Insect and mold resistant chemicals added to particles	Applications requiring protection against insects and decay

Even the "roughest" particleboard can be brought to paintable condition by applications of thin wood-paste. Sand smooth between coats. Pay special attention to edges. You can eliminate the procedure if you obtain panels that have been factory-prepared for painting.

A unique application for particleboard—preparing edge-beveled pieces for arrangement in an ashlar pattern. I used the idea to cover walls in a hallway. It was a great way to make use of a quantity of scrap I obtained from a local lumberyard.

Terms That Apply to Plywood and Some Other Panel Materials

APA Abbreviation for AMERICAN PLYWOOD ASSOCIATION. Organization representing most of the structural wood panel manufacturers in the nation.

BACK-PRIMING Priming the back of a panel. For example, back-priming the back of cabinet doors will prevent them from warping.

BACKSTAMP Identification stamp on the back of some panels.

BATTEN A plywood or lumber strip that conceals and protects the joint between panels. Often used decoratively.

BEVEL (JOINT) Makes a smooth joint when edges or ends of panels are butted.

BLOW A localized delamination of plies that can be caused by a buildup of steam pressure during the pressing procedure. Can be caused by moisture or excessive glue spread.

BOND Veneers are *bonded* to form a panel of plywood. Heat or pressure, sometimes both, are used so the glue will cure properly.

BOW A distortion. The lengthwise plane of the panel isn't flat.

BRUSHED A surface treatment that accents the grain pattern to create an interesting and attractive texture.

CAULK A sealant, usually waterproof, that is used to fill joints or seams. Available as a putty, in rope form, and as cartridge-contained compounds.

CENTER The inner piece of a panel that has five or more plies. The grain of the center runs parallel with the grain of the face and back.

CHECKING Exposure to changing conditions of dryness and moisture can cause cracks or "checks." Eliminate or minimize by sealing edges and priming, or sealing surfaces before installation.

COMPOSITE PANEL A panel with veneer surfaces but a reconstituted wood core.

CORE The inner plies of conventional plywood. The constituted wood in composite panels.

CORE GAP Open veneer joint that results when core sections are not butted together during manufacturing. Sizes of gaps is controlled by product standards.

CROSSBAND Core plies placed so grain is at right angles to surface veneers.

CUP A distortion. The panel is concave across its small dimension.

DELAMINATION Bond failure that causes separation between plies or within reconstituted wood cores.

EDGE SEALING Coating edges of panels with a sealant (paint or similar product) to reduce possibility of water absorption.

EDGE VOID A gap in the edge of a plywood panel. A defect caused by inner plies splitting or breaking away.

EMBOSSED Special treatment that provides textured effects in the surface of the panel. Usually done by heat and pressure against a master pattern.

EXTERIOR TYPE Plywood designed for outdoor or marine use. Bonding is 100% waterproof.

FACE GRAIN Grain direction of a panel's outer plies. Greatest strength is parallel to the face grain.

GRADES (VENEER)
A Smooth and can be painted. Permissible repairs must be neat. Can take a natural finish when project is not critical.
B Solid surface veneer. Can obtain tight knots and circular repair plugs.
C Can contain knotholes but totals within a specified area are limited by standards. The minimum veneer grade used in exterior type plywood.
C (plugged) An improved C veneer manufactured to standards that limit sizes of splits and knotholes.
D Can contain knots and knotholes up to 2½″ and sometimes larger. Some splits are also permitted.
N Selected heartwood or sapwood. Some repairs permitted but no open defects. Usually a special order, natural finish material.

HDO (HIGH DENSITY OVERLAY) Exterior plywood with resin-impregnated fiber overlay. Surface is hard and smooth, and resistant to chemicals and abrasion. Stands up to punishing applications.

INTERIOR TYPE Plywood manufactured for indoor use or construction subjected to temporary moisture. Interior types are often bonded with exterior glue.

LUMBER CORE Plywood with a core of lumber strips. Face and back plies are veneer.

MDO (MEDIUM DENSITY OVERLAY) Exterior plywood with an opaque resin-treated fiber overlay. Surface is smooth and excellent as a base for paint.

NON-VENEERED PANELS Panels of reconstituted wood such as "waferboard", "oriented strand board", or "particleboard." Panels manufactured without veneer plies.

ORIENTED STRAND BOARD Panels of reconstituted, mechanically-oriented wood strands that are bonded with resins under heat and pressure. The material may also be used as a center layer in composite panels.

PARTICLEBOARD Panels of reconstituted wood *particles* that are bonded with resins under heat and pressure.

PEELER LOG Selected log, debarked, and then turned against a long knife to produce thin, continuous sheets of veneer which are then sized, dried, and graded.

REPAIR One of several methods of covering defects. A "patch" is a sound wood insert. "Boat" patches are ovals with pointed or rounded ends. "Router" patches have parallel

(Continued on next page)

sides and rounded ends. "Sled" patches are rectangles with feathered ends. A "plug" may be a circle of wood or a synthetic filler. A "Shim" is a long, narrow repair that can be wood or a synthetic material. There are standards for repairs in particular veneer grades.

TEXTURED   Panels with surface textures. Available in exterior and interior types. Examples are: "brushed", "rough-sawn", "kerfed", "channel groove" and "reverse board & batten".

TOUCH SANDED   Light surface sanding during manufacture brings panels to a uniform thickness but sander "skips" are admissable.

TYPES—EXTERIOR

A-A   Sanded panels with A-grade face and back and C-grade inner plies. Used where appearance on both sides is important. Typical applications include built-ins, cabinets, signs, boats, and fences.

A-B   Sanded panels with A-grade face and B-grade back. Often used in place of A-A when appearance of one side is not critical.

A-C   Panels with A-grade face and C-grade back; inner plies usually C-grade. Use when appearance of only one surface is important. Typical applications include fences, soffits, and building exteriors (farm).

B-B   Panels with B-grade veneer on both surfaces. Utility panel that is paintable.

B-C   Face is B-grade, back is C-grade. Utilitarian material that is often used as a base for exterior coatings.

C-C (plugged)   Face is C-plugged grade; back and inner plies are C-grade. Panels are touch sanded. Often used for severe moisture conditions.

TYPES—INTERIOR

A-A   Panels with A-grade veneers on face and back, with D-grade inner plies. Used when appearance of both sides is important. Often bonded with exterior glue. Applications include built-ins, furniture, cabinets, and partitions.

A-B   A reasonable substitute for A-A when the appearance of one side is not critical. A-grade face, B-grade back, D-grade inner plies.

A-D   A-grade face, D-grade back. Used on projects where smoothness and appearance of only one side is important.

B-B   Utility panel with B-grade veneer on face and back.

B-D   B-grade face, D-grade back. A utility panel often used as a backing material or shelving when appearance is not critical.

C-D (plugged)   Face veneer is C-plugged grade; back is D-grade. Surface is touch sanded. Often used in hidden areas.

UNSANDED   Interior or exterior sheathing grade panels. Made for utility applications.

WAFERBOARD   Non-veneered panels composed of reconstituted wood *wafers* as opposed to *particles* or *strands*. The wafers are bonded under heat and pressure with resins.

Wood Species Used in Plywood Manufactured Under Specific Product Standards

Many wood species can be used in the manufacture of plywood. These species are divided into groups according to relative strength and stiffness. The species in Group 1 are the strongest and stiffest; Group 2 is next and so on. Each group is designated by number in the APA trademark stamped on the back of the panel and tells, generally, the species used for the *face* and *back* veneers. The consumer should check local availability if a particular species is desired.

Group 1

Apitong; American beech; sweet and yellow birch; Douglas fir (A); kapur; keruing; western larch; sugar maple; caribbean and ocote pine; loblolly, longleaf, shortleaf, and slash pine; tanoak.

Group 2

Port Orford cedar; cypress; Douglas fir (B); balsam, California red, grand, noble, pacific silver, and white fir; western hemlock; almond, bagikan, mayapis, red, tangile, and white lauan; black maple; mengkulang; red mereanti(C); merwawa; pond, red, Virginia, and western white pine; black, red, and sitka spruce; sweetgum; tamarack; yellow poplar.

Group 3

Red alder; paper birch; Alaska cedar; subalpine fir; eastern hemlock; bigleaf maple; jack, lodgepole, ponderosa, and spruce pine; redwood; englemann and white spruce.

Group 4

Bigtooth and quaking aspen; cativo; incense and western red cedar; eastern and black cottonwood; eastern white and sugar pine.

Group 5

Basswood; balsam poplar.

Notes:

A   Douglas fir trees from Washington, Oregon, California, Idaho, Montana, Wyoming, and provinces of Alberta and British Columbia.

B   Douglas fir trees from Nevada, Utah, Colorado, Arizona, and New Mexico.

C   This species (red meranti) is limited to those with a specific gravity of .41 or more based on green volume and oven dry weight.

Courtesy of APA

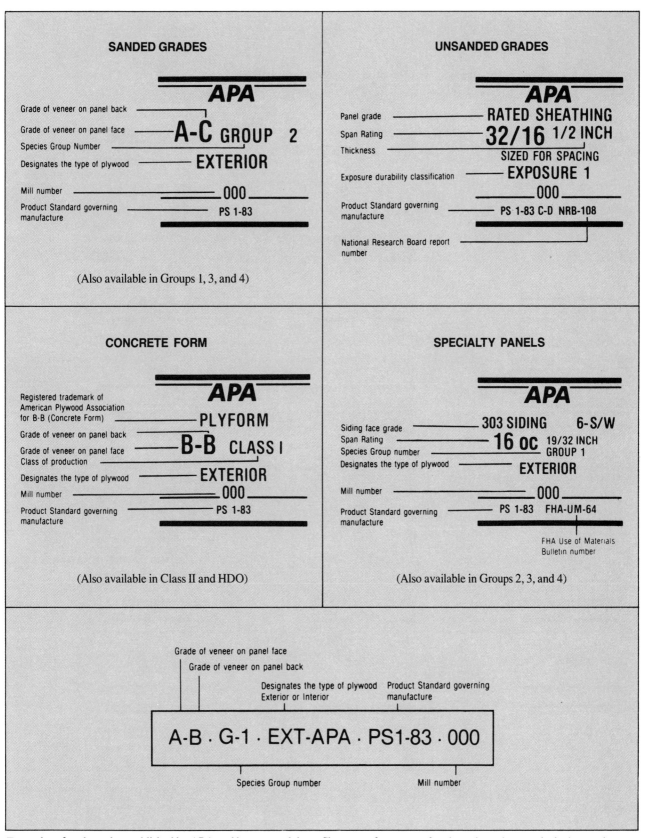

SANDED GRADES

Grade of veneer on panel back
Grade of veneer on panel face
Species Group Number
Designates the type of plywood

APA
A-C GROUP 2
EXTERIOR

Mill number
Product Standard governing manufacture

000
PS 1-83

(Also available in Groups 1, 3, and 4)

UNSANDED GRADES

Panel grade
Span Rating
Thickness

Exposure durability classification

Product Standard governing manufacture

National Research Board report number

APA
RATED SHEATHING
32/16 1/2 INCH
SIZED FOR SPACING
EXPOSURE 1
000
PS 1-83 C-D NRB-108

CONCRETE FORM

Registered trademark of American Plywood Association for B-B (Concrete Form)
Grade of veneer on panel back
Grade of veneer on panel face
Class of production
Designates the type of plywood
Mill number
Product Standard governing manufacture

APA
PLYFORM
B-B CLASS I
EXTERIOR
000
PS 1-83

(Also available in Class II and HDO)

SPECIALTY PANELS

Siding face grade
Span Rating
Species Group number
Designates the type of plywood
Mill number
Product Standard governing manufacture

APA
303 SIDING   6-S/W
16 OC 19/32 INCH
GROUP 1
EXTERIOR
000
PS 1-83 FHA-UM-64

FHA Use of Materials Bulletin number

(Also available in Groups 2, 3, and 4)

Grade of veneer on panel face
Grade of veneer on panel back
Designates the type of plywood Exterior or Interior
Product Standard governing manufacture

A-B · G-1 · EXT-APA · PS1-83 · 000

Species Group number   Mill number

Examples of trademarks established by APA and how to read them. Shown are four types of trademarks and one typical edge mark. Notations tell the meaning of each of the elements.

A-A·G-1·EXPOSURE1·APA·PS1-83·000

APA A-A

Use where appearance of both sides is important for interior applications such as built-ins, cabinets, furniture, partitions; and exterior applications such as fences, signs, boats, shipping containers, tanks, ducts, etc. Smooth surfaces suitable for painting. EXPOSURE DURABILITY CLASSIFICATIONS: Interior, Exposure 1, Exterior. COMMON THICKNESSES: 1/4, 11/32, 3/8, 15/32, 1/2, 19/32, 5/8, 23/32, 3/4.

A-B·G-1·EXPOSURE1·APA·PS1-83·000

APA A-B

For use where appearance of one side is less important but where two solid surfaces are necessary. EXPOSURE DURABILITY CLASSIFICATIONS: Interior, Exposure 1, Exterior. COMMON THICKNESSES: 1/4, 11/32, 3/8, 15/32, 1/2, 19/32, 5/8, 23/32, 3/4.

B-B·G-2·EXPOSURE1·APA·PS1-83·000

APA B-B

Utility panels with two solid sides. EXPOSURE DURABILITY CLASSIFICATIONS: Interior, Exposure 1, Exterior. COMMON THICKNESSES: 1/4, 11/32, 3/8, 15/32, 1/2, 19/32, 5/8, 23/32, 3/4.

APA
UNDERLAYMENT
GROUP 1
EXPOSURE 1
000
PS 1-83

APA UNDERLAYMENT

For application over structural subfloor. Provides smooth surface for application of carpet and possesses high concentrated and impact load resistance. Touch-sanded. For areas to be covered with thin resilient flooring, specify panels with fully sanded face. EXPOSURE DURABILITY CLASSIFICATIONS: Interior, Exposure 1. COMMON THICKNESSES: 3/8, 1/2, 19/32, 5/8, 23/32, 3/4.

APA
A-C   GROUP 1
EXTERIOR
000
PS 1-83

APA A-C

For use where appearance of only side is important in exterior applications such as soffits, fences, structural uses, boxcar and truck linings, farm buildings, tanks, trays, commercial refrigerators, etc. EXPOSURE DURABILITY CLASSIFICATION: Exterior. COMMON THICKNESSES: 1/4, 11/32, 3/8, 15/32, 1/2, 19/32, 5/8, 23/32, 3/4.

APA
B-C   GROUP 1
EXTERIOR
000
PS 1-83

APA B-C

Utility panel for farm service and work buildings, boxcar and truck linings, containers, tanks, agricultural equipment, as a base for exterior coatings and other exterior uses or applications subject to high or continuous moisture. EXPOSURE DURABILITY CLASSIFICATION: Exterior. COMMON THICKNESSES: 1/4, 11/32, 3/8, 15/32, 1/2, 19/32, 5/8, 23/32, 3/4.

APA
C-C PLUGGED
GROUP 2
EXTERIOR
000
PS 1-83

APA C-C PLUGGED

For use as an underlayment over structural subfloor, refrigerated or controlled atmosphere storage rooms, pallet fruit bins, tanks, boxcar and truck floors and linings, open soffits, and other similar applications where continuous or severe moisture may be present. Provides smooth surface for application of carpet and possesses high concentrated and impact load resistance. Touch-sanded. EXPOSURE DURABILITY CLASSIFICATION: Exterior. COMMON THICKNESSES: 3/8, 1/2, 19/32, 5/8, 23/32, 3/4.

APA
A-D   GROUP 1
EXPOSURE 1
000
PS 1-83

APA A-D

For use where appearance of only one side is important in interior applications, such as paneling, built-ins, shelving, partitions, flow racks, etc. EXPOSURE DURABILITY CLASSIFICATIONS: Interior, Exposure 1. COMMON THICKNESSES: 1/4, 11/32, 3/8, 15/32, 1/2, 19/32, 5/8, 23/32, 3/4.

APA
B-D   GROUP 2
INTERIOR
000
PS 1-83

APA B-D

Utility panel for backing, sides of built-ins, industry shelving, slip sheets, separator boards, bins and other interior or protected applications. EXPOSURE DURABILITY CLASSIFICATIONS: Interior, Exposure 1. COMMON THICKNESSES: 1/4, 11/32, 3/8, 15/32, 1/2, 19/32, 5/8, 23/32, 3/4.

APA
C-D PLUGGED
GROUP 2
EXPOSURE 1
000
PS 1-83

APA C-D PLUGGED

For built-ins, cable reels, walkways, separator boards and other interior or protected applications. Not a substitute for Underlayment or APA Rated Sturd-I-Floor as it lacks their puncture resistance. Touch-sanded. EXPOSURE DURABILITY CLASSIFICATIONS: Interior, Exposure 1. COMMON THICKNESSES: 3/8, 1/2, 19/32, 5/8, 23/32, 3/4.

A guide to sanded and touch-sanded plywood. The trademarks shown here are typical facsimiles. (APA standards)

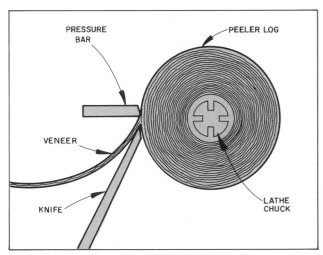

Continuous, thin sheets of veneer are sliced from a selected log that has been debarked and mounted on a lathe. The veneer is then sized, dried, and graded.

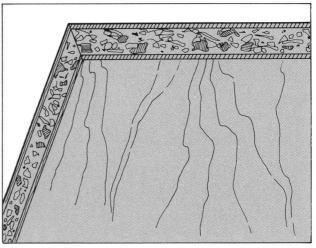

Composite panels are faced with veneers but have cores of reconstituted wood as opposed to conventional plywoods that have veneer cores.

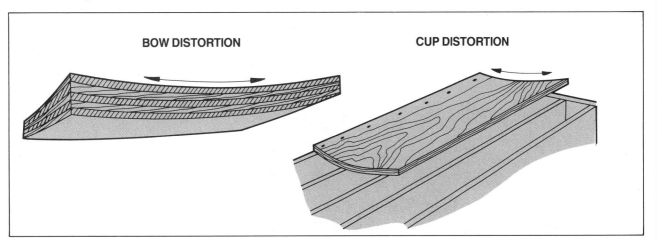

The panel is not flat lengthwise.

The panel is not flat crosswise.

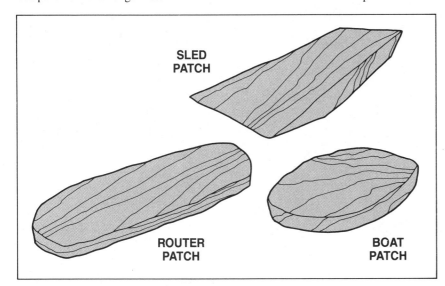

Examples of patches that are used to replace defects in veneers. The sizes, numbers, and shapes of repair pieces in given veneer grades are subject to established standards.

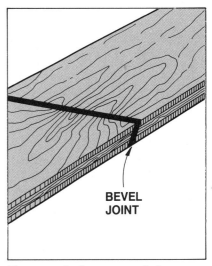

The connection between panels that are joined edge-to-edge or end-to-end is smoother when a bevel joint is used.

Available Panel Material

A. STANDARD PLYWOOD   Panels are all veneer, usually an odd number placed so the grain in each ply is at right angles to the next one. Grain of front and back veneers runs parallel to panel's long dimension.

B. COMPOSITE PANELS   Face and back veneers are bonded to a reconstituted wood core. Another design has a core of solid wood.

C. WAFERBOARD   Thin, wafer-like wood flakes are mixed with phenolic resin and treated with heat and pressure to form a solid material. Flakes can be randomly or directionally oriented.

D. ORIENTED STRAND BOARD   Panels consisting of small particles; usually arranged in layers by particular size. Particles are usually randomly oriented.

E. PARTICLEBOARD   Panels consisting of small particles; usually arranged in layers by particle size. Particles are usually randomly oriented.

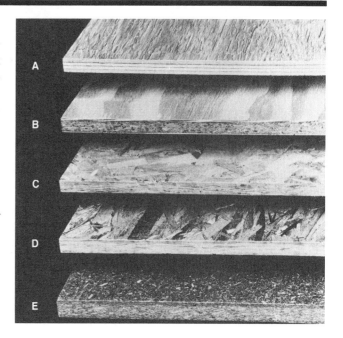

How house-siding plywood can be used to make an attractive project. Kerfed, rough-sawn plywood was used on this patio barbecue stand.

Textured panels. Plywood is available with surface textures and patterns. While essentially a house siding material, the panels can be used effectively for many home craft projects. The photo shows a "rough-sawn" texture. "Brushed", "kerfed", and "channel groove" are among other available designs.

Hardboard

Hardboard is a man-made product manufactured from natural wood materials (sometimes waste) that are reduced to basic fibers by special processes. One involves steaming and grinding; another places wood chips in a high-pressure enclosure into which steam is introduced in a manner that causes an explosion and reduces the chips to fibers.

The fibers are bonded with adhesive lignin, also a wood by-product, and then arranged in thick blankets on mats which carry them through a heat and pressure procedure that forms the fibers into solid, very dense, smooth panels. Particular materials may be added during the panel-forming steps that affect, among other things, the rigidity and the density of the final product.

Hardboard is available in various sizes and thicknesses. Those most likely to be available in local lumberyards, aside from decorative hardboards used as paneling, are 4' x 8' panels in thicknesses of ⅛" and ¼". Perforated hardboard (pegboard) comes in ¼" and sometimes ⅜" thicknesses.

Although hardboard is not as tough on cutting tools as particleboard, it is still a good idea to use carbide-toothed saw blades. Use a plywood blade or something similar if you use an all-steel blade. A combination blade will work but edges will be rougher than you might like. Because of the material's density, it is a good idea to drill pilot holes for nails. Casing nails are preferable to finishing nails when the fasteners must be concealed.

Always use a backup block when drilling. You'll find that hardboard has a greater tear-out problem when the bit breaks through than other materials.

The easiest way to achieve a successful finish on hardboard is to work with a *primed* or *sealed* type. Surface density makes it difficult to apply paint, so un-primed panels must be sanded to provide some "tooth". A fine sandpaper, about #380, wrapped around a wood block will do. You're not trying to renew the surface, just roughing it a bit, so heavy pressure isn't necessary.

Always use an undercoat that is compatible with the finish coat. It's good procedure to sand the undercoat before applying the final one.

Of course, hardboard can be used as the "core" for veneering materials such as plastic laminates, vinyls, and contact papers or plastics.

Types of Hardboard

TEMPERED   Hardboards with moisture inhibitors and other materials that were added before the manufacturing procedure to increase surface hardness, resistance to abrasion, and stiffness. These panels can take more punishment than untreated panels.

STANDARD   Do not resist moisture as well as tempered panels.

SERVICE-TEMPERED   Much the same as tempered hardboard but with a lower percentage of the additives.

SERVICE   Made without additives. Panels will have less tensile strength and resistance to moisture than other types.

INDUSTRIALITE   Special hardboards that are of medium density and lighter than others.

PRIMED   Panels with a base coat that makes them easier to paint. Sometimes the word "coated" is used in place of "primed".

SEALED OR FILLED   Panels with a special manufacturing treatment that allows them to take paint more easily.

PERFORATED   Panels with uniform holes that are used with special hooks and other types of hardware to form storage walls. Often called "pegboard".

EMBOSSED   Panels with a pattern that has been pressed in during manufacture. The embossing can resemble materials like basketweave, woodgrain, and leather.

FILIGREE   Panels that have through geometric or other types of designs. Typical applications are room dividers and cornices—wherever a light, airy feeling is desirable.

PATTERNED   Panels with pressed or machined surface patterns. Used to provide decorative touches. Applications include wainscots and dividers. Available as house siding.

STRAITED   Surface of panel has shallow, randomly-spaced grooves that run the long dimension. Some plywoods are also treated in this fashion.

GROOVED   Panels with grooves that run lengthwise. A siding material that can be used imaginatively elsewhere.

Hardboard Terms to Know

SURFACE   The condition of the face and back of the panel.

S1S   Means the panel has one smooth surface. The opposite side will have a mesh pattern or other rough texture.

S2S   Panels that are smooth on face and back.

WATER RESISTANCE   The amount of swelling that can occur when panels are subjected to extreme exposure. Standards testing requires that panels be fully submerged in water for a specific period of time.

MODULUS OF RUPTURE   What it takes to break a panel across its face. Tested in terms of number of pounds per square inch required to cause failure.

TENSILE STRENGTH   Tested by the force in pounds per square inch of pull that is needed to rupture internal bonding.

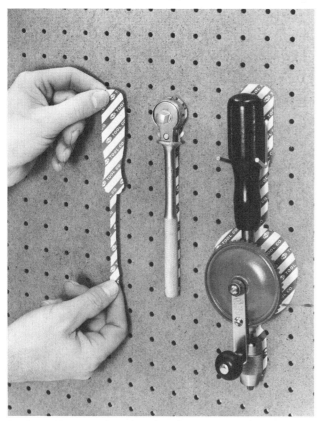

Perforated hardboard (pegboard) makes a good storage wall or cabinet back for placing tools. A paper silhouette helps keep things neat and organized—also lets you know when a tool is not in its proper place.

One example of many types of prefinished hardboard—Masonite's "Woodfield". Although created as wall paneling, the products can be used on other projects or merely to supply decorative accents. The panels are available in 4′ x 8′ sheets, ¼″ thick and can be applied with nails or adhesive. Other panel finishes include various wood species and surface grains, even brick and stone. Some of the panels are available perforated.

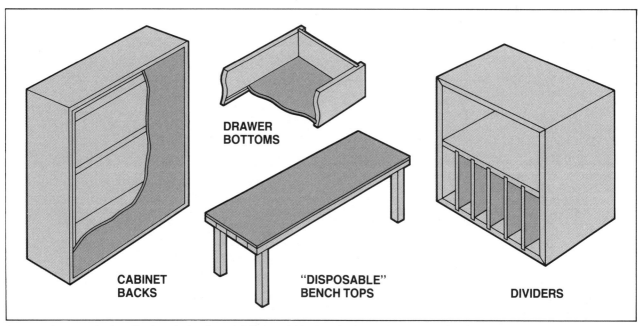

CABINET BACKS

DRAWER BOTTOMS

"DISPOSABLE" BENCH TOPS

DIVIDERS

Some typical, practical applications for hardboard. S1S material is okay for drawer bottoms, cabinet backs, and bench tops. Use S2S for dividers or partitions. Use tempered material, tacked down with nails for easy removal, for bench tops.

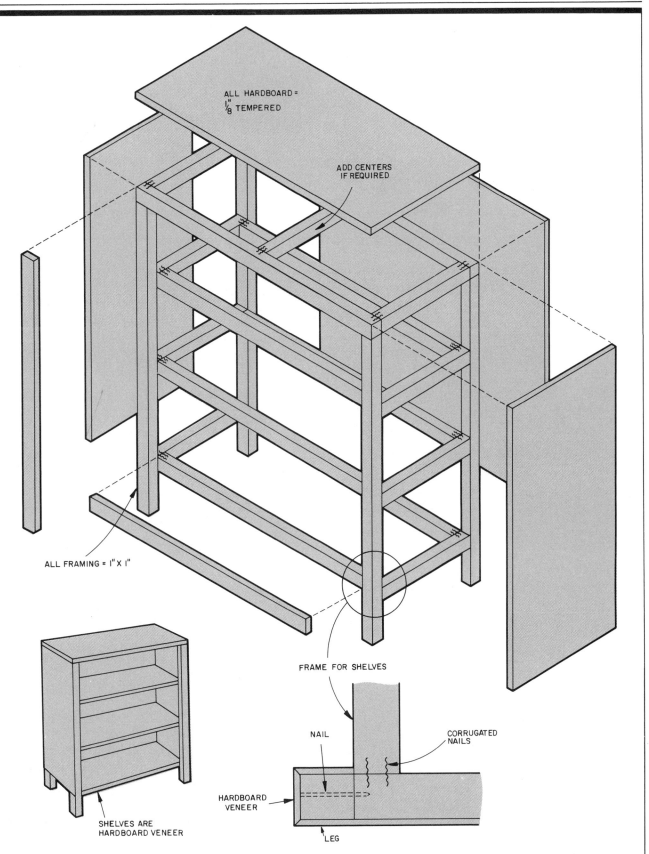

ALL HARDBOARD =
$\frac{1}{8}$" TEMPERED

ADD CENTERS
IF REQUIRED

ALL FRAMING = 1" X 1"

FRAME FOR SHELVES

NAIL

CORRUGATED
NAILS

HARDBOARD
VENEER

LEG

SHELVES ARE
HARDBOARD VENEER

One way to make a project using hardboard. The frame assembly should be strong even though attaching the covering will stiffen it. Decorative hardboards can be used on projects like this.

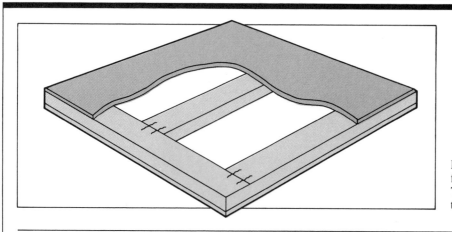

Make panels by constructing a sturdy frame then covering with thin hardboard. The hardboard can be attached with contact cement or glue.

HARDBOARD SPECIFICATIONS*								
TYPE	SURFACE	THICKNESS IN INCHES	WATER RESISTANCE				MODULUS OF RUPTURE (PSI)	TENSILE STRENGTH	
			ABSORPTION (%)		SWELLING (%)			PARALLEL TO SURFACE (PSI)	PERPENDICULAR TO SURFACE (PSI)
			S1S	S2S	S1S	S2S			
TEMPERED (1)	S1S	1/12	30		25		7000	3500	150
	S1S and S2S	1/10	20	25	16	20			
		1/8	15	20	11	16			
		3/16	12	18	10	15			
		1/4	10	12	8	11			
		5/16	8	11	8	10			
		3/8	8	10	8	9			
STANDARD (2)	S1S and S2S	1/12	40	40	30	30	5000	2500	100
		1/10	25	30	22	25			
		1/8	20	25	16	18			
		3/16	18	25	14	18			
		1/4	16	20	12	14			
		5/16	14	15	10	12			
		3/8	12	12	10	10			
SERVICE TEMPERED (3)	S1S and S2S	1/8	20	25	15	22	4500	2000	100
		3/16	18	20	13	18			
		1/4	15	20	13	14			
		3/8	14	18	11	14			
SERVICE (4)	S1S and S2S	1/8	30	30	25	25	3000	1500	75
		3/16	25	27	15	22			
		1/4	25	27	15	22			
		3/8	25	27	15	22			
		7/16	25	27	15	22			
		1/2	25	18	15	14			

*Most readily available types.

Oriented Strand Board (OSB)

OSB is a manufactured panel with a composition of strand-like particles of wood that are placed in layers and then compressed and bonded with phenolic resin. While the material was designed specifically for construction applications, its appearance and the fact that the panels are good on both sides have prompted its use in areas that range from wall paneling to shelving. Common panel size is 4' x 8'—thickness range is ⅜" to ¾".

The panels will take stain or paint and can be finished in natural tones. Semi-transparent stain will allow grain and other natural characteristics to show through, but oil-base types are recommended to prevent discoloration that can be caused by water-soluble compounds in the wood.

Oil-base or water-base (latex) paints can be used but a primer should be applied before the finish coat. Light-colored latex stains should be applied over a stain resistant undercoat.

Varnish or oils can be used for a natural finish. A popular treatment is two coats of penetrating sealer with a light sanding between applications and after the final one—then wax.

A variety of wood species can be used in the manufacture of OSB, but a soft-grain hardwood, usually aspen, is most often used. Logs are debarked and cut into short "bolts" which then go to the "flaker". Waste material is removed, and the flakes are sorted by size and then dried.

When dry, the flakes are combined with a phenolic resin, placed on mats, and then passed through a hydraulic press where heat and pressure transform them into solid wood panels. The panels are then trimmed to size and, if made to a particular standard, are sanded.

APPENDIX 3.

Other Wood Products

In addition to lumber, plywood, and common building materials, there are many other wood products that you may want to use. Of these, the most common are ready-made turnings and moldings. Both of these can save you an enormous amount of work. They can also expand your woodworking capabilities if you have limited tools.

Although this section only covers turnings and moldings, it should be noted that there are many more wood products available. They aren't discussed here because they are normally used for very specific types of projects. For example, several companies manufacture wooden 'people', wheels, and axle pegs for toymakers. Some make wooden drawer pulls and other furniture parts for cabinetmakers. There are also overlays and inlays for chess and backgammon boards, wooden wheels for carts, 'Shaker' pegs for closets and hallways—the list goes on and on. Should you wish to locate a supply of a particular wood product, consult a local building center or check the advertisements in various woodworking magazines.

Ready-Made Turnings

Of the many relatively new products available to woodworkers, one of the most practical and intriguing is the variety of ready-made turnings that are available at lumberyards and handyman supply centers. The products are especially useful to folks who work mostly with portable power tools, since such equipment doesn't include a lathe. Even stationary tool users who don't care much for lathe work find the materials practical. The point is, you don't have to be limited to straight lines when designing. Turned legs, lamp bases, posts, railings, finials, and other components can be part of your output when you use the ready-made, turned materials.

Most of the items are designed for specific purposes. For example, legs for tables and chests, newel posts and balustrades for stairways, sets of spacers and finials for shelves, similar sets for two-tiered tables, and so on. However, all can be used imaginatively as individual projects or parts of a major assembly merely by modifying or by culling out sections that suit the purpose.

The illustrations show typical items that are available. Your best bet is to visit local sources to see what fits your needs or suits your imagination. You can also send for catalogues.

Ready-made spindles like those used on the doors of this project increase the design scope of folks who work mostly with portable power tools.

Examples of ready-made turnings. They can be used as-is or sections can be culled out. Slicing items like these in half, longitudinally, provides two half-round moldings.

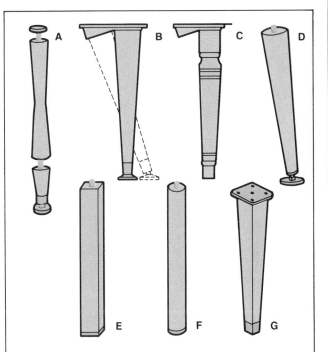

A   Combination leg; spacer and cap can be used for tables or shelves.

B   Tapered legs equipped with a ferrule and leveler can be mounted vertically or slanted.

C   Early American style version of B.

D   Screw-top, round tapered leg with leveler for slanted mounting.

E   Screw-top, square leg.

F   Screw-top, round leg.

G   Square, tapered leg with ferrule and mounting plate.

Note: Metal plate which is screwed to underside of structure is used with items E and F.

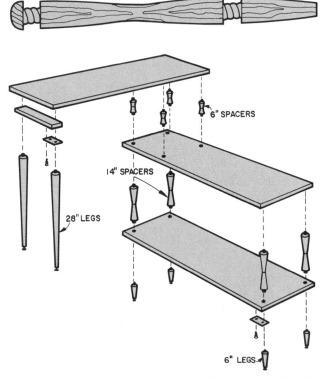

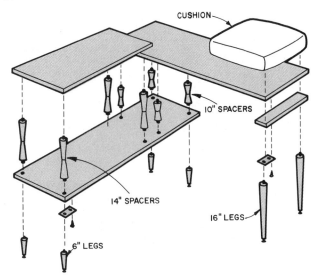

Sets of legs, spacers, and finials can be used to construct tables, shelves, bookcases, and other projects. Such items are available in different lengths and styles.

Turnings designed for stairway constructions can be adapted to other uses. Such components are available in many sizes and styles.

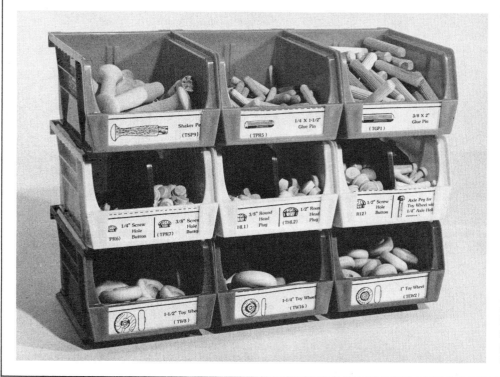

Kit of ready-made turnings includes wheels, hole buttons and plugs, Shaker pegs, even grooved dowels for edge-to-edge joints.

Facts About Molding

Ready-made moldings are available in a great variety of shapes and sizes. Generally, they can be classified as "decorative" or "structural" but the names describe applications more than they do the shape or appearance of the product. For example, **cove** molding was designed for use at the joint between a wall and a ceiling, but many craftspeople, by modifying it with a glass rabbet, use it as picture framing. The same is true for **picture** molding, a design created for use on a wall.

In practical applications, moldings are used to hide and to seal the normal gaps between door jambs and walls and those around window installations, or to finish in good fashion the joint between walls and floors or walls and ceilings. Esthetically, they are used to transform a flush door, add detail to cabinets and chests, or make a blank wall appear paneled. What is obvious is that even when molding is used for architectural purposes, it adds to the appearance of the construction.

Always cut molding with a fine-tooth saw blade. In fact, for the best possible job, it's wise to saw a fraction oversize and to finish to the line by sanding. General rules call for using miters on outside corners but coped joints on inside corners (see sketch). The coped joint requires a little more attention than a straight forward miter but it's good practice to use this joint where, for example, baseboards abut at an inside corner since shrinkage won't result in an obvious gap. A coped joint is one where the end of one piece is shaped to match the cross-sectional shape of the piece it must join with.

Moldings are attached with either finishing or casing nails depending on the size of the material and the application. For example, use casing nails to secure trim around doors and windows, finishing nails if you are adding to furniture or flush doors. Both types of nails are set below the surface of the wood and concealed with wood dough. Don't use nails if you are embellishing a hollow-core door since the plywood surfaces are too thin for any kind of nail to grip. Instead, attach the molding with contact cement or regular glue. If you are working on an outside door, which will probably be solid-core, use finishing nails and a water-proof glue like resorcinol.

Molding can be painted, but you get better results if an undercoat is applied first, followed by a light sanding before finish applications.

For clear finishes, do a light sanding first and then apply the end material. If using more than one coat, do a light sanding between them and after the final one.

Molding can be stained to match or contrast paneling. It's a good idea to cut the piece to size and do a test installation without nailing for all the pieces you need. Then stain before final attachment. This system will also work with clear finishes and even with painted projects, especially if the molding will be a contrasting color.

Here are some molding installation rules that are generally applicable:

- Use a common miter joint on outside corners.
- Use a cope joint on inside corners.
- For tight joints, use glue as well as nails.
- When attaching moldings to walls and in similar situations, locate nails so they will penetrate solid backing members like studs and plates. Use only glue when attaching to thin materials.
- When the backing has slight irregularities, use nails at those points to pull the molding in tightly.
- Driving nails into corners of profiles will help to conceal them. Stain wood dough with the same material used to finish the molding. Colored wax sticks are available for filling nail holes after the finish has been applied.
- At least one of the moldings should be symmetrical when the pattern has an intersection. A "butt block" may be used at an intersection when the moldings are not similar or symmetrical.
- Try to use moldings in one-piece runs. When this isn't possible, use a "scarf" joint at the connection instead of a butt joint.

Standard Moldings and Typical Uses

CROWN   Usually used at the joint between walls and ceilings, also under exterior eaves. Does a good job of eliminating sharp lines where two planes meet.

BED   Serves functions similar to CROWN. The term usually applies to specific shapes. For example, a combination of cove and bead.

COVE   Applications are similar to those of CROWN and BED. The face of the molding has a concave shape.

CASING   Provides decorative trim around doors and windows. This type of molding is "relieved" with a shallow back groove. It is used for interior and exterior work.

CASING and BASE   These moldings resemble CASING and can be used around doors and windows or as the finishing strip where a wall meets the floor. The edge that rests on the floor is usually beveled a few degrees in the direction of the back face.

STOOL   Most common use is as part of a window sill to provide a snug joint with the sash.

CASING and BASE (ROUND EDGE)   When the molding has two rounded edges it serves as casing for doors and windows and other trim applications. When it has one square and one rounded edge it serves as a baseboard.

CAP   Used to top off wainscots and other horizontal installations.

BRICK   Used as an attractive finish where brick or stucco butts against wood in exterior walls.

ROUNDS AND FULL-ROUNDS   Used as closet poles, curtain rods, bannisters, and so on. HALF-ROUNDS can be used to cover joints or for creative embellishments. QUARTER-ROUNDS are generally used at inside corners. They can provide a "shaped" connection where a panel is set into or abuts a square edge.

BALUSTERS   Square stock in various sizes designed as uprights in railings but which are handy for many other uses.

BANDS   Shaped material that is often used to top off base-boards and wainscotting. BANDS make good, ready-made cleats for shelves.

SHINGLE   Provides a decorative joint where siding or shingles butt against eaves or window sills. Can be used as BAND molding or as shelf cleats.

BATTEN   Decorative pieces that can be used to cover joints in flat surfaces. Often used with interior paneling and exterior siding.

LATTICE   Strips with a rectangular cross-section. Can be used as BATTEN but will serve any other decorative or practical purpose.

BEADS (GLASS)   Used to secure glass, wood, or other materials in frames.

STOPS   Make snug joints and keep doors and window sash in correct position. A closed door should be snug against the STOPS.

CASING (MULLION)   Generally used between windows when there is more than one in an installation. Provides a decorative break.

BASE SHOE   Was designed for the joint where the base-board meets the floor but can be used for many trimming chores.

DRIP CAP   A typical structural molding. Usually used over the exterior side of windows and doors to guard against moisture seeping inside walls.

CORNER GUARD   Used to cover interior or exterior out-side corners. Provides a neat finish and protects the corner construction.

BACK BAND   Can be used as caps on some types of BASEBOARD and CASING. Also, as a CORNER GUARD when only one edge of the construction is exposed.

PICTURE   Designed to be used on walls some distance below the ceiling so pictures can be hung. Not in wide use in modern construction.

SCREEN STOCK   Pieces of various sizes with a rectangular cross-section. Can be viewed as a ready-made material for constructing door or window screens. Also useful for various cabinetmaking applications.

SCREEN   Slim strips, usually with a shaped top surface, that are used over screen edges to hold the screen firmly and neatly.

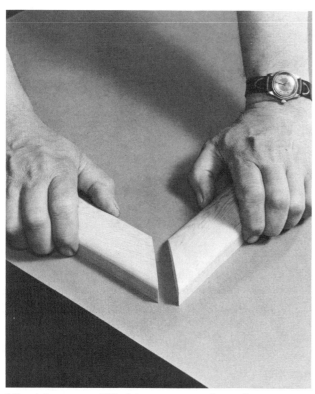

Miter joints are not difficult but accuracy and smooth cuts are essential for parts to mate correctly and form a 90° corner.

Some moldings that meet at right angles can be joined like this: a V-cut in one piece and a matching pointed shape on the other. Any sharp edges that might remain can be blended with fine sandpaper.

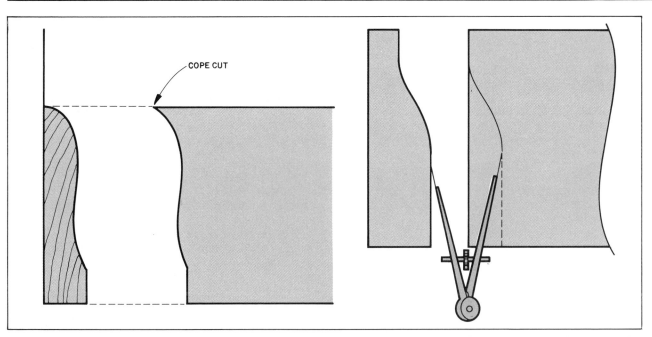

In a coped joint, one piece is shaped to match the cross-sectional profile of the other piece. The shape that must be cut can often be traced by using a compass as shown here.

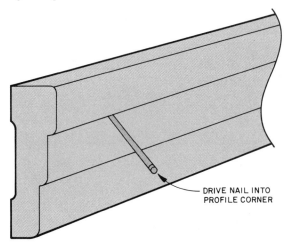

Driving nails into the corners of profiles helps to conceal them.

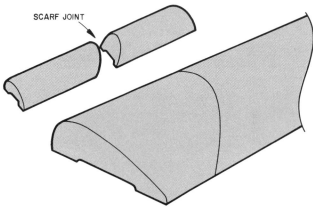

Always try to run moldings in continuous strips. If you must join pieces, use a *scarf* joint instead of butting the ends. It's less likely that the joint will separate, especially if you use glue and drive a finishing nail at an angle through the mating ends.

INTERSECTIONS

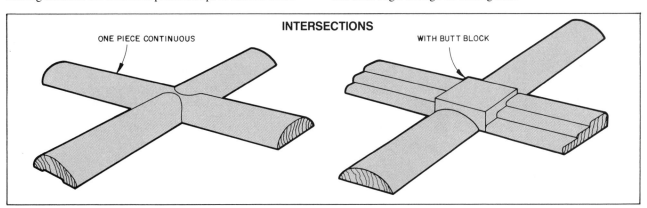

If possible, it's a good idea to let one of the strips be continuous. Another system involves a "butt block". It can be used with similar or dissimilar moldings and provides an additional decorative detail.

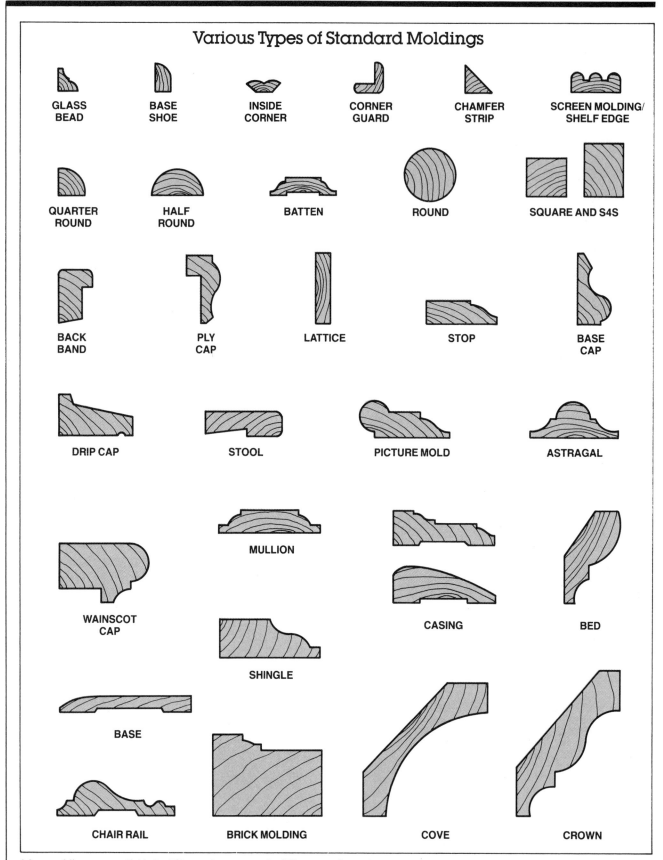

Various Types of Standard Moldings

GLASS BEAD

BASE SHOE

INSIDE CORNER

CORNER GUARD

CHAMFER STRIP

SCREEN MOLDING/ SHELF EDGE

QUARTER ROUND

HALF ROUND

BATTEN

ROUND

SQUARE AND S4S

BACK BAND

PLY CAP

LATTICE

STOP

BASE CAP

DRIP CAP

STOOL

PICTURE MOLD

ASTRAGAL

MULLION

WAINSCOT CAP

CASING

BED

SHINGLE

BASE

CHAIR RAIL

BRICK MOLDING

COVE

CROWN

Most moldings are available in different sizes—many in different configurations.

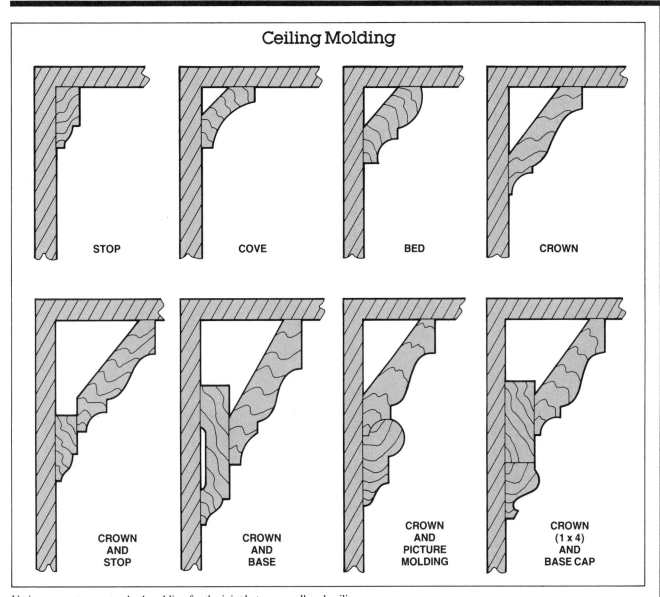

Ceiling Molding

STOP

COVE

BED

CROWN

CROWN
AND
STOP

CROWN
AND
BASE

CROWN
AND
PICTURE
MOLDING

CROWN
(1 x 4)
AND
BASE CAP

Various ways to use standard molding for the joint between wall and ceiling.

Molding Measurements

Molding is measured by its thickness, width, and length. Measurements are listed in that order just as with lumber. A typical order might be ¾″ x 3⅝″ crown molding x 10′. Of course, standard moldings are of specific thicknesses and widths. Your best bet is to check availability at a local source or to work from a chart that illustrates types and sizes (see Glossary for charts available from various sources).

Generally, molding lengths run from 6′ to 16′. Always order to the next rounded foot that suits your needs. It's better to be left with a short cutoff than have to form splices to complete a run. Don't forget to add the extra length required for miters when doing outside corners. For example, when framing a 36″ square window and the molding is 3″ wide, each frame piece needs to be 42″.

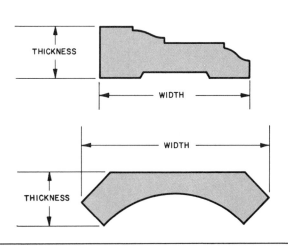

THICKNESS

WIDTH

WIDTH

THICKNESS

Structural (Practical) Uses for Molding

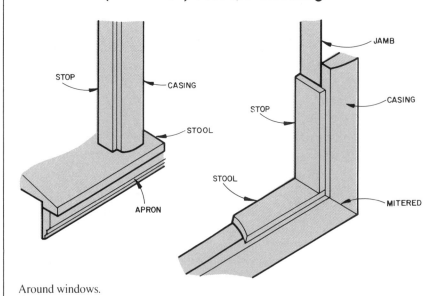

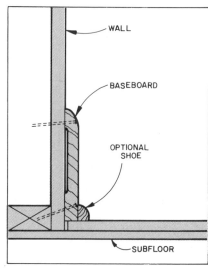

Around windows.

At the base of a wall.

Decorative Uses for Molding

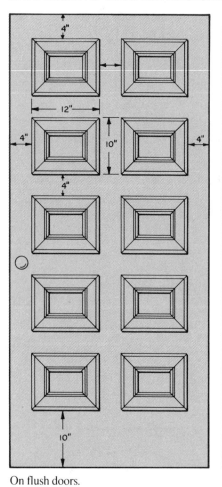

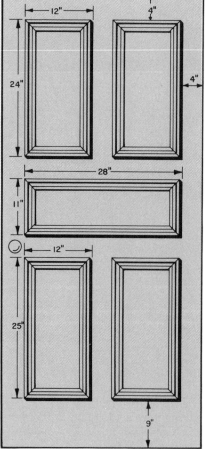

On flush doors.

On cabinets.

APPENDIX
4.

Abrasives

We conveniently use the words "sanding" and "sandpaper", but sandpaper isn't really "sand" paper at all. The off-white color and somewhat sandy texture of flint, (actually the natural mineral "Quartz") which was one of the first abrasives applied to paper, probably led to the terms we now accept. Even the word "paper" is often erroneous since the abrasives in common use, for power sanding anyway, are bonded to a cloth backing for durability (Figure A4-1).

Flint is not impressive as an abrasive because it dulls and wears rapidly. But because it is one of the cheapest materials, it is often used for chores like the removal of existing finishes, especially paint, that clog the paper very quickly.

More efficient abrasives are natural ones like garnet and emery, and artificial ones like aluminum oxide and silicon carbide. The natural abrasives are mined like any mineral, whereas the artificial abrasives are essentially products of an electric furnace. Aluminum oxide is fused bauxite; silicon carbide results from a sand-coke fusion.

Each type of abrasive is especially good for a particular application, but in practice overlaps do exist. A particular grit in one abrasive will often do the job when the recommended abrasive is not available. It's a good idea to know something about the various types and what they do best.

A4-1. Coated abrasives may have a paper or cloth backing. Those used on power tools, like the portable or stationary belt sander, should be the cloth types for durability.

Types of Abrasives

Aluminum oxide is available with either cloth or paper backing. The cloth backing is always stronger and more flexible. It can be used dry or with a lubricant and is excellent for machine sanding wood, plastics, and metal. The material is hard and tough and can take a lot of abuse. Paper-backed aluminum oxide can be used on machines—sheets for pad sanders are often made this way—but is generally recommended for hand work. Aluminum oxide is one of the most popular abrasives available today for all-around shop use.

Garnet is another popular woodworker's abrasive. It's a hard, natural material which is mined from the same source that holds the semi-precious jewel bearing the same name. Garnet may be used with machines or by hand, but it does fracture easily and its use is often limited to soft materials. It is a respectable, all-purpose shop abrasive, even though aluminum oxide is favored for power tool use.

Silicon carbide is widely available on waterproof backings and is excellent for wet sanding either by hand or machine. In finer grades, it is commonly used for smoothing finish coats of varnish, lacquer, or enamel on furniture and on automobiles. In most cases you'll find that it is the better abrasive to use on metals.

Emery, which is a combination of iron oxide and corundum, is frequently used for metal finishing but is comparatively dull and tends to wear quickly. It shouldn't be shunned for metal-polishing jobs. In fact, it's often found in powder or stick form so it can be applied to cloth discs for buffing applications.

Tungsten carbide, which has made its mark as hard-working, long-lived cutting edges on saw blades and router bits, is appearing on abrasive products. You'll find that the backing for the abrasive is usually a thin sheet of metal (Figure A4-2). The products don't have the flexibility of paper- or cloth-backed abrasives and their use is confined mostly to flat surfaces.

Flint is the least durable of all abrasives. It's also the cheapest and, therefore, often chosen for preliminary work that is bound to clog the paper very quickly. It's not made for power sanding but, in a pinch, no law says you can't cut up a sheet for use in a pad sander.

A4-2. New tungsten carbide sheets are very durable, but since the abrasive particles are bonded to thin sheets of metal they are not as flexible as regular materials and are best used on flat surfaces.

Grit Sizes

The grit number of an abrasive is actually a *mesh number* that indicates the particular wire or silk screen that was used to filter the abrasive particles during the manufacturing process. For example, particles that pass through a number twelve screen would total twelve to the inch if they were placed in a line. When the screen-control method becomes impractical, because of the size of the particles, then a fairly complex flotation system is used to accomplish the same thing. Grit sizes can range from the coarsest, Number 12, to the finest, Number 600.

How smooth a project will be depends on the grit you use. Number twelve would produce results similar to what you would get by rubbing wood with tiny, sharp stones. Using the finest grit is almost like rubbing with flour (Figures A4-3 and A4-4).

The usual recommendation of working through progressively finer grits of abrasive until you achieve the smoothness you want is okay, but only to a point. A critical factor is the grit you *start* with, and this can be judged by the original condition of the surface you must work on. There is little point in routinely working from "very coarse" to "very fine", with a half dozen steps between, if the project is in respectable condition to begin with. It certainly isn't necessary on the plywood and most of the yard lumber that is available today.

The charts shown in Figures A4-5 and A4-6 are offered as guides to help you select the type of abrasive and the grit best suited for a particular application on various materials. The emphasis is on the word "guides", since in each of the steps there is a range of grit sizes.

Remember that abrasives are cutting tools. They do their job by removing material almost like tiny chisels. The "chisel" you start with will leave ridges and grooves that, if

necessary, can be made into smaller ridges and grooves by working with smaller "chisels". There will always be striations; you work to the point where you can't feel them, or see them without magnification.

Imperfections will be most obvious after cross-grain sanding that hasn't been followed with sufficient with-the-grain sanding. In the extreme, flaws will appear as cross-grain swirls. Use a cross-grain pattern, regardless of the grit of the abrasive, only when you wish to remove a lot of material quickly. Orbital pad sanders do a lot of cross-grain sanding, but orbits are so tiny and such fine abrasive particles can be used, that imperfections are virtually non-existent.

Abrasive Coatings

"Closed coat" is the term used to describe coated abrasives that are densely covered with cutting particles. The result is a fast-cutting surface, but one that can clog quickly under certain conditions. When the abrasive particles are applied with spaces between them so that only about 50 to 70% of the backing material is covered, the product is called "open coat". Open-coat products won't cut as fast as closed-coat products simply because there aren't as many abrasive particles per given area. On the other hand, there is less tendency for open-coat products to clog; facts to consider when determining the type that is best for a particular job. Closed coats cut faster, usually stand up longer, and do a smoother job. Open coats are best for soft materials, gummy materials, and for removing existing finishes.

TYPE	VERY FINE	FINE	MEDIUM	COARSE	VERY COARSE
Flint	4/0	2/0 - 3/0	0 - ½	1 - 2	2½ - 3½
Garnet	6/0 - 10/0	3/0 - 5/0	0 - 2/0	½ - 1½	2 - 3
Aluminum oxide and silicon carbide	220 - 360	120 - 180	80 - 100	40 - 60	24 - 36

8/0 = 280	3/0 = 120	1½ = 40
7/0 = 240	2/0 = 100	2 = 36
6/0 = 220	0 = 80	2½ = 30
5/0 = 180	½ = 60	3 = 24
4/0 = 150	1 = 50	

A4-3.   This chart groups different abrasives into five classes of word/grit descriptions and indicates the number of the grits that fall in each. Quite often, the word description is enough on which to base a choice.

A4-4.   Here are the number equivalents of the various grit sizes.

ABRASIVE	USE	GRIT			REMARKS
		ROUGH	MEDIUM	FINE	
Aluminum oxide	Hardwood	2½ - 1½	½ - 0	2/0 - 3/0	Manufactured, brown color, bauxite base, more costly than garnet but usually cheaper to use per unit of work.
	Aluminum	40	60 - 80	100	
	Copper	40 - 50	80 - 100	100 - 120	
	Steel	24 - 30	60 - 80	100	
	Ivory	60 - 80	100 - 120	120 - 280	
	Plastic	50 - 80	120 - 180	240	
Garnet	Hardwood	2½ - 1½	½ - 0	2/0 - 3/0	Natural mineral, red color, harder and sharper than flint.
	Softwood	1½ - 1	0	2/0	
	Composition board	1½ - 1	½	0	
	Plastic	50 - 80	120 - 180	240	
	Horn	1½	½ - 0	2/0-3/0	
Silicon carbide	Glass	50 - 60	100 - 120	12-320	Manufactured, harder but more brittle than aluminum oxide, very fast cutting.
	Cast iron	24 - 30	60 - 80	100	
Flint	Removing paint, old finishes	3 - 1½	½ - 0		Natural hard form of quartz, low cost, use on jobs that clog the paper quickly.

A4-5.   This chart is offered as a guide to help you select a type and grit of abrasive for a particular material and finish. Which grit you start with has much to do with the original state of the surface you work on.

MATERIAL	FIRST STEP	SECOND STEP	FINAL
Oak	2½ - 1½	½ - 0	2/0 - 4/0
Maple	2½ - 1	½ - 0	2/0 - 4/0
Maple (curly)	2½ - 1½	½ - 0	2/0 - 4/0
Birch	2½ - 1	½ - 0	2/0 - 4/0
Mahogany	2½ - 1½	½ - 0	2/0 - 3/0
Walnut	2½ - 1½	½ - 0	2/0 - 4/0
Fir	1½ - 1	½ - 0	2/0
Pine	1½ - 1	0	2/0
Gum	2½ - 1½	½ - 0	2/0 - 3/0
Willow	2	½ - 0	2/0
Cypress	2½ - 1½	½ - 0	2/0
Plaster			5/0 - 8/0
Hardboard		3/0 - 4/0	5/0 - 7/0

A4-6.   This chart suggests grit sizes to choose for progressive steps on various materials. Again, it's a "guide". If the material is in reasonable condition to begin with, it's usually okay to skip step number one.

Care of Coated Abrasives

The cost of coated abrasives can add up if you are too casual with how you use them and neglect some simple maintenance chores. When the paper is worn enough so it just doesn't cut, the only choice you have is to discard it. However, a coarse-grit paper used to the point where it no longer does the job it was designed for can be used further as a finer grit.

Dry cleaning with a brush will slow the accumulation of stubborn waste on an abrasive surface. When the accumulation is powdery and loose, a bristle brush will do. When the accumulation is thick and sticky, a wire brush may be used. Work the brush in all directions to uncover particles that might still be sharp enough to work. When you are doing such work on a power tool, don't have the machine running or you will soon have a "brushless" brush; brush over the abrasive surface while the tool is still. You can rotate a belt sander, drum sander, or disc sander by hand as you apply the brush.

A new product from the Granlund Engineering Co. provides a practical and very efficient way to keep abrasives clean and to prolong their life. The units, which resemble oversize gum erasers as much as anything else, are available mounted on handles so they can be applied to the tool, or with a backing so they can be held to a solid surface while the coated abrasive is moved against them (Figures A4-7 and

A4-8). I have found them to do an impressive job even on drum sanders, whether they are powered by a portable drill or a drill press (Figure A4-9). The idea is to use the cleaners frequently to prevent the waste buildup that clogs paper and covers the cutting points of the abrasive particles.

There are times when a smoothing job can't be done with a power tool, or is more convenient to do by hand. The ideas that are shown in Figures A4-10 through A4-14 are some that I have used and which you may find helpful.

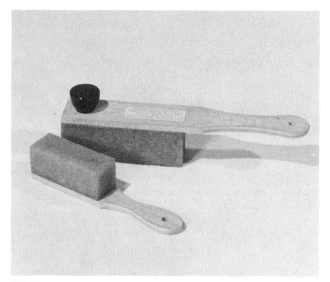

A4-7.   Gum-eraser type cleaners for coated abrasives are efficient and easy to use. Those with handles are designed to be applied to the abrasive.

A4-8.   Other "sanding insurance" products, as they are called by the manufacturer, can be secured to a solid surface. The abrasive, in motion, is held against the cleaner.

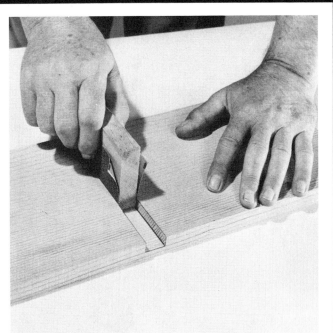

A4-9. The gum-type cleaners can be used on drum sanders regardless of how they are powered. Use the cleaners frequently as you work to keep waste from clogging the cutting particles. Operations like this, as well as sanding, throw off particles, so always wear safety goggles and a dust mask.

A4-11. Use fine sandpaper wrapped around a block of wood to increase the width of a dado that would otherwise be too tight for the insert piece. If you use a very fine sandpaper, the wood block can have the same thickness as the part that must fit the dado. Don't overdo this—what you want is a slip fit.

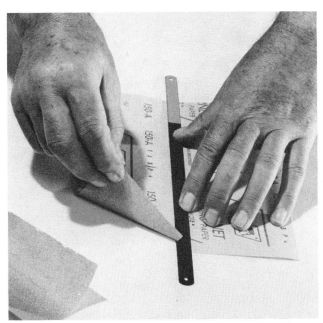

A4-10. By using a hacksaw blade as a guide, you can cut pieces from regular sheets of sandpaper accurately to use with a pad sander. The teeth on the blade help to produce a clean cut. A strip of wood can also be used, but there will be a greater tendency for the paper to tear unevenly.

A4-12. A piece of molding that must be sanded can be used as a sanding block with matching contours. In this case, the edges of the block have been sawed off so it will conform to major contours.

A4-13. To smooth tight radii or sharp corners, you can wrap sandpaper around a sharpened, thin piece of wood, or a piece of thin carpeting. It's easier to smooth hard-to-reach areas when the abrasive "carrier" is shaped to suit the job.

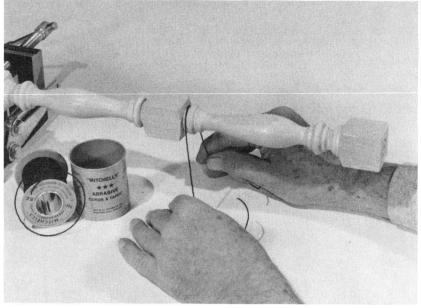

A4-14. A line of abrasive cords and tapes, introduced by E. C. Mitchell Co., lets you get into spots that might be inaccessible with other means. The cords and tapes are available in various diameters and widths, and with coatings that include silicon carbide, aluminum oxide, and crocus. Thus, they can be used on metal as well as wood, and for polishing.

APPENDIX

5. Hardware

There is an old woodworker's saying that the reason early American furniture has such complicated joinery is that hardware was hard to come by. It was cheaper to make a dovetail than use a screw. Whether or not that's true is open to debate. But what is true is that since the beginning of this country, the availability and the variety of hardware has grown steadily. Today, there is a bewildering array of hardware on the market, and most of it at reasonable prices.

This section will help you sort out some of the more common types of nails, screws, and other fasteners. You'll find that within each type of fastener, there is an amazing variety. There are nails for common construction, finishing, concrete work, flooring, paneling, siding, and upholstery, just to name a few. There are also special decorative 'cut' nails available for antique restoration and reproduction. Under the heading of screws, there are not only the usual flathead and roundhead screws, but also hanger bolts, dowel screws, security screws, tapping screws, and the new 'square drive' screws. All of these have different applications. Finally, there are many types of ingenious fasteners that you can use instead of the usual assortment of nails and screws—corrugated nails, 'Skotch' jointers, 'Tite Joint' fasteners, 'Molly' bolts, 'Tee' nuts, and on and on. Some of these are permanent fasteners; you have to destroy the wood to disassemble the project. Others are 'knock-down' fasteners; they are made especially so that you can assemble and disassemble the project for easy storage or shipping. With a good working knowledge of what's out there on the market, you can use the best fastener for the particular job you have to do.

There is a lot of hardware that wasn't included in this section. This isn't an oversight. Hinges, drawer and door pulls, drawer slides, latches, shelving supports, and the like are often specific to a particular project. By contrast, the hardware that was included in this section is more general in its application. You can use each of the fasteners listed here on many different kinds of projects. However, should you need a specific type of hardware, your local hardware store will usually have catalogues that you can look through to find and order what you need.

Basic Nailing Techniques

- Choose a nail that is three times longer than the piece being secured—this is a general rule that can't always apply, but stay close to it when you can.
- Start nails with light taps and get your fingers out of the danger zone as soon as possible—don't drive nails as if you were trying for a prize in a carnival. Nails driven "calmly" will hold better because they cause minimum distortion in wood fibers.
- Let up on the force of hammer blows when the nail head nears the surface of the wood—this is the way to avoid marring wood surfaces.
- Drive finishing and similar nails to within ⅛″ of the work surface—use a nail set to complete driving the nail below the work surface (¹⁄₁₆″ to ⅛″). Use a set that is compatible with the nail-head diameter.
- You may be able to straighten a bent nail by tapping it gently upright with the hammer but it's usually better to

remove it and start a new one. A nail bent in the wood where you can't see it can cause problems.
- There is nothing wrong with using a small drill to form pilot holes for nails—this is very useful when nailing hardwoods and when nailing near edges.
- Use a staggered pattern when driving many nails in a confined area—nails driven on the same line are likely to cause splits.
- Nails driven at a slight angle grip better than nails driven straight.
- When clinching, bend the nail *across* the grain of the wood rather than *with* it.
- You can help avoid splitting if you tap the point of the nail with the hammer to dull it slightly.
- A fine way to hide a nail is to use a sharp chisel to lift a thin sliver of wood, then drive the nail in the depression and glue down the sliver.

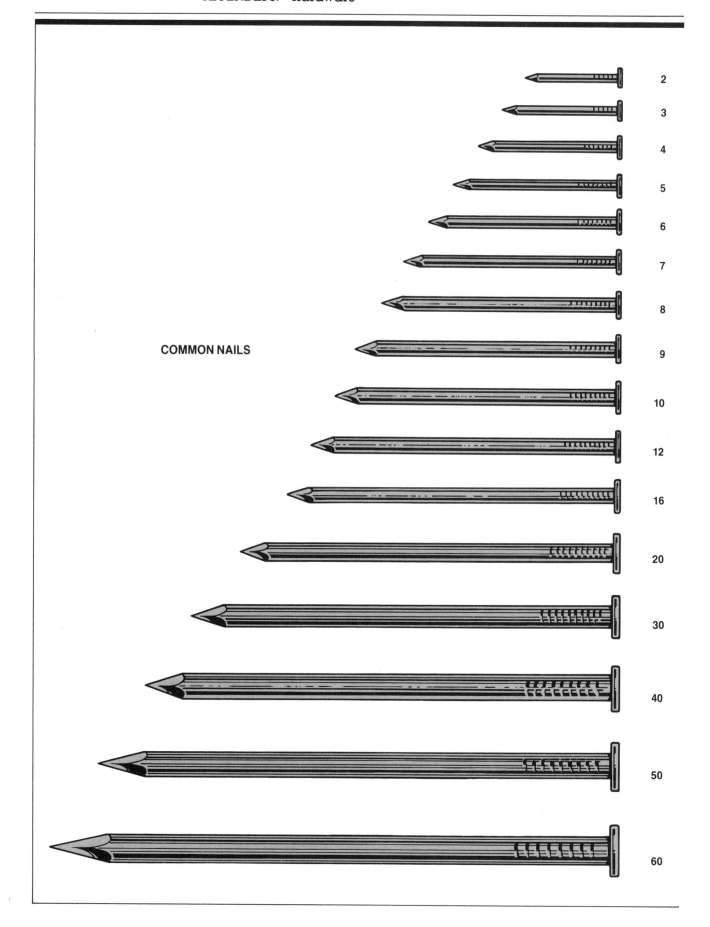

COMMON NAILS

2
3
4
5
6
7
8
9
10
12
16
20
30
40
50
60

SIZES OF COMMON AND BOX NAILS						
SIZE d= "penny"	COMMON			BOX		
	GAUGE	LENGTH	# - LB.*	GAUGE	LENGTH	# - LB.*
2	15	1	845	15½	1	1010
3	14	1¼	540	14½	1¼	635
4	12½	1½	290	14	1½	473
5	12½	1¾	250	14	1¾	406
6	11½	2	165	12½	2	236
7	11½	2¼	150	12½	2¼	210
8	10¼	2½	100	11½	2½	145
9	10¼	2¾	90	11½	2¾	132
10	9	3	65	10½	3	94
12	9	3¼	60	10½	3	88
16	8	3½	45	10	3½	71
20	6	4	30	9	4	52
30	5	4½	20	9	4½	46
40	4	5	17	8	5	35
50	3	5½	13	—	—	—
60	2	6	10	—	—	—

*Approximate length in inches.

GAUGE EQUIVALENTS (NAIL SIZES)			
GAUGE	INCHES (IN DECIMALS)	GAUGE	INCHES (IN DECIMALS)
2	.2625	9	.1483
3	.2437	10	.1350
4	.2253	11	.1205
5	.2070	12	.0985
6	.1920	13	.0915
7	.1770	14	.0800
8	.1620	15	.0673

TYPES OF POINTS ON NAILS

	KEY	NAME	COMMENTS
	A	Diamond (regular)	A most common point design that is good for general purpose use but which can cause splitting in dense woods.
	B	Diamond (long)	Easier to drive because of long, tapering point—often found on nails for drywall construction—sharp point penetrates easily and cleanly.
	C	Diamond (blunt)	Especially good for dense wood since blunt point is less likely to cause splitting than a sharp point.
	D	Chisel (or wedge)	Found on large nails, especially spikes—point makes it easier to drive nails into timbers—also found on gutter spikes.
	E	Needle (short)	Similar to diamond but points have circular cross section—easy to start—often used to avoid tearing of fibrous material; carpeting, and fiberboard.
	F	Needle (long)	

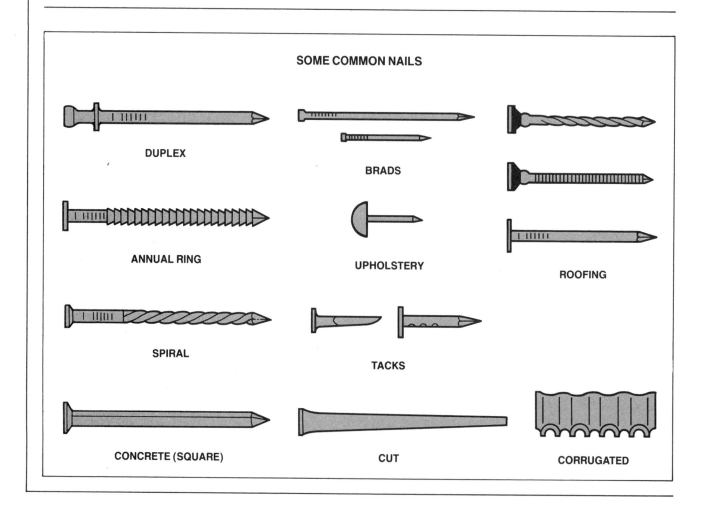

SOME COMMON NAILS

DUPLEX

BRADS

ANNUAL RING

UPHOLSTERY

ROOFING

SPIRAL

TACKS

CONCRETE (SQUARE)

CUT

CORRUGATED

"OLD FASHIONED" CUT NAILS			
SIZE	KEY	NAME	COMMENTS
8d (2½)	3	Clinch rose head	Often used for face nailing of wide-board flooring.
8d (2½)	2	Hinge	
8d (2½)	7	Common rose head	
4d (1½)	3	Clinch rose head	For antique decorative effects on paneling, cabinet, doors.
6d (2)	3	Clinch rose head	
8d (2½)	3	Clinch rose head	
¾"	1	Clout	Works well when making or restoring early American furniture.
4d (1½)	5	Fine finish	
7d (2¼)	5	Fine finish	
4d (1½)	2	Hinge	For attachment of antique hinges and similar jobs.
8d (2½)	2	Hinge	
10d (3)	2	Hinge	
6d (2)	3	Clinch rose head	For decorative touches on exterior work such as siding and fences—available zinc plated.
7d (2¼)	6	Common	
Note: Supply source for cut nails: Tremont Nail Co., Wareham, MA 02571			

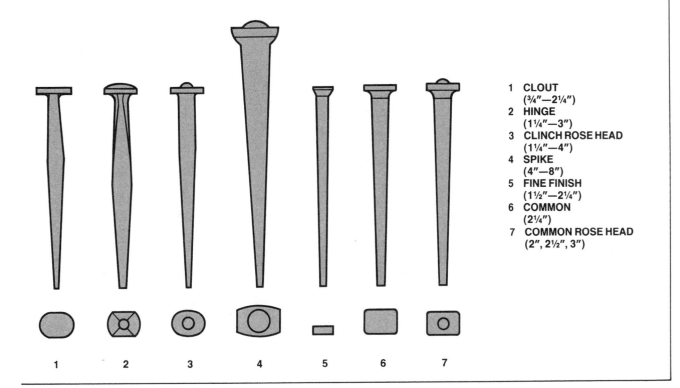

1 CLOUT
   (¾"—2¼")
2 HINGE
   (1¼"—3")
3 CLINCH ROSE HEAD
   (1¼"—4")
4 SPIKE
   (4"—8")
5 FINE FINISH
   (1½"—2¼")
6 COMMON
   (2¼")
7 COMMON ROSE HEAD
   (2", 2½", 3")

FINISHING NAILS

	SIZE d= "penny"	GAUGE	LENGTH IN INCHES	APPROX. NO. PER POUND
	2	16½	1	1350
	3	15½	1¼	880
	4	15	1½	630
	6	13	2	290
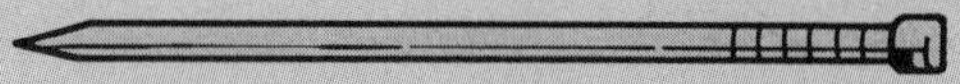	8	12½	2½	196
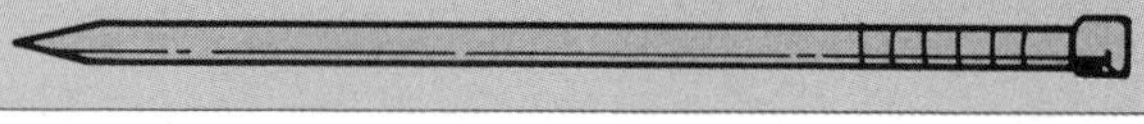	10	11½	3	125

CASING NAILS

	SIZE d= "penny"	GAUGE	LENGTH IN INCHES	APPROX. NO. PER POUND
	3	14½	1¼	630
	4	14	1½	490
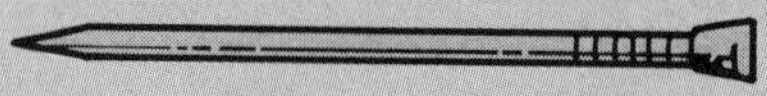	6	12½	2	245
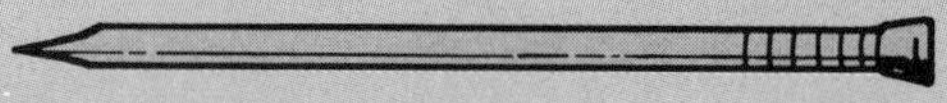	8	11½	2½	149
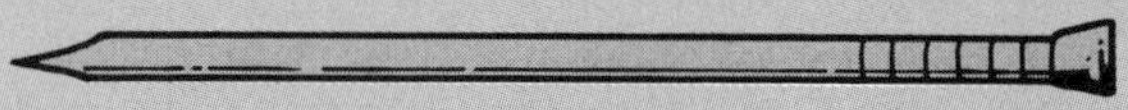	10	10½	3	94
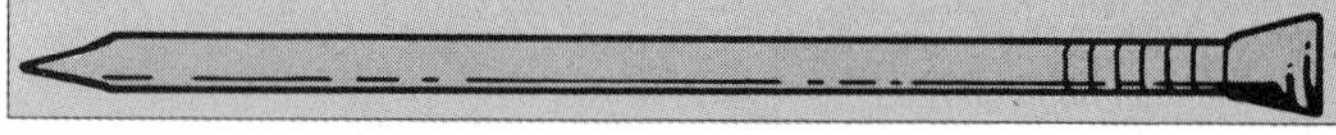	16	10	3½	75

WIRE BRADS (SMALL)

	LENGTH IN INCHES	GAUGES		LENGTH IN INCHES	GAUGES
	3/16	20-24		¾	13-21
	¼	19-24		⅞	13-20
	⅜	18-24		1	12-20
	½	14-23		1⅛	12-20
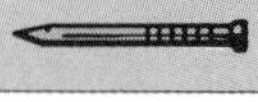	⅝	13-22			

TACKS							
SIZE (NUMBER	LENGTH (INCHES)	SIZE (NUMBER)	LENGTH (INCHES)	SIZE (NUMBER)	LENGTH (INCHES)	SIZE (NUMBER)	LENGTH (INCHES)
2	1/4	4	7/16	10	5/8	16	13/16
2½	5/16	6	1/2	12	11/16	18	7/8
3	3/8	8	9/16	14	3/4	22	1

VARIOUS NAIL TYPES AND TYPICAL APPLICATIONS	
IDENTIFIED AS	TYPICAL USE
COMMON	A general purpose nail used extensively in house framing and general carpentry. BOX nail (slimmer) is often substituted when splitting is a problem.
DUPLEX OR DOUBLE-HEADED	For temporary structures such as scaffolding—second head projects so fastener can be removed easily.
CONCRETE	Specially hardened for driving into concrete or masonry—also for attachment of furring strips and sole plates.
ROOFING	Special heads, usually larger than normal for securing roofing materials; some with washers attached for waterproof seal.
FINISHING	For cabinetmaking, attachment of trim, and so on—usually driven below the surface and hidden with wood dough.
CASING	Used like a finishing nail but has more holding power—attachment of casing or trim around doors and windows.
CUT (FLOORING)	For edge, blind nailing of flooring—thin, rectangular shape guards against splitting.
SPIRAL	Threaded shank so nail turns like a screw—more holding power—often used in place of CUT nails for flooring.
PANELING	Hard and thin and often ribbed—available in colors to match the paneling.
SIDING	Often in aluminum to guard against rusting—available in colors.
CAPPED	Attachment of insulation sheathing—has large plastic or metal cap—usually with spiral shank.
BRAD	Slim nails resembling finishing nails—usually light duty applications such as attachment of moldings—set and hidden with wood dough.
UPHOLSTERY	Used in upholstery work where nails are not hidden—have large, decorative heads.
TACK	Common for attachment for carpeting and upholstery—used in hidden areas—differ from THUMB TACKS which are not driven with a hammer.
STAPLE	U-shaped fastener for attachment of screening, wire fencing, and so on—also for electrical wiring, some with insulated shoulders.

General Screw Driving Techniques

- Drill shank and pilot holes especially in hardwoods and when using large screws (see chart)—you might get by without these holes when using very small screws in softwood; forming a starting hole with an awl might do the trick.
- Use a screwdriver with a blade-tip that seats snugly the full width of the slot in the screw head—a blade tip that is *too* wide will damage the material.
- You can apply greater leverage by using the longest, suitable screwdriver.
- Keep the screwdriver at right angles to the work surface.
- Use one hand to guide the screw until it is firmly started.
- Be careful when it becomes necessary to exert excessive pressure; you might break the screw—solve the problem by using "threading screw" (see sketch)—sometimes, the solution is as simple as coating the threads of the screw with soap or wax (don't use oil)—enlarge the pilot hole only as a last resort—it's rarely necessary to enlarge the shank hole.
- Countersink to full depth in hardwoods—in softwoods driving the screw will sink it flush.
- Once the screw is started, concentrate on the torque needed to turn it—it's no longer necessary to bear *down* on the screw—it will pull itself into the wood.

Screw Types

A. FLATHEAD
Screw is driven until head is flush with surface of work. Most sizes, especially in hardwoods, require countersunk holes. Can be driven in counterbored holes when hiding with wood plug is desirable.

B. PHILLIPS HEAD
Similar to flathead screws except for cross slots which minimize screwdriver slippage. Special Phillips screwdriver is needed.

C. SQUARE HEAD
New design with fast spiral thread for quicker penetration in soft or hard woods. Square head minimizes driver slippage. Require square-tipped screwdriver.

D. SECURITY (ONE-WAY)
Special slot allows driving screw but screwdriver slips to prevent removal.

E. ROUNDHEAD
General utility screws. Can be used alone or with washers. Often used to secure material that is too thin for countersinking.

F. OVAL HEAD
Combine oval head and flathead configurations. More attractive than flathead screws. Require some countersinking. Often used with raised or flush countersunk washers.

G. DOME HEAD
Flathead screw with threaded hole for attachment of decorative dome. Not common. Usually available on special order.

H. LAG SCREW (BOLT)
For heavy-duty applications. Available with square or hex heads. Usually used with a washer. Driven with a wrench or socket.

I. HANGER SCREW (BOLT)
One end drives like a screw, the other is threaded so a nut can be used to secure the attachment. Can be used in wood and in expansion shields in masonry.

J. DOWEL SCREW
Useful for some end-to-end joints and similar applications.

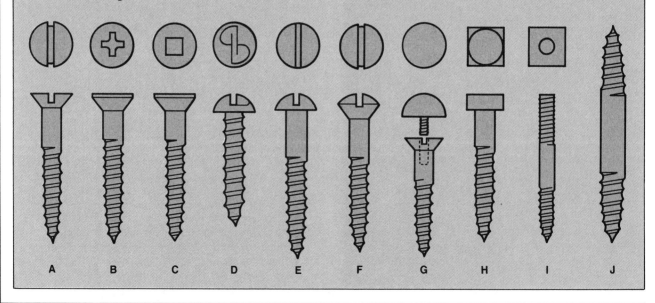

A   B   C   D   E   F   G   H   I   J

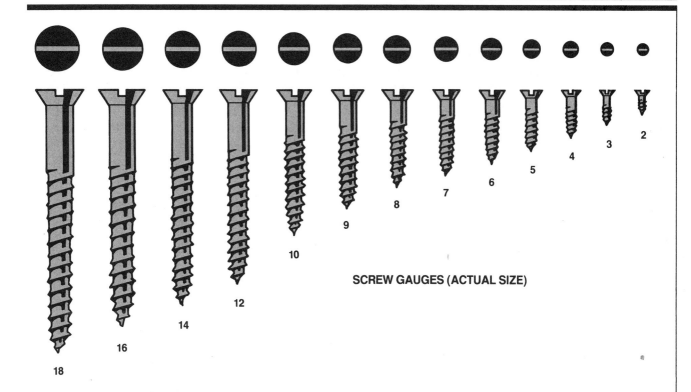

SCREW GAUGES (ACTUAL SIZE)

18 16 14 12 10 9 8 7 6 5 4 3 2

Common Head Styles on Wood Screws

A. FLATHEAD
Can be set flush to surface of work when hole is counter-sunk or can be hidden with a wood plug when hole is *counterbored.*

B. ROUNDHEAD
Head is left exposed—often used with a flat washer.

C. OVAL HEAD
Left exposed—requires a partial countersink.

D. FILLISTER
Left exposed—often used with a flat washer.

E. PHILLIPS HEAD
Used with Phillips head screwdriver—design is available on all wood screws.

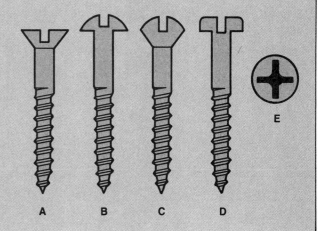

A   B   C   D   E

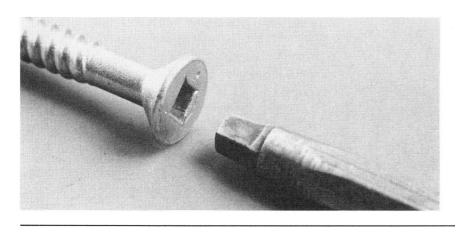

New screw design has a square recess and is driven with square-tipped drivers which are available for manual or power driving. An advantage of the screw is that the driver is less likely to slip and damage adjacent surfaces. At this writing the screws are available in gauges and lengths that run from #3 x ⅜ to #14 x 3.

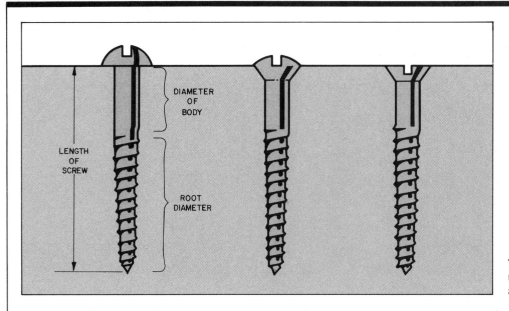

The length of a screw is measured from where the head bears against the work.

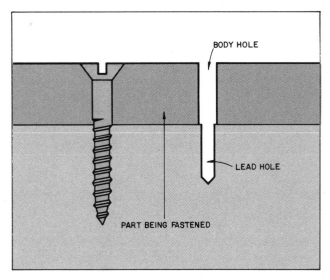

General Recommendations for Screw Holes

Ideally, the length of a screw should be ⅛″ to ¼″ less than total thickness of materials being joined. The pilot or lead hole should be about one half the length of the threaded portion of the screw. The shank or body hole may penetrate the part being fastened.

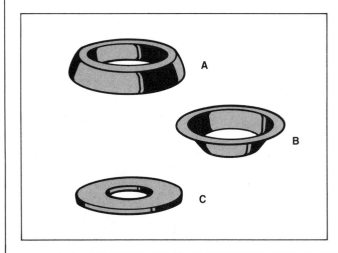

Washers

A.   COUNTERSUNK
Can be used with flathead or oval head screws.

B.   FLUSH (COUNTERSUNK)
Use with flathead or oval head screws to reduce projection of fastener above surface of work.

C.   FLAT (OR PLAIN)
Can be used with flathead or fillister head screws.

Note: Washers are used to improve appearance or to add to the bearing area of the screw so strength is increased.

Screws Can Be Concealed by Counterboring the Screw Hole

- The counterbore is filled with a *plug* which is sanded flush to adjacent surfaces, or with a *button* that provides a decorative detail.
- Plugs and buttons can be purchased in various sizes.
- Also, you can make plugs with cutting tools called "plug cutters".

WOOD PLUG

WOOD BUTTON

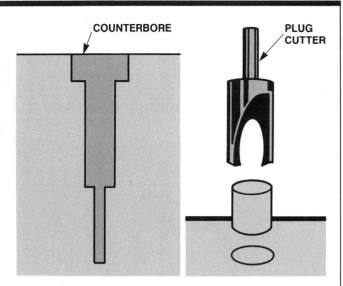

COUNTERBORE

PLUG CUTTER

Special Portable Drill Bits for Drilling Screw Holes

A. Forms shank hole, pilot hole, and countersink.
B. Forms shank hole, pilot hole, and counterbore.

Note: Both cutters are available in sizes to suit various screws.

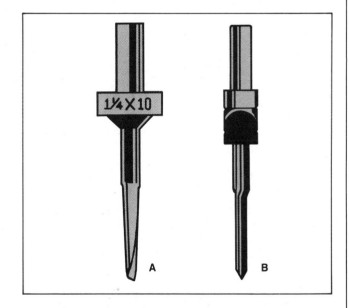

1/4 X 10

A

B

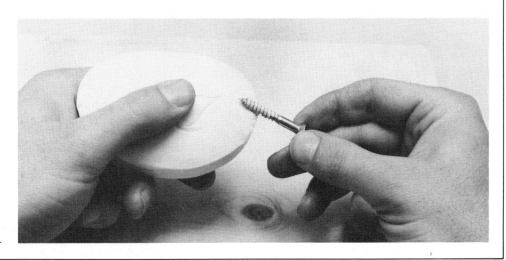

Try coating threads with soap when a screw is difficult to drive. Don't use oil or other materials that might stain wood.

A "Threading Screw" Can Be Useful

Sometimes it can be difficult to drive a screw even when shank and pilot holes have been drilled correctly. This can happen in hardwoods like birch or maple. Before you try to solve the problem by enlarging the holes, file one of the screws to the shape shown in the sketch and turn it into each of the holes. It will act somewhat like a tap, pre-forming threads so the regular screws will be easier to drive.

Save the "threading screw" as you would any tool; you may have use for it at a later date.

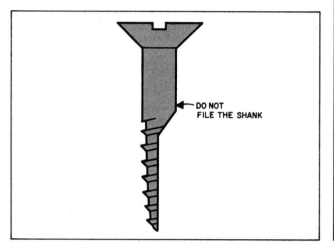

Two Ways to "Lock" a Screw

- Drill a hole at about a 45° angle and drive a brad through the hole and into the wood.
- Use a staple that fits the slot in the screw.

Hanger screw (or bolt) can be used in wood or, with a correct shield, in masonry. The fastener allows attachments by means of a conventional nut.

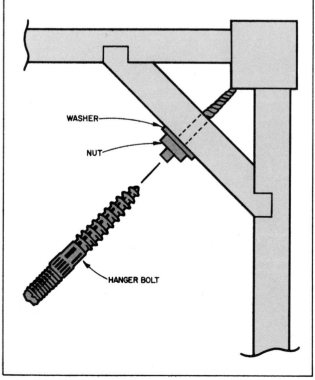

Secure corner blocks or braces on leg and rail assemblies to apply a hanger screw or bolt.

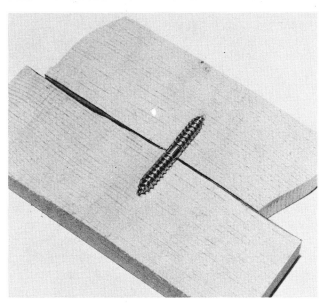

Dowel screws have screw-type threads at both ends. Common applications include joining spindles or squares end-to-end, attaching posts to bases, and reinforcing leg joints. A single one can be used in an edge-to-edge joint.

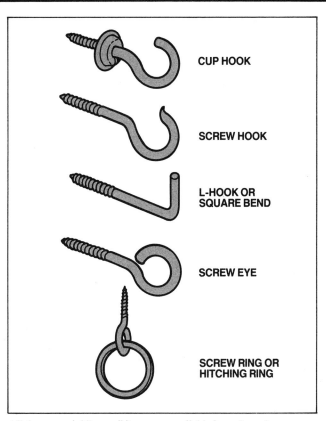

All these special "screw" items are available in various sizes.

LAG SCREWS (LAG BOLTS)	
DIAMETER IN INCHES	LENGTH IN INCHES
¼	1 to 10
5/16	
⅜	1 to 12
7/16	
½	1 to 12
⅝	1¾ to 16
¾	1½ to 16
⅞	2 to 16
1	2 to 16

Note: Lag screws have square or hex heads and are used for heavy duty connections—are driven with a wrench—usually with flat washers—often used with expansion shields for attaching items to masonry.

Sheet Metal Screws ("Tapping Screws")

Screws that cut or form their own threads. Especially useful for joining thin sheet metal, but can provide greater gripping power than nails or conventional screws when used in plywood, hardboard, particleboard, and even some plastics. Most require a pilot hole sized to suit the screw's diameter (see charts). Gripping strength in very soft materials can be increased by reducing the size of the pilot hole.

Most useful types, "A" and "AB", have gimlet points and are available in lengths up to about 2″. The threads on AB are finer than those on A.

Type "B" is similar to A but has a blunt point and finer threads. It's designed for adequate gripping power when working on thicker sheet metals. Sizes are similar to those available for A.

Another useful type is the "Drive Screw". It works something like a blind rivet, being tapped into place for permanent attachment of thin materials to heavier components. A typical application—nameplate on a tool. Available in lengths from ⅛″ to ¾″.

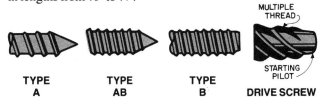

HOLE SIZES RECOMMENDED FOR SHEET METAL SCREWS (TYPES A & AB)				
NUMBER AND EQUIV.	METAL THICKNESS		HOLE REQUIRED	
	GAUGE	EQUIVALENT	DRILL	EQUIVALENT
4	28	.0156	44	.0860
	26	.0188		
	24	.0250	42	.0935
.112	22	.0313		
	20	.0375	40	.0980
6	28	.0156	39	.0995
	26	.0188		
	24	.0250		
.138	22	.0313	38	.1015
	20	.0375	36	.1065
7	28	.0156	37	.1040
	26	.0188		
	24	.0250	35	.1100
.155	22	.0313	33	.1130
	20	.0375	32	.1160
	18	.0500	31	.1200
8	26	.0188	33	.1130
	24	.0250		
	22	.0313	32	.1160
.165	20	.0375	31	.1200
	18	.0500	30	.1280
10	26	.0188	30	.1285
	24	.0250		
	22	.0313		
.191	20	.0375	29	.1360
	18	.0500	25	.1495
12	24	.0250	26	.1470
	22	.0313	25	.1495
	20	.0375	24	.1520
.218	18	.0500	22	.1570
14	24	.0250	15	.1800
	22	.0313	12	.1890
	20	.0375	11	.1910
.251	18	.0500	9	.1960

HOLE SIZES RECOMMENDED FOR SHEET METAL SCREWS (TYPE B)				
NUMBER AND EQUIV.	METAL THICKNESS		HOLE REQUIRED	
	GAUGE	EQUIVALENT	DRILL	EQUIVALENT
4	28	.0156	44	.0860
	26	.0188		
	24	.0250	43	.0890
.112	22	.0313	42	.0935
	20	.0375		
6	28	.0156	37	.1040
	26	.0188		
	24	.0250	36	.1065
.137	22	.0313		
	20	.0375	35	.1100
7	26	.0188	32	.1160
	24	.0250		
	22	.0313		
.151	20	.0375		
	18	.0500	31	.1200
	16	.0625	30	.1285
8	26	.0188	32	.1160
	24	.0250		
	22	.0313		
.163	20	.0375		
	18	.0500	30	.1285
10	26	.0188	27	.1440
	24	.0250		
	22	.0313		
.186	20	.0375		
	18	.0500		
12	24	.0250	19	.1660
	22	.0313		
	20	.0375		
.212	18	.0500	18	.1695
14	22	.0313	13	.1850
	20	.0375		
	18	.0500	11	.1910
.243	16	.0625	8	.1990

SCREW LENGTHS THAT ARE AVAILABLE																
SCREW	**LENGTH IN INCHES**															
	¼	⅜	½	⅝	¾	⅞	1	1¼	1½	1¾	2	2¼	2½	2¾	3	3½	4
0	X																
1	X																
2	X	X	X														
3	X	X	X	X													
4		X	X	X	X												
5		X	X	X	X												
6		X	X	X	X	X	X	X	X								
7		X	X	X	X	X	X	X	X								
8			X	X	X	X	X	X	X	X	X						
9				X	X	X	X	X	X	X	X	X					
10				X	X	X	X	X	X	X	X	X					
11					X	X	X	X	X	X	X	X					
12						X	X	X	X	X	X	X	X				
14							X	X	X	X	X	X	X	X			
16								X	X	X	X	X	X	X	X		
18									X	X	X	X	X	X	X	X	X
20										X	X	X	X	X	X	X	X
24																X	X

RECOMMENDED HOLE SIZES FOR WOOD SCREWS						
	DRILL TO USE FOR PILOT HOLE				DRILL TO USE FOR SHANK HOLE	
SCREW	HARDWOOD		SOFTWOOD		FRACTION SIZE	NUMBER OR LETTER
	FRAC. SIZE	NO. OR LETTER	FRAC. SIZE	NO. OR LETTER		
0	$1/32$	66	$1/64$	75	$1/16$	52
1		57	$1/32$	71	$5/64$	47
2		54	$1/32$	65	$3/32$	42
3	$1/16$	53	$3/64$	58	$7/64$	37
4	$1/16$	51	$3/64$	55	$7/64$	32
5	$5/64$	47	$1/16$	53	$1/8$	30
6		44	$1/16$	52	$9/64$	27
7		39	$1/16$	51	$5/32$	22
8	$7/64$	35	$5/64$	48	$11/64$	18
9	$7/64$	33	$5/64$	45	$3/16$	14
10	$1/8$	31	$3/32$	43	$3/16$	10
11		29	$3/32$	40	$13/64$	4
12		25	$7/64$	38	$7/32$	2
14	$3/16$	14	$7/64$	32	$1/4$	D
16		10	$9/64$	29	$17/64$	I
18	$13/64$	6	$9/64$	26	$19/64$	N
20	$7/32$	3	$11/64$	19	$21/64$	P
24	$1/4$	D	$3/16$	15	$3/8$	V

Note: Recommended hole sizes are for easiest driving and maximum holding power, especially in hardwoods.

MACHINE BOLTS	
DIAMETER IN INCHES	LENGTH IN INCHES
¼	½—8
5/16	½—10
⅜	¾—12
7/16	1—12
½	1—25

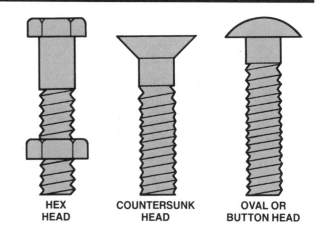

HEX HEAD   **COUNTERSUNK HEAD**   **OVAL OR BUTTON HEAD**

STOVE BOLTS	
DIAMETER IN INCHES	LENGTH IN INCHES
⅛ & 5/32	⅜—2
3/16	⅜—6
¼	½—6
5/16 & ⅜	¾—6
½	1—4

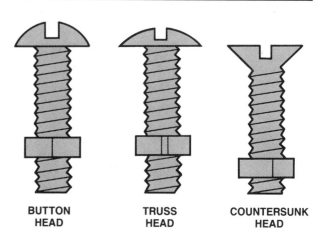

BUTTON HEAD   **TRUSS HEAD**   **COUNTERSUNK HEAD**

CARRIAGE BOLTS	
DIAMETER IN INCHES	LENGTH IN INCHES
3/16	½ to 4
¼	½ to 8
5/16	¾ to 10
⅜	¾ to 12
7/16	1 to 12
½	1 to 20

Carriage Bolts

Carriage bolts, which were frequently used in the assembly of carriages, are ideal for woodworking projects because of the shoulders under the oval head. They sink into the wood and keep the nut from turning while the nut is fastened. Secure them before tightening the nut by tapping them with a hammer until the shoulders are seated.

Washers

Washers are used to spread the gripping power of the bolt and to prevent damage to the work surface. It's especially important to use washers when bolts are used to secure wood components.

Lock washers are designed to prevent a bolt from loosening. Use a flat washer under a spring-lock washer when bolting wood components.

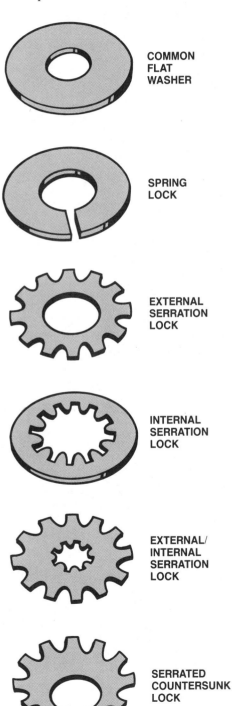

COMMON FLAT WASHER

SPRING LOCK

EXTERNAL SERRATION LOCK

INTERNAL SERRATION LOCK

EXTERNAL/ INTERNAL SERRATION LOCK

SERRATED COUNTERSUNK LOCK

Types of Nuts

Wing Nuts are used when a project might require disassembly or when a component must be tightened or loosened frequently.

Cap nuts or "acorn nuts" are used when appearance is important.

Castellated nuts are kept from turning through the use of a cotter pin. The pin passes through a hole in the shank of the bolt.

Note: Nuts used most often are the square or the hexagon.

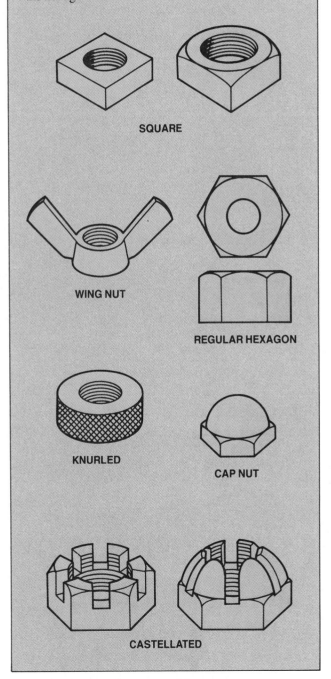

SQUARE

WING NUT

REGULAR HEXAGON

KNURLED

CAP NUT

CASTELLATED

INSTALLATION INFORMATION FOR MACHINE SCREWS							
DIAMETER (GAUGE)	THREADS PER INCH	NC	NF	THROUGH HOLE		HOLE FOR TAPPING	
				BIT	DIA.	BIT	DIA.
2	56	X		43	.089	50	.070
3	48	X		37	.104	47	.079
4	40	X		32	.116	44	.086
6	32	X		27	.144	36	.107
8	32	X		18	.170	29	.136
10	24	X		9	.196	25	.150
10	32		X	9	.196	21	.160
12	24	X		2	.221	16	.177
12	28		X	2	.221	13	.185
¼	20	X		F	.257	7	.201
¼	28		X	F	.257	3	.213
5/16	18	X		P	.323	F	.257
5/16	24		X	P	.323	I	.272
⅜	16	X		W	.386	5/16	.313
⅜	24		X	W	.386	Q	.332

NC = National Coarse Threads
NF = National Fine Threads
Note: Screws and bolts with national fine threads (more threads per inch) have greater holding power.

Corrugated Nails

Popular use is to reinforce miter joints but they can be used on edge-to-edge and similar connections. Special "nail sets" are available so the fasteners can be driven below the surface of the wood and concealed with wood dough.

Common sizes are:
⅜" high x 1⅛" long
½" high x 1⅛" long
⅝" high x 1⅛" long

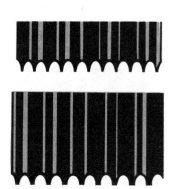

Skotch Wood Jointers

A strong "staple" with eight prongs that penetrate easily and spread in the wood to provide a firm grip. Used on butt joints and miters.

Available in various sizes by number:
#0 = ⅜" x 1"
#1 = ⅜" x 1 5/16"
#2 = ½" x 1 11/16"
#3 = ½" x 1⅛"

Special Dowels for Miter Joints

These 90° degree angle plastic dowels are specially designed for miter joints. Depressions on all sides of the units allow generous glue spread. Can be used with available adhesives.

Overall size is 1⅜″ and they come in diameters of ¼″ and ⅜″. Drill holes to match diameters but a fraction deeper than the length of one leg of the dowel.

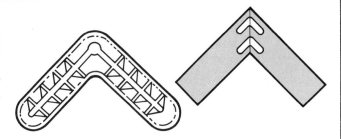

Clamp Nails

Clamp nails are specially shaped steel splines with divergent flanges that grip and pull together the parts of the joint. They are popular with manufacturers who use them on miter, bevel, butt, and other joint designs. The Clamp Nails are driven into matching 22-gauge kerfs that are required in each part of the joint. When the fasteners are installed correctly it is virtually impossible to separate the joint without destroying the wood.

The items are about ⅝″ wide and available in lengths from ½″ to 2″. They can be used in wood thicknesses from ⅝″ to 1″.

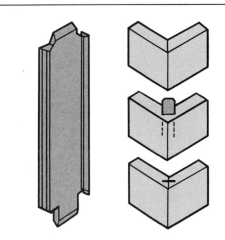

Tite Joint Fasteners

A mechanical means of pulling mating edges together with controlled pressure so parts have less tendency to twist or buckle. Can be used on panel edge-to-edge joints; often used on workbench leg-to-rail assemblies and similar projects where vibration may make retightening necessary. In such cases the fasteners are used without glue.

Installation requires two holes for the tubular "nuts" and a horizontal hole between them for the threaded rod. A drill guide is available so the holes can be drilled accurately.

They cost about $1.75 when purchased in single units.

Right Angle Connector

Consists of a ¼″-20, 2″-long steel bolt with flat head, and hex socket and a steel "dowel" with a threaded hole. Installation requires accurately sized and positioned holes for the dowel and the bolt.

Can be used with glue or alone for assemblies you may wish to break down. Very good for joints that may have to be retightened occasionally.

Cost about $.50 when purchased in units; about $4.50 for sets of ten.

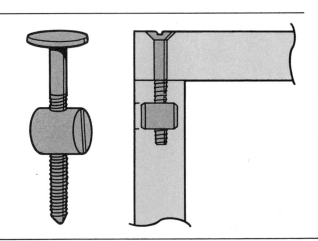

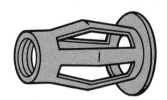

JACK NUTS			
NUT (NUMBER)	DUTY	USE ON MATERIAL THICKNESS	USE MACHINE SCREW
4S	Light	To $3/16''$	6-32
4L	Light	To $3/8''$	6-32
6S	Medium	To $3/16''$	10-24
6L	Medium	To $3/8''$	10-24
8S	Heavy	To $3/16''$	$1/4$-20
8L	Heavy	To $3/8''$	$1/4$-20

Note: Jack nuts pull together to grip the material when the screw is tightened. They provide metal threads in thin materials, hollow walls, and hollow-core doors.

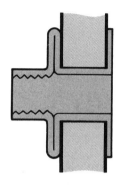

TEE NUTS	
SIZE (INTERNAL THREADS)	INSTALLATION HOLE REQUIRED
6-32	$3/16''$
8-32	$7/32''$
10-24	$1/4''$
10-32	$1/4''$
$1/4$-20	$5/16''$
$5/16$-18	$25/64''$
$3/8$-16	$29/64''$

Note: A tee nut is a fastener that permits the installation of machine screws in wood and similar materials. To install, drill hole and then hammer tee nut into place so the prongs penetrate.

THREADED INSERTS	
SIZE (INTERNAL THREADS)	INSTALLATION HOLE REQUIRED
6-32	$11/64''$
8-32	$13/64''$
10-24	$7/32''$
10-32	$7/32''$
$1/4$-20	$5/16''$
$5/16$-18	$3/8''$
$3/8$-16	$15/32''$

Note: Use these to install permanent machine threads in wood and similar materials. The inserts have slots so they can be turned into a hole with a screwdriver.

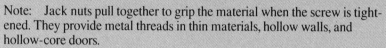

Molly® Bolts (Hollow-Wall Anchors)

The item is passed through a hole and tapped to imbed the gripping prongs. The screw is tightened to spread the anchor so it grips the wall. Then the screw is removed and reinserted after it is passed through the fixture. The screw can be removed without losing the anchor.

   Available for wall thicknesses from ¼″ to 1¼″.

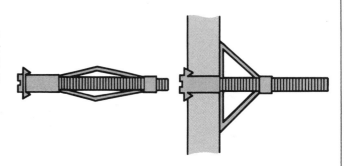

Toggle Bolts

Toggle bolts are used to secure items to hollow structures such as tile walls and concrete block. The hole must be large enough to allow passage of the spring-activated wings on the bolt. The wings spread and grip so the screw can be tightened. The screw cannot be removed without loosening the wings which in effect, act as a nut.

   Available in diameters from ⅛″ to ½″, and in lengths from 2″ to 10″.

   To use, pass the bolt (or screw) through the item to be fastened and then add the wings. Pass the wings through the hole and add the wings. Pass the wings through the hole and tighten the bolt.

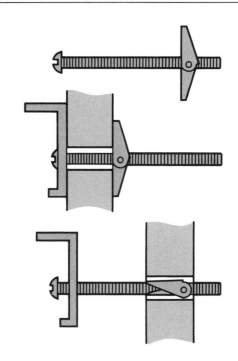

Fiber Anchors

Fiber anchors allow wood screws to be used in masonry. They are available for No. 6 to No. 20 screws, in lengths ranging from ⅝″ to 2″. For maximum strength only the threaded portion of the screw should enter the anchor.

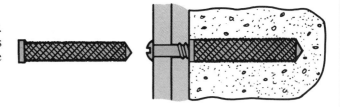

Expansion Shields

Expansion shields, used with lag screws, are driven into holes drilled in masonry. Driving the screw spreads the shield to provide a firm grip.

   Short shields are okay in hard masonry but use longer ones when the material is porous.

   The hole required equals the diameter of the shield.

   Available in diameters of ¼″ to 1¼″ and in lengths from 1″ to 8″.

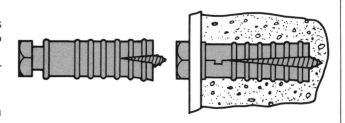

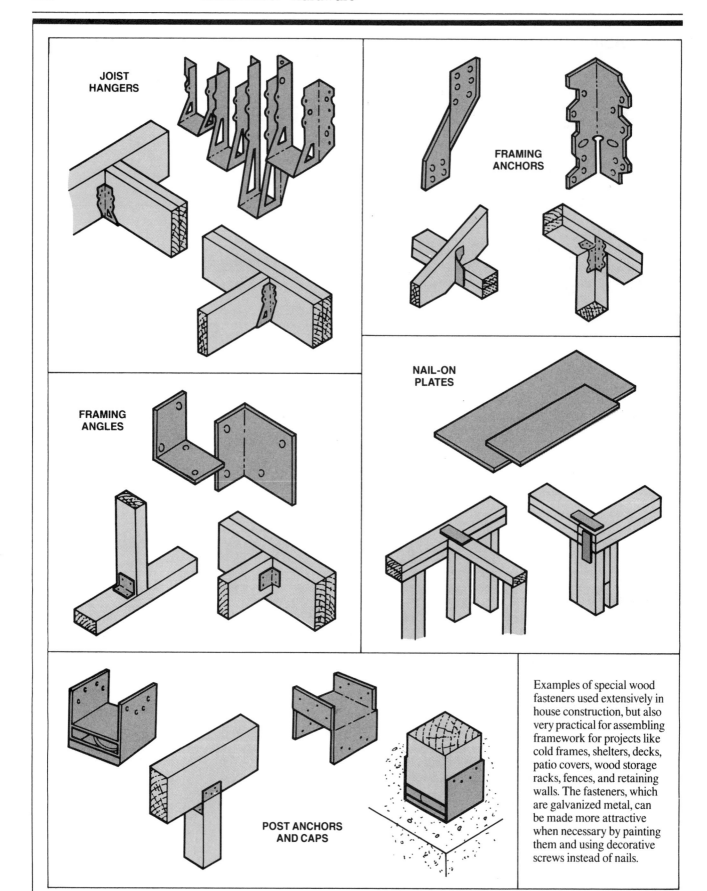

JOIST
HANGERS

FRAMING
ANCHORS

FRAMING
ANGLES

NAIL-ON
PLATES

POST ANCHORS
AND CAPS

Examples of special wood fasteners used extensively in house construction, but also very practical for assembling framework for projects like cold frames, shelters, decks, patio covers, wood storage racks, fences, and retaining walls. The fasteners, which are galvanized metal, can be made more attractive when necessary by painting them and using decorative screws instead of nails.

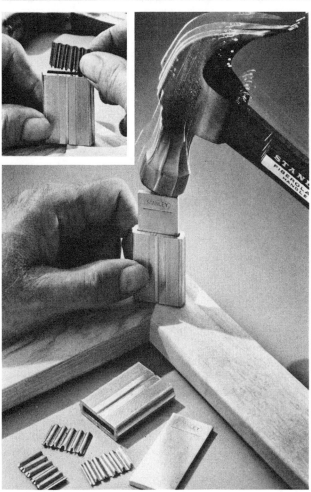

This special tool makes it easy to drive corrugated fasteners accurately. The fastener is held in a sleeve and set by tapping the ram.

APPENDIX

6.

Shop Math

Don't let the title of this section scare you off. There isn't so much figuring in 'shop math' as there is common sense and a few unique tricks.

In order to plan a project, you have to manipulate and manufacture simple geometric shapes; this is what most woodworking is all about. The boards you purchase at the lumberyard are simple squares and rectangles. Depending on how you machine these boards, you may turn them into triangles, circles, or—most likely—smaller squares and rectangles. These geometric shapes are joined in a way that somehow becomes a finished project, such as a storage shed (rectangles and triangles), a table (rectangles and circles), or a built-in cabinet (just rectangles). Shop math is a collection of methods to accurately measure and draw the geometric shapes you want to reproduce.

There are four indispensable measuring tools that you'll need to do this 'math'—a straightedge, a compass, a protractor, and a square. Don't skimp when you purchase these tools. You'll quickly find that a good straightedge is every bit as important (if not more so) than a good saw. What's the use of being able to cut a straight line if you can't scribe one? Once you have good measuring tools, always use the same tool to measure when laying out a project. Don't measure some parts with one straightedge, and other parts with another.

You may also want to invest in an awl for marking. It's hard to get used to an awl, but you'll quickly find that it offers two advantages over a pencil. First, the scribed line is always crisp and even; it doesn't broaden like a pencil line. This makes it easier to make accurate cuts. Second, an awl scores the wood grain before you cut it, helping to prevent tear-out.

The Circle

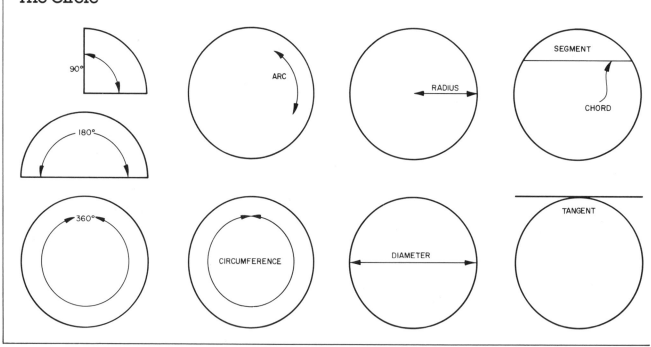

The Triangle

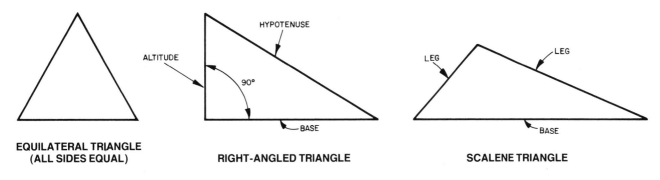

EQUILATERAL TRIANGLE (ALL SIDES EQUAL)   **RIGHT-ANGLED TRIANGLE**   **SCALENE TRIANGLE**

Figures

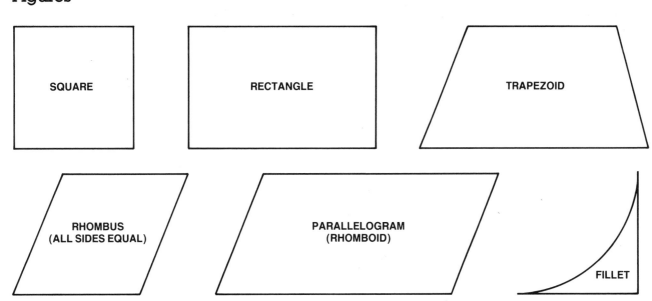

SQUARE   RECTANGLE   TRAPEZOID

RHOMBUS (ALL SIDES EQUAL)   PARALLELOGRAM (RHOMBOID)   FILLET

How to Find the Center of a Circle

- Draw two lines AB and CB from a common point on the circumference of the circle—direction of the lines is not critical.
- Construct a perpendicular bisector (D and E) for lines AB and CB.
- Point F, where lines D and E intersect, is the center of the circle.

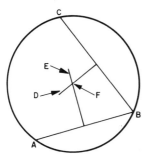

How to Construct a Square in a Circle

- Draw lines to connect the ends of perpendicular diameters.

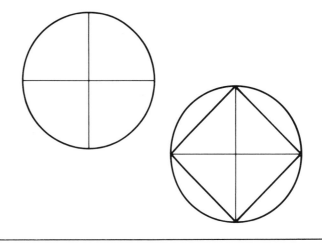

How to Construct a Circle in a Square

- Draw intersecting lines from opposite corners.
- Set the compass to equal the distance from the intersection of the lines to one side of the square.
- Use the intersection as the center of the circle.

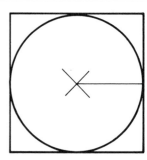

How to Construct a Hexagon (Six Sides)

- Set the compass so it equals the radius of the circle.
- Strike six arcs on the circumference using each intersection as the center point of the following arc.
- Draw lines to connect points where the arcs cross the circumference.

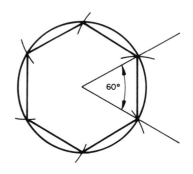

How to Construct a Pentagon (Five Sides)

- Form perpendicular diameters and then bisect a radius (AB).
- Form a line from point C to point D.
- Using the line CD as a radius and point C as a center, strike the arc E.
- Set the compass to equal the distance from point D to where arc E crosses the diameter.
- Use the settings to strike arcs on the circumference of the circle—each arc is the center of the following one.
- Draw lines to connect points where arcs cross the circumference.
- H is equal to the distance from D to where arc E crosses the diameter.

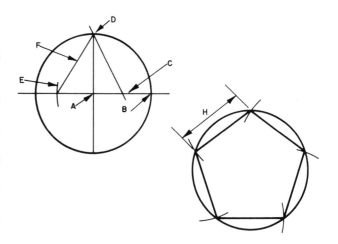

How to Construct a Five-Point Star

- Scribe a circle that represents the overall size of the star.
- Divide the circumference into five equal parts—360 divided by 5 = 72°.
- Connect the points as shown.

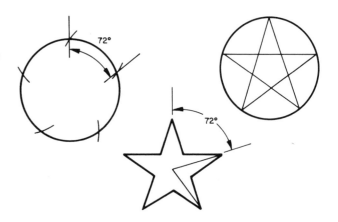

How to Form an Inside Corner (Concave)

- First, bisect the angle of the corner (line D).
- Establish a point on line D (E) and use it as the radius (F) for the arc.

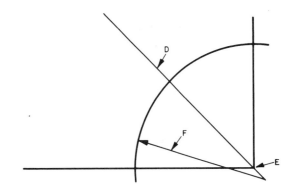

How to Round Off a Corner

- First, bisect the angle of the corner (line A).
- Select a point on line A (B) and set the compass to equal the distance from B to a side of the corner (C).
- Strike the arc using B as a center.

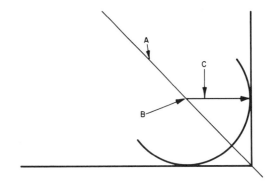

How to Construct Tangent Arcs

- Find the centers of the existing arcs (or circles) and draw a line through them (A).
- Establish point B by bisecting line A between the existing arcs.
- Use the distance between point B and one arc as a radius (C).
- Use point B as the center to strike the new arc or circle (D).

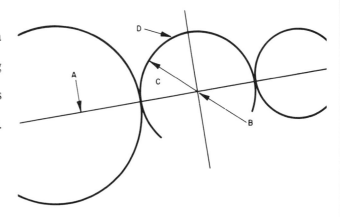

How to Construct an Equilateral Triangle

- Draw base line AB (equals one side of triangle).
- Set compass to equal distance between A and B.
- Use A as a center to strike arc D.
- Use B as a center to strike arc C.
- Draw lines from A and B to the intersection of arcs C and D (E).

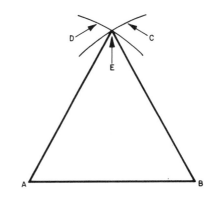

How to Bisect an Angle

- Set the compass arbitrarily and using A as a center strike arcs B and C.
- Set the compass arbitrarily and using points D and E as centers, strike arcs F and G.
- A line (H) drawn from A and through the intersection of arcs F and G will bisect the angle.

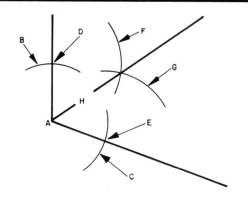

How to Find the Correct Cut Angle for Segmented Forms

The Formula: Divide 360 by the number of segments, and divide the result by 2.

- The example shows a 12-sided figure:
  360 divided by 12 = 30
  30 divided by 2 = 15
  15° is the correct *cut* angle.
- The cut angle is always ½ of the joint or included angle.

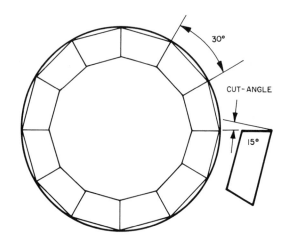

How to Bisect a Line

- Set the compass arbitrarily and using each end of the line as a center point, strike arcs C and D.
- A line (E) drawn through the intersection of arcs C and D will bisect the existing line.
- The new line will also be perpendicular to the existing line.

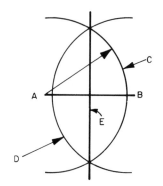

How to Construct a Perpendicular Line

- Mark the base-point of the perpendicular (A).
- Set compass arbitrarily and use A as a center to strike arcs B and C.
- Set compass arbitrarily and use points E and D as centers to strike arcs F and G.
- The perpendicular (H) will be a line drawn from A through the intersection of arcs F and G.

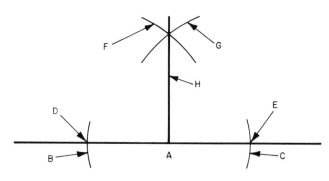

How to Draw a Line Parallel to an Existing Line

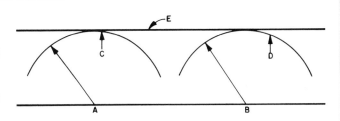

- Set the compass to equal the distance that is required between the lines.
- At arbitrary points A and B, strike arcs C and D.
- A line drawn tangent to the arcs (E) will be parallel to the existing line.

How to Make a Pattern for an Arbitrary Ellipse

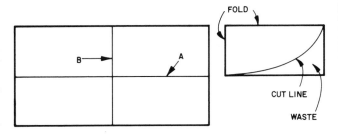

- Draw a rectangle using lines A and B as the major and minor axes of the ellipse—length of rectangle = major axis—width of rectangle = minor axis.
- Fold the paper on the minor axis and again on the major axis.
- Draw a smooth curve or use a slim, flexible strip of wood as a guide—then cut off the waste.
- Unfold the paper to have the pattern for the ellipse.

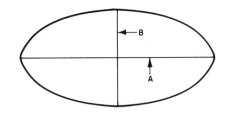

How to Use the String Method to Form an Accurate Ellipse

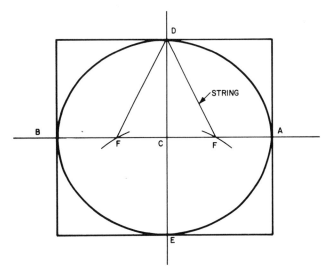

- Draw a rectangle with length and width to equal the major and minor axes of the ellipse.
- Divide the rectangle into four equal parts—lines AB and DE.
- Set compass to equal AC and use E as center to strike arcs F.
- Drive brads at point D and where arcs F cross line AB.
- Tie string tightly around the three brads and then substitute a pencil for the brad at D.
- Allow the pencil to be guided by the string as you move it to mark the ellipse.

Decimal Equivalents

To find the decimal equivalent of a fraction, divide the numerator by the denominator.

$$\frac{\text{NUMERATOR}}{\text{DENOMINATOR}} = \text{DECIMAL EQUIVALENT}$$

Examples: ¾   3.000 divided by 4 = .750
            ³⁄₆₄ 3.000 divided by 64 = .046875
            ⅝   5.000 divided by 8 = .625

A Quick Look at Metrics

Most Common Prefixes

Milli = .001   (one thousandth)
Centi = .01   (one hundredth)
Kilo = 1000   (one thousand)

SYMBOLS AND RELATIONSHIPS

NAME	SYMBOL	RELATIONSHIP
Millimeter	mm	10mm = 1cm
Centimeter	cm	10cm = 1dm
Decimeter	dm	10dm = 1m
Meter	m	10m = 1Dm
Decameter	Dm	10Dm = 1Hm
Hectometer	Hm	10Hm = 1Km

CONVERSIONS

mm x .03937 = inches
mm divided by 25.4 = inches
cm x .3937 = inches
cm divided by 2.54 = inches
m x 39.37 = inches
m x 3.2809 = feet
m x 1.094 = yards
Km x .621377 = miles

EQUIVALENTS

1mm = .03937 inches	1Km = .62137 miles
1cm = .3937 inches	1 inch = 2.54cm
1dm = 3.937 inches	1 foot = 30.48cm or .3048m
1m = 39.37 inches (also 3.281 feet or 1.094 yards)	1 yard = 91.44cm or .9144m
	1 mile = 1.6093Km

Using a Carpenter's Square as a Protractor

If you draw a line from the 12″ mark on the tool's tongue to a point on its blade you will have the hypotenuse of a right triangle. The idea is to use the correct dimension point on the blade to get the angle you need.

The drawing shows dimension points for some commonly used angles. The angles formed by the line you draw are complementary. If, for example, the line forms a 30 degree angle with the horizontal plane, then the angle between the line and the vertical plane will be 60 degrees.

As shown in one of the charts, the same system can be used to discover correct joint angles for multi-sided figures.

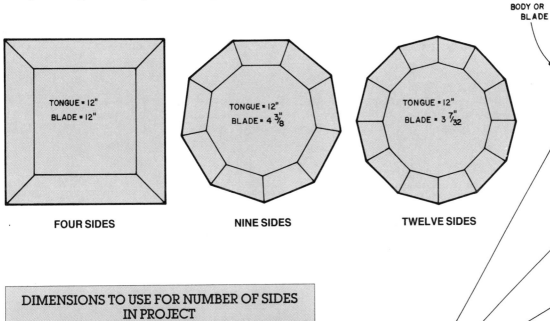

FOUR SIDES   NINE SIDES   TWELVE SIDES

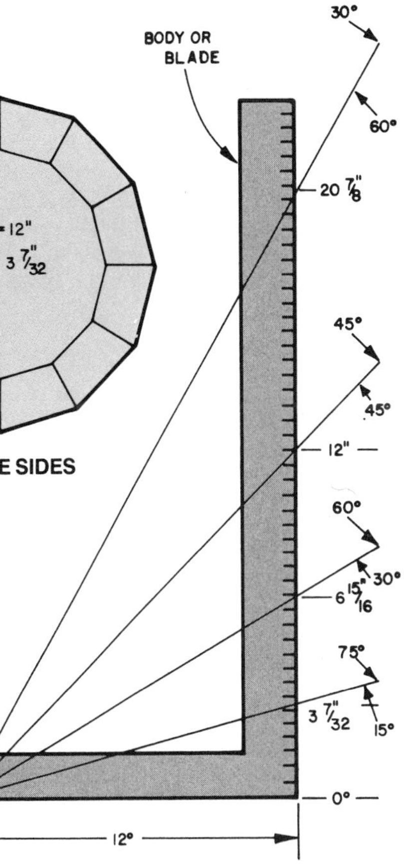

DIMENSIONS TO USE FOR NUMBER OF SIDES IN PROJECT		
NO. OF SIDES	DIMENSION ON TONGUE	DIMENSION ON BLADE
3	12″	20⅞″
4	12″	12″
5	12″	8²⁵⁄₃₂″
6	12″	6¹⁵⁄₁₆″
7	12″	5²⁵⁄₃₂″
8	12″	3³¹⁄₃₂″
9	12″	4⅜″
10	12″	3⅞″
11	12″	3¹⁷⁄₃₂″
12	12″	3⁷⁄₃₂″
14	12″	2¾″
16	12″	2¹³⁄₃₂″
18	12″	2⅛″
20	12″	1²⁹⁄₃₂″

EXAMPLES OF DIMENSIONS TO USE FOR PARTICULAR ANGLES		
ANGLE REQUIRED	DIMENSION ON TONGUE	DIMENSION ON BLADE
30°	12″	20⅞″
45°	12″	12″
60°	12″	6¹⁵⁄₁₆″
70°	12″	4⅜″
72°	12″	3⅞″
75°	12″	3⁷⁄₃₂″
80°	12″	2⅛″
81°	12″	1²⁹⁄₃₂″

DECIMAL EQUIVALENTS OF COMMON FRACTIONS			
FRACTION	DECIMAL	FRACTION	DECIMAL
1/64	.015625	33/64	.515625
2/64 1/32	.03125	34/64 17/32	.53125
3/64	.046875	35/64	.546875
4/64 2/32 1/16	.0625	36/64 18/32 9/16	.5625
5/64	.078125	37/64	.578125
6/64 3/32	.09375	38/64 19/32	.59375
7/64	.109375	39/64	.609375
8/64 4/32 2/16 1/8	.1250	40/64 20/32 10/16 5/8	.6250
9/64	.140625	41/64	.649625
10/64 5/32	.15625	42/64 21/32	.65625
11/64	.171875	43/64	.671875
12/64 6/32 3/16	.1875	44/64 22/32 11/16	.6875
13/64	.203125	45/64	.703125
14/64 7/32	.21875	46/64 23/32	.71875
15/64	.234375	47/64	.734375
16/64 8/32 4/16 2/8 1/4	.2500	48/64 24/32 12/16 6/8 3/4	.7500
17/64	.265625	49/64	.765625
18/64 9/32	.28125	50/64 25/32	.78125
19/64	.296875	51/64	.796875
20/64 10/32 5/16	.3125	52/64 26/32 13/16	.8125
21/64	.328125	53/64	.828125
22/64 11/32	.34375	54/64 27/32	.84375
23/64	.359375	55/64	.859375
24/64 12/32 6/16 3/8	.3750	56/64 28/32 14/16 7/8	.8750
25/64	.390625	57/64	.890625
26/64 13/32	.40625	58/64 29/32	.90625
27/64	.421875	59/64	.921875
28/64 14/32 7/16	.4375	60/64 30/32 15/16	.9375
29/64	.453125	61/64	.953125
30/64 15/32	.46875	62/64 31/32	.96875
31/64	.484375	63/64	.984375
32/64 16/32 8/16 4/8 2/4 1/2	.5000	64/64 32/32 16/16 8/8 4/4 2/2 1	1.0000

Index